SHRM

Society for Human Resource Management

Resource Management

Complete Study Guide
SHRM-CP Exam and
SHRM-SCP Exam

Sandra M. Reed, SHRM-SCP

SYBEX®
A Wiley Brand

This book is dedicated to the tireless HR professionals that show up every single day and try to make their workplaces—and themselves—better. I see you.

Acknowledgments

I would like to start by acknowledging the efforts of the incredible editorial team I had the privilege of working with on this project! It would not have happened without the guidance (and nudging) from my project manager, Gary Schwartz, who barely digitally reacted when I added four chapters halfway through the project and submitted content in such a nonlinear fashion. Similarly, thanks to my editor, Kenyon Brown, whose "flexibility-with-accountability" approach is exactly what my INTP (Introverted, Intuitive, Thinking, and Perceiving) personality requires.

Whenever I start a new book, I put in a special request for Pantelis Markou as the technical editor. Having him review my work gives me confidence that, if I make an error, he will not only catch it, but he will also provide feedback on how to make the content stronger. I was also fortunate to call upon his expertise for the special features in Chapter 11, "Diversity and Inclusion," along with the professional expertise of Reut Schwartz-Hebron, Jeffrey Pietrzak, and Dawn Kelley. I am grateful that they understood my vision for that chapter and for their generosity in sharing their work.

I have had the absolute luxury of working with clients and students whom I adore. Thank you to the businesses and students who put their trust in me and allowed me to conduct my experiments in their "petri dishes." We have learned together the incredible value of heartfelt leadership over these last 18 months, and they (the leaders and employees) were my role models.

Finally, I'd like to acknowledge my family, Chris, Clara, Calvin, and Jen. I tend to disappear when writing, and yet they continue to support and encourage and love and demand and enrich my life beyond any professional work I could imagine. This last year was intense beyond belief, and I wouldn't want to "do life" without them!

About the Author

Sandra M. Reed, SPHR, SHRM SCP is a leading expert in the certification of human resource professionals. She is the author of *HRCI: A Guide to the Human Resource Body of Knowledge (HRBoK)* (Wiley, 2017), *PHR and SPHR Professional in Human Resources Certification Complete Deluxe Study Guide: 2018 Exams, Second Edition* (Wiley, 2019), and *PHR/SPHR Exam For Dummies with Online Practice, Second Edition* (For Dummies Press, 2021). Reed has trained adult learners at the University of California, Davis; the University of the Pacific, and California State University, Stanislaus. She holds an undergraduate degree in industrial-organizational psychology and a graduate degree in organizational leadership. She is a master practitioner of the Myers–Briggs Type Indicator (MBTI) personality assessment, and the owner of a business consulting group that specializes in strategy, organizational effectiveness and design, and leadership development for small businesses. You can find her at www.sandrareed.co.

About the Technical Editor

Pantelis Markou, PhD, is the chief administrative officer for Mikimoto America and an adjunct professor of business psychology at the Chicago School of Professional Psychology. He has over 20 years of corporate experience managing human capital in the fashion and luxury jewelry industries, and some of his specialties are business strategy, executive selection and coaching, talent management and leadership development, change management, organizational design and restructuring, and cultural integration for mergers and acquisitions. In addition to his responsibilities in human resources, he oversees information technology, real estate, legal, and operations at t=company headquarters in New York.

Markou holds a bachelor of science in psychology from Brooklyn College, a master's degree in organizational psychology from Columbia University, and a PhD in business psychology from the Chicago School of Professional Psychology.

Contents at a Glance

Contents

Introduction

Writing a book at any time is always exciting; writing a book in the middle of a pandemic is an extreme adventure. Toward the beginning of this project, I became ill with Covid-19. Six months later, my Type 1 diabetic husband also caught the virus. Five months later my oldest son got married. In between these major events, my daughter began her independent study at high school, there were a couple of job changes in the house, a cancelled vacation to New York, a strategic rebrand, an added 10 pounds, and a switch to a vegetarian diet. Oh, and one other small item: I let my SHRM SCP certification expire and had to retest—not because I didn't have the credits, but because I simply did not register them. My first thought when I found out was "Am I an adult or not?" Anxiety, joy, lack of balance, a healthy dose of curiosity, and the original cast of "Hamilton: An American Musical" were the companions inside my head.

As I navigated these circumstances and thoughts that informed my perspective: I am you, and you are me. Your experiences may bedifferent, but we have weathered this time in history, and all of its uncertainties, together.

During the pandemic, my LinkedIn message box filled daily with questions about certification, specifically: "Is now the right time to take the exam?" Other concerns included pass rates, fear of failure, finances, job security, and perhaps the most common of concerns—capacity and time. The truth is, doing anything of significance is never convenient, even in the absence of a global shutdown. Those issues have always been barriers to taking a first step toward professional certification. The pandemic simply spotlighted them in a more emotionally intensive way.

If the exam concerns and my experience are familiar to you, consider the words of Lao Tzu, who asked, "Do you have the patience to wait until your mud settles, and the right course of action comes along?" (*Tao Te Ching*, Stephen Mitchell translation, 1995). When I read this, I visualize myself thrashing about in a stream, blocking my own vision by stirring up the mud. It was in one of these underwater moments that the theme for my writing process (and quite frankly, life), declared itself: *Be still, not idle.* I encourage you to do the same. Read this book. Take practice exams. Reach out to your network. Set the worry aside. Wander when stuck. Rest before you quit. Life will happen whether you prepare, pass, or fail. The key to success of all sorts is to plant your feet firmly on the ground and stop thrashing about. This will allow you to be on your path with a still mind and a clear vision. This is important because, as a therapist told me, "We are not human *thinkers*, we are human *beings*, meant to do, to act." Stop thinking, start doing, and enjoy the people you meet and the perspectives you gain along the way. I truly wish you the best of luck!

How This Book Is Organized

The goal of this book is to serve two outcomes: prepare for a difficult exam and be a go-to resource as you practice the craft of human resources. For these reasons, a few structural features were included.

Applied Examples

As you may be aware, these exams are experience-based, and thus it is critical that you see examples of how the content applies to the workplace. This is accomplished in three main ways:

Exam Notables: Each chapter opens with a section entitled "Exam Notables." The purpose of this section is to introduce SHRM's definition of the exam functional area and to provide a relevant example that demonstrates how the concepts apply in real life. You will also see a list of key terms within each chapter. Some of these terms are drawn straight from SHRM's Glossary of Terms, whereas others are drawn from the best practices of HR.

Chapter Feature: Titled "Note," "Case Study," or "Tip," these sidebars feature relevant examples of an exam concept as it is being practiced in the field or as it may appear on the exam.

Review Questions: Chapters 5–19 closes with 10 Review Questions that are designed to test your knowledge. A few are written to place you into the workplace, requiring that you use critical thinking skills to apply what you just read.

Parts

As you begin to prepare for the exams, your main tool from SHRM will be the exam Body of Competency and Knowledge (BoCK). This document outlines the content focus of the exams, and it is divided into behavioral competencies, technical competencies, and functional areas. These are further sorted into clusters and sub-competencies. More on this will be found in the coming chapters. For our purposes here, though, I sought to organize the book into parts to reduce the confusion that the BoCK can produce. The five main "parts" of this book are briefly reviewed next.

Part I: Preparing for the Exams   In Part I, you will find a review of the certification process and take a closer look at the BoCK.

Part II: Understanding Human Resource Competencies   In Part II, we break down the various competencies that are reviewed throughout the content areas. This includes a look at the differences between the behavioral competencies and the domains of knowledge competencies (also called technical expertise), which are further broken down into HR functional areas.

Part III: The People Knowledge Domain   Part III takes a deep dive into the functional areas related to the workers we trust to achieve organizational goals.

Part IV: The Workplace Knowledge Domain   The technical competencies of the workplace focuses on the internal and external environments where work gets done and how workplace practices affect achieving organizational results. It is in Part IV that SHRM's behavioral competencies begin to be introduced at the end of each chapter.

Part V: The Organization Knowledge Domain   This part's major focus is on the structures and relationships that drive organizational behavior and successful strategies.

Other Resources

Finally, I took care to ensure that each chapter includes additional resources to augment your studying efforts. Hearing from multiple perspectives, in multiple voices, and in multiple ways will increase the odds that you will retain information on exam day and beyond. I encourage you to build additional time each week into your study plan to access the website links, watch the recommended videos, read summaries of the cited authors, or even chase down a headline about a topic of interest. Context matters with these exams.

Interactive Online Learning Environment and Test Bank

The interactive online learning environment that accompanies the *SHRM® Society for Human Resource Management Complete Study Guide: SHRM-CP Exam and SHRM-SCP Exam* provides a test bank with study tools to help you prepare for the certification exams—and increase your chances of passing them the first time! The test bank includes the following:

Sample Tests

All the questions in this book are provided, including the chapter review questions at the end of each chapter. In addition, there are two practice exams (one each for the SHRM-CP and SHRM-SCP). Use these questions to test your knowledge of the material. The online test bank runs on multiple devices.

Flashcards

Two sets of questions are provided in digital flashcard format (a question followed by a single correct answer); one set is for the SHRM-CP and the other set is for the SHRM-SCP. You can use the flashcards to reinforce your learning and provide last-minute test prep before the exam.

Other Study Tools

A glossary of key terms from this book and their definitions is available as a fully searchable PDF.

Go to www.wiley.com/go/sybextestprep to register and gain access to this interactive online learning environment and test bank with study tools.

SHRM CP Assessment Test

1. Which of the following intervention strategies would work best for an employee who had low engagement with their job?

   A. Offer training.

   B. Place them on a performance improvement plan.

   C. Have a conversation with them about career development.

   D. Engage a coach or mentor.

2. Which of the following is an equity challenge for performance management systems?

   A. Lack of supervisor training

   B. Lack of efficacy

   C. Being tied to pay increases

   D. How time-consuming they are to complete

3. Which of the following is the best example of a team in the workplace?

   A. Individuals who work for the same organization

   B. Individuals who report to the same boss

   C. Individuals who share responsibilities

   D. Individuals who work in the same department

4. Which of the following examples best represents an organization that competes using knowledge as a core competency?

   A. A people-analytics corporation

   B. A staffing agency

   C. An automobile manufacturing company

   D. A financial services company

5. Which of the following is necessary for an internship to be legal?

   A. The intern's effort cannot materially produce the work of a paid employee.

   B. The intern must agree in writing that the work will be unpaid.

   C. The work must be tied to the student's field of study.

   D. The student must come from an accredited college or university.

6. You manage HR for a large employer that has just broke ground on their first global facility, which will be operational within the next 2 years. The national cultures are significantly different, as are the host-country labor laws. Which of the following HR service models should you recommend?

   A. Centralized

   B. Decentralized

   C. Offshoring

   D. Outsourcing

7. Which of the following HR metrics is used to establish the department's annual budget?

  A. HR expense-to-revenue

  B. Revenue per FTE

  C. Return on investment

  D. A balanced scorecard

8. Which of the following statements about the primary purpose of employee handbooks is true?

  A. Handbooks are required by various labor laws.

  B. Handbooks are used to communicate the expected standards of employee behaviors.

  C. Handbooks are used to help employers manage risk.

  D. All of the above.

9. The behavioral competencies required of a human resource professional is best described by which of the following?

  A. HR professionals must be active listeners to understand needs.

  B. HR professionals must be competent in their work.

  C. HR professionals must be geared toward taking action.

  D. HR professionals must be highly educated.

10. Which of the following best describes the value of HR networking?

  A. Networking builds relationships that may be mutually beneficial.

  B. Networking helps create a pipeline of talent from which to recruit.

  C. Networking identifies best HR practices from which to draw upon.

  D. Networking is an effective way to socialize with like-minded individuals.

11. Of the four dimensions of diversity, where does a person's religion and age belong?

  A. Demographics

  B. Organizational

  C. Internal and external

  D. Personality

12. Which of the following represent a demographic barrier to success?

  A. Transgenderism

  B. Age

  C. Religion

  D. All of the above

13. What is the age group identified for protection under the Age Discrimination in Employment Act (ADEA)?

   A. Individuals over the age of 40

   B. Individuals over the age of 50

   C. Individuals over the age of 60

   D. Individuals over the age of 65

14. Which of the following statements regarding the failing of diversity initiatives is true for most organizations?

   A. Most fail because there continues to be systemic racial and other bias in the workplace.

   B. Many fail for the same reasons most business strategy fails, including lack of resource and leadership commitment.

   C. Many fail because organizations do not understand the true value of diversity at work.

   D. Most fail because HR teams themselves lack diversity.

15. Why do individuals with high STEM skills self-select into routine work?

   A. They tend to have lower social skills.

   B. They are smart enough to navigate complex technology.

   C. There is an abundance of routine jobs within the United States that drives employment patterns.

   D. There are not enough nonroutine jobs to keep people employed.

16. Which of the following data collection methods would be most useful to understand how employees perceive their company's pay practices?

   A. Conduct online research to see what competitors are paying.

   B. Purchase an external salary survey.

   C. Conduct an employee survey.

   D. Use an online service, such as `salary.com`.

17. What was the primary outcome from the Lilly Ledbetter Fair Pay Act of 2009?

   A. The filing period for a claim of wage discrimination resets with every pay period.

   B. Gender-based wage disparity is a form of unlawful discrimination.

   C. Employers must pay jobs of comparable worth equally.

   D. Nothing; Lilly Ledbetter lost her case against her employer.

18. _____ plans focus on keeping critical operations running in the event of an emergency.

   A. Injury and illness

   B. Risk management

   C. Emergency response

   D. Business continuity

19. What is the primary difference between corporate governance and corporate citizenship?

 A. Governance is focused on sustainability, whereas citizenship is focused on compliance.

 B. Governance is focused on social responsibility, whereas citizenship is focused on risk management.

 C. Governance is focused on compliance, whereas citizenship is focused on sustainability.

 D. Governance applies only to corporations, whereas citizenship applies to all businesses.

20. Which of the following is covered by the Fair Labor Standards Act?

 A. Employees who work interstate

 B. Enterprises with at least two employees

 C. Public agencies

 D. All of the above

21. As the recently hired HR manager at a 52-employee manufacturing company in South Carolina, you have discovered that separated employees are not being offered the option to continue healthcare after termination. Which labor law is the employer violating?

 A. HIPAA

 B. COBRA

 C. ERISA

 D. OSHA

22. Which of the following is the most rapidly growing technology adoption for HR service delivery?

 A. Self-service

 B. Mobile

 C. Cloud

 D. Global systems

23. Which of the following is a best security practice for holding more online meetings at work?

 A. Making sure that the presentation materials are easily understood online

 B. Focusing on high levels of engagement

 C. Decreasing the number of meetings held online

 D. Initiating meeting passcodes and waiting rooms

24. As the HR manager for a nonprofit organization that offers free tutoring and other educational resources to underserved communities, you have been tasked with identifying how many full-time volunteers are necessary to staff next week. Calculate the FTE ratio using the following data:

 24 students per day, 60-minute sessions over a 5-day period.

 A. 1.3 FTEs

 B. 2 FTEs

 C. 3 FTEs

 D. 4 FTEs

25. Of the following, which would be the most effective action HR could take for employees who wish to use their own computer and mobile equipment at work or while remotely working?

    A.   Consult with a labor attorney to identify risk.

    B.   Develop a policy to establish guidelines of use.

    C.   Ask senior leaders which technology they would prefer their teams use.

    D.   Survey teams to see what they are already using.

Answers to SHRM CP Assessment Test

1. C. Finding ways to engage team members with their work is part of the role of HR. Once a clear career path has been identified, other intervention strategies such as training or coaching may be considered.

2. A. Many organizations rely on their managers and supervisors to complete performance appraisals. If steps are not taken to properly train the raters, bias is introduced that has a disproportionate effect on individuals.

3. C. Teams and workgroups are best defined through shared responsibilities or outputs.

4. D. Knowledge as a core competency relies on employees who are subject matter experts in their field.

5. C. When structured properly, internships have positive outcomes for the employer and the student. Key to these outcomes is compliance with various laws and so the work performed by the intern must complement the student's field of study.

6. B. A decentralized HR service model allows for a tie to corporate headquarters while maintaining cultures and compliance with labor laws within the host country.

7. A. The HR expense-to-revenue ratio is used to identify the costs associated with HR activities within the context of annual revenue and is used to set the HR department's budget.

8. B. The primary purpose of an employee handbook is to communicate employment rights and responsibilities, including the expected standards of behavior. They are often used to demonstrate compliance with labor laws; however, they are not explicitly required.

9. C. Behavioral competencies are what an HR professional does in their role, how they behave, and the actions they take to align HR strategy with business strategy.

10. A. Networking as an HR competency provides value in many ways, all through developing relationships. These relationships often lead to mutually beneficial outcomes such as recruiting, learning and development, and socializing with like-minded individuals.

11. C. Gardenswartz and Rowe defined internal dimensions of diversity as factors such as age, health, and national origin as well as external factors such as religion, education, and income.

12. D. Demographic barriers to success are diversity factors that, when unmanaged, result in under-representation of groups based on sexual orientation, age, religion, national origin, and mental health, just to name a few.

13. A. The Age Discrimination in Employment Act protects individuals over the age of 40.

14. B. Diversity and inclusion as a business strategy leads to many positive outcomes. As with any strategic initiative, many fail due to lack of adequate resource and/or leadership commitment.

15. A. David Deming of Harvard University noted that individuals self-select into roles that are best suited to their natural skills. Individuals with lower social skills such as teamwork and collaboration, but high technical skills such as those found in science, technology, engineering, and math (STEM), are more likely to work in routine roles. This is significant because as more U.S. jobs become nonroutine, HR will need to help employees develop their social skills.

16. C. Using employee surveys can help HR teams gather data related to pay practices, including satisfaction and perceptions of fairness, factors that influence retention.

17. A. Although Lily Ledbetter did lose her claim of wage discrimination against her employer, she inspired the act establishing that the filing period for a claim of wage discrimination resets with every pay period.

18. D. HR is responsible for leading the effort in developing business continuity and other disaster preparedness plans. These plans are focused on continuing critical operations in the event of an emergency.

19. C. Corporate governance is a risk management practice that focuses on compliance with business laws. Corporate citizenship is part of corporate social responsibility initiatives such as sustainability and doing no harm to the environments in which a business operates.

20. D. The Fair Labor Standards Act applies to enterprises with two or more employees, to public agencies, and to employees who regularly work between states.

21. B. The Consolidated Omnibus Budget Reconciliation Act (COBRA) was passed to ensure that employees who had healthcare coverage while employed have the option to continue healthcare coverage upon a qualifying event, such as termination. COBRA requires that the employer provide notification of this right at the time of separation.

22. C. Adoption rates for cloud technology is growing. This is because employers are moving more and more of their services online, requiring a change to how data is stored and secured.

23. D. With the increased use of online meetings there have been several security challenges. HR works closely with IT and presenters to ensure that there are security protocols in place such as requiring meeting passcodes and working with virtual waiting rooms.

24. C. Full-time equivalent (FTE) is calculated by dividing the total workweek hours by 40 hours. In this example, the weekly work hours equals 120 hours, which, when divided by 40, equals 3 FTEs.

25. B. Bring your own device (BYOD) policies exist to help manage the risk that occurs when employees use their own laptops, cell phones, or home-based equipment.

SHRM SCP Assessment Test

1. Under what conditions would senior leadership recommend an ethnocentric staffing strategy?
   A. When an MNE is in its first year of operations
   B. When an MNE needs to follow home-country procedures
   C. When host-country labor law differs significantly from home-country laws
   D. When there is a need to save on costs

2. Which of the following is *not* an operational consideration for human resource information systems?
   A. The ability to streamline payroll
   B. The ability to track succession plans
   C. The ability to manage the performance management process
   D. The ability to house and secure compliance records

3. Which PESTLE force is represented by China's restrictions on Internet website availability?
   A. Political
   B. Economic
   C. Social
   D. Environmental

4. What is the primary purpose of an OSHA accident and injury investigation?
   A. To determine who is at fault
   B. To determine if an accident or injury is recordable
   C. To identify the root cause for use in the design of prevention strategies
   D. To determine if an injury is compensable under an employer's workers' compensation program

5. What is the first step in preventing a cybersecurity attack on an organization?
   A. Lobbying the government for greater online controls
   B. Prohibiting personal mobile device use on the company servers
   C. Designing training to educate employees on how to prevent threats from occurring
   D. Having a written policy and procedure on Internet and email protocols

6. Which of the following should be the first step in the development of a positive employee feedback system?
   A. Decrease the frequency of feedback.
   B. Increase the frequency of feedback.
   C. Phase out the annual performance review.
   D. Train managers on rater bias.

7. In which of the following structures is the bell curve used to map employee performance?

   A. Forced distribution

   B. Graphic rating scales

   C. Narrative methods

   D. Likert scale

8. Which of the following job attitudes is the most widely studied in terms of employee engagement?

   A. Job enrichment

   B. Job indexing

   C. Organizational commitment

   D. Job satisfaction

9. Which of the following organizational structures are best characterized by standard operating procedures?

   A. Authoritarian

   B. Transformational

   C. Participative

   D. Decentralized

10. _____ is the metric used to understand the costs of recruitment and selection activities.

   A. Time-to-hire

   B. Cost-per-hire

   C. Attrition

   D. Selection costs

11. Biographical data, cognitive ability tests, and application forms are all examples of which of the following?

   A. Protected class data

   B. Options for selection testing at assessment centers

   C. Preemployment tests covered by the UGESP

   D. Selection tests that measure traits

12. When Apple partnered with Mastercard to process payments across all of their platforms, what kind of agreement did they enter into?

   A. Acquisition

   B. Merger

   C. Divestiture

   D. Strategic alliance

13. _____ is defined as HR's ability to provide results beyond the initial cost or expected outcomes.

   A. Measurement of impact

   B. Value-added

   C. Utility

   D. Business impact

14. Which of the following project management tools would be best when there is a need to manage a large project over time?

   A. Critical path analysis

   B. SWOT analysis

   C. Gantt charts

   D. Variance analysis

15. Which the following tools would be most useful for an organization that wants to understand the skillset of their workforce?

   A. A PESTLE analysis

   B. A SWOT analysis

   C. A gap analysis

   D. A needs assessment

16. Which of the following is considered the operational framework for an organizational system?

   A. The succession planning process

   B. The workforce planning process

   C. The strategic planning process

   D. A human resource information system

17. Quality, features, and high price point of a product or service are most closely related to which of the following competitive strategies?

   A. Cost leadership

   B. Differentiation

   C. The value proposition

   D. Market entry

18. If an enforcement action is brought against an employer for a labor law violation, how long must the employer retain the records related to the dispute?

   A. For at least 7 years

   B. For as long as the enforcement agency directs

   C. For as long as the dispute remains active

   D. For 30 years

19. Which of the following statements is true about ERISA?

    A. It requires that employers offer retirement savings programs.

    B. It does not apply to all employers.

    C. It governs the use of retirement plans as part of an executive compensation package.

    D. A major feature of ERISA is holding executives accountable.

20. There have been rumblings of union organization activity at your place of work, and you recently saw a pamphlet that had been left on a table in the break room. When you brought it up at the management meeting, a senior leader said that you needed to send out a communication to all employees that anyone caught organizing on the premises would be immediately terminated. This is an example of which of the following unfair labor practices?

    A. Threatening

    B. Interrogating

    C. Spying

    D. Promising

21. Why is wealth distribution an issue for employers to address?

    A. Wealth distribution is a function of corporate social responsibility.

    B. Wealth distribution affects the ability of employees to meet their basic needs.

    C. Wealth distribution is a human rights challenge that all citizens should be concerned with.

    D. Wealth distribution is a perception of equity and it will drive consumer and employee behavior.

22. Which of the following is an important characteristic of a holistic risk management system?

    A. Having a long-term risk assessment horizon

    B. Taking a global view

    C. Having an enterprise-wide focus

    D. Building a focus on continuous improvement

23. Which of the following is an outcome of a poor-quality management program?

    A. High employee turnover

    B. Increased risk

    C. A compromised employer brand

    D. All of the above

24. As the HR manager for the nonprofit organization that offers free tutoring and other educational resources to underserved communities, you have been tasked with identifying how many full-time volunteers are necessary to staff next week. Calculate the FTE ratio using the following data:

40 students per day, 60-minute sessions over a 5-day period

- **A.** 1 FTE
- **B.** 3 FTEs
- **C.** 5 FTEs
- **D.** 7 FTEs

25. Annualized loss expectancy is an example of which of the following data analysis methods?

- **A.** Quantitative
- **B.** Qualitative
- **C.** Regression
- **D.** Lagging indicator

Answers to SHRM SCP Assessment Test

1. **B.** An ethnocentric staffing strategy uses home-country nationals to staff global locations of a multinational enterprise. This strategy is appropriate when host-country operations must closely align with or follow headquarters.

2. **B.** A human resource information system (HRIS) is a technology solution that helps to streamline processes related to the life cycle of the employee. Succession planning is the only option that relates more to business strategy.

3. **A.** There are many political, economic, social, technological, legal, and environmental (PESTLE) forces that affect an organization's ability to compete on a global scale. China's restrictions on Internet website availability is an example of governmental influence, which in turn is influenced by the political and global climates.

4. **C.** The primary focus of any accident, injury, or incident investigation should be on identifying the root cause of the issue and designing solutions to prevent a similar incident from occurring in the future.

5. **D.** The first step in any sort of risk management technique is to conduct a needs assessment, and then develop standards of behavior that are communicated in writing. From this, employee training may occur on both the threat and the policies designed to mitigate the threats.

6. **B.** The first step to building a positive feedback system is to increase the frequency of informal and formal feedback that is focused on what is working and what needs to be developed.

7. **A.** A bell curve is used to compare employees by forcing supervisors to place them along a curve.

8. **D.** Job satisfaction is the job attitude that is most associated with levels of employee engagement.

9. **A.** Authoritarian cultures are characterized by top-down leadership and are more likely to insist upon standard operating procedures and roles.

10. **B.** Cost-per-hire is the metric related to calculating the true cost of recruitment and selection activities.

11. **C.** Any preemployment requirement is considered a test under the Uniform Guidelines on Employee Selection procedures. All preemployment tests must be valid and reliable predictors of performance on the job.

12. **D.** A strategic alliance is formed when two organizations join competencies to leverage strengths without a change in ownership.

13. **B.** Value-added is the ability of human resource and other business initiatives to provide results beyond the initial expected outcomes.

14. A. Critical path analysis is focused on mapping out a large project by identifying the end result and the smaller steps that will be necessary to be successful.

15. B. A SWOT analysis assesses internal strengths and weaknesses and may include a review of employee skill sets.

16. C. The strategic planning process provides the framework for how an organization will compete and address internal and external forces that drive organizational strategy.

17. B. A competitive strategy of differentiation is going to focus more on quality, features, benefits, and higher price points than a strategy of cost leadership, which is focused on competing based on low cost.

18. C. As a general rule, employer records related to a labor law dispute must be kept until the final disposition of the action.

19. B. The Employee Retirement Income Security Act (ERISA) applies only to employers that offer retirement savings plans.

20. A. The National Labor Relations Act exists to protect a worker's right to concerted protected activity or collective effort toward organizing. When faced with union organizing activity, an employer may not make threats to obstruct a worker's right to organize.

21. D. The consumer and the employee are not so much separated, and perceptions are shaping purchasing behavior along with the employer brand. People want to work for and patronize organizations that they perceive as being fair.

22. D. Senior leaders must orient risk management practices that are built on continuous improvement that address current issues and anticipate future threats.

23. B. Poor quality not only affects an organization's ability to compete, but it also creates risk such as increased warranty expense and defective products or services that impact the customer.

24. C. Full-time equivalent (FTE) is calculated by dividing the total workweek hours by 40 hours. In this example, the weekly work hours equals 200 hours, which, when divided by 40, equals 5 FTEs.

25. A. Quantitative analysis methods rely on data to interpret or predict behaviors. An annualized loss expectancy tool is used to anticipate loss every time a condition occurs within a 12-month period.

Preparing for the Exams

> We are what we repeatedly do. Excellence, therefore, is not an act, but a habit.
>
> *Aristotle*

The desire to move to the next level of one's career by taking a professional exam is a mark of excellence. This excellence comes from continuously reaching for new technical knowledge and then applying it to your work. It is likely that, as a successful professional with the experience necessary to qualify for these exams, you have brought a passion and commitment to your career that sets you apart. The characteristics that have brought you to this professional stage are the same ones that you will use as you prepare for the test: determination, resilience, strong organizational skills, time management, and solid resources. In this part, you will learn about the following:

The Society for Human Resource Management's (SHRM) certification process

Best practices for preparing to take a professional-level test

Which exam is the best choice for you based on your knowledge and experience?

The importance of the SHRM CP and SCP Body of Competency and Knowledge (BoCK)

The SHRM Certification Handbook describes the journey that you are now beginning:

> By deciding to pursue SHRM certification, you join a growing number of professionals seeking to meet and exceed the higher expectations of HR in today's complex global economy. SHRM certification is designed to help HR professionals assume more-strategic leadership positions and perform more effectively as they earn a credential recognized worldwide for its focus on behavioral competencies as well as technical HR knowledge.

Chapter 1

The Basics of SHRM Certification

Exam Notables

Look around, look around, at how lucky we are to be alive right now.

Lin-Manuel Miranda from Hamilton: An American Musical

As this book will highlight, organizations of all sizes are experiencing tremendous changes and challenges. By reading through these pages, you will discover that we are entering the fourth industrial revolution. The way that work is structured is changing. The challenge to find qualified talent is consistent across all industries. Front-loading education at the beginning of a career through college and university studies is no longer serving long-term talent needs. Social justice is driving change. These are just some examples used to make one point: the strategies and solutions to our world of work run straight through human resource (HR) systems. This is an exciting time to be in HR!

Certification provides a consistent standard of knowledge and a common language through which to practice HR. When HR pros are certified, we align with our organizations and our industry to define strategy and deliver results. Although the individual achievement of becoming certified is important, the collective impact of a group of professionals aimed toward the same targets—using similar tools, best practices, and shared values—is immeasurable.

The Society for Human Resource Management's Certified Professional (SHRM CP) and Senior Certified Professional (SHRM SCP) exams are recognized by employers across the globe for their excellence. This is because preparing for the exams helps HR professionals become stronger resources for their teams, accelerate career earnings, and build a strategic mindset that serves both people and results.

Exam Overview

The Society for Human Resource Management (SHRM) is one of the premier agencies responsible for promoting the industry of HR management over the last 70 years. Their purpose, mission, and vision are noted on their website, www.shrm.org, and illustrate why they exist:

Our purpose is to elevate the HR profession. Our mission is to empower people and workplaces by advancing HR practices and by maximizing human potential. Our vision is to build a world of work that works for all.

SHRM accomplishes these things in several ways, including through education. In addition to the case studies and learning modules that were already a part of their educational initiatives in 2015, SHRM launched their own professional certification exams.

The SHRM Certified Professional (SHRM CP) exam is described by SHRM as appropriate for applicants who have operational experience in human resources. This includes roles with responsibilities described with verbs such as "implement," "execute," "support," and "perform." The SHRM Senior Certified Professional (SHRM SCP) is a good choice for individuals with job responsibilities that "design," "advise," "oversee," and "align." Here are the exam descriptions from SHRM's website to help you decide:

SHRM CP

This credential is designed for HR professionals who are engaged primarily in operational roles—implementing policies, serving as the HR point of contact for staff and stakeholders, and/or performing day-to-day HR functions.

SHRM SCP

The SHRM-SCP certification is designed for HR professionals at a senior level who operate primarily in a strategic role—developing policies and strategies, overseeing the execution of HR operations, analyzing performance metrics, and/or contributing to the alignment of HR strategies to organizational goals.

The SHRM CP had a pass rate in 2021 of about 67 percent, and the SCP exam had a pass rate of 51 percent. These numbers have remained consistent for each exam over the annual testing windows.

Exam Eligibility

Both exams have eligibility requirements that are based on education and work experience. Note that title does not matter; rather, the important thing is the work being performed. Table 1.1 shows the eligibility requirements for both exams. As you review the table, consider the following:

- One year of experience is equivalent to 1,000 hours of HR work performed in the calendar year. If you are in a blended role, at least 1,000 hours of your work must be HR-related to be counted toward this requirement.
- Experience can be exempt or nonexempt.
- The category "less than a bachelor's degree" includes working toward a degree, some college, qualifying HR certificate program, high school diploma, or GED.

Individuals who have felony convictions are not eligible for certification if their conviction affects their suitability for an HR role.

TABLE 1.1   Exam eligibility criteria

Type of credential	Less than a bachelor's degree		Bachelor's degree		Graduate degree	
	HR program	Non-HR Program	HR program	Non-HR Program	HR program	Non-HR Program
SHRM CP	3 years HR experience	4 years HR experience	1 year HR experience	2 years HR experience	Current role	1 year HR experience
SHRM SCP	6 years HR experience	7 years HR experience	4 years HR experience	5 years HR experience	3 years HR experience	4 years HR experience

 Take a moment to download SHRM's Certification Handbook. It is here that you will find answers to *non-content*-related exam questions. It is free of charge and an important resource. Find the most current version at https://www.shrm.org/certification.

Exam Basics

In addition to getting your mind ready to take a professional-level exam, there are some practical considerations. For example, testing for both exams is only offered twice a year. The exam windows are spring and winter. You will need to select when you plan to test and then register by the deadline. Figure 1.1 highlights the main steps on the path to certification.

My Portal

Your main point for all things exam-related is SHRM's website. This is where you will first need to create your account and register for the exam that you choose. This step is crucial. Many HR pros believe that they should sit for the exam for which they are most eligible, and this logical approach is often successful. It is also okay to treat certification as a journey that builds upon itself. This approach allows for maximum retention of the exam concepts, which is useful to ensure that the learning achieved through the preparation process adequately transfers to your job.

You will need a few things to ready your application for the test. This includes your full name as shown on your legal identification and your work history, along with the descriptions of your tasks, duties, and responsibilities. SHRM conducts random audits of applications to ensure that they are truthful. Submitting false information is grounds for denial.

FIGURE 1.1   Certification steps

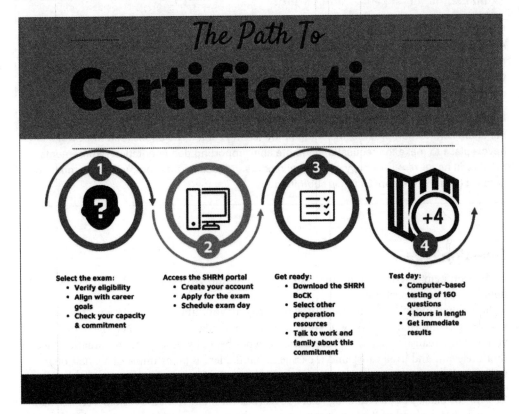

The Path To

Certification

Select the exam:
- Verify eligibility
- Align with career goals
- Check your capacity & commitment

Access the SHRM portal
- Create your account
- Apply for the exam
- Schedule exam day

Get ready:
- Download the SHRM BoCK
- Select other preparation resources
- Talk to work and family about this commitment

Test day:
- Computer-based testing of 160 questions
- 4 hours in length
- Get immediate results

Exam Fees

Two fees apply at this stage of the application process: the processing fee and the exam fee. The application processing fee is $50–$75 and is nonrefundable. Although you do not have to be a member of SHRM to take their exams, members enjoy a discount on the exam fee. The exam fee for SHRM members is $300 USD, and for nonmembers the exam fee is $400 USD. All fees must be paid at the time of the application.

Computer-Based Testing

A Prometrics Testing Center is where you will take your exam. Once you have received your authorization to test (ATT), you will be directed to their website to find a location near you and to schedule the test date and time. We recommend that you do this as soon as possible! More on this process is covered in Chapter 2, "Preparing for the Exam."

Each exam is 4 hours in length and includes 160 multiple-choice questions.

Exam Language and Accommodations

If Spanish is your native language, SHRM offers the exam at least once a year in Spanish. An advantage is that that you may gain a better understanding of question context if you aren't having to translate, which in turn saves time and increases understanding. A disadvantage is that most preparation materials, including the SHRM Learning System and other practice tests, are written in English.

Reasonable accommodations for physical or mental disabilities are also made throughout the entire certification process, including at the testing center. The application form will have a place to make the request(s) and note any supporting documentation requirements. SHRM will never require a copy of medical records. Requests for accommodations must be made at the time the application is submitted.

Question Type

Each exam item is written to measure application or knowledge. Figure 1.2 breaks down the item by type and distribution.

Situational judgment items are written to measure your ability to apply your behavior or knowledge competencies. You will know a situational judgment item when the item "places" you within a realistic scenario. These question types begin by describing the situation, details (both relevant and irrelevant), and the issue at hand. Here is an example of a situational judgment item:

1. An HR manager of a technology start-up has heard rumors from the customer service manager that the head of R&D is pushing projects through too quickly, causing quality defects. The customer service manager thinks this is because the R&D team gets higher incentive pay if they deliver early on a project timeline. The manager knows that a team meeting will not be possible; these managers do not naturally get along. Which of the following strategies would work best to investigate?

   A. Conduct individual interviews with each manager.

   B. Talk to the R&D manager's employees to see if the rumors are true.

   C. Check in with the quality department to collect data related to product defects.

   D. Nothing. Line managers should have complete autonomy.

   The best answer is A, conducting individual interviews. This is because in this scenario, the HR manager is only hearing rumors. Thus, to take action immediately would be premature. If HR goes directly to the line manager's team members, they are compromising trust and potentially undermining the department head, so option B is not correct. Option C, checking in with the quality department, may be a good course of action if, after interviewing the managers, HR discovers more than just rumors. HR teams serve as advisers and support for all departments and must be able to design and deliver HR programs that drive quality results, so option D is incorrect.

FIGURE 1.2   Item content distribution and type

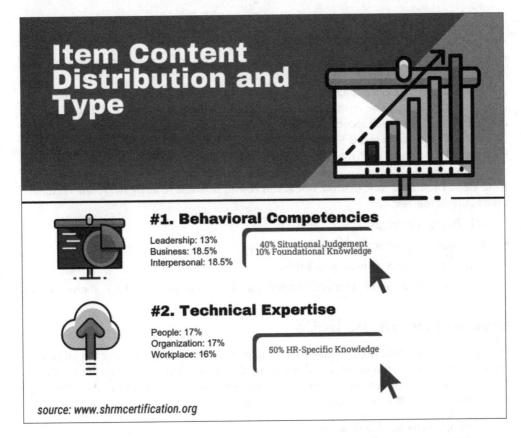

Item Content Distribution and Type

#1. Behavioral Competencies

Leadership: 13%
Business: 18.5%
Interpersonal: 18.5%

40% Situational Judgement
10% Foundational Knowledge

#2. Technical Expertise

People: 17%
Organization: 17%
Workplace: 16%

50% HR-Specific Knowledge

source: www.shrmcertification.org

Foundational knowledge items are designed to measure the key concept items of the behavioral competencies. HR-specific knowledge items are designed to measure the key concepts and proficiencies described throughout the functional area section of the exam BoCK. A foundational knowledge question would look something like this on the exams:

2. Which of the following is the best example of the principled approach to negotiation?

    A. A focus on solution, not the problem

    B. A focus on individual interests

    C. A focus on the problem at hand, not personal interests

    D. A focus on minimizing the compromises of each party

The best answer is C. In principled negotiation, the parties focus on the problem at hand and what is best for the situation, not what is best for the individual (option B). This shift in focus will allow the parties to understand what compromises (option D) may be necessary to produce a win-win solution. In a negotiation, there cannot be a focus on the solution without understanding the problem, so option A is incorrect.

The SHRM Exam Objectives

> If everything is important, then nothing is.
>
> *Patrick Lencioni*, Silos, Politics and Turf Wars, *Jossey-Bass, 2006*

As with all instructional design, it is important to understand the goal of the training effort—what results are we trying to achieve? An exam objective is similar in that it describes the focus of each section. For this reason, one of the primary tools that you should use to study for these exams is SHRM's Body of Competency and Knowledge (BoCK). This foundational document describes the content that will be measured on the tests. The good news is that this means that you have the framework from which to prepare and keep your focus clear. The challenge is that the BoCK can be cumbersome to navigate. A few reasons for this are as follows:

- It is 70 pages in length.
- It is organized with multiple layers.
- Several terms are used interchangeably.
- It can be difficult to differentiate between the CP proficiencies and the SCP proficiencies.

Breaking Down the BoCK

As with any professional domain, human resources has its own language. For the purposes of the exam, there are specific terms related to what is being measured. This is important, because the exams will test you on knowledge and application of that knowledge. The macro view is that the BoCK is organized into three sections:

Section 1: Behavioral competencies

Section 2: HR/technical expertise

Appendix A: Glossary of key HR terms

The BoCK references Appendix B, a 36-page list of resources that is available via download. These resources are sorted into general, competency-based, and HR expertise books and articles that can help get you prepared.

The BoCK does not teach content. For this reason, you will need multiple resources (such as this book) to learn what you need to know for success on exam day. Preparation is covered in more detail in Chapter 2.

 You can find the exam Body of Competency and Knowledge (BoCK) as well as other downloadable resources at www.shrm.org. There is only one document for both the CP and the SCP exams. I recommend printing out or saving an easily accessible copy of the BoCK and using it to orient your studying. In short, it should be at the center of all your preparation efforts.

There are specific terms used throughout the BoCK that are part of the framework, not the exams. It is important to understand these terms, however, so that the way the BoCK is organized does not detract from your learning.

Competencies

Competencies are groups of highly interrelated *knowledge, skills, abilities, and other (KSAOs)* that are necessary for successful performance in HR. Competencies are both behavioral (what we do) and technical (what we know).

Behavioral Competencies

As shown in Figure 1.3, there are three clusters of the *behavioral competencies* and their relevant sub-competencies, which are Leadership, Interpersonal, and Business. The behavioral competencies are reviewed in greater depth in Chapter 4, "The Business Competency Cluster," and throughout the relevant chapters in Part 3, "The People Knowledge Domain," of this book to help you connect the behavioral competencies with the technical expertise necessary to pass the exam.

FIGURE 1.3   SHRM's behavioral competencies

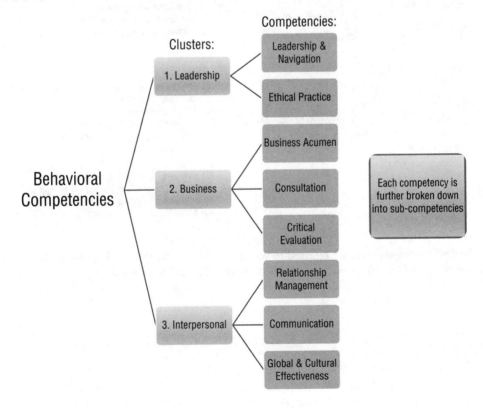

Technical Competencies

Technical competencies refer to the three knowledge domains identified in SHRM's model. They include People, Organization, and Workplace. Figure 1.4 shows the functional areas covered within each of these knowledge domains.

FIGURE 1.4   HR functional areas

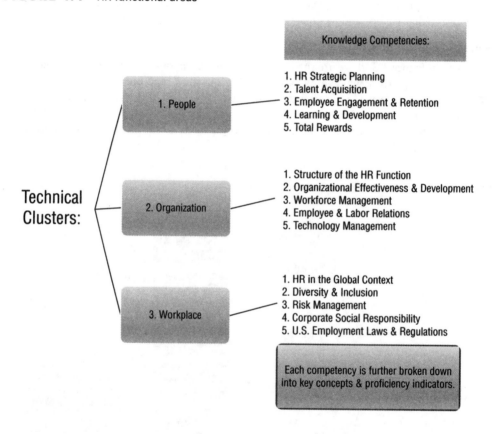

Technical competencies are referred to within the BoCK and this book by the terms *HR expertise, knowledge domains, knowledge competencies*, and *functional areas*.

Within each functional area, SHRM describes what knowledge an HR professional should have at various stages of their career. Remember, these exams have experience requirements that determine eligibility to take the test, so a baseline of knowledge gained through experience is already assumed to be present. The BoCK sorts these technical components as follows:

Key Concepts   The general knowledge necessary as it relates to the functional area. CP and SCP exam takers must be able to apply this general knowledge.

Proficiency Indicators   Statements that describe the behaviors and attributes a professional should have at certain points in their career. CP candidates are expected to have deep knowledge of the first set of proficiency indicators, labeled "For All HR Professionals." SCP candidates are expected to have a thorough understanding of the first category, along with the content found under the second category, labeled "For Advanced HR Professionals."

Acronyms

As experienced HR practitioners, you well know the comprehensive use of acronyms within our field. The exams are no exception. Although memorization of acronyms is not the main purpose of the tests, you will see them throughout the BoCK and in the question items. Table 1.2 is a list of the most likely acronyms that you will encounter on the test and throughout this book.

TABLE 1.2   Common HR acronyms

ADDIE	Analysis, design, development, implementation, evaluation	HRM	Human resource management
ADA	Americans with Disabilities Act	KPI	Key performance indicator
ADEA	Age Discrimination in Employment Act	KSAO	Knowledge, skills, abilities, and other characteristics
ADR	Alternative dispute resolution	LMRA	Labor Management Reporting Act
ATS	Applicant tracking system	M&A	Merger and acquisition
CHRO	Chief human resource officer	MNC	Multinational corporation
COBRA	Consolidated Omnibus Budget Reconciliation Act	NLRA	National Labor Relations Act
COO	Chief operating officer	NLRB	National Labor Relations Board
CSR	Corporate social responsibility	OSHA	Occupational Safety and Health Act/ Administration

TABLE 1.2   Common HR acronyms *(continued)*

EAP	Employee assistance program	PESTLE	Political, economic, social, technological, legal, and environmental
EEOC	Equal Employment Opportunity Commission	PPACA	Patient Protection and Affordable Care Act
EPA	Equal Pay Act	PTO	Paid time off
ERISA	Employee Retirement Income Security Act	ROI	Return on investment
EVP	Employee value proposition	SWOT	Strengths, weaknesses, opportunities, threats
FCRA	Fair Credit Reporting Act	UGESP	Uniform Guideline on Employee Selection Procedures
FLSA	Fair Labor Standards Act	ULP	Unfair Labor Practice
FMLA	Family Medical Leave Act	WARN	Worker Adjustment and Retraining Notification
GINA	Genetic Information Nondiscrimination Act		
HIPPA	Health Insurance Portability and Accountability Act		
HRBP	HR business partner		

The Value of HR Certification

In Ricklyn Woods's fabulous podcast, titled "So You Want to Work in HR?," she interviews HR professionals at all stages of their career to hear about their experiences in our field (Apple Podcasts). Many of the guests share that HR certification was not only a personal goal, but a defining moment in their career. This is not just because of pride of achievement. The process of preparing for these exams makes the individual better at their jobs, regardless of a pass or fail on exam day.

Not all growth, however, is equal. There are degrees of growth that are dependent on several factors, such as test anxiety, commitment to the preparation process, work experience, and selecting the right exam—all topics covered throughout Part I of this book, "Preparing for the Exams."

PayScale, a compensation research organization, collects data every few years or so to determine the value of HR certification. Their last survey of more than 100,000 HR professionals was published in 2018. Key findings included the following:

- About 30 percent of HR professionals are certified.
- Certified professionals enjoy a pay boost of about 30 percent compared to their noncertified counterparts.

These two factors combined mean one very important thing: achieving certification makes you more competitive in the HR world. Download the full survey, "The 2018 Market Value of HR Certifications for HR Pros," which includes statistics by industry and by certification type, at `https://www.payscale.com/hr/worth-it-infographic`.

 Real World Scenario

Is It Worth It?

The question "Is it worth it?" is difficult to answer, because everybody has different outcomes that they value. For this reason, I share my personal thoughts and experience here.

I did not have the opportunity to go to college right out of high school. For someone with drive and potential, a lack of education was a barrier—both real in terms of the jobs that I wanted but wasn't qualified for and perceived in terms of my own self-esteem. I limited myself most by feeling inferior to others who did have a college degree. HR certification was the equalizer. Once I had the required years of experience, it was only a matter of time before I passed the PHR, and then the SPHR (exams administered by the Human Resource Certification Institute), was grandfathered in through tutorial to the SHRM SCP, and then recertified by exam. Achieving these certifications gave me confidence and built my knowledge and skill sets so that I began having more success in my work. In fact, I would not have had the opportunity to write these books, support others on their journey toward certification, and coach leaders and teams—my absolute passions—if I didn't have my HR and other credentials.

Getting certified changed my perspective, from thinking that "school just wasn't for me," to believing that I was smart enough, capable enough, and worth enough to finish what I started. As a lifelong learner, I realized that it did not matter that it took me 30 years (almost to the day of my high school graduation) to finish my master's degree. Certification was the mechanism for a shift in mindset, the key to overriding my own hardwiring and limiting beliefs to activate more of my potential. For me, it truly was life changing and definitely worth it.

Summary

The fourth industrial revolution is here, and it is about much more than digital innovation. We are living in an era ripe with possibilities of how to shape and re-shape business practices. Many of the forces demanding these shifts require human resources solutions. These solutions are built within the functional areas covered on the SHRM CP and SCP exams administered by the Society for Human Resource Management.

Understanding the basics to certification is the first step on your journey toward the credentials. The SHRM Certification Handbook and the exam Body of Competency and Knowledge are must-have resources as you get organized. These documents are found on SHRM's website, and it is here where you will create the portal where you will manage the entire credentialing process.

Becoming certified is a mark of professional excellence that has multiple value, not the least of which is our industry's ability to influence collective action through shared knowledge and competencies and the career-enhancing value that those credentials bring.

Key Terms

Behavioral competencies

Competencies

Technical competencies

Exam Essentials

Become familiar with the Society for Human Resource Management website.   SHRM's website, www.shrm.org/certification, is where you will create your certification portal and find answers to many of your questions that will come up during this process. This is also where you will log your recertification activities to maintain your credentials over time.

Select the right exam.   HR at all professional levels will benefit from getting prepared for either the Certified Professional or the Senior Certified Professional exam. If your work experience has been mostly operational, the CP may be best. If strategy has been your focus, consider instead the SCP.

Choose multiple preparation resources.   In addition to the exam Body of Competency and Knowledge (BoCK), it is imperative that you access multiple resources to prepare for these exams. Chapter 2 is focused on getting ready for exam day.

Orient studying to the exam Body of Competency and Knowledge.   Although the BoCK does not teach content, it is the road map to what will be tested on the exam. Be familiar with the different types of competencies that will be measured, along with the glossary of terms that bring context to exam items.

Know your values and value.   Once the process is over, most HR professionals are happy that they chose to get certified. This is for many reasons, including personal achievement, accelerated career earnings, and upskilling. Take a few moments to understand your own reasons for taking the exam and what you value the most about these credentials. Perhaps most important is to remind yourself why you are worth the investment. As one of the amazing individuals in my network said to me at a turning point in my own HR career, "Burn the bridges that no longer serve you. I have matches. We ride at dawn." (Becky Lee, `https://qaffect.co`)

Chapter 2

Preparing for the Exam

Exam Notables

Robert K. Cooper, in his book *The Other 90%: How to Unlock Your Vast Untapped Potential for Leadership and Life* (Three Rivers Press, 2001) describes research showing that humans use not 10 percent, not 1 percent, not even 1/10th of a percent of our capabilities—we access only one-ten-thousandth of a percent of our potential! This is because the same mechanism that kept our ancestors safe from the sabertooth tiger still lives deep within our brain's amygdala. This wiring "promotes a perpetual reluctance to embrace anything that involves risk, change, or growth. Your amygdala wants you to be what you have been and stay just the way you are" (Robert K. Cooper, *The Other 90%*, Three Rivers Press, 2001).

At the base of the word "potential" is "potent." *Potency* is a source of powerful, concentrated energy that, when released, allows us to do what we perhaps never thought we could do before—like land our dream job, negotiate work/life balance, or pass a challenging exam. The key is to develop, through consistent mindset and process, mechanisms that activate that potential and that free our stored energy until we reach our full (or even 1/10th) of our potential.

This chapter sets out to describe the tools, resources, and preparation techniques that serve as mechanisms to override this hardwiring so that you have success on exam day and beyond.

Study Plans

It is amazing how strong the voices in our heads are able to keep us from doing something. "I should be happy to have a job," "I don't need certification," or "What if I try and fail? How embarrassing!" A simple mechanism to change your mindset is to stop thinking about all the reasons why you can't and instead start focusing on what you can do to be successful. One of the first things that you can do is to get organized, and that starts with a study plan.

A *study plan* is a written document that outlines the steps that you will take over the 6-, 8- or 12-week study period. For these exams, I recommend 12 weeks. Start backwards: select the exam window for which you plan to sit, identify the target date, and then count backward 12 weeks. Be sure to adjust for holidays, vacations, or particularly busy times at work, such as open enrollment periods or peak hiring seasons.

Break down activities by week. For example, for Week 1, download additional study materials, set up your study space, take an assessment exam, and apply for your exam of choice. The assessment exam should be an exam simulation where possible, and it should be timed. The goal of this phase is not to see if you can pass the test; rather, it is to assess your exam readiness. In fact, I have not once had a student pass an assessment test at the beginning of their preparation activities. If they did, they would not need 12 weeks to get ready! Do not get discouraged by these scores; instead, use them to define the activities necessary for success. Change your mindset from "I can't do this" to "here is what I can do." From these scores, you can allocate the appropriate amount of time per content area. If you are an experienced total rewards practitioner, you may only want to allocate a small amount of time to this functional area. If you have never worked in a union environment, you will need to dedicate more time (and additional resources) to this content. The best way to determine this is with the assessment, so don't skip this step.

Group vs. Self-Study

A common question regarding all professional certifications is whether to self-study or join an instructor-led study group, such as those offered by universities and SHRM chapters. This is largely a function of personal preference, although both have pros and cons, as shown in Table 2.1. A hybrid approach is often the best, because even if you do choose to join a study group, you will have to set aside individual time to prepare.

TABLE 2.1   Pros and cons of self- vs. group study

	Pros	Cons
Self-Study	▪ Allows you to work at your own pace ▪ Less expensive than group programs ▪ Generates more concentrated effort and independent resourcefulness	▪ Less accountability for a disciplined study routine ▪ Is limited by not knowing what you don't know, which can result in too narrow of a focus ▪ An increased sense of isolation without access to social encouragement from similar people
Group Study	▪ Often has sample tests, study plans, and other resources ▪ Creates an opportunity to learn from those with diverse experience ▪ Allows for a connected experience, testing each other, and sharing tips ▪ Adult learners do well through facilitated discussion and debate	▪ Is generally more expensive ▪ Often turns into a social gathering, diluting the learning ▪ Differing levels of readiness that can slow down the group

The SHRM Exam Objectives

Going to the source is always the preferred method to identify areas to include in your study plan. For these exams, the best place to start is the Society for Human Resource Management (SHRM). As described in Chapter 1, "The Basics of SHRM Certification," the two guiding documents for these exams is the Body of Competency and Knowledge (BoCK), which includes a glossary of terms, and the most current SHRM Certification Handbook. Be sure to have both of these downloaded and accessible throughout the weeks of preparation.

Preparation providers only have access to the exam body of knowledge and other information that is available to the public. SHRM offers their own exam prep bundles, and they make it very clear that they maintain a firewall between their preparation instructional designers and the exam item writers. Not only is this an act of integrity, but it also protects their accreditation. For this reason, it is wise to have multiple resources from which to prepare. Each chapter of this book references additional study resources such as videos, websites, articles, and books to ensure that you are hearing and seeing exam content from different voices.

Using Exam Weights

The CP and SCP exams are not scored using the traditional percentages with which you are probably most familiar, where anything under a 60 percent is considered a failing grade.

The SHRM exams use a weighting protocol called the *Angoff method*, which considers the probability of an examinee answering the question correctly. This probability drives a point system for each exam item (question) that indicates the degree of difficulty. According to Pearson Vue, a major provider of exam assessments, judges of each item consider "out of one hundred minimally competent people, how many would answer the item correctly?" They then score the item accordingly (`http://examdevhelp.pearsonvue.com`).

There are thousands of weighted exam items in the CP and SCP database. You will see only 160 of these, and it is impossible to predict the mix of questions that you will receive. You may get a randomized exam that is made up of easier questions, or for some, a lot of difficult questions. Two points about this are as follows:

- The more difficult the question mix, the lower the threshold for passing. This is to ensure that those who receive a more difficult mix of questions are not penalized. Try not to psych yourself out on exam day if you begin to struggle a bit. Shut down the negative self-talk, such as "I don't know any of this," or "I knew I wasn't ready." More strategies on mental readiness are coming up in a later section.

- You will prepare for content that will not show up on the exam or be represented by only one or two questions. This frustrates a lot of students! Instead of getting flustered, know that what you learned will likely come in handy at some point in your work.

The only certainty regarding the exam that you will take is that you will get an approximate number of items within each content area. This is identified in the exam BoCK. Consider this: the exam has 160 questions, and content is evenly distributed between the knowledge competencies and behavioral competencies further sorted by clusters.

In the behavioral competencies, this appears as follows:

Leadership: 13 percent, 20 questions

Interpersonal: 18.5 percent, 30 questions

Business: 18.5 percent, 30 questions

For the knowledge competencies, it looks more like the following:

People: 17 percent, 27 questions

Organization: 17 percent, 27 questions

Workplace: 16 percent, 25 questions

When considering that the outcome of 12 weeks of study time (two weeks per competency cluster) will only be measured by 20 or so questions per cluster, it seems quite startling. This book alone comes in at more than 500 pages! If you are in a rush, again consider the assessment score, your work experience, and any specialization that you are bringing to your baseline and adjust accordingly.

Remember, the purpose of certification is not just to pass the test successfully (although you need strategies for this also). The CP and SCP credentials signal to employers that you have a baseline of knowledge and behavioral competencies to have impact within their organizations. Becoming a valued contributor is achieved through work experience, education, and preparation for the exam. Truly, the preparation process is the most valuable part of this journey.

Conversely, for high achievers, this is for you: the purpose of dedicated preparation is to pass the exam, *not pass with a perfect score*. Give yourself permission to go a bit easier in one content area that is particularly difficult for you. For example, I am horrible at math, especially mental math. Instead of losing sleep over trying to get a handle on fractions, I gave myself permission to miss items related to the 4/5ths rule used to calculate adverse impact. The odds were probable that I would get only two or three of these questions based on the content distribution, so I relaxed. This would have been a flawed strategy if I hadn't counterbalanced it with exceptional preparation in other exam content areas. So, don't go too easy on yourself, but play to your strengths where possible.

Practice Exams

The best way to understand your special strengths and challenges is to take practice exams. In addition to studying for content, it is important to set time aside to prepare for the exam structure itself. The best tool for doing this is the practice exams.

There is a science behind structuring a coherent item (question). An item writer must consider the following when writing:

Content area: Pulled from the BoCK

Question type: Multiple choice, fill in the blank, true-false, or matching

Competency: Behavioral (application) or knowledge (technical expertise, foundational)

Not all practice exams are created equal! It is understandable that preparing for this exam can become quite pricey—do not skimp on your choice of practice exams, however. Too often, a student fails the test, not because they do not have the technical expertise or experience, but because they were unprepared for the way that items are written, or they fell victim to taking a timed test under pressure. For this reason, it is useful to understand the different types of practice items that you will encounter as you search for this preparation resource.

Simulation practice exams are written to be as close to the actual exam as possible. The best of these are full-length (160-question), timed, and weighted to the BoCK.

Self-assessments are useful for measuring progress as you go along. Think about chapter or unit reviews as opposed to full-content areas. Look for resources that sort questions by competency area where possible.

Another way to use practice questions as you prepare is to take them first using an open-book strategy. This way, you learn as you go and focus your attention on what the exam question is asking, an important feature of success on exam day.

Exam-Taking Strategies

You will have four hours to take the SHRM CP or SCP exam. Both tests have 160 questions, which means that you have approximately 1.5 minutes to find the answer.

The total test time is more than 4 hours:

1. **Confidentiality reminder**: 2 minutes
2. **Introduction and tutorial**: 8 minutes
3. **Exam** *(2 sections at 120 minutes per section)*: 4 hours
4. **Survey**: 5 minutes

The sections are timed separately; any additional minutes left over from one section will not roll over to the next, and you cannot go back once the section is closed. You will be able to track your time by the countdown clock on your screen.

All this information and more can be found in the SHRM Certification Handbook that you (hopefully) have already downloaded from www.shrm.org.

The following are a few best practices to help you on exam day.

Understand the Stem

This seems like a simple directive, but many test takers stumble because they did not understand what the question was asking. An exam item has three main components: the stem, the options, and the correct (or best) answer. Here is an example of these components:

Item Stem

As the HR manager for a company with 300 FTEs, you have recently completed a market wage survey for all job categories. Several employees within the IT department have been identified as being green-circled. Which of the following strategies would be best if your employer wants to save on costs?

Options

A. Do nothing for now if the pay rates are compliant with state and federal laws.

B. Increase the pay rates so that they are aligned with market competitiveness.

C. Freeze the pay rates so that they are aligned with market competitiveness.

D. Work with the managers to create performance-based and other incentives.

Answer: D

The SHRM exams will not give you an answer explanation. In this question, D is the best option because the stem was asking for the best strategy if the employer wanted to save costs; option A and option D does that. Option A, however, will result in increased costs if turnover occurs as the result of being paid under-market wages, and option B increases labor costs. Option C is an answer distractor, since it refers to a strategy to address red-circled employees.

Note the knowledge and behavioral competencies that are necessary to successfully answer this question:

- Knowledge of the acronym "FTE," full-time equivalent employee.

- Experience in HR trends and how difficult (and competitive) it is to recruit for these roles.

- Knowledge of the definition and differences between green-circled and red-circled employees; green-circled employees are being paid below the labor market midpoint, and red-circled employees are being paid above market midpoint.

- Option A can distract you if you don't know that market wages are what competitors are paying in the relevant market (geographic location, industry), not what is required by law.

- Option A does not draw upon the HR behavioral competency of business acumen, specifically, aligning HR strategy and practices with core business needs. HR must communicate that if the organization is not competitive on compensation, the turnover rate will go up and thus increase the cost of recruiting. This does not achieve the goal of cost savings.

- Option B may solve the immediate issue at hand, but it does not address the request of management. Market competitiveness in this space is likely to continue to be a challenge in recruiting, so a short-term solution, such as B, is not the best choice.

To understand what the question is asking and apply your knowledge, read the question twice and then answer the question in your mind before reading the options. Generally, the option that most aligns with your first thought should be the answer you go with.

Guess When Necessary

On a multiple-choice question with four answer options such as these, the candidate has a 25 percent chance of guessing correctly. For the CP and SCP exams, you automatically miss the question if you leave it blank. This means that your best guess is better than not answering the question at all. Take your best guess and then mark for review the questions about which you are unsure of the answer and come back to them if time permits.

As mentioned earlier, the options to each question will include clearly wrong answers and other types of distractors. The most difficult distractors are the options that, in addition to the correct choice, could also be right. These exams will challenge you often to select the *best* of the correct answers. Be sure to pare down your choices to the two most likely, and then guess from those two. This increases your odds of guessing correctly.

It is a myth that on a multiple-choice exam it is beneficial to guess "C" as the correct choice. For example, starting with Chapter 5, "Strategic Human Resource Management," you will begin to study content areas. At the end of these chapters, there are 10 review questions, each with four multiple-choice options: A, B, C, and D. Item writers use a key balancer to ensure that the options are equally distributed.

Exam Day Basics

Whether you are taking this exam remotely or on-site at a Prometric facility, consider a few best practices before and during the exam.

In the days leading up to the exam, spend your study time reviewing the areas where you feel the least confident. Don't try to learn new concepts! Our short-term memories have limited capacity—they can only hold so much new information. Trying to add new data will result in the loss of other stored information. Be sure to get enough rest the night before and avoid the dehydrating effects of alcohol. Dehydration can cause fuzzy thinking and other challenges, so be sure and drink enough water in the days leading up to the exam—not just on the day of the exam.

On exam day, eat before your test. Nerves can make you lose your appetite, but your brain needs good, strong fuel to perform optimally. Eat foods high in proteins, such as eggs or quinoa, and add in foods that are high in omega fats and antioxidants where possible. A blueberry smoothie with oat milk and flaxseed is a good option for vegetarians; eggs or fish alongside broccoli better serves meat eaters. Both groups can benefit from the mood boost of dark chocolate, so go ahead and indulge!

For many, the best release of nervous energy is achieved through physical exercise. If this is you, don't skip your routine on exam day! Even for those who don't regularly exercise, a brisk walk around the testing facility or bear hugs in the parking lot can release some of the pent-up energy and fire up the brain-boosting endorphins that come from an increased heart rate. Note that visual processing takes up more than 50 percent of our brain's energy. If you start to feel "brain fog" during the exam, close your eyes. This gives your brain a few moments to rest, and it can provide the boost necessary for the duration of the exam.

If testing at a brick-and-mortar facility, drive the route that you will take to get there during the days before so that there are no unexpected surprises, like construction detours that will need to be considered. You will need to arrive at least 30 minutes prior to your appointment. Pack carefully—you will not be allowed any snacks, mobile phones, or other devices in the examination room, although you will be given a locker to store your personal items. For check-in, you must bring valid identification with a name that matches the name on your application. This website offers other useful on-site testing protocols to help you be ready on exam day: https://www.prometric.com/test-takers/what-expect. As of September 2021, masks are required at the testing facility.

If you are taking the exam remotely, you will need specific digital equipment, including a computer with a camera, because you will be monitored during the exam. Check and double-check your Internet connection and equipment, making sure you have a functional keyboard, mouse, and comfortable headphones if you will be using them. Ahead of test day, set up and/or clear your desk of all papers and other items, and ensure that you have good lighting. Place a "do not disturb" notice on your door. Have easy access to your confirmation email, since it contains the link to the exam portal, where you will first be asked to download the app to your computer. Check-in follows, along with comprehensive security procedures to ensure exam integrity. See a more detailed description of the remote exam day at https://www.prometric.com/proproctorcandidate.

Socially, touch bases with the people in your group who are your biggest champions, positive influence, and supporters. Embrace and believe their feedback!

Mental Mechanisms

There is no passion to be found playing small, in settling for a life that is less than the one you are capable of living.

Nelson Mandela

As the opening suggests, our bodies are designed with systems of survival; these systems may be conscious and unconscious.

A *limiting belief* is a thought, attitude, or identity that originated as a survival asset but that no longer serves that outcome. These beliefs are based on fear of failure, fear of success, fear of inadequacy, feelings of being unworthy, past failures, past conditioning. . .so many layers of what was and what could be. Here are a few examples of limiting beliefs that are activated in times of growth:

- "I can't do this."
- "I'm not smart enough."
- "I'm not good at taking tests."
- "I'd never make a good HR leader."
- "I shouldn't be taking time/money/energy away from my family."

Closely related to limiting beliefs is the *imposter syndrome*, a condition where you may feel as though you are a fraud, don't belong, or have not earned the right to be where you are, particularly when compared to others who you perceive as being better, smarter, or more deserving of success.

Both limiting beliefs and the imposter syndrome are ways that our brains keep us from taking the next step on the path to living out our capabilities. The following are a few techniques that may be just the right mechanism for overcoming the voices in your head that are holding you back. After all, limiting beliefs and other syndromes only become true if you don't take the first step. As Henry Ford said, "Whether you think you can, or think you can't, you're right." Mindset matters.

Mindset

"Phelps was emotional. He had trouble calming down before races. His parents were divorcing, and he had problems coping with the stress." So wrote *Power of Habit* (Random House, 2012) author Charles Duhigg about young swimmer Michael Phelps when a coach realized Phelps's potential. How did the 28-time Olympic medalist overcome what we all have experienced at one time or another—stress, anxiety, and fear? What were the mechanisms he used to overcome the internal and external barriers to living out his full potential? Many would argue that it was mindset, guarded by habit. According to Duhigg, Phelps began to practice a tension-releasing exercise where, every night, he would tighten his hand into a fist and then release it, imagining his tension being released along with it. Visualization, combined with dedication to a process, developed a habit that overrode the impact of the stress.

To apply this technique while preparing for this exam, first set aside a specific time every day or every week that you will study. Perhaps it is each morning before your household wakes up, or every Thursday after work. Find a quiet place where you will study—one without constant interruptions or potential distractions. Go to your dedicated space, without your phone if possible, and turn off email notifications.

Before getting started, close your eyes and regulate your breathing. As thoughts crowd in, acknowledge and then release them, perhaps by imagining them scuttling across a blue sky like a cloud in the wind or floating away like a sailboat on a lake. Try not to judge yourself for having too many thoughts; simply press a mental "release" button and continue breathing.

When you are ready, visualize a door in your mind. There is something behind the door that is important to you, that is made just for you, that is yours to claim. All you must do to get in is walk through the door. Before you go, place a powerful message upon the door—one that matters to you. Suggestions are "It is okay for me to be exceptional," or "I serve others by living my purpose." Once you have this vision firmly rooted in your mind, take a deep breath, open the door, and visualize yourself walking through it.

This is but one example of the many types of visualization techniques that exist. If it does not resonate with you, that's okay! Take some time and research others until you find the one to which you are ready to commit.

The Power of Positive Psychology

Note that any mindset visualization statements should be positive. This is an important part of mindset management. Practice catching yourself with a negative mindset and shifting it to positive language at any time during the day. For example, instead of saying "Sorry I'm late," say, "Thank you for waiting." Here are some examples of switching the limiting beliefs statements from the "Mental Mechanisms" section into a positive internal message:

- "I can't do this" to "I am more capable than I think."

- "I'm not smart enough" to "I have everything I need to be successful."

- "I'm not good at taking tests" to "I am a resilient learner."

- "I'd never make a good HR leader" to "I am the leader I needed when I was younger."

- "I shouldn't be taking time/money/energy away from my family" to "I am modeling passion and hard work to those I care about."

As with any other skill, changing a mindset from negative to positive takes practice and discipline. Keep at it until positive thinking becomes natural.

Confidence Building

Often, when champions win, they raise their arms with fingers in the "V" position—for victory. This nonverbal demonstration of confidence is signaling to others that they are powerful and at the top of their game! The question posed by a group of researchers was whether these physical, nonverbal power poses could signal power and success to our internal observers as well.

In Amy Cuddy's fantastic research and TED Talk, she discusses how when you pretend to be powerful, you begin to feel more powerful; body language can literally change our own minds. Cuddy's research found that power poses held for about two minutes before an important task reduces cortisol, the stress hormone, and increases testosterone, the confidence hormone. Standing with your chest pushed out, hands on hips, legs slightly held apart, feet planted firmly (the Wonder Woman pose) in the bathroom for two minutes before studying or right before the exam changes the hormones enough to make you feel more powerful—and confident. It is well worth 20 minutes of your study time to watch the TED Talk "Your Body Language May Shape Who You Are"—and be sure to watch until the end! Find it on YouTube here:

```
https://www.ted.com/talks/amy_cuddy_your_body_language_may_shape_
who_you_are
```

Success or failure on this exam does not indicate your value, purpose, or future achievements. The exams are simply a measurement of your representative knowledge over four hours in time, not your entire past and future career. Professional development is a journey, not an event, and getting ready through strong preparation is moving you forward as a competent human resource business partner, regardless of the initial outcome. As you prepare, strive for a healthy perspective and development mindset.

Summary

Taking a professional certification exam is an exciting development activity that anybody can achieve with the right preparation. Eligibility to sit for the CP and SCP exams is based on years of experience or education, so you already have the minimum requirements to be successful!

The preparation process serves to round out your knowledge by building on your strengths and shoring up the areas where you are least ready. A study plan is the organizational tool that maps out the activities that you should undertake throughout the recommended 12 weeks of preparation time.

Getting ready for an exam such as the CP and SCP requires resources beyond your own knowledge or experience. For some, accessing these resources is best done through a formal study group, such as those offered by universities or SHRM chapters across America. For others, the preference may be to self-study and utilize resources accessed independently, such as through online videos or articles from subject matter experts. For most, a blended approach works best.

Proper planning requires that you have benchmarks from which to establish targets and measure progress, so taking a quality practice exam should be one of the first things you do to get ready for exam day. Choose from credible resources that align the practice tests with exam weights and question style where possible.

Readiness to test is not just measured by practical knowledge of the exam BoCK. Mental fortitude and the development and application of multiple mechanisms will be required to overcome many of the beliefs and attitudes that can keep us from achieving the successes of which we are capable.

Exam Essentials

Prepare to get prepared.   A good, solid study plan will map out the resources and behaviors necessary to be ready on exam day and to learn new content to apply on the job.

Practice makes permanent.   Practice exams are necessary to identify exam readiness and to help you become familiar with the structure of exam items. Taking multiple exams over 12 weeks is an excellent way to become more comfortable so that the question structures do not get in your way on exam day.

Take advantage of exam day strategies.   Getting ready for a rigorous exam requires attention before and during the exam. This includes managing the clock, reading the question stem twice to ensure that you know what is being asked, and understanding the logistics of on-site versus remote exam facilitation. It's also important to eat right and get a little physical boost on the day of your exam to ensure optimal cognitive performance.

Develop mental mechanisms.   Developing mental mechanisms to activate our potential is an effective way to build successful habits. These mechanisms include the power of positive thinking, visualization, and physical steps that you can take to build confidence. Don't undervalue the mental preparation steps that will help you on exam day and beyond.

Understanding Human Resource Competencies

The SHRM Body of Competency and Knowledge is structured specifically around HR knowledge and behaviors. Being able to demonstrate both are necessary for exam-day success and for transfer of learning to your career.

In this part, you will find information related to the following:

The work environment where these knowledge, skills, abilities, and other characteristics will be applied

The behavioral competencies necessary to act as a valued business partner

An overview of the Leadership and Interpersonal competencies prominent within other parts of the exam

The content related to the three clusters of behavioral competencies—Business, Leadership, and Interpersonal—is layered throughout the book. Part II takes a deep look at the behavioral competencies related to Business in Chapter 4. This is to accommodate the most recent updates to the exam BoCK, where the original domain of "Strategy" was removed, and content was absorbed into other areas. Chapters 5–19 align the Leadership and Interpersonal competencies with the most relevant knowledge domains so that readers may begin to see how both technical expertise (knowledge) and behaviors (actions) work together for success.

Chapter 3

The Dynamic Environment of Human Resource Management

Exam Notables

In 2019, the World Health Organization (WHO) classified burnout as an occupational phenomenon, defining it as "a syndrome . . .resulting from chronic workplace stress that has not been managed . . ." (https://www.who.int/news/item/28-05-2019-burn-out-an-occupational-phenomenon-international-classification-of-diseases).

Even before the Covid-19 pandemic, these leaders identified three dimensions of burnout:

- Feelings of exhaustion
- Feelings of negativity about their job or company
- Feeling personally inadequate or ineffective at their jobs

It could be argued that HR professionals are at a high risk of burnout. Over the last several years, the work of HR teams has become increasingly difficult, characterized by an environment that is all at once *volatile, uncertain, complex,* and *ambiguous* (VUCA). Covid-19 amplified what was already apparent for many HR teams: political, technological, social, and other forces are changing the way that work gets done.

The activities of HR must change to keep pace with the evolution of workplace practices. This is because we must continue to meet the needs of our organizations, our industry, our employees, and ourselves. As Peter Drucker said, "The greatest danger in times of turbulence is not the turbulence—it is to act with yesterday's logic."

An Evolving Landscape

Human resource management—the practice and the people—has always had to evolve. As with any other profession, a framework of practice that aligns with educational institutions, business, and government helps keep practitioners pointed at the same targets. A body of knowledge, such as the exam BoCK developed by SHRM, identifies the knowledge, skills, abilities, tasks, duties, and responsibilities that are required to be successful.

As in the study of industrial-organizational psychology, the work of human resources is practiced in the field. Human resources is a professional service industry that draws from the principles of business, psychology, finance, sales, data management, and more. All these principles are used by HR teams to do one thing: understand and influence the relationship between the organization and its employees to drive business results. Consider this quote:

> 100 percent of customers are people. 100 percent of employees are people. If you don't understand people, you don't understand business.
>
> *Simon Sinek*

In recent years, there have been significant developments that have changed the way that HR is practiced. These developments are covered next.

Strategic Alignment

As each chapter will demonstrate, most HR systems must align with business strategy. For example, upskilling current employees has strategic benefit, because it positions the business for the future. A strategic intervention will generally be built around people, processes, or the organization, and it will require HR practices that support business operations to drive results. Best case scenarios occur when HR is part of the strategic planning process.

Global Operations

The world of work is much more accessible than ever before. Economic changes, technological advances, organizational offshoring/outsourcing, and local recruiting challenges all have contributed to a work environment that crosses borders. The implications for human resource management include managing diversity, building cultural awareness, and directing a dispersed workforce. HR advises senior leaders and builds HR practices that account for the impact of these issues within the workforce.

Diversity, Equity, and Inclusion

Diversity, equity, and inclusion (DEI) is another human resource responsibility that has evolved in recent years. The social justice movement has required that organizations go beyond compliance with equal opportunity laws. HR is responsible for advising and implementing DEI interventions to drive change at a systemic level. This is done through the employer's hiring practices, opportunities for learning, mentoring programs, and measuring of progress.

Talent Acquisition and Workforce Management

Talent supply and demand is a major influencer of how HR practices are designed and administered. When there is a shortage of qualified workers, employers must get creative to attract the people necessary to remain competitive. Amazon's "returners" program is one example that targets software engineers. Individuals who have been out of the workforce for more than two years may apply for the program, and if selected, they are immersed in mentoring and other training designed to upskill to fill future openings. It's not enough just to get them through the door; HR takes the lead on retention practices that serve the needs of employees. HR also keeps track of social trends that drive retention, from offering popular perks to more systemic changes, such as redesigning jobs to accommodate hybrid work.

Regulatory Environment

It seems that January 1st of each year is the great equalizer—new labor laws go into effect that HR professionals at all stages of their career must learn and adapt to. In addition to foundational laws such as the Americans with Disabilities Act and the Fair Labor Standards Act, HR must also keep abreast of state and local regulations. Agencies such as the Equal Employment Opportunity Commission release guidance documents, and court cases change the rights and responsibilities of the employer and the employee. Many employers report that most of their training budget goes toward compliance with the many labor laws that exist. HR serves in an advisory and operational role when working within the regulatory environment.

Measuring Results

As with any other business unit, HR must be able to demonstrate the value and return-on-investment of their contributions. This is done using qualitative and quantitative measures that aid in evidenced-based decision-making. Metrics exist for each functional area of human resources, including hiring, training, and employee relations.

Corporate Social Responsibility

Of particular significance in these times is the need for businesses of all sizes to contribute to employee health and wellness in ways that go beyond the paycheck. Corporate social responsibility (CSR) and governance initiatives seek to find ways to positively sustain vital conditions or avoid doing harm. To do so, organizations must have a clear understanding of all stakeholders and the impact of their business practices. CSR has strategic value in that many people are seeking purpose in their work, and the employer brand is a driver of consumer behavior. Building sustainable work practices supports a company's resource pipeline, ensuring that adequate resources are available when needed.

In addition to the environmental factors that influence the work of HR, specific characteristics exist that help HR professionals navigate these conditions. These are described at length throughout the pages of the exam BoCK, and they generally reflect what the environment demands of their HR teams.

HR Demographics

Recruiter, employment specialist, chief happiness officer, specialist, generalist, investigator, culture champion, event planner, problem-solver, negotiator. . .HR by any other name is still fundamentally about serving as a bridge between business and people. Figure 3.1 highlights a few demographics of HR, including the average pay for these professionals. Unfortunately, the data will show that HR teams across the United States have a way to go in balancing a lack of equity within their own departments including lack of diversity and the significant pay gap between male and female HR professionals.

FIGURE 3.1   Who we are 2019–2020

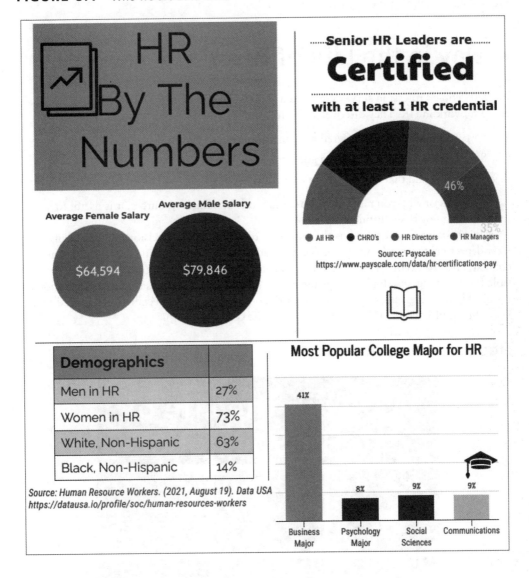

Social changes are also driving the makeup of an HR professional. For example, more employers are hiring DEI professionals as part of their executive suite and within their HR teams. Many protected class groups have not had access to educational opportunities, and so requiring multiple years of experience or a formal education in this area is counterproductive since this role is still emerging. The need for bilingual skills will also continue to grow, particularly as more organizations go global and immigration patterns shift.

The exam BoCK does an excellent job of describing the knowledge and behavioral competencies that HR professionals must have or develop to succeed in these environments; all are covered in detail in the chapters of this book.

A Day in the Life of HR

A 2020 People Profession survey conducted by SHRM looked at the reasons why individuals chose to work in HR. They discovered the following:

- 95 percent said that HR offered a meaningful career.
- 88 percent said that HR offered good career prospects.
- 79 percent said that HR had good earning potential.

Regardless of why you may have chosen to work in human resources, it is useful to understand a few basic distinctions.

A *line manager* is one who has the authority to act and make decisions on behalf of their department. A *staff manager* is one who advises and supports line managers. In this context, HR professionals are staff managers (and individual contributors) who are responsible for designing, developing, implementing, and evaluating systems that drive operational results. Figure 3.2 gives examples of the work context of an HR Specialist, as reported by the Department of Labor's O*Net site (`https://onetonline.org`).

FIGURE 3.2 HR Specialist role

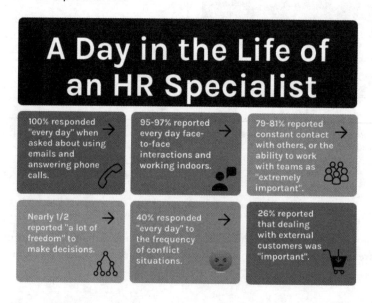

A Day in the Life of an HR Specialist

100% responded "every day" when asked about using emails and answering phone calls.

95-97% reported every day face-to-face interactions and working indoors.

79-81% reported constant contact with others, or the ability to work with teams as "extremely important".

Nearly 1/2 reported "a lot of freedom" to make decisions.

40% responded "every day" to the frequency of conflict situations.

26% reported that dealing with external customers was "important".

The role of HR occurs within three distinct yet related categories: strategic, operational, and administrative.

In the strategic role, HR teams contribute to organizational development, design, and building of intervention strategies that are closely tied to the company's mission, vision, values, and goals. Although it is the job of line managers to implement and manage many of these systems within their departments, HR serves in an ongoing advisory and support capacity. Policies, procedures, and rules are designed to support business strategy and employees throughout all stages of the employee life cycle. Here are a few examples:

- Developing the employer brand and using it to recruit and retain team members
- Designing total rewards systems that attract qualified talent and reward performance
- Designing learning and development programs that support the workforce's current skill sets and upskills or reskills to prepare the workforce for future needs
- Managing the relationships within the workplace, including the relationship with a labor union
- Effectively managing risk to the organization and protecting the safety and health of the employees
- Conducting workforce research to collect data related to job attitudes and workforce needs, remaining up-to-date with employment trends, and making a business case for change when necessary

The operational role of HR professionals includes advocating for the needs of the employees. Necessary behavioral competencies, such as conflict management, negotiation, communication, and relationship management, are used on a daily and a weekly basis. Individuals in an operational role will also require the ability to navigate organizational politics and work with other departments and personnel to gain buy-in and support for HR intervention strategies. HR operations also refers to the functional aspect of an HR team, such as processing payroll and recruiting.

Becoming overwhelmed with data is a daily threat to HR departments in all industries. Administratively, HR must build data and knowledge management systems that are organized and secure. Personnel files must be properly managed and human resource information systems selected that optimize integration with other employer systems.

Internally, the administrative data management efforts of HR help protect employee confidential information. Applicant tracking, training records, performance feedback, and maintaining of accurate time records all fall within this functional role of HR. Employment law is the main driver of the external forces affecting personnel record management. This includes maintaining of safety records, retirement documents, hiring statistics, and accommodation management. These records must be stored and secured, and the appropriate reports submitted, depending on the size of the organization. The administrative function also includes properly destroying records in accordance with various recordkeeping requirements.

Chapter 15, "Structure of the HR Function," takes a deep dive into the educational and experience requirements of an HR professional, along with the various ways that an HR department can be integrated with other business units.

HR Professional Development

SHRM's BoCK is instructive in more ways than just preparing for the exam. The document outlines the knowledge, skills, and abilities that must be developed to perform the various tasks, duties, and responsibilities on a day-to-day basis. Because these exams are all about "real-world" applications, the following examples are aligned with the BoCK and highlight an informal and formal learning and development opportunity for HR practitioners.

As the leading advisory group for the human resources industry, SHRM gives us important insights into the dynamic environment in which HR performs. These a few of the featured topics from the Society for Human Resource Management's annual conference in 2021 (https://annual21.shrm.org).

Workplace   A breakout session was focused on the important issue of alcohol, drugs, and mental health. This is an example of how deeply interrelated many issues are, and the resulting impact in the areas of risk management, social responsibility, diversity, inclusion, and employment law.

People   The keynote feature at the 2021 conference was delivered by a chief-team from Chipotle. Their topic focused on the importance of a partnership between HR and senior leadership, and the influence of workplace culture and relationships on talent acquisition strategies.

Organization   Another in-person event featured how HR can leverage technology to build people systems, scale HR departments, collect data, and improve organizational effectiveness.

In addition to SHRM's commitment to researching and developing HR best practices, they designed a curriculum template for university business programs that concentrate on HR management. These guides focus on the knowledge and behavioral competencies of HR that businesses need from their HR professionals.

The Department of Labor reports that in 2019, 47 percent of HR students graduate with a bachelor's degree, and as noted in an earlier section, the top degree choice for HR practitioners is in business administration.

Here is an example of content from California Southern University's Bachelor of Business Administration with a concentration in Human Resources Management that aligns with SHRM's curriculum recommendations (https://www.calsouthern.edu/business-management/bba):

Leadership   Describe the importance of integrity and professional ethical responsibilities in business operations.

Interpersonal   Describe the interaction between effective leadership, organizational culture, and human relationships.

Business   Formulate strategies to solve business problems using appropriate methodologies and tools.

Landing Your First Job in HR

It can be difficult to land that first job in human resources, especially without work experience or education. Too often, people think that they want to go into HR because they "like people." And it's true—a passion for people must be at the heart of everything we do. However, it is also important that individuals develop knowledge of business, operational efficiencies, technology, metrics, and more. When starting out, don't be afraid to accept a position that gives you exposure to all the business units within an organization. As you grow, ask for opportunities to lead teams, participate in committees, and gain exposure to the transactional or administrative tasks of management, particularly the ones that will transfer into an HR role. Be sure to round this out by joining a local SHRM chapter and networking for exposure, advice, and volunteer activities. Get professionally certified in any HR credential for which you qualify. This could be a specialized credential, such as a becoming a certified coach, or a generalist credential, such as the aPHR (Associate Professional in Human Resources), which does not have an experience or education requirement. When you find a desirable HR opportunity, align your work experience, professional networking, and credentials with HR competencies to demonstrate that you are ready to take on a formal HR role.

Managing Burnout

WHO's report referenced in the introduction to this chapter suggests that burnout should not be classified as a mental or workplace disease, but rather as a human condition. An HR professional's risk for burnout is higher than it has ever been before, accelerated by the chaos from the Covid-19 pandemic, which began in 2020. Many of our teams are experiencing the exhaustion, stress, and hostility toward their jobs that characterize burnout. It is the task of HR to support employees experiencing burnout while also taking care to manage their own needs.

In the American Psychological Association's podcast "Why we're burned out and what to do about it," with Christina Maslach, the host talks about how employers are *coping* with burnout but not actually *fixing* burnout. Dr. Maslach, professor of psychology at the Graduate School at U.C. Berkeley, discusses how taking time off, employee wellness programs, and other strategies targeting employee burnout do not fundamentally address the problem. The WHO report does not suggest that it is only up to the individual to solve the problem, but that a multi-resourced approach that looks at individual, job, and organizational factors is necessary. Learn more here:

http://sopapa.apa.libsynpro.com/why-were-burned-out-and-what-to-do-about-it-with-christina-maslach-phd

At an individual level, it has been in my personal experience that HR professionals put themselves last. I am not just referring to self-care, such as stepping away from the desk to eat lunch, although that is certainly a factor. Many individuals in HR do not benefit from the recognition and rewards systems that they design and implement. It may be as simple as removing themselves from an employee raffle in order not to appear unethical, to eating last at the holiday banquet because they are busy organizing.

On a deeper level, HR pros may be less likely to have a mentor or a coach, even though they coordinate these resources for other business units. Professional development is not always a priority, and nearly 100 percent of the employed students in my exam prep classes report difficulty in finding time to study because work is so busy. Gender comes into play here, especially as numerous reports found that women shouldered the bulk of childcare responsibilities during the stay-at-home orders of the Covid-19 pandemic, leaving the female-dominated role of HR with both occupational and parental burnout. Women also tend to have lower negotiating skills, which may account for some of the disparity in pay between the men and women noted by the demographic figure in an earlier section.

At a job level in human resources, there is often more work to be done than personnel to do it. Taking time off from an HR desk usually means coming back to a voice mailbox that is full and to unmet employee needs. Because these employee needs are important, such as payroll errors or questions about benefits, many HR professionals never truly disconnect; they continue to answer calls and respond to emails during "off" time. Other individuals experience occupational exhaustion not because they are overworked, but because they spend the bulk of their days putting out fires or dwelling on negative situations. True burnout strategies will require that the job be restructured to some degree, the workload better distributed, or the ratio of HR to full-time employees more reasonable.

Organizationally, if there is a lack of trust in leadership or a toxic environment, HR's positive influence will be severely limited. If HR does not have the autonomy and respect necessary to make changes and address relational needs, burnout is likely to follow. This is particularly the case for HR individuals who desire to make a difference and thus begin to second-guess their own talent or occupational choice. Companies with high turnover due to systemic issues can also frustrate an HR pro, since they are left to deal with avoidable consequences such as responding to lawsuits, addressing employee morale, and handling separation meetings. All this negativity does take its toll.

Resilience, grit, and passion, in addition to technical competence, are necessary characteristics of an HR pro who can last. When true dysfunction exists without any support for change, it may be time to switch companies to one where there is greater respect for the important work of HR.

Of course, there is no perfect person, job, or organization, and the conditions described in this chapter are true for many roles. When HR is perceived as a credible business partner, they can play a key role in helping to develop job, task, and individual interventions to stop the negative influence that work can have on employee mental health. Redesigning jobs, offering social support, designing flexible work arrangements such as job sharing, and empathetic leadership are all ways that HR can resolve burnout throughout their teams. The key is advocacy, for others as well as for themselves.

Summary

The exam BoCK describes the human resources technical and behavioral competencies that are applied in an HR management environment that is volatile, uncertain, complex, and ambiguous (VUCA). These VUCA disruptions are driven by the evolution of industrial practices, such as the rise of global competitiveness, the shortage of qualified workers, and social issues demanding a collective response. HR must shift their own performance to align with the needs of the business's stakeholders, including employees, clients, shareholders, vendors, and the communities where they operate.

The ability to be a contributing and valued HR business partner involves several common characteristics. From a demographic perspective, education seems to be concentrated in business management, with nearly three-quarters of practitioners being women. Industry and departmental inequities should be addressed as part of an organization's overall DEI activities.

Many of the skills and abilities that are used by HR practitioners are applied throughout the life cycle of the employee. From recruiting to separation and all activities in between, research is used to inform evidenced-based decision-making that drives necessary change. People interactions through phone calls and face-to-face interactions are used every day by HR teams, requiring strong communication, relationships, and problem-solving competencies.

Developing competencies is achieved through formal and informal professional development activities. Too often, HR stays focused on their customer at the expense of their own opportunities for development. Attending networking events, taking classes, or achieving professional certification that is relevant for their stage of the career path can help ensure that HR teams have the most up-to-date knowledge to perform successfully.

Employees in industries that were significantly affected by the rapid changes forced on their workplace by Covid-19 continue to be at high risk for burnout. First responders, grocery store personnel, and teachers are some examples of industries that were severely disrupted because of the pandemic. These disruptions required rapid adaptations to the way work was performed. A driving force of implementing these changes involved HR professionals completing tasks such as policy development, activating remote equipment, advising employees about unemployment, securing personal protective equipment, researching tax credits, and more. HR individuals often experience burnout themselves, and they are charged with designing meaningful programs that address the underlying cause of burnout, for themselves and their teams.

Exam Essentials

Identify the environmental factors that affect HR practices.   As the business landscape changes, HR practices must adapt in response. This is so that HR teams continue to be effective by aligning people practices with business strategy that drives results. Other environmental conditions such as global practices, social movements, and talent availability all demand real-time changes to HR activities.

Prepare for demographic changes to HR teams.   The makeup of a typical HR professional demonstrates challenges within their own departments that will also require an evolution. This is to reflect inequities that exist within the industry as well as how the role of HR continues to develop. Knowledge and behavioral competencies will also evolve as the needs of business and individuals change.

Perform in a typical HR environment.   HR roles across all industries are built around the strategic, operational, and administrative tasks of a practitioner. These tasks and responsibilities exist within all the traditional functions of an HR job.

Engage in ongoing professional development activities.   Because the business landscape changes so rapidly, HR must engage in ongoing professional development activities that help them stay relevant. These activities can be informal, such as attending educational networking events, or formal, such as getting a degree in human resources or achieving professional certification.

Understand ways to manage burnout.   Burnout is a condition that is characterized by stress, exhaustion, feelings of hostility, and inefficacy. Burnout can occur in any organizational role, including that of HR. HR teams should lead the way in finding individual, job, and organizational intervention strategies that address the root cause of these issues.

Chapter
4

The Business
Competency Cluster

Exam Notables

Fun fact! Google got its name from a typo. The founders had planned to name their new company *googol* (a mathematical term for the number 1 followed by 100 zeroes), but an opportune misspelling changed the name for good. What's behind that name is brand recognition, the fastest search engine in the world, and a technological infrastructure that handles more than 70 percent of global online searches (William L. Hosch, *Google: An American Company*, Brittanica.com). These business competencies are part of Google's competitive advantage.

Figure 4.1 defines the individual components of competencies: the knowledge, skills, and abilities required to perform at an organizational level (such as Google's core competencies) and an individual level (such as the exam BoCK).

FIGURE 4.1   Review of competency components

Competencies
The knowledge, skills, abilities, and behaviors that contribute to individual and organizational performance.

Knowledge
Information developed or learned through education, experience or research.

Skills
The outcome of regularly applying knowledge or ability.

Abilities
The innate potential to perform mental and physical tasks.

Behaviors
Observable actions of an individual at work.

Proficiency Indicators: The level of competency defined for each stage of an HR career.

Fundamental to the relationship between human resources and their organizations is business management. HR teams apply relevant theories (knowledge) to design HR systems (behaviors) that drive results through business management principles and best practices. For this reason, the business competencies are the focus of this chapter.

SHRM defines this cluster as follows:

> Ensuring that HR contributes to the strategic direction of the organization; understanding the business and the environment in which it operates; designing and implementing business solutions to meet human capital needs; contributing to and leading change management initiatives; and gathering and analyzing data to inform business decisions.

Business Competencies

The U.S. gross domestic product (GDP) is an economic indicator that is monitored across the world. It includes the value of goods and services produced by businesses. In 2020, about a million workers generated a GDP of more than $20 trillion, down just a bit from 2019, but increasing every quarter of 2021 (`https://www.bea.gov/data/gdp/gross-domestic-product`).

Where there are employees, there are personnel needs that must be managed, and this is at the heart of the responsibilities of HR teams. Human resources departments exist within most industries, including the largest U.S. employer, the federal government. Other industries include technology, healthcare, education, manufacturing, and entertainment. The ability of HR people to perform within these industries requires the thorough development of business knowledge and competencies that support competitiveness, advise leaders, and use data to solve organizational problems.

Business Acumen

The BoCK defines the competency of Business Acumen as follows:

> The KSAOs needed to understand the organization's operations, functions and external environment, and to apply business tools and analyses that inform HR initiatives and operations consistent with the overall strategic direction of the organization.

Business and Competitive Awareness

HR's understanding of business management tools and techniques, in addition to the specifics of HR management, is critical to the development of a *human capital strategy*. Human capital refers to the collective employee knowledge and other skills that are deployed toward the execution of business strategy. The term "capital" refers to the wealth of an individual or a business. In this context, employee talents are a form of capital that is strategically utilized to achieve results. Here are two formulas designed to measure the effectiveness of human capital strategies:

Human Capital Value Add

Revenue – (Operating expense – Total Reward costs) / Number of Full-Time Employees

Human Capital Return-on-Investment

Revenue – (Operating expense – Total Reward costs) / Total Reward costs

In addition to understanding the effect of human capital efforts, other factors affect organizational competitiveness. Michael Porter, Professor at Harvard University and well-renowned business strategist identified five major forces that influence an organization's competitive position. These forces are as follows:

Threat of New Entry   In an episode of the show *Billions*, a principal character wanted to buy a bank. Despite being a wealthy and influential CEO of a multibillion-dollar hedge fund, this character could not get approved by the Securities and Exchange Commission (SEC) (*Season 5, Episode 3*, written by Ben Mezrich, directed by John Dahl. Showtime, May 2020). In industries with high barriers to entry, such as government regulation or cost, the competitive threat of new entry is low.

Threat of Substitute Products or Services   In the mid-2000s teachers across America were tormented by the wildly popular children's toy, the fidget spinner. At the height of the craze, the toys were being manufactured in China, the United States, and Switzer-land. Because of the simple design and lack of clear ownership, it was easy for manufac-turers to create substitute models, preventing any single company from fully profiting from this trend.

Bargaining Power of Supplier   "Surge pricing" is a method of adding a premium to the cost of Uber rides when demand is high and available drivers are low. In some cases, the price increases by 50 percent (Kate Konger, "Prepare to Pay More for Uber and Lyft Rides," *The New York Times*, June 2021). This is an example of high supplier power.

Bargaining Power of Buyer   Many experts advise that the best time to buy a home is in the spring because a variety of inventory is coming on to the market. This is a case of the bargaining power of the buyer, as supply levels are high in many markets.

Rivalry Among Existing Competitors   When buying a car, consumers have a choice between affordability and luxury, and there are thousands of makes and models to choose from in both categories. Because industry rivalry is high, car manufacturers will compete by lowering prices, increasing services, or offering high quality.

Analyzing the five forces as part of an organization's strategic process allows for a real-time response to changing conditions. Other analysis tools include the strengths, weaknesses, opportunities, and threats (SWOT) audit and an analysis of the political, economic, social, technological, legal, and environmental (PESTLE) forces affecting businesses, both covered in more detail in Chapter 5, "Strategic Human Resource Management."

Financial Analysis

Financial analysis is an objective review of inputs and outputs that are organized and communicated through financial reports. As the GIGO principle asserts "garbage in, garbage out," so a company's overall enterprise management or other systems, such as inventory and timekeeping, must be accurate. Table 4.1 lists the fundamental accounting terms that you should understand, including a short description of the three main financial reports: the *balance sheet, statement of cash flow* and *the profit and loss statement.*

TABLE 4.1   Basic accounting terms

Assets	The financial holdings of a business including cash, investments, inventory, tools, and equipment.	Liabilities	The financial debts that the company owes, including outstanding payables and bank loans or other financing.
Balance Sheet Statement	A financial report that shows assets and liabilities over a given time.	Net Loss	When expenses exceed revenue.
Cash Flow Statement	Net amount of cash and cash equivalents that moves into and out of a business over a given time.	Net Profit	Total revenue minus expenses.
Cost of Goods Sold (COGS)	Represents the material and labor costs that are used to produce goods or services.	Payables	Outstanding billing that is owed to vendors and other lenders.
Debt	Money borrowed from a lender that accrues interest.	Profit and Loss statement (also called an Income statement)	A statement that summarizes income and expenses over a given time.
Depreciation	An accounting method that calculates the cost of a tangible or physical asset over its life expectancy.	Receivables	Outstanding billing that is owed by customers.

TABLE 4.1   Basic accounting terms *(continued)*

Equity	Different from the term used in terms of equal employment, equity is the degree of ownership in the business.	Return-on-Investment	The amount of profit earned from an investment calculated by dividing net profit by the cost of the investment.
Expenses	Operating and other costs of doing business.	Revenue	The amount of income coming in at any given time, such as monthly or quarterly.
Interest Rate	The amount charged by a lender for debt calculated as a percentage against the total or remaining balance owed.		

In addition to the terms related to understanding financial statements, human resources, especially advanced HR professionals, should understand the formulas used to analyze the health of the business and aid in decision-making. These are shown in Table 4.2.

TABLE 4.2   Financial ratios

Financial Measure	Calculation
Accounts Receivable Turnover	Net Terms Sales/ Average Accounts Receivables
Debt to Asset Ratio	Total Liabilities/ Total Assets
Debt to Equity Ratio	Total Debt/ Equity
Earnings Before Interest, Taxes, Depreciation, and Amortization (EBITDA)	Earnings before interest, tax, depreciation/ Total Sales
Gross Margin	Total Sales-Cost of Goods Sold (COGS)/ Total Sales
Profit Margin	Net Terms Sales / Average Accounts Receivables

Strategic Alignment

It used to be that the fundamental purpose of for-profit businesses was to be financially competitive within their markets and to deliver maximum shareholder value. This is still true to a large extent. However, just as employees currently hold the power in the labor market, consumer needs and attitudes are driving the strategic focus of many businesses today. From operational issues such as free shipping for online orders to a more global demand for corporate social responsibility, organizations must develop business strategies that go beyond revenue generation.

The psychological contract between an employee and their employer looks completely different than it did even five years ago, and it continues to change as employee attitudes about work, social issues, and collective values evolve. HR's expertise in the people-oriented programs in the workplace have become even more valuable as a result. HR and business strategy are interdependent and thus must be aligned.

Company Culture

> Culture eats strategy for lunch.
>
> *Peter Drucker*

Sociologists and anthropologists have long studied the effect of group belonging and how it shapes shared values and beliefs. These shared elements have a direct effect on how people behave and what is considered acceptable or normal. This research has been expanded to include the effect of culture within organizations.

Company culture affects many organizational outcomes, including employee morale, job satisfaction, diversity, motivation, and more. Changing an organizational culture is necessary when it is no longer serving the people or results, and thus HR is generally charged with navigating the conflict that comes with such change. To develop this competency, organizations must understand the foundational theories of culture.

Edgar Schein

Edgar Schein is a well-known leader on the theory of organizational culture and culture change. A professor at MIT and educated at both Stanford and Harvard, he provided an important foundational perspective. Schein defines culture as follows:

> A pattern of shared basic assumptions—invented, discovered, or developed by a given group as it learns to cope with problems of external adaptation and internal integration—that has worked well enough to be considered valid and, therefore be taught to new members as the correct way to perceive, think and feel in relation to those problems.

> *Edgar Schein* (in Stuart Crainer, *The Ultimate Business Library*, Capstone Publishing, 2006)

Schein believed that culture constrains any organizational strategy, regardless of resource availability. The absence of a positive culture, or indeed, a toxic workplace, will decrease the odds of a successful strategic initiative.

Schein presents culture as a series of assumptions that a person makes about the group in which they participate. He suggests that there are three levels of corporate culture:

- At the center of organizational culture are *basic assumptions* about human behavior, which are usually so deeply embedded into the culture that it becomes difficult to isolate.

- Encompassing the assumptions are *expressed values* taken from those assumptions. These usually emerge in the form of standards, rules, and public expressions of the organization's philosophy.

- At the surface level are *artifacts*, which are the outcome of the assumptions and values, which reflect as actions, policies, the physical environment, office jokes, and so forth.

Schein notes that culture is not a static but rather a fluid state that adopts and adapts as new information is discovered. From a strategic perspective, organizations with cultures that fail to adapt are entrenched and less able to respond to the following:

- Porter's five forces and other external, environmental conditions as represented by PESTLE and SWOT analyses

- What is real versus what is perceived

- The different characteristics of people, including personality and personal cultures

- The changing nature of relationships at work

Regardless of the stage of culture development, Schein noted that there were five categories of agreement that were necessary for culture evolutions:

- The company mission

- Goals

- How the goals will be accomplished

- How progress will be measured

- How to make repairs and/or redirect

Geert Hofstede

Geert Hofstede is another pioneer in the space of company culture. His work includes references to how cultural characteristics manifest at different stages of development. Values are at the center of any culture, and they are communicated through observable practices, such as rituals, heroes, and symbols. Other insights from Hofstede's work include the following:

- No group can escape culture.

- Culture is contagious.

- Culture is beyond race, family, and other demographics.

Perhaps Hofstede's main contribution to the theories of culture is his identification of cultural dimensions. For example, in the dimensions of indulgence versus restraint, cultures that value restraint are less emotionally demonstrative, whereas in more indulgent cultures, more demonstrative expressions are acceptable—and even expected. Figure 4.2 illustrates Hofstede's five other cultural dimensions.

FIGURE 4.2 Hofstede's dimensions of culture

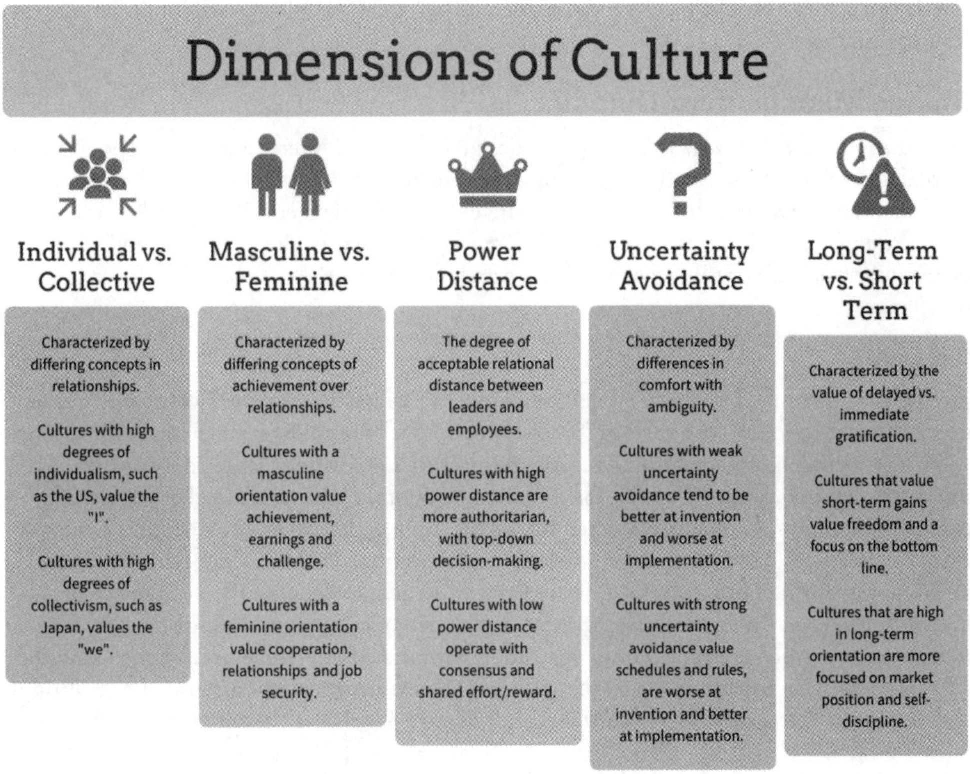

Dimensions of Culture

Individual vs. Collective	Masculine vs. Feminine	Power Distance	Uncertainty Avoidance	Long-Term vs. Short Term
Characterized by differing concepts in relationships.	Characterized by differing concepts of achievement over relationships.	The degree of acceptable relational distance between leaders and employees.	Characterized by differences in comfort with ambiguity.	Characterized by the value of delayed vs. immediate gratification.
Cultures with high degrees of individualism, such as the US, value the "I".	Cultures with a masculine orientation value achievement, earnings and challenge.	Cultures with high power distance are more authoritarian, with top-down decision-making.	Cultures with weak uncertainty avoidance tend to be better at invention and worse at implementation.	Cultures that value short-term gains value freedom and a focus on the bottom line.
Cultures with high degrees of collectivism, such as Japan, values the "we".	Cultures with a feminine orientation value cooperation, relationships and job security.	Cultures with low power distance operate with consensus and shared effort/reward.	Cultures with strong uncertainty avoidance value schedules and rules, are worse at invention and better at implementation.	Cultures that are high in long-term orientation are more focused on market position and self-discipline.

Source: *Cultures and Organizations: Software of the Mind.* By Geert Hofstede, Gert Jan Hofstede and Michael Minkov. McGraw-Hill, 2010

Fons Trompenaars and Charles Hampden-Turner

Fons Trompenaars and Charles Hampden-Turner added their views on culture via the dilemmas that occur when making choices or assigning value. These dilemmas are as follows:

Achieved vs. Ascribed (assigned): Merit over network

Individual vs. Group: The focus of decision-making

Internal vs. External: Control over one's destiny

Neutral/Affective: Expressions of emotions

Specific vs. Diffuse (broad): Degree of boundaries

Sequential vs. Synchronic (concurrent): Sense of time

Universal vs. Particular (precise): Rule flexibility

In business strategies such as mergers and acquisitions (M&A), or in building global operations, HR adds value by helping to identify and resolve these dilemmas to create a more cohesive structure. As Schein referenced earlier, failure to align cultures will limit the success of such a venture.

Change Management Theories

Organizational development is built on the design of planned interventions to respond to internal and external forces affecting company performance. Interventions at a business, department, process, or individual level require change management. Particularly with human resource solutions, HR acts as the change agent—that is, the champion and advocate for the intervention. For this reason, we must understand the theories behind effective change.

Kurt Lewin

Kurt Lewin's force-field analysis model for change is like Michael Porter's competitive theories in that he describes the various forces at work that help to determine which direction behavior—including organizational behavior—will go. Like water that erodes rock over time, forces that constantly flow in one direction or another will result in change. The key to controlling this phenomenon is when the forces driving change in one direction are met equally with forces driving change in the opposite direction. This process begins by identifying what is getting in the way of a desired state and acknowledging the need for change, thereby "unfreezing" a commitment to current behavior. Doing so allows for new behaviors to be introduced that produce the change, along with the counterforce necessary to stop the old behaviors. This tension between the old and the new brings about a sense of equilibrium, allowing for a "refreezing" of the new behavior. Figure 4.3 shows the three stages of Lewin's model.

Force-field analysis has been very useful when planning and executing organizational changes. The model separates between external and internal forces for change and external and internal forces resisting change. Forces for change could be sociocultural, based on governmental regulations, as well as changes in market share and production economics. Forces resisting change can stem from the organization's prior commitments, culture, or limited resources.

Whenever an organization is considering an episodic change, the most appropriate sequence to follow is the unfreeze-change-refreeze. Episodic change should be implemented for organizations that are characterized by inertia and the inability to change as rapidly as their environment. In the unfreeze stage, we must disconfirm employees' expectations, consider the induction of learning anxiety, and provide employees with psychological safety that turns their anxiety into motivation. During the change phase, we need to use cognitive restructuring to redefine new concepts, expectations, and standards. Finally, during the refreeze stage, practitioners should develop social norms supportive of the new behaviors that are expected of the employees.

FIGURE 4.3   Unfreeze, change, refreeze

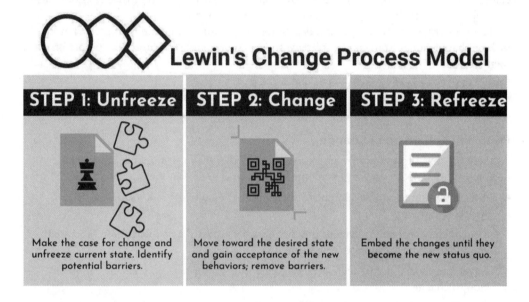

Continuous change should be considered for organizations that accept change to be a constant. When it comes to continuous change, freeze-rebalance-unfreeze should be considered as the optimal sequence. During the freeze stage, change agents need to provide employees with tools such as maps and schemas that will reinforce the desired behaviors and practices. During the rebalance stage, change agents should try to reframe issues and concerns as opportunities and new endeavors. Finally, during the unfreeze stage, learning and improvisation should continue in a way that is meaningful and understood by all employees.

John Kotter

According to John Kotter, there is a preferred order to follow when leading change management efforts. This eight-step process looks like this:

1. Create a sense of urgency and justification for the change.
2. Build a leadership team or coalition to guide the change.
3. Formulate a strategic vision and initiatives to reach it.
4. Communicate the vision and its benefits to generate support.
5. Empower action and remove barriers to change.
6. Generate short-term wins early in the process to build momentum.

7. Be patient and persistent to sustain and accelerate progress.

8. Institutionalize changes to ensure their permanence.

McKinsey's 7 S's

McKinsey and Company is a well-regarded leader in the world of management consulting. Part of their work includes conducting research, and this includes research in the field of change management. Their 7-S model provides a framework for change that considers the multiple factors influencing (or getting in the way of) strategy.

The 7 S's are of equal importance; one is not more compelling than the other. They include shared values, staff, skills, strategy, style, systems, and structure. Learn more about their work at:

```
https://www.mckinsey.com/business-functions/
strategy-and-corporate-finance/our-insights/enduring-ideas-the-7-
s-framework
```

Overcoming Barriers to Change

As these theories show, there are no shortages of challenges to sustainable change. HR will need to call upon techniques to overcome barriers to change that include the following:

- Utilizing training and development to ensure that employees understand what is expected of them

- Using behavioral reinforcement practices, such as reward and recognition (and sometimes discipline), to support new behaviors

- Leveraging social needs, such as belonging and peer pressure, to create the motivation to change

- Identifying a change agent to model new behaviors and inspire others to do the same

Having a linear process is helpful when managing complex change and overcoming barriers. While there are always variables that cannot be accounted for, a systematic, step-by-step process can mitigate the effects of the unexpected. For purposes of the SHRM exams, gaining buy-in from leadership by making a business case for change, followed by action plans to engage employees in the changes, effectively communicating through the change management process, and addressing any barriers to the new behaviors during and through evaluation after the changes take effect, are recommended. These basic principles hold true regardless of which of the change management theories you choose to adopt.

Consultation

The BoCK defines the competency of Consultation as follows:

> The KSAOs needed to work with organizational stakeholders in evaluating business challenges and identifying opportunities for the design, implementation and evaluation of change initiatives, and to build ongoing support for HR solutions that meet the changing needs of customers and the business.

Evaluating Business Challenges

One of the main responsibilities of human resources is to serve as an adviser. This requires the ability to collaborate and partner effectively with other departments in order to identify business challenges and create HR solutions. Common areas for troubleshooting include performance management, recruiting, training, and relationships.

As with any strategic or operational initiative, it is a necessary first step to identify the gaps between current and desired state. This involves interviewing all stakeholders to ensure that the appropriate perspectives are considered. HR takes this information and makes a business case for one or two possible solutions.

Key to this process is understanding and effectively communicating the risk of taking, or not taking, action. Compliance, lost opportunities, and increased exposure to threats and liabilities must all be factored into evaluating a best course of action.

It is important to note that HR does not often have authority in these matters. We facilitate, gather data, identify multiple solutions, and communicate risks using our unique expertise. Once an informed decision has been made, HR will design and implement solutions.

Designing and Implementing HR Solutions

It is understandable that an HR desk is often overflowing with the current delivery of services, and operationally, this is necessary. When serving in a consulting role, though, HR casts a wider net to understand the challenges that other department leaders are having with their teams to drive change. Effective consulting is a mix of art and science, intuition, and thinking. Informed consulting begins with a discovery process that is innovative and unlimited, a form of "intentional wandering" designed to understand, not resolve, and flowing between an organic and systematic state. HR consultants will need to practice nonjudgment and stay within the boundaries of their own expertise. Once the problem is sufficiently understood and targets have been established, HR helps to design and then implement intervention strategies. Figure 4.4 shows the life cycle of a business, and it gives examples of HR solutions to the challenges that are unique to each stage.

HR intervention strategies are delivered through HR systems; HR systems are managed within the HR department. Fundamental to delivery of these services is the structure of an HR department. This is covered in detail in Chapter 15, "Structure of the HR Function." When designing and implementing solutions, HR teams will draw upon skills such as listening, empathy, and follow-up to the organizational and individual performance challenges getting in the way of results.

Motivation Theories

At the heart of many individual performance challenges often lies a lack of motivation or desire to change. The survival instincts of humans include a deeply rooted need for the status quo, and it is this that must be overcome to effect lasting change. Employees may be motivated from intrinsic factors, such as a belief that they can be successful (called *self-efficacy*), or from extrinsic factors, such as recognition. There are several theories that include examples of intrinsic and extrinsic motivators.

FIGURE 4.4   Business and product life cycle

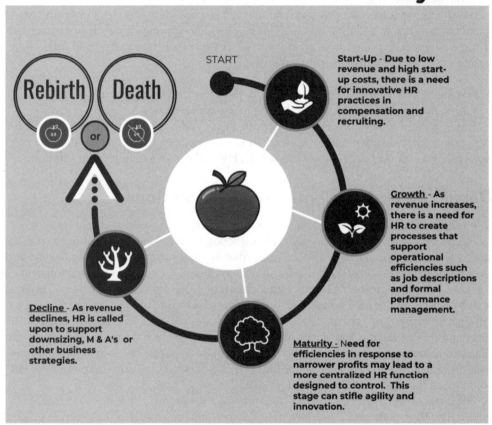

Business and Product Life Cycle

START

Start-Up - Due to low revenue and high start-up costs, there is a need for innovative HR practices in compensation and recruiting.

Rebirth   Death

or

Growth - As revenue increases, there is a need for HR to create processes that support operational efficiencies such as job descriptions and formal performance management.

Decline - As revenue declines, HR is called upon to support downsizing, M & A's or other business strategies.

Maturity - Need for efficiencies in response to narrower profits may lead to a more centralized HR function designed to control. This stage can stifle agility and innovation.

Self-determination theory (SDT) makes a distinction between intrinsic and extrinsic motivation. Intrinsic motivation involves doing an activity for the inherent satisfaction of the activity itself, such as seeking out novelty and challenges. Cognitive evaluation theory (CET) within SDT describes the supportive conditions that can help maintain and enhance people's intrinsic motivation. These are described as competence, autonomy, and relatedness. People need to feel competent that they can do the job. Also, they need to feel autonomous, which says that the individual must experience their behavior as self-determined. Finally, the individual must feel connected and related to others, especially those providing the motivation. When people are extrinsically motivated, they are doing an activity not because they value it, but because there are strong external forces, such as rewards and punishments.

There are different forms of extrinsic motivations, and they vary in the extent to which their regulation is autonomous. Extrinsically motivated behaviors can become self-determined through internalization and integration, but for this to happen, people need to feel competence, autonomy, and relatedness.

When it comes to goal-setting theory, goals affect performance by serving a directive, energizing, persistence, and strategizing function. When people have goals, it helps them direct their attention to goal-relevant activities, helps them increase and prolong their efforts, and leads them to discover and use task-relevant knowledge.

People's performance will be the strongest when they are committed to their goals. This can be accomplished by making people understand that goal attainment is important, and by enhancing their self-efficacy. In addition, it is important for the goals to be difficult and specific. According to Edwin Locke and Gary Latham, "Specific, difficult goals consistently lead to higher performance, than urging people to do their best" [Locke, E. A. & Latham, G. P. (2002). "Building a practically useful theory of goal setting and task motivation: A 35-year odyssey," *American Psychologist*, 57(9), pp. 705–717]. Also, for goals to be effective, people need to receive feedback that reveals their progress.

Hierarchy of Need

Abraham Maslow is perhaps most famous for his contribution of the hierarchy of needs to the studies of motivation. Maslow believed that individuals have an "order" of needs that serve as motivators. Until the lower needs are met, they will not be motivated up through the hierarchy toward self-actualization, thus fulfilling their potential. Figure 4.5 shows the hierarchy along with a brief description of each level. Individuals may move up from the base line of needs, and in some cases drop back down through the hierarchy as conditions change.

Two-Factor (Motivation and Hygiene)

Herzberg's two-factor theory of motivation states that certain factors are likely to make employees feel satisfied or dissatisfied with their work:

- Satisfiers are the factors that drive effort, and they include the nature of the work itself, such as purpose and increased responsibilities, achievement, and recognition.

- Dissatisfiers are called the hygiene factors, and they include elements such as policies, salaries, and working conditions. Hygiene factors will not increase individual effort, but the absence of a hygiene factor can decrease motivation levels. For example, the presence of a restroom in working order does not motivate individuals; however, take away a working restroom and employees will become dissatisfied.

Theory X and Theory Y

Douglas McGregor's theories focused on the behavior of managers toward their employees and the manager's efforts to motivate them.

Theory X managers believe that employees are lazy and uninterested, and they require constant direction to complete their work. This results in a leadership style that is authoritarian and micromanaging.

Theory Y managers believe that most people are motivated by rewarding or challenging work. This presents a leadership style that is participative and collaborative.

FIGURE 4.5   Pyramid of needs

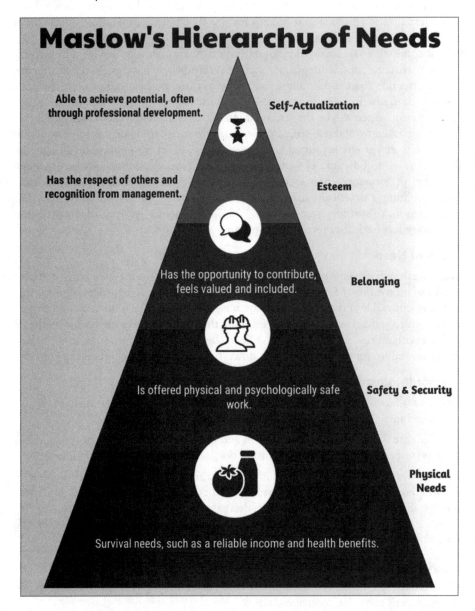

Expectancy Theory

Victor Vroom is the thought leader behind the expectancy theory of motivation. His theory maintains that people are motivated by what they expect to receive in return for their efforts. These expectations are shaped by what they believe about their ability to complete the work, the perceived return (ends) for their efforts (means/instrument used), and whether the reward is worth it.

A similar theory comes from J. Stacey Adams's equity theory; employees measure the value of what they receive compared to their efforts.

Achievement, Affiliation, Power

David McClelland defined motivators as falling within one of three categories: achievement, affiliation, and power. Achievement-oriented individuals may be motivated by earning degrees or credentials. Affiliation-oriented team members are more likely to enjoy collaborative work. Those driven by power would appreciate the word "senior" being added to their title, or face time with the CEO. Knowing your team preferences can help leaders better understand how to manage them effectively.

Critical Evaluation

The BoCK defines the competency of Critical Evaluation as follows:

> The KSAOs needed to collect and analyze qualitative and quantitative data, and to interpret and promote findings that evaluate HR initiatives and inform business decisions and recommendations.

Data Advocate

At first glance, it may not be clear what becoming a "data advocate" means. The use of the word "advocacy," as opposed to "support" or technician," is informative. Advocacy implies becoming a champion of data, promoting its benefits, and modeling its use.

Business Intelligence

Organizations that can collect and harness data to drive strategic and operational initiatives enjoy success in their markets. Companies that value HR and their ability to use business intelligence to align people strategy with business strategy become powerhouses in their field. Management consultant Patrick Lencioni puts it this way:

> [I]f you could get all the people in an organization rowing in the same direction, you could dominate any industry, in any market, against any competition, at any time. (https://conventionconnection.net/personnel/patrick-lencioni).

HR uses data to predict turnover, measure engagement, and identify hiring trends that will support business strategy. This requires a way to gather, store, access, and analyze information.

In addition to the enterprise and department specific technology systems described in Chapter 19, "Technology Management," companies use business portals to store data. These *portals* are a data warehouse that stores and organizes business intelligence. Employees can access this data based on hierarchies of authority.

It is of little use to employers if the stored data is too vast to organize, analyze, and eventually apply efficiently. For this reason, data analytics systems are key. Individuals create queries (requests for information based on specific criteria), and the system retrieves the data and delivers it in a standard or customized report. These systems can also analyze data using qualitative and quantitative methods, which are described next.

Data Gathering and Analysis

Data itself is defined as objective measures communicated through facts and reports. Similarly, there are widely used data gathering and analysis tools. Key data analysis terms are described in Table 4.3, and they are important to understand for the exam.

The type of method to use is dependent on several factors, among them:

- The need for confidentiality or anonymity to control for bias

- The sensitivity of the topic being studied

- The level of ease or difficulty of data extraction

- The number of variables that must be accounted for

- The purpose

The last bullet point is perhaps the most important question to ask when mining for data. Gathering data for the sake of having the information is not a best practice, and in some cases it is not an ethical choice. Additionally, collecting too much data makes it more difficult to analyze and use in evidenced-based decision-making. Data collection should be controlled to ensure that it is reliable, credible, and unbiased for use in decision-making.

TABLE 4.3   Data analysis terms

Quantitative terms to know		Qualitative terms to know	
Focused on graphs, charts, and mathematical analysis.		Focused on depth of information. Often used to evaluate judgments, attitudes, and feelings.	
Correlation	Compares two variables to determine whether there is a relationship between them.	Judgmental Forecasts	Educated guesses used to predict future conditions.
Correlation Coefficient	A correlation coefficient describes the relationship between two variables, and it is stated as a number between −1.0 and +1.0.	Delphi Technique	Method in which input is obtained from a group of individuals, summarized, and resubmitted to the group for additional input until consensus is reached.

Quantitative terms to know		Qualitative terms to know	
Measures of Central Tendency	Looking for the center of the data. Methods include mean, mode, median, moving average, weighted average, and weighted moving average.	Nominal Group Technique	A structured meeting format designed to elicit participation from all members of a group to arrive at the best possible solution to a problem.
Time-Series Forecasts	Used to measure data over a period of time to identify trends. Methods include trend analysis, simple linear regression, and multiple linear regression.	Focus Groups	A facilitated discussion used to gather data from diverse groups on a specific topic.

Evidence-Based Decision-Making

When Dale Carnegie set out to write his best-selling book, *How to Win Friends and Influence People* (Simon and Schuster, 1936), he interviewed the most successful people of the time, including business leaders. One of the questions that he asked was "What percentage of time are you correct?" With very near perfect consensus, most leaders answered, "About 50 percent of the time." This number is supported by empirical evidence as well. Let's assume that our leaders are above average in all respects and accord them a right-rate of 75 percent. This still means that at least 25 percent of all organizational decisions are in some way inadequate. *Evidenced-based decision-making (EBDM)* is the practice of using objective data based on credible sources to inform a course of action. A best practice in EBDM is consistently to use a linear model, identifying specific steps to take when faced with an important decision. This may include creating a list of "absolutes" and "nice-to-haves," and then systematically reviewing the available options to identify the one(s) that best meets the criteria. For advanced EBDM, weighted points may be determined and assigned to each factor. It is also helpful to ask the experts. Taking an outside view by seeking out subject matter experts improves the credibility of the data, which will help build a business case for an effective option.

Since data advocacy and EBDM are behavioral competencies, it's important for HR to remember the following:

- Stay up-to-date on the research being done in the organizational sciences. Listen to podcasts, read journals, and network with credible groups to keep learning.

- Be curious and ask questions using key business terms to understand how data may be applied.

- Model the ethical use of data to inform, not destroy.

- Build a business case using data to manage change through human resource interventions.

- Use technology solutions to streamline and control data gathering, and then distill it down to its most easily understood form.

Summary

The need for human resources to act as true business partners continues to evolve as an important component of a successful business strategy. As organizations respond to the changing psychological contract and employee expectations about work, they depend on a human capital strategy that supports the success of their teams and company. To do so, HR must develop the business competencies necessary to help manage the business and be credible advisers.

HR uses financial and other business intelligence to design HR programs that are aligned with the larger plan for business development and growth. When new organizational strategies are developed, HR leads the way in managing the necessary changes required for success.

As businesses adapt to remain competitive, HR demonstrates their knowledge of theories, models, frameworks, and other types of subjective and objective data. HR helps leaders understand and apply theories of motivation to help keep employees and the business moving in the same direction. They also advocate for the use of data to drive decision-making so that changes are supported by sound business practices and research, which in turn will increase the odds of success. These business competencies apply to all the functional areas of human resource management that are covered throughout the remaining chapters of this book.

Key Terms

Balance sheet	Portals
Evidenced-based decision-making (EBDM)	Profit and loss statement
Financial analysis	Self-efficacy
Human capital strategy	Statement of cash flow
Organizational Development	

Exam Essentials

Understand how human resources supports organizational competitiveness. Acting as human resources' business partners requires an understanding of business management principles and best practices. This includes practical knowledge of competitive and other factors that drive strategy.

Be able to design and implement business solutions to meet human capital needs. People are a form of capital that may be used to achieve business results. A human capital strategy measures the value of the collective competencies of the workforce and recommends ways to continue to align the needs of the employees with business goals.

Contribute to and lead change management efforts. An organizational intervention is the tool used to bridge the gap between the current and future state. Interventions at a business, department, process, or individual level require change, and HR often acts as the change agent leading the effort.

Advocate for the efficient and ethical use of data. Making ethically and empirically sound decisions requires the capability to collect, store, manage, secure, access, and analyze information. HR professionals act as data advocates and model the ethical application of information to support people and business outcomes.

The People Knowledge Domain

As described in Chapter 1, "The Basics of SHRM Certification," the exam's Body of Competency & Knowledge (BoCK) is organized by three clusters of behavioral competencies and three distinct knowledge domains. The expertise that an HR professional must have to perform well is in the knowledge domains of the People, the Workplace, and the Organization.

Within these chapters, you will learn concepts related to the domain of the People:

Supporting organizational success by aligning HR and business strategies

Acquiring the necessary talent to compete

Creating a sustainable company culture to engage team members

Enhancing employee capabilities to advance professional and organizational goals

Designing competitive compensation and benefits programs that attract and retain qualified workers

SHRM summarizes the domain of the People in the following way:

Create and set the strategic direction of the HR function; acquire or develop the talent necessary for pursuing organizational goals; maintain a satisfied and engaged workforce while minimizing unwanted employee turnover; and develop a total rewards program that maximizes the effectiveness of the organization's compensation and benefits.

The content related to the three clusters of behavioral competencies—Business, Leadership, and Interpersonal—is layered throughout the book.

Chapter 5

Strategic Human Resource Management

Exam Notables

The U.S. economy is divided into three broad categories: agriculture (which includes mining, construction, and utilities), manufacturing, and service. The evolution of human resources (HR) has paralleled the changes to these sectors over the last several decades. As shown in the accompanying graphic, the service sector now makes up around 70 percent of the U.S. economy, with manufacturing second and agriculture a distant third. This trend is in addition to the rise of all three sectors on a global scale, such as manufactured goods from China, services provided by the United Kingdom, and agricultural imports from Mexico. This shift has required that HR professionals become as well versed in business and industry as they are in human resources. It also requires organizations to be highly intentional and systematic when setting strategy related to how they do business, where they do business, and what they must focus on at any given time. This practice is best reflected in SHRM's definition of the functional area of HR Strategic Planning:

> HR *Strategic Planning* involves the activities necessary for developing, implementing, and managing the strategic direction required to achieve organizational success and to create value for stakeholders.

This chapter serves as a guide, not only for exam preparation purposes, but to help you understand the very real implications of the strength, or weakness, of our abilities to perform as strategic business partners.

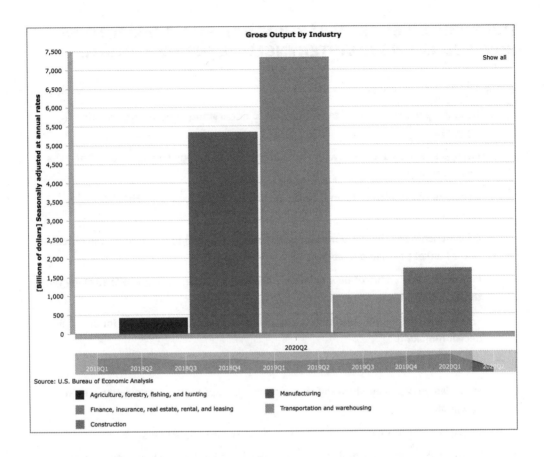

Source: U.S. Bureau of Economic Analysis

The SHRM Exam Objectives

SHRM's *Body of Competency and Knowledge (BoCK)* not only summarizes this functional area, but also defines the proficiency indicators and key concepts. No matter your career level, pay special attention to the exam concepts defined "For All HR Professionals" and the "Key Concepts." If seeking the SHRM-SCP designation, you must expand your efforts to include those labeled "For Advanced HR Professionals."

THE SHRM-CP EXAM AND SHRM-SCP EXAM OBJECTIVES COVERED IN THIS CHAPTER INCLUDE THE FOLLOWING:

✓ **For All HR Professionals**

- Uses the perspective of systems thinking to understand how the organization operates.

- Informs business decisions with knowledge of the strategy and goals of HR and the organization.

- Develops and implements an individual action plan for executing HR's strategy and goals.

- Uses benchmarks, industry metrics and workforce trends to understand the organization's market position and competitive advantage.

- Informs HR leadership of new or overlooked opportunities to align HR's strategy with the organization's.

- Provides HR leadership with timely and accurate information required for strategic decision-making.

✓ **For Advanced HR Professionals**

- Identifies the ways in which the HR function can support the organization's strategy and goals.

- Engages other business leaders in strategic analysis and planning.

- Evaluates HR's critical activities in terms of value added, impact and utility, using cost-benefit analysis, revenue, profit-and-loss estimates and other leading or lagging indicators.

- Provides HR-focused expertise to other business leaders when formulating the organization's strategy and goals.

- Develops and implements HR strategy, vision, and goals that align with and support the organization's strategy and goals.

- Ensures that HR strategy creates and sustains the organization's competitive advantage.

✓ **Key Concepts**

- Approaches to project management (e.g., traditional, Lean Six Sigma, Agile, Critical Chain) and processes (e.g., initiating, planning and design, launching/executing, monitoring and controlling, closing).

- Concepts of systems thinking (e.g., related parts, Input-Process-Output) and components of an organizational system (e.g., interdependence, necessity of feedback, differentiation of units).

- Organizational mission, vision and values, and their relation to strategic management and planning.

- Project planning, monitoring and reporting methods and tools (e.g., critical path analysis, Gantt charts, variance analysis, outcome monitoring).

- Project leadership, governance and structures (e.g., team roles, team management, work breakdown structures).

- Role of strategic management and planning in creating and sustaining competitive advantage.

- Strategic planning analysis frameworks (e.g., PESTLE analysis, SWOT analysis, industry analysis, scenario planning, growth-share matrix).

- Strategic planning process (e.g., formulation, goal-setting, implementation, evaluation).

- Systems theory and Input-Process-Output models.

Strategic Business Management

A *competitive advantage* exists when an organization is able to produce their goods or services more efficiently or for less money than their competitors. Successful organizations focus their competitive strategy in one of two areas:

Cost Leadership   Focusing on cutting costs and leading the market based on low price is the nature of this competitive approach. This strategy will require a business to focus on high productivity, purchasing power to negotiate the lowest cost on production inputs, and streamlined distribution channels.

Differentiation   A differentiation strategy is less focused on cost and more likely to invest in high-quality elements such as material, functionality, or durability. The product or service's brand is highly developed and well communicated.

A competitive strategy is but one factor of business management. A seasoned HR professional must understand the organizational design factors that set up the environment in which to achieve this strategy.

Systems Theory

An *organization* is an environment that relies on interdependency in order to survive. The whole is greater than the parts, so if the parts are deficient, the environment breaks down. Similar to a body's nervous system or a technical switchboard, there are specific components that work based on inputs which lead to outputs. In between the inputs and outputs are the processes from which the work is done.

HR teams work in both a diagnostic and a prescriptive way. When a part of a whole system is broken, HR may lead teams to identify whether the deficiency is in the people, the process, or the organizational design. Driving down to the root is necessary so that any intervention strategy—the prescription—addresses the cause as opposed to only the symptoms. HR also serves the system by defining each role and the knowledge, skills, and abilities of the people required to do the work so that redundancies are reduced and efficiencies are improved.

When a decision is made at any level within an organizational system, there is a ripple effect. *Systems theory* thus requires a holistic approach, with an eye on the full system as opposed to the broken component only.

Differentiation of units speaks to the idea that each part of the organization has a specific role to play, with unique strengths and challenges and subcultures that must be managed. Optimizing that diversity is often the task of the strategic planning process. It is not the same as the competitive strategy of differentiation.

Systems Thinking

As the world becomes more interconnected and business becomes more complex and dynamic, work must become more learningful . . .It's just not possible any longer to "figure it out from the top . . ."

> *Peter Senge, senior lecturer at MIT's Sloan School of Business and author of* The Fifth Discipline: The Art and Practice of the Learning Organization (Image Books, 2006)

When learning new concepts, you will find it helpful to view them from opposite perspectives—in this case, silos versus systems. In business, *silos* refer to independent business units that have little to no shared information. Conversely, *business systems* are those systems that are designed to optimize connectedness of information, people, and innovative solutions.

Systems thinking is what Peter Senge called the "fifth discipline" of a learning organization. *Systems thinking* is a mind shift from seeing only the parts to the whole and then creating an environment where employees take ownership. This environment is one where employees feel free to express opposing views, are open to new ideas, and know that they must work together to achieve organizational aims. Systems thinking is built on a foundation of agency, the idea that successful organizations are made up of teams that are "continually enhancing their capability to create their own future" (Peter Senge, Image Books, 2006. *The Fifth Discipline: The Art and Practice of the Learning Organziation*). This requires a level of flexibility, adaptability, and creative sourcing of new ways to achieve results at all levels of the organization. It also requires a change to the traditional structure of *management as directors*, recasting leaders as system architects. In this way, employees are expected to seek out feedback and are allowed to tap into their natural motivators, individual drive, and creativity to solve problems and achieve outcomes.

As noted earlier, systems thinking is the fifth discipline, so we must ask the question, "Well, what then are the other four disciplines?" Senge's research team developed the concept of a learning organization, a place where groups seek out new knowledge and then apply change and project management planning to adopt new ways of doing things. It is deep-level work that requires intentional focus.

The five disciplines that characterize a true learning organization are as follows:

1. **Personal Mastery:** An individual process that clarifies and deepens our personal vision, followed by action steps to achieve that vision.

2. **Mental Models:** The deeply seated attitudes and beliefs formed by employees in response to their organization. It often presents as a form of bias that blinds their ability to see reality clearly.

3. **Shared Vision:** According to Senge, "People are not playing according to the rules of the game but feel responsible for the game." The mark of an effective employee is one who can hold the vision without ignoring reality. Systems thinking anchors the vision in the realistic needs of what it will take to achieve the desired outcome.

4. **Team Learning:** Activating learning as a team in order to solve organizational problems and drive change.

5. **Systems Thinking:** As discussed earlier, systems thinking refers to building processes that take care of the entire organization, not just individual parts. This fifth discipline is what binds the other four disciplines together.

Every organizational system must have an operating framework, and it is in this way that the strategic planning process drives output.

Strategic Planning

A *strategy* is a planned course of action. Building that plan of action requires the identification of inputs from which a leadership team may then coordinate efforts to achieve the desired outputs. This process requires a level of analysis that begins with collecting data and ends with evaluating outcomes, the framework for the strategic planning process.

Strategic Analysis

Several well-known tools are used to scan the environment. The purpose of *environmental scanning* is to identify the forces that shape organizational decision-making. These are categorized as the internal and external forces that must be accounted for when setting a course.

Internally, an organization should have a clearly formulated *mission, vision, and values (MVV)*. The company *mission* defines the purpose to which organizational effort will be applied. The *values* define what the company believes in—the attitudes and beliefs that they are unwilling to compromise on in the course of day-to-day business. The *vision* is future-oriented, describing the place the company wants to be. A well-crafted and authentic MVV serves the organization in many ways. As Patrick Lencioni, author of *The Five Dysfunctions of a Team* (Jossey-Bass, 2002), says, "If everything is important, then nothing is." Defining the MVV ahead of the strategic planning process and then using it to guide action planning ensures that the company is applying its resources (people, time, and money) to the best use. And though the MVV remains relatively stable over time, the strategic planning process must be more agile, using the MVV as a tether from which to launch efforts appropriate for the current environment.

 In strategic planning, a stakeholder may serve as a bridge between the internal and the external environment. A *stakeholder* is anyone within or outside an organization who will be affected by the organizational strategy. Stakeholders include employees, vendors, contractors, and communities where the business operates.

Numerous outside forces drive organizational decision-making. These forces are conditions and events that require an organizational response. You can plan for some of these forces whereas others require a more reactive approach. Next, we review several analysis tools that are useful when scanning the external environment.

IPO Model

The *Input-Process-Output (IPO) model* is a useful tool for scanning the environment. A look at the inputs will unearth factors of constraint, such as an unskilled management team. Process review will include looking at functional needs to achieve organizational strategy, such as having efficient enterprise software. The outputs are best described as results of the strategic intervention, such as gaining new market share, increased sales, cost reduction, or improved diversity.

PESTLE

PESTLE is an acronym for the external forces that demand attention when shaping strategy. They are as follows:

Political   These are the forces shaped by government regulations and political agendas. In the two-party political system of the United States, the priorities shift based on which party is in office and as often as every four years. Issues with impact include immigration, taxation, and global trade.

Economic   The economy has significant impact on strategic business decisions. Expansion plans, for example, may need to be scaled based on labor supply and demand. Other economic factors that drive strategy include household income, consumer confidence, and interest rates on business loans.

Social   Social factors drive organizational behavior in many ways. Current examples include the impact of racism on workplace diversity, an aging or younger workforce, and the cost of earning a college degree.

Technological   Technology is perhaps the most rapidly changing of all external forces and is an area of significant HR spending in the next several years. Factors include securing employee and customer data, technological trends, and innovative iterations that may improve competitiveness.

Legal   These forces are similar to the political forces in that they are built from regulations passed by the government. Compliance with laws is the focus of this force, as is fighting labor lawsuits and patent infringements.

Environmental   Environmental forces are those related to responsible business practices that sustain our environmental resources. Consider water usage, pollution, and global warming.

Social Justice Philosophy

Social justice is a movement designed to promote economic or social equity through many of the PESTLE factors described here. Proponents of social justice seek to effect change through the political system by nominating candidates who share their viewpoint and policy changes to the distribution of land or the tax treatment of corporations. Economic parity is a pillar of this theory, in some cases seeking to abolish capitalism in the United States completely and move toward a government-sponsored economy. Buddhist socialism and Jewish socialism are social justice movements based on religious principles, and the #MeToo movement of 2017 spoke to the social issues of sexual assault. Technically speaking, the digital divide represents geographic locations within the United States that have little to no access to broadband Internet, limiting corporations moving to those areas and individual job search ability. Legally, the social justice philosophy drives initiatives such as establishing a living wage or better family leave policies. Finally, social justice philosophy's supporters seek to address environmental issues, such as when Patagonia pledged all of its profits from Black Friday to combat global climate change.

SWOT Analysis

Assessing an organization's or department's internal strengths and weaknesses, as well as the external threats and opportunities, is the focus of the *SWOT analysis*. A tool for strategic analysis, SWOT (strengths, weaknesses, opportunities, and threats) is used to drill down into what is most important at any given time. From this, action plans may be developed to max-imize internal strengths, minimize the impact of internal weaknesses, mitigate or eliminate external threats to competitiveness, and take advantage of external opportunities.

Growth-Share Matrix

The *growth-share matrix* was developed by Bruce Henderson and first published in 1964 by The Boston Consulting Group in an essay titled "Perspectives." This information gives us the context to understand the tool in that it shifts one's perspective toward *growth* as opposed to decline or status quo. From this point of view, a business can determine a strategy for products, services, or investments. The horizontal perspective indicates the direction of market share, with the vertical axis delineating the market growth rate. See Figure 5.1 for more on this prioritization tool and its responses.

FIGURE 5.1   The Growth Matrix tool

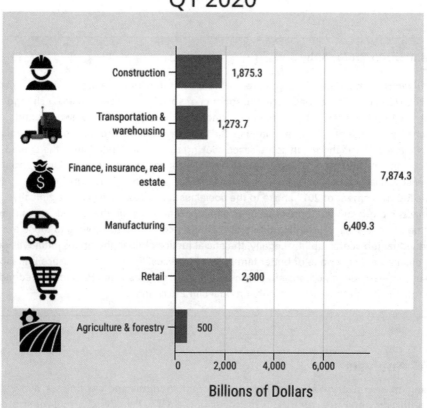

Scenario Planning

Running *scenarios* is a qualitative approach to analysis that may include quantitative data. Brainstormers meet to evaluate possibilities and then identify different responses based on factors such as risk management, profitability, and the likelihood of the event. Facilitators often outline a five-box plan that seeks input for no more than three scenarios at a time. The categories include key assumption(s), system impact, risk assessment (financial, legal), people impact, and summary. Table 5.1 provides an example of scenario planning.

TABLE 5.1   Five-box scenario analysis

Issue: Addressing a Covid-19 stay-at-home order

Key Assumptions	When does a stay-at-home-order begin and how long do we need to plan for it?
System Impact	How will critical infrastructure be managed?
Risk Assessment	What risks will need to be addressed before, during, and after the shutdown? (Consider financial, compliance, inventory, and other.)
People Impact	How will we call employees back to work? How will we service our customers?
Summary	Summarize the findings here.

The Strategic Planning Process

The outcome of the *strategic planning process* is a coherent road map that serves as a guide for organizational decision-making. *Environmental scanning* identifies the conditions from which strategy may be formulated and then translated into actionable plans for implementation and evaluation.

Strategy Formulation

Simon Sinek, author of *Start With Why* (Penguin Audio, 2017) and *The Infinite Game* (Penguin Audio, 2019), notes that business is a creative process requiring continuous improvement and adaptation. He argues that the outcome is actually less important than the process. If Sinek is right, the *formulation* stage of the strategic planning process becomes a key factor to competitiveness and achieving excellence through disciplined process management.

Sinek's opinion also takes into account the entire view that is at the heart of systems theory. It requires consideration of not only the transactional components of business, such as growth targets, but also the less tangible (yet just as important) concepts like ethical behavior. In this way, strategy formulation must take into account the needs of all stakeholders.

Ultimately, *strategy formulation* is about taking the internal and external data collected through environmental scanning and defining the targets over time. It includes conversations about the following:

Budgets: Both operational and strategic

Tracking Tools: How will progress be measured?

Personnel Required: The people resources necessary to achieve outcomes

Training Needs: Identifying short- and long-term objectives necessary to achieve the strategy

Technology Needs: Understanding current system capabilities and what may need to be upgraded or replaced

Communication: Planning for how strategy will be communicated at all organizational levels

Once the strategy has been formulated, the process of setting goals can begin. The focus of *goal setting* is to align the efforts of each business unit to achieve synergy. True alignment can serve as a multiplier of efforts. From organizational strategy, department and individual goals are set to achieve a focused effort on what has been identified as being the most important.

For example, consider a strategic initiative to grow sales by 7 percent in the new fiscal year. Human resources may support this goal by hiring quality team members to handle additional sales. Learning and Development may support this goal by designing training programs for the new products or services that will be necessary for results. Marketing may create campaigns to drive consumer messaging. Production will identify what is necessary to support additional output. In short, setting goals that cascade down from the master strategy and align with other business units will increase the odds of positive results.

It is not enough simply to talk about setting goals. Teams must write out goals in a way that increases the odds of success. A common acronym used to do just that is SMARTER:

Specific: A goal that defines the desired outcome.

Measurable: What does success look like?

Attainable: On a scale of 1 to 5, with 5 being the most likely, how likely are you to achieve this goal?

Relevant: In what ways does this goal align with the strategic objective?

Time-Based: When will this goal be complete?

Evaluated: What are the key milestones?

Revised: What needs to be adjusted in response to new information?

Strategy Implementation and Evaluation

Once the strategy has been formulated and goals defined, it is time for implementation. Simply put, *implementation* is about creating action steps to move toward the defined goal.

Implementation requires the use of several control tools. These tools allow for data tracking so that real-time adjustments can occur.

Critical Path Analysis

Imagine for a moment that you were a member of the project team that was tasked with ending World War II. Where would you begin? Consider that this project will require that you marshal the talents of over 130,000 people with a $2 billion budget. So describes the initiatives of the 1940s Manhattan Project, which is credited with the birth of the *critical path method (CPM)* from which CPA developed.

Critical path analysis (CPA) is a project planning technique that is focused on project mapping. Fundamentally, it is about breaking up a large project into smaller steps and identifying the estimated time to complete each task. It begins by identifying the high-value tasks, creating a detailed timeline, and using a visual tool to mark the path that the team will take to achieve the goal.

Gantt Charts

The most common of the visual tools used to track project progress is the *Gantt chart*. Named after its inventor, Henry Gantt, the Gantt chart is designed to show the progress of a project. Modern-day versions include *dependency factors*, which describe a relationship of the tasks that are dependent on one another for completion. Dependency may also indicate conditions that must exist or come before an action may be taken. Take a look at Figure 5.2 for a sample Gantt template built in Microsoft Excel.

FIGURE 5.2 An Excel Gantt chart

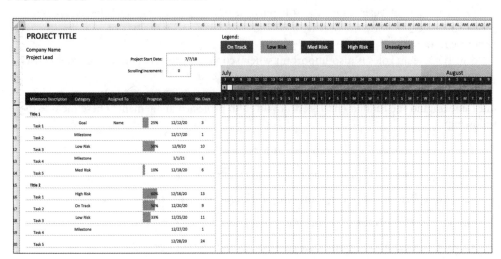

It is important to evaluate the success or failure of strategic initiatives for several reasons. A form of reflection, taking the time to evaluate performance demonstrates to all stakeholders that the company cares about how it spends its resources; it is a matter of trust in leadership. Strategic evaluation is important because some initiatives have greater impact than others; knowing what worked or didn't work will set the stage for future efforts. Timing also matters. For example, one company set a strategic initiative to grow revenue by sourcing parts from China beginning in March 2020. When Covid-19 changed the world, the strategy failed for reasons outside the organization's control, not necessarily because the strategy was flawed. Let's look at a couple of tools used to evaluate strategy.

Variance Analysis

Actual versus planned behavior is the focus of a *variance analysis*. It is a tool that helps to identify variances in outcomes that allow for real-time adjustment, often communicated using trend lines. The most common variances measured include cost, labor rates or labor efficiencies, scheduling, and overhead.

Outcome Monitoring

The purpose of *outcome monitoring* is to track the performance of an initiative over a period of time. This tool is dependent on the practice of *benchmarking*, a process where data is collected about current state or competitor performance prior to a project beginning. This data is then used at the end of a project for comparison.

Project Management

The implementation and evaluation stages of the strategic planning process are closely related to *project management*. The work requires a robust review of the structure of a project team, including identifying the project manager. From this, roles can be established and the work can be dispersed.

A project leader does not necessarily have to be the most competent person in the room. IDEO, a company in business for the sole purpose of innovating for their clients, appoints project managers that are the best with people—not necessarily the person who has the most expertise in the project scope.

Identifying team roles is also important when scoping a project. This step creates clarity among members and allows for accountability for outcomes.

Although HR professionals are not called upon to be master project managers, we must understand the fundamental steps involved in project management. These include the following:

Initiating   Identifying the problem and deliverables

Planning/Design   Defining the scope and creating action steps

Launching/Executing   Beginning the work and reporting on progress

Monitoring/Controlling   Tracking status and refining as needed

Closing   Documenting outcomes and summarizing findings

In addition to the project management framework, you should be familiar with three other models.

Lean Six Sigma

Lean is a business philosophy originally developed and used by Toyota in the 1970s. Focused on the elimination of waste through continuous improvement efforts, it is designed to streamline production to maximize efficiencies. *Lean* is a collaborative effort that requires all team members to engage in root cause analysis to solve problems. According to the Project Management Institute (PMI), the most likely short-term outcomes of implementing a Lean focus are as follows:

90 percent inventory reduction

90 percent lead time reduction

60 percent floor space reduction

Agile

Agile project management is focused on the iterative process, which evolves and builds as the project progresses. Used often in creative environments, a project team will deliver a chunk of a project, gather input from the stakeholders, and then refine or push forward into the next project phase.

Critical Chain

The Theory of Constraints notes that all projects have limitations from a small number of specific constraints. If this were not the case, then all strategic initiatives would be accomplished all of the time by all organizations with a vision! These constraints can be cost, time, personnel, or any other factor in the categories of equipment, people, or policy. *Critical Chain project management* is focused on managing or breaking the constraints so that throughput (the process) does not break or impede. This is accomplished through the use of buffers to offset the impact of the constraints, such as slowing down a line so that downstream can keep up.

SHRM SCP Only

Although all the functional areas of human resource management require a different level of effort from senior HR leaders, there is particular emphasis in the function of business strategy. This is because all HR systems must be designed to align with organizational strategy and serve the people responsible for achieving results. HR has been criticized time and again of being advocates only for the employer, but this is not supposed to be the case. In fact, HR is at its best when it serves as a neutral party to the relationship between the employer and the employee (and union where applicable), designing systems that attract and retain the talent necessary to drive organizational results.

Becoming Strategic Business Partners

It has never been more important to remember that we must not only be HR leaders, but business leaders as well. In their job description series on SHRM.org, the Society for Human Resource Management defines an *HR Business Partner (HRBP)* as one who is:

> Responsible for aligning business objectives with employees and management in designated business units. The position formulates partnerships across the HR function to deliver value-added service to management and employees that reflects the business objectives of the organization. The HRBP maintains an effective level of business literacy about the business unit's financial position, its midrange plans, its culture and its competition.

The world of HR has been marked these past several years by rapid change, requiring the ability to work in a VUCA environment—that is, one that is volatile, uncertain, complex, and ambiguous. For example:

- Discussions of politics in the workforce have become much more divisive, and HR pros have found themselves paying special attention to the factors that can create a hostile workplace. This affects our policies, procedures, rules, and culture.

- The increasing cost of benefits every year has left HRBPs needing to find new ways to manage these costs for the employer and employees. This affects employee burden and the cost of labor.

- The Covid-19 pandemic kept many HR professionals working late as they called back employees from stay-at-home orders and managed the health and safety of our teams. Diversity and social justice also played an important role for HR. These all affected the way that work is organized.

- Advances in employee monitoring systems and the need to shift to a virtual workforce brought to the fore privacy issues and the need to communicate large amounts of data. This affects our ability to use data to compete and motivate employees.

- Compliance with labor laws continues to be a large part of HR's job responsibilities. Laws exist for business, employee relations, equal opportunity, leave, safety and health, and wage and hours. This affects how well or how poorly we manage organizational risk.

- Young professionals make up the second-largest labor force population, and they want to work for organizations that have a purpose. For many, this includes the need to support environmental issues such as global warming, plastic in the ocean, and other forms of pollution. This affects our ability to recruit top talent.

All of these factors must be considered as HRBPs work to align HR strategy with organizational strategy.

Engaging Leaders

Another interesting piece of SHRM's job description for HRBPs is their assertion that the role has "no direct supervisory responsibilities but does serve as a coach and mentor for other positions in the department." Although this may not be true for the average HRBP who wears many hats, each with an HR staff of their own, it is telling. Our ability to model appropriate behavior, engage leaders, and coach performance drives business success and must be accounted for in our daily efforts.

C-suite executives have their own particular brand of needs. Many have experienced high degrees of success and may be reluctant to change. Others are governed by boards of directors and make decisions based on short-term rewards. Still others are both the CEO and founder, meaning that a corporate purpose drives their decisions, just as much as data. HR must counsel the C-suite with courage and conviction, serving as an advocate for all stakeholders.

Evaluating HR Activities

The concept of alignment comes up through the entire CP and SCP exam BoCK. An HR best practice is to use analysis tools to evaluate our efforts. The focus of these evaluative tools should be on how well the HR systems serve organizational outcomes. These tools include the following:

Value-Added   *Value-added* refers to the ability of HR systems/teams to provide value beyond total cost or individual effort. For example, if an HR professional is able to coach multiple employees to higher degrees of success, they have brought value beyond their own efforts by increasing the performance of others.

Measurement of Impact   The *measurement of impact* is an indication of the affect an HR activity has on strategic objectives. For example, if HR is charged with reducing the cost of employee health insurance and so they shift to a captive insurance plan, did the quality of care change? If so, how did that affect the employees?

Utility Analysis   The term *usefulness* may be substituted for *utility*. In this way, a *utility analysis* takes a look at the usefulness of a decision when it comes to managing employees or other outcomes. For example, consider when employers were tasked with preventing the spread of Covid-19 by conducting health screenings prior to employees starting work, and thus HR proposed temperature checks. A utility analysis would review the effectiveness of this activity when compared to the desired goal.

Cost-Benefit Analysis   *Cost-benefit analysis* is a simple comparison of the cost of taking action to the results. One may also consider the cost of not taking action and comparing that to the risk or benefit.

Business Analysis   Being familiar with *business analysis tools* enhances an HR professional's value to the organization. Understanding financial reports, such as the profit and loss statements and budgets, allows HR to use its competencies to enhance financial decision-making. For example, providing executive teams with the employee burden costs or market wage data allows for the creation of effective budgets. Digesting marketing or customer satisfaction trends helps HR understand job roles—information that the hiring and performance management systems are highly dependent on.

Leading/Lagging Indicators   *Indicators* are a form of performance analysis that tells us something about the past (lagging) or helps us predict the future (leading). For example, indicators about the employer brand strength would be leading indicators about recruiting prospects. Claims costs paid out of an employer's self-insured workers' compensation program would be a lagging indicator.

Ultimately, HR's performance as a business partner is about creating HR systems that support their company's core competency. A *core competency* is a company's strategic strength, whether it be *people*, such as in a service environment, *product*, such as in a manufacturing environment, or *systems*, such as Airbnb or Uber. Our job in accordance with the BoCK is to reaffirm the competitive advantage, which means designing employee engagement and relations, total rewards, and learning and development systems that support success.

Summary

Strategic human resource management involves going outside of the regular, day-to-day operations of a busy HR office. It demands a sharp focus on business management and the factors and forces that influence its ability to create or maintain a competitive advantage. This focus should be on the system as a whole, rather than just on a single business unit.

The strategic planning process is a formal way to identify initiatives that a company must take in response to several internal and external factors. These include the company's competitive philosophy along with its mission, vision, values, the needs of the stakeholders, and the external forces to which a company must respond. Project planning tools and models allow for a structured approach to strategy implementation.

Senior leaders have an elevated responsibility as strategic business partners. This includes developing the need to work in an environment that is volatile, uncertain, complex, and often ambiguous (VUCA). Developing these skills sharpens HR's ability to align HR systems with organizational needs.

Organizational strategy is built on people, process, and project management, none of which can be achieved without critical talent acquisition strategies. This is the focus of the next chapter.

Key Terms

Benchmarking

Business analysis/Intelligence

Business unit

Cost-benefit analysis

Regulation

Six Sigma/Lean Six Sigma

Stakeholders

Strategic management

Critical path

HR business partner

Lagging indicator

Leading indicator

Mission statement

Organizational values

Strategic planning

Strategy

SWOT audit

Systems thinking

Vision

Exam Essentials

Understand how systems theory and systems thinking influence an organization's competitive advantage. A competitive advantage exists when an organization can produce their products or services more effectively than their competitors. Systems theory and systems thinking takes a holistic approach to organizational health. This approach builds and protects the competitive advantage, capitalizing on strengths and minimizing weaknesses.

Know how to participate in the strategic planning process. As true business partners, HR is able to help frame organizational strategy through the planning process, using the company mission, vision, and values as its guide. Models to follow include Input-Process-Output, PESTLE, SWOT, the Growth-Share matrix, and scenario planning.

Be able to implement and evaluate strategic initiatives. Using SMARTER goals to create action plans, HR often leads the effort of implementing strategy. This requires the use of project planning tools, such as critical path analysis, GANTT charts, variance analysis, and outcome monitoring within a project planning framework.

Be familiar with project planning concepts. Project planning at any level may be done using models, such as Lean Six Sigma, Agile, and Critical Chain. Knowing the key components to each method will ensure that HR advises organizational leadership with the best option.

Be able to identify what is important for SCP exam takers. SHRM SCP preparers must take note of the elevated efforts that are part of being an HR bsiness partner. This includes aligning HR efforts with strategic initiatives and engaging leaders throughout the process. Senior leaders will also need to be familiar with evaluating HR activities to ensure that they are achieving desired results.

Review Questions

1. The car company you work for recently became the most valuable car company in the world. They compete by emphasizing the uniqueness of their brand in a high-priced market. Which of the following best describes their competitive strategy?

    A. Buyer power

    B. Differentiation

    C. Competitive advantage

    D. Cost leadership

2. A client services leader is resisting the need to restructure their department to include off-shoring a portion of the call center to India. They say it is because they are not confident that they will have access to the financial or people resources they need to make the new department structure effective. In which of Peter Senge's disciplines does this leader most likely need support?

    A. Personal mastery

    B. Systems thinking

    C. Team learning

    D. Mental modeling

3. The company you work for publishes the following on their About Us section of their web-site: "We exist to help improve lives through business—it is embedded in everything we do." This is the best example of which of the following?

    A. Mission statement

    B. Values statement

    C. Corporate governance compliance

    D. Social justice commitment

4. One of your company's strategic initiatives this year is to move to a self-insured "captive" health insurance plan. You have been asked to identify the key milestones that will need to be achieved in order to implement the new program effectively. Which step of setting SMARTER goals are you most likely in?

    A. Specific

    B. Attainable

    C. Time-based

    D. Evaluated

5. What should be the next step after a strategy has been formulated?

    A. Strategic planning

    B. Goal setting

    C. Strategy alignment

    D. Strategy evaluation

6. The use of key assumptions and risk assessment are characteristics of which of the following business analytics tools?

   A. Scenario planning

   B. SWOT audit

   C. Growth-share matrix

   D. SMARTER goals

7. In a SWOT analysis, strengths and weaknesses are to internal processes as opportunities and threats are to _____ processes.

   A. Cognitive

   B. Centralized

   C. External

   D. Outward

8. Which of the following terms best characterizes the Agile model of project management?

   A. Customer-driven

   B. Iterative

   C. Microbursts

   D. All of the above

9. The United States officially categorized China's restrictions on Internet use (specifically, site blocking) a trade barrier, affecting how American businesses are able to compete in China's marketplace. This is the best example of which of the following PESTLE forces?

   A. Political

   B. Economic

   C. Social

   D. Environmental

10. The company you work for has decided to implement customer relationship management (CRM) software as a strategic objective for the new fiscal year. The purpose is to organize the data associated with the company's sales and marketing efforts. The company most likely used what strategic analysis tool to arrive at this decision?

    A. SWOT audit

    B. PESTLE analysis

    C. Input-Process-Output (IPO)

    D. Growth-share matrix

Chapter

6

Talent Acquisition

Exam Notables

Imagine a turnover rate of 37 percent. If you are in the medical industry, you don't have to imagine it—you have felt the pain of the nationwide nursing shortage. Regardless of your market, factors such as retirement, burnout, and relocation, combined with industry growth, has led many organizations to wonder how they will acquire the necessary talent to supply current and future needs. This is reflected in SHRM's definition of the Talent Acquisition functional area:

> Talent Acquisition encompasses the activities involved in building and maintaining a workforce that meets the needs of the organization.

This chapter takes a look at best practices when it comes to attracting, sourcing, and selecting employees.

The SHRM Exam Objectives

SHRM's *Body of Competency and Knowledge (BoCK)* not only summarizes this functional area, but also defines the proficiency indicators and key concepts. No matter your career level, pay special attention to the exam concepts defined "For All HR Professionals" and the "Key Concepts." If seeking the SHRM-SCP designation, you must expand your efforts to include those labeled "For Advanced HR Professionals."

THE SHRM-CP EXAM AND SHRM-SCP EXAM OBJECTIVES COVERED IN THIS CHAPTER INCLUDE THE FOLLOWING:

✓ **For All HR Professionals**

- **Understands the talent needs of the organization or business unit.**

- **Uses a wide variety of talent sources and recruiting methods to attract qualified applicants.**

- Uses technology (e.g., social media, applicant tracking software [ATS]) to support effective and efficient approaches to sourcing and recruiting employees.

- Promotes and uses the EVP and employment brand for sourcing and recruiting applicants.

- Uses the most appropriate hiring methods to best evaluate a candidate's technical skills, organizational fit, and alignment with the organization's competencies needs.

- Conducts appropriate pre-employment screening.

- Implements effective onboarding and orientation programs for new employees.

- Designs job descriptions to meet the organization's resource needs.

✓ For Advanced HR Professionals

- Analyzes staffing levels and projections, to forecast workforce needs.

- Develops strategies for sourcing and acquiring a workforce that meets the organization's needs.

- Establishes an EVP and employment brand that supports recruitment of high-quality job applicants.

- Designs and oversees effective strategies for sourcing, recruiting and evaluating qualified job candidates.

- Designs and oversees employee onboarding and assimilation processes.

- Designs and oversees valid and systematic programs for assessing the effectiveness of talent acquisition activities that meet the organization's needs.

✓ Key Concepts

- Approaches to employee onboarding.

- Approaches to sourcing (e.g., external talent pipelines).

- Employment categories (e.g., salaried/ hourly, contract, temporary, interns).

- Job analysis and identification of job requirements.

- Job offer contingencies (e.g., background investigations, credit checks).

- Job offer negotiations (e.g., salary).

- Methods for creating and maintaining a positive employer value proposition (EVP) and employment brand.

- Methods for external and internal employee recruitment (e.g., job ads, career fairs).

- Methods for selection assessment (e.g., ability, job knowledge, non-cognitive tests, assessment centers, interviews).

- Talent acquisition metrics (e.g., cost per hire, time to fill).

Aligning Strategy

The ability of human resource teams to deliver talent acquisition plans that align with business strategy has a direct impact on organizational competitiveness. For human resource professionals, this will require the development of several key competencies from each functional area of the exam. These competencies include the ability to create workforce strategies to understand the talent acquisition needs at organizational and business unit levels.

Mergers and Acquisitions

Chapter 5, "Strategic Human Resource Management," reviewed organizational strategy in detail, focusing on business development. Similarly, there are numerous talent acquisition strategies that may be considered based on the structure of the organization.

Talent need not always be acquired through traditional hiring. Talent may also be purchased through a merger and acquisition (M&A). An M&A is defined by SHRM as "the process by which two separate organizations combine, either by joining together as relative equals (merger) or by one procuring the other (acquisition)." When two firms in the same industry integrate, it is known as a horizontal merger, such as when Walt Disney and Pixar Animation Studios merged in 2006. Vertical integration occurs when two firms with complementary products or services join, such as the one between eBay and PayPal in 2002. A conglomerate exists when multiple businesses types exist under one flagship company, such as within Atari Games.

According to a McKinsey report, more than 75 percent of large companies rely on M&As to grow. M&As are designed so that the acquiring company can gain a competitive advantage in their market. The advantage may be buying up market share, gaining valuable assets (product, knowledge, or people), or simply taking out a competitor. Although the headline-making M&As are often large in scope and cost, companies that use a programmatic strategy (smaller deals more often) tend to perform better over time. Organizations that use this strategy are constantly exploring opportunities, have a step-by-step plan to collect the objective data, and then act.

Whether HR employees work for the acquiring company or the target company, they actively participate in the due diligence process. In an M&A, due diligence involves the collection and review of data used for evaluation. As a legal process, the target company must act with transparency and provide an honest view of the company's financials, employee records, legal action, assets, and liabilities.

M&As most often fail because senior leaders focus on transactional alignment at the expense of the consideration of the cultural alignment that is necessary for success. For this reason, HR is a critical resource to evaluating factors of culture prior to making a deal and helping the newly acquired talent assimilate into their new business units.

Joint Ventures

Joint ventures occur when two or more companies enter into a contract to combine resources or expertise toward a shared goal. It may result in the formation of a corporation or other legal entity that outlines the specifics of the venture. One high-profile example in 2020 was the announcement by Ford and Volkswagen to leverage their unique strengths to produce three new vehicles—a commercial vehicle, an electric vehicle, and a self-driving vehicle. The CEO of Volkswagen Group, Herbert Diess, summed up the benefits of a joint venture as follows:

> In light of the Covid-19 pandemic and its impacts on the global economy, more than ever it is vital to set up resilient alliances between strong companies. This collaboration will efficiently drive down development costs, allowing broader global distribution of electric and commercial vehicles, and enhance the positions of both companies (`http://www.cnbc.com`).

A key distinction between M&As and joint ventures is that joint ventures may be short-term and do not result in a change of ownership. HR supports both strategies through their recruiting and talent management efforts and compensation structures, and by defining the jobs and the talent that will be necessary to achieve results.

Strategic Alliance

A *strategic alliance* is created when two or more companies come together to achieve a specific result. A key difference between a joint venture and a strategic alliance is that in a strategic alliance, the partners continue independent business operations and thus staffing strategies may not be affected at all. One example of a strategic alliance is that between Apple Pay and Mastercard. When Apple decided to offer a digital payment platform, it made more sense to partner with an expert as opposed to building an entirely new business unit (with resulting job descriptions, staffing needs, performance management, and so forth) and having to compete with the forces that already dominated that space.

Divestitures and Downturns

Alignment of a talent acquisition strategy is not only important for growth plans, such as with an M&A, joint venture, or strategic alliance. Companies may also choose to divest a portion of their business or an entire business unit, such as when PepsiCo sold off its fast-food chain brands in order to focus more on the competitive beverage market. In a divestiture, HR is called upon to re-home the talent where possible throughout the remaining business units.

Many industries are struggling with having to lay off people in some areas while hiring talent for other business units. This is driven by both economic and *demographic* factors.

These unpredictable inconsistencies can leave an HR pro tasked with building a talent plan with more questions than answers.

Reskilling and *upskilling* are growing trends for companies juggling the talent in a world where the way work gets done is shifting so rapidly. This requires that HR become familiar with complementary skill sets that are used between seemingly unrelated jobs and then building programs to round out the employee competencies for use in other jobs.

Additionally, upskilling has become necessary for entire workforces as technology has changed the way that work gets done. Some experts note that many of the jobs of tomorrow don't even exist yet. A talent acquisition plan must focus on the needs of today while also building in targeted skill development tools to prepare their current workforce for future needs.

According to the book *Long Life Learning: Preparing for Jobs That Don't Even Exist Yet,* by Michelle R. Weise (Wiley, 2020), some experts predict that the first human to live to 150 years of age has already been born! What this suggests for the workplace is a force of disruption equal to the Industrial Revolution—it's a true game changer. Strategic HR professionals understand that many of the jobs being performed today did not exist 20, 10, or even 5 years ago. For talent acquisition, this means that defining jobs and the skills necessary to perform will be fundamental to an employer's success. This also means that we must build learning opportunities for the existing talent if we are to have a pipeline to support strategic initiatives. You'll see more about this topic and the implications on an employer's learning and development activities in Chapter 8, "Learning and Development."

Talent Planning

Conducting a talent needs assessment has evolved from the traditional skills inventory. As with many HR techniques, the process of assessing and predicting talent has become more digitized. Artificial intelligence (AI) models are now used to predict what job—and skill sets—will be in demand by industry and title. For example, the data analytics company Faethm (`faethm.ai`) predicts that 38 percent of the tasks of a payroll and accounting clerk will be automatable in just five years. That does not necessarily mean that the job will become fully automated or that humans will no longer be needed to perform the important work of paying and communicating about pay to team members. It simply points organizations in the direction of the types of skills that will be necessary for these clerks to continue to perform in a future work context, which are skills in human relations.

Many other digital tools are available that HR can use to support talent planning long before the first job ad is posted. This includes the use of applicant tracking systems (ATSs). ATS applications have some mixed results. ATSs that only serve to store résumés are too limited for today's recruiting needs because they do not enhance the candidate experience. Robust systems now have capabilities that link an ATS to a recruitment management system (RMS) (also called candidate relationship management [CRM] software) to support strategic hiring, from communicating the employer brand during the recruiting process all the way through onboarding new talent.

The Employer Brand

Brand is a marketing term used to communicate standards and expectations of a company's product or service. The *employer brand* does the same thing, only it focuses on what an individual may expect from an employer. Factors such as reputation are much easier to discover now with websites such as `glassdoor.com` providing an anonymous review system for businesses—not for their services, but whether they are a 1-star or 5-star employer.

Becoming an employer of choice requires thoughtful action on the part of HR. For example, it is often noted that younger professionals crave work with a purpose. When seeking to attract this talented generation, employers would do well to include purpose-driven messages in their employer brand communications.

A Korn Ferry study found that 63 percent of millennials said that the primary purpose of work should be "improving society"—not profit. A SHRM study noted that 94 percent of millennials want to use their skills toward work with a purpose, and 57 percent of millennials believe that there aren't enough volunteer days built into employer's benefit packages. With 75-million members of this generation now in the workforce, a strategic HR team should take these stats to senior leadership, craft policies where possible, and then use the data to inform the employer's brand.

Employee Value Proposition

In order for the employer brand to have impact on talent acquisition strategies, a detailed plan must be in place. This plan should capture the essential and often unique elements that would cause an individual to want to work for the organization. The employee value proposition (EVP*)* promotes the positive aspect of joining—and then staying with—an organization. It includes information about the tangible benefits, such as paid time off, and the more subjective employment factors that often outweigh compensation and benefit factors. The key is for organizations to do their research to identify what their *target* applicant both needs and wants. This is done through traditional labor market research at a local, a regional, and a global scale where necessary. Companies must be sure that what they communicate is in alignment with actual practices, or they face the risk of a higher-than-average turnover in the first six months statistics.

The Work Institute (`workinstitute.com`) has found that over one-third of newly hired professionals quit their jobs within the critical first six months of employment. The primary reason? The job was not what they expected. HR can combat this by using realistic job previews during the recruiting process and ensuring that what they say the company values in terms of the EVP is what is actively practiced at all levels of the organization.

In addition to attractive facets such as recognition and flexible work arrangements where available, the EVP should focus on what the company values and how those values exist in the workplace. For example, Warby Parker has a dedicated corporate culture team that designs programs, such as Leap Day, to strengthen organizational culture and increase fun at work. Squarespace touts a matrix-like organizational structure that reduces levels of management to promote creativity and ownership. Chani Nicholas makes a point to communicate how, when developing her popular astrology app, she partnered with an agency whose engineers were predominantly survivors of gender exploitation and violence. These are just a few examples of how organizations can harness their uniqueness to attract qualified and values-aligned talent to their teams.

HR can communicate the EVP through their website, employee word-of-mouth, social media, at local and university job fairs, and through traditional advertising efforts. Employee video testimonials used in online recruiting is also another effective way to get the word out about your organization's EVP. In short, in a highly competitive market for qualified talent, an EVP communication plan should be just as important as the job design process is at work.

Job Analysis and Descriptions

As an experienced HR professional, you are probably already familiar with the acronym KSAO—the knowledge, skills, abilities, and other characteristics that are necessary in order to perform a body of work. But how are these KSAOs quantified and communicated? A *job analysis* is the process of breaking down the whole of a job into its individual and complementary parts. Job analysis is a process by which HR identifies the tasks, duties, and responsibilities of the job, which, in addition to the KSAOs, are then formalized into a *job description. Job specifications* are the fundamental requirements of the work that are used to recruit, select, and ultimately manage the performance of the team member.

The job analysis process identifies the tasks, duties, and responsibilities (TDRs) of the job, and the KSAOs required of the people performing the job. The selection process seeks to identify the best fit between KSAOs (characteristics of applicants) and TDRs (characteristics of the job).

Job descriptions are not specifically required by law, but they do serve many compliance outcomes, such as justifying pay systems or understanding how to modify work if an employee is injured. Regardless of its purpose, most job descriptions share common elements, usually found in the following order:

1. **Job Identification:** This part gives the job title, the work location/department, to whom the job reports, and the employment category.

2. **Summary:** This section identifies what constitutes the purpose of this role or what makes the position unique from all other jobs within the company.

3. **Essential Duties and Responsibilities:** This part is critical for purposes of compliance with the Americans with Disabilities Act (ADA). This section identifies, in order of importance, the essential TDRs of the job.

The ADA defines several factors used to determine whether a task is essential or not, such as the following:

- Whether or not the reason that the position exists is to perform that function
- The number of other employees available to perform the function, or among whom the performance of the function can be distributed
- The degree of expertise or skill required to perform the function

4. **Mental and Physical Requirements:** This section is often expressed as the percentage of time spent standing, walking, breathing, lifting, and the other physical and mental requirements of the role.

Ultimately, a job description is the place to house the required job competencies, defined by the ADA as the "measurable pattern of knowledge, skills, abilities, behaviors, and other characteristics that an individual needs in order to perform work roles or occupational functions successfully."

Part of the job analysis and job description process is to place the job in the proper employment category. This is important because it defines the employer of record as well as how a worker performing the job is to be paid.

The employment categories are strictly defined by the Department of Labor (DOL) and the Internal Revenue Service (IRS). They include the following:

Exempt Employees   These employees are "exempt" from the overtime and rest period requirements of the Fair Labor Standards Act (FLSA).

Non-Exempt Employees   These are hourly workers who are due overtime and minimum wage from their employer under the FLSA requirements.

Contract Worker   This is an individual who is not an employee of the employer, but who performs work under a defined contract. Individuals are defined as independent contractors by the IRS based on the degree of behavioral and financial control an employer has over the individual and whether a contract for services is in place.

Temporary Worker   The DOL defines a temporary worker as one who is hired to work for 12 months or less and with a specific end date.

Interns   These are individuals who are in school and are not considered employees. Thus, they are not covered by the FLSA's overtime or minimum wage requirements. The key to ensuring that you have an intern as opposed to an employee is identifying who stands to benefit the most from the relationship.

To help employers, the DOL created a seven-factor test to classify these workers properly:

1. The extent to which the intern and the employer clearly understand that there is no expectation of compensation. Any promise of compensation, express or implied, suggests that the intern is an employee—and vice versa.

2. The extent to which the internship provides training that would be similar to that which would be given in an educational environment, including the clinical and other hands-on training provided by educational institutions.

3. The extent to which the internship is tied to the intern's formal education program by integrated coursework or the receipt of academic credit.

4. The extent to which the internship accommodates the intern's academic commitments by corresponding to the academic calendar.

5. The extent to which the internship's duration is limited to the period in which the internship provides the intern with beneficial learning.

6. The extent to which the intern's work complements, rather than displaces, the work of paid employees while providing significant educational benefits to the intern.

7. The extent to which the intern and the employer understand that the internship is conducted without entitlement to a paid job at the conclusion of the internship.

Hop online to find the complete briefing of the September 2020 updates from the FLSA titled "Fact Sheet 13: Employment Relationship Under the Fair Labor Standards Act (FLSA)" here:

www.dol.gov/agencies/whd/fact-sheets/
13-flsa-employment-relationship

Recruiting

As the chapter title implies, one of the major tasks of human resource professionals is sourcing qualified talent to fill current and future job opportunities. *Recruitment* is the practice of actively seeking out talent and encouraging such talent to apply for open positions. *Sourcing* has a definition of its own, implying that it is no longer enough for employers simply to post a job opening online and wait for the qualified résumés to come pouring in. The role of sourcing is assertively to hunt for passive candidates—those who are not actively looking for work and, in many cases, are already employed. Some estimate that more than 90 percent of all recruiting activities are now done via websites and social media, so the development of a strong online presence is key to securing qualified talent.

The nature of the candidate experience is also a marker for many positive outcomes that go beyond acceptance of a job offer. Research suggests that a successful candidate experience is positively correlated with the length of tenure if hired, a favorable employer brand through social media, and the job seeker's likelihood of consuming a company's product post-application, whether hired or not. Many job seekers report barriers to these outcomes that include excessively long response times or no interview follow-up. This is more than just lack of courtesy on the employer's part; it communicates a message about how the employer feels about human beings—within and outside the organization.

Recruiting Methods

Recruiters can source qualified candidates in several ways. These methods are generally classified as internal and external.

Internal sources are those that are found within the company itself. They include employee referrals, hiring family members, job postings (allowing current employees to apply for open positions before opening them up to the outside), and *job bidding* (the process of allowing employees to express an interest in a position and work toward skill-building prior to the role becoming available). The advantages to using internal sources for talent acquisition is that the applicant usually has a good sense of who the company is and how they treat their employees. A disadvantage is that an over-reliance on internal sources may create a lack of diversity in the employee groups. In a potential promotion situation, an overlooked employee may also experience low morale or a lack of clarity on why they did not get a position.

Using external sources to find talent is really a function of advertising and outreach. Employers may advertise using any traditional medium, such as posting on job seeker websites, social media, university and community college job boards, trade schools, former employees, and labor unions. Hosting or participating in job fairs is a common activity for employers who practice a continuous recruitment strategy for hard-to-fill positions. Targeted advertising is also a practice that continues to grow in importance. As technology evolves, these methods are becoming more effective. The practice of geofencing, for example, allows employers to create targeted recruiting campaigns. Target applicants may live in a particular area, frequent certain business, watch particular television shows, have a specific level of education, or earn a minimum income level.

Many companies continue to use a formal job application process to capture the pertinent details related to each candidate. Unfortunately, the process continues to receive negative ratings from a candidate experience perspective. Common complaints include the following:

- Asking for redundant information in multiple places
- The length of the application
- Lack of information about the job responsibilities, pay, and other details that a candidate needs to know before deciding to apply
- Company responds only if there is interest or lack of any communication at all

If HR is truly going to support organizational goals that are reliant on a qualified workforce, these issues will have to be addressed.

Selection

Once a pool of qualified talent has been found, it is HR's responsibility to attempt to predict "fit"—person-to-job fit and person-to-organization fit. Traditionally, this is done through the use of a series of preemployment tests. Experienced professionals know, however, that the term *test* in this context goes beyond a skills exam. The Uniform Guidelines on Employee Selection Procedures (UGESPs) define any requirement that will be used to make an employment decision as a test. This includes applications; interview questions; skills tests, such as keyboarding or math; minimum education requirements; performance tests; and probationary periods as tests that must be nondiscriminatory in both intent and outcome. More on the UGESPs is found in Chapter 14, "U.S. Employment Laws and Regulations."

Employment Interviews

The interview continues to be the most common method for making a hiring decision. For the purpose of the SHRM exams, it is useful to have an understanding of the various interview methods, all of which have particular advantages and disadvantages.

Structured vs. Unstructured   The terms *structured* and *unstructured* refer to the way that interview questions are designed and used. In a *structured interview*, the interviewer asks a series of prewritten questions that are asked of all candidates applying for the same role. The advantage of the structured interview is that it decreases the chance of interviewer bias and has the highest rate of *predictive validity* (the success of a preemployment test at predicting successful future performance). The disadvantage is that it inhibits the flow of information. An *unstructured interview* is one where the questions being asked are built from the candidate answers to a previous question. The advantage of the unstructured interview is that the flow of information is more specific to the individual. A disadvantage is that using different interview questions for each candidate results in inconsistent collection of data. Employers see the value in both structured and unstructured interviews, and so blending the two and conducting a semi-structured interview is a successful way to get the best of both interview methods.

Behavior Based   *Behavior-based interview* questions seek to understand how a candidate has reacted in a past situation. These questions often begin with phrases such as "Tell me about a time when you had to . . ." The goal of behavioral questions is not so much to ascertain whether or not they have a particular skill, but rather to determine the degree of capability that is necessary for the job.

Panel and Peer   A form of group interview, *panel and peer interview* setups are designed to gather multiple perspectives. This is valuable so that the presence of any interview bias, whether conscious or not, does not decrease the chance of a good hire. The downside to this structure is that many candidates report walking into a room of 3–5 strangers as highly stressful in a situation where they are already nervous.

Stress   The *stress interview* is used for roles that require taking action or applying critical thinking skills under high pressure. Industries such as law enforcement or air traffic controllers benefit from creating emotionally chaotic scenarios to see how the applicant reacts. A disadvantage is that a stress interview can leave candidates feeling put off from the process, thus decreasing hiring rates.

Assessment Centers

In a competitive, candidate-driven labor pool, HR or recruiters are being constantly challenged to be building a labor pipeline from both internal and external sources. As discussed earlier, technology can help a great deal with this. An *assessment center* is not (as the name suggests) an actual place but rather an administrative process of legally valid and reliable exercises that help managers make a selection choice—whether that is a new hire, a promotion, or selection to receive training. For example, the U.S. Office of Personnel Management (OPM) includes in their assessment centers work sample tests that simulate job tasks, non-cognitive tests, leaderless problem-solving group work, and personality assessments. OPM (OPM.gov) notes that for internal candidates, the tests should be aligned with competencies. For external candidates, the assessments should be written to align with the job or industry. Because of their complexity, assessment centers require experienced raters to ensure that the administration process and assessment development remain valid and reliable predictors of behavior.

Several options for preemployment tests may be used to predict candidate performance on the job:

- *Cognitive ability tests* are instruments used to measure thinking skills, such as reasoning or memory.

- *Biographical data (biodata)* measures are based on the principle that past behavior is the best predictor of future behavior. Therefore, *biodata assessments* seek to identify patterns of attitudinal or behavioral responses to past events.

- *Predictive personality assessments*, which are designed to measure traits accurately, have been shown to drive behavior and continue to be used by many employers to great effect.

- *Application forms*, if required as part of the selection process, are also considered tests under the UGESPs, and thus must be reliable and valid predictors of performance on the job.

Job Offers

Once a qualified candidate has been identified, a formal job offer is extended. This can be done verbally or in writing. Regardless of how the offer is extended, there are several key HR competencies for which HR must be proficient, including, the use of contingencies, and the risk of creating unintended employment contracts.

> **Contingencies**   *Contingent job offers* are made when there are certain post-offers or pre-hire requirements that must be met before officially starting work. Conditions may include passing a drug screen, verifying educational credentials, or passing a health screen to ensure that the candidate can safely perform the essential duties of a job.
>
> **Employment Contracts**   The *doctrine of employment at-will* states that the employer or the employee may at any time, and for any reason, with or without notice to each other, terminate the relationship. Conversely, an *implicit or explicit contract for employment* states the terms and conditions of the relationship, including pay, benefits, work being performed, and under what conditions a contract may be terminated without further obligation. Employers must be careful not to form a written contract for employment in their job offers. They must also avoid creating an implicit contract for employment based on statements made to the team member, such as "You'll have a job here for life if you just show up every day." Doing so means that the employer may only terminate for cause.

In other cases, an employment contract is desirable. This may be the case for difficult-to-recruit positions, or positions that require tenure for performance, such as at the executive level.

Regardless, it is a good practice to ensure that a job offer template, the employee handbook, and a formal contract be vetted by a labor attorney for proper risk management.

Education, Certification, and Licensing

A word about educational requirements: The goal of the UGESPs is to make sure that any preemployment test is a valid and reliable predictor of success on the job. This is extended to any education, certification, or licensing requirements. Unless an employer can demonstrate that a minimum level of education is necessary for performance, the requirements may be found to be discriminatory, regardless of intent. *Griggs v. Duke Power* (covered in more detail in Chapter 14) was a landmark case that found that a high school diploma requirement for entry-level work was discriminatory in effect because it disproportionately affected the employment of people of color.

Certification and licensing have become a political issue as well. For example, in Indiana a change.org petition was launched to remove the state licensing requirements for hairstylists, barbers, and nail technicians as a matter of freedom of choice. Utah proposed licensing exemptions for cosmetologists who only wash and dry hair. Proponents of these exemptions argue that the state has self-interest because they profit from license and relicensing fees that may be unnecessary or overly restrictive. Those against these activities argue that consumer health and safety are at risk without them.

Additionally, the rising cost of education and the alarming amount of student loan debt is causing many to have second thoughts about a traditional college education. Elon Musk made news when he announced on social media that you don't need a college degree to work at Tesla. This tracks with the many stories of tech giants who famously dropped out of universities, such as Steve Jobs, Bill Gates, and Larry Ellison. For talent acquisition pros, this requires strategic conversations with business leaders about what roles truly require specific knowledge or skill that is demonstrated only through a college degree.

Negotiation Techniques

Although many other components help to make up a qualified candidate's mind, the answer to the question "What are the salary and benefits?" is a critical piece of information. Studies have shown that transparency matters; employers should be up front about the pay range. *Negotiation* is the process by which the employer and the potential hire work together to come to an agreement on salary and other conditions of work.

As you will see in Chapter 7, "Employee Engagement and Retention," market wage surveys are an important function of establishing legally compliant pay systems. However, salary is not the only valuable aspect of a job offer. Creative employers may negotiate instead with offers of equity in ownership for startups who perhaps cannot afford the high salaries or extra paid volunteer time for a younger generation craving balance.

In a tight labor market, it is not uncommon for an applicant to accept a job offer from a new employer, put in notice to their current employer, and have the current employer make a counter-offer to keep them. When this happens, HR may need to use negotiating skills to re-iterate why the applicant was looking in the first place- better pay, schedule, feeling valued, challenging work . . . It differs for each candidate and if HR wants to successfully land the hire, they must get to know the applicants intrinsic and extrinsic needs.

In their phenomenal book, *Getting to Yes: Negotiating Agreement Without Giving In* (Penguin Books, 2011), authors Roger Fisher and William Ury remind us that successful negotiations occur over interests, not positions. The authors recommend that to identify interests, negotiators should first ask, "Why?" For example, "Why does this engineer want a sign-on bonus?" The answer may be that they have another job offer on the table and need to know that you are willing to demonstrate the value of their choice. The second question a negotiator should ask is, "Why not?" In this same scenario, the recruiter may answer that they have three other qualified engineering candidates who are willing to accept the starting pay without the bonus. Or they may come to the conclusion that in such a difficult-to-fill role that also brings diversity to the team, the cost of the sign-on bonus will be offset by the saved recruiting costs and perspective that diversity brings. Regardless, HR should have the authority to act within a reasonable timeframe so as to secure top talent when it comes their way.

Acculturation, Socialization, Orientation, and Onboarding

So many words to describe the processes that welcome a new team member to their first days of work!

Orientation is an administrative process. It is focused on completing new-hire paperwork, working through security protocols, and getting the new team member oriented to the new workspace.

Employee *acculturation* (also called *socialization*) is a much more comprehensive and dynamic psychological and physical onboarding process that focuses on a gradual introduction of the employee to the work and culture. Depending on the learning curve for the job and company, these efforts can take many months. Factors such as training for their new job, meeting the team, and figuring out the logistics of the physical space are all important in those first weeks. As the employee becomes more comfortable, acculturation shifts to an awareness of the unspoken protocols related to items such as *face-time bias* (perceptions of loyalty and commitment for those working on-site versus working remotely) and the presence of informal yet influential power structures.

Once again, technology can have a deep impact on the processes. For example, onboarding portals gives new hires access to the mountain of paperwork, including benefits information and the employee handbook, all in one place that can be completed via electronic signature. The portal may also include pictures of the team so that the employee has a resource to help put names to faces. New-hire welcome messages from the president or CEO can be a friendly reminder that the employee made the right choice to begin work with the organization.

Finally, as discussed in the section on the employer brand, the employee experience starts long before their first day of employment. How they are treated during the recruitment and selection process goes a long way toward setting expectations for Day 1 and beyond, affecting early turnover, long-term retention, and return on investment from recruiting and training a new employee.

Workforce Analytics

Workforce analytics impacts all functional areas of human resources. For talent acquisition, the data that needs to be collected revolves around the recruiting and selection processes:

Headcount   Understanding how many full-time employees or full-time equivalents (FTEs) you need is important. From a business perspective, an employer will forecast labor costs based on the average number of employees it takes to operate over a given year. From a compliance perspective, the number of FTE workers determines which labor laws an employer must comply with. For example, compliance with the major provisions of the Affordable Care Act (ACA) is dependent on the number of FTEs an employer has annually. This can be measured on a month-to-month basis or by looking back at the prior year. An FTE is one who worked at least 30 hours a week, or 130 hours in a month. According to the IRS, an hour of service includes the following:

- Each hour for which an employee is paid, or entitled to payment, for the performance of duties for the employer
- Each hour for which an employee is paid, or entitled to payment, by the employer for a period of time during which no duties are performed due to vacation, holiday, illness, incapacity (including disability), layoff, jury duty, military duty, or leave of absence

Cost per Hire   *Cost per hire (CPH)* is a measure of the financial expenses associated with filling open positions. For purposes of the exam, you need to understand SHRM's method of calculating the CPH, which includes expenses related to recruiting, sourcing, and selection. This includes external costs, such as advertising fees, and internal costs, such as the salary of the recruiter. CPH is found by adding together the internal and external costs and then dividing it by the total number of hires for the period being evaluated.

Time to Fill   This metric is designed to understand the level of ease or difficulty to hire sorted by type of position. This data can be used in strategic planning to plan for the necessary recruiting window and set expectations. It is a simple metric that merely tracks the day a job order was received to the day of a candidate's acceptance of a formal job offer. The *time-to-fill ratio* has a relationship to other measures of workforce reporting, such as turnover in the first six months (a faster hire may result in a lower-quality candidate) and cost to hire (the longer the position is open, the greater the cost).

Turnover and Attrition   Expressed as a percentage, *turnover* is a metric designed to understand the ratio of employees that exit the company, both voluntarily and involuntarily. It is found by dividing the average number of employees by the total number of separations for the time being measured and then multiplying that by 100 in order to arrive at a percentage.

Attrition is different from turnover in that it calculates the rate of exits for non-employer-generated events. This includes employees who quit and those who retire. This value is important, especially for the positions that have a higher-than-average cost to hire. Attrition is calculated by dividing the average number of employees by the total number of non-employer-related separations, then multiplying the total by 100 to convert the number into a percentage.

Both turnover and attrition can be calculated by department, by number of new hires, or by the whole organization over any given time (month, quarter, or year).

Levels, Groups, and Subgroups   Knowing the different organizational layers can help HR audit whether their hiring, promotion, and other practices are nondiscriminatory. For example, an almond producer is proud of the fact that 65 percent of their workforce are Hispanic women. Upon closer examination, however, only one member of the entire management team is of that same demographic (group characteristics such as age, ethnicity, position, income, geographic location, and so on). This fact suggests that their hiring and promotion practices are out of balance. HR can support a more diverse field by creating a plan to increase the number of individuals who are qualified to work at all levels of the organization. This plan may include initiatives aimed at recruiting, promotion, and learning/development opportunities.

SHRM SCP Only

Practicing senior-level activities within the domain of talent acquisition includes a lot of oversight. Talent acquisition is a highly operational task, and so it can be easy to get lost in the weeds of working "in" the department as opposed to "on" the department. The SHRM BoCK tells us what that looks like with terms such as *analyzing, developing, establishing, designing,* and *overseeing.* In this way, senior leaders must be thinking strategically.

For example, the chapter opened with concepts related to aligning talent acquisition strategies to organizational goals. For senior leaders, this means analyzing the current staffing levels and understanding current employee skill sets. The purpose of this step is to forecast the talent needs based on organizational growth or decline strategies. Understanding trends in learning and development at a university and on-the-job level will help senior leaders more adequately predict where their acquisition resources should be spent. This includes directing the HR team toward sourcing and recruiting methods that will manage metrics, such as cost-per-hire and time-to-fill, both of which directly contribute to an organization that competes based on knowledge assets.

The EVP is another area that will require a senior-level review that goes beyond promoting the brand. HR leaders must develop the critical thinking and strategic skills to target high-quality applicants using creative and diverse solutions. Agility matters here. As technology and social movements drive change, an EVP may also need to flex. Senior leaders will need to advise executives and coach managers to ensure that the company is living its EVP at an operational level.

The value of acculturation and socialization activities cannot be underestimated. In a tight labor market with shifting candidate needs and flexible work locations, the new hire experience is a marker of both short- and long-term retention efforts. For senior leaders, this means that onboarding systems are directly tied with meeting the goals of organizational strategy, which is then tied to the achievement of organizational results.

As with all HR activities, the ability to measure results does more than justify HR activities. It certainly communicates the value of having HR in senior leadership, but the United States and other countries continue to be challenged to respond rapidly to external conditions. The design of systematic programs to measure results allow for real-time adjustments to economic, social, political, and technological forces driving change. Data allows leaders to make a valid business case for the necessary changes to compete for talent in a near constantly changing environment.

Summary

Finding the talent necessary for an organization to compete in the current market as well as for the work of the future is the primary function of talent acquisition. It begins by aligning acquisition plans with business strategy and then selecting sources that will produce a selection of qualified individuals. To do so, HR must lead the job analysis process that results in clearly defined job descriptions that outline the tasks, duties, and responsibilities of a job along with the necessary knowledge, skills, and abilities of a qualified worker. These will be used in the recruitment process.

Many candidates are initially attracted to an employer because of their brand. A strong brand that is true in message and practice can be the deciding factor for a candidate to accept an offer of employment and then stay long enough for their talent to be harnessed in a mutually beneficial way.

Once a pool has been developed, HR initiates the process of selection using a variety of preemployment tests, negotiation techniques, and crafting of job offers without unintentionally creating an employment contract.

As new hires begin work, the process of acculturation begins to help them transition into their new role and the company culture. Turnover in the first six months of employment is but one of many metrics a qualified HR professional will calculate in order to support their company's talent acquisition efforts.

Key Terms

Acculturation

Assessment center

Behavior-based interview

Contingent job offer

Cost-per-hire

Demographic

Doctrine of employment at will

Employer brand

Face-time bias

Implicit or explicit contract for employment

Job analysis

Job bidding

Job description

Job specifications

Joint ventures

Negotiation

Orientation

Panel interview

Peer interview

Predictive validity

Recruitment

Reskilling

Stress interview

Structured interview

Sourcing

Strategic alliance

Time-to-fill

Turnover

Upskilling

Unstructured interview

Workforce analytics

Exam Essentials

Understand how talent acquisition strategy aligns with organizational strategy.   All HR systems should seek to be in alignment with overall company strategy. For talent acquisition, this means focusing on creating and maintaining a workforce that meets organizational goals.

Be able to develop and communicate the employer brand.   The employer brand is a form of messaging that tells individuals about who you are as a company. In the case of talent acquisition, the brand communicates the employee value proposition, which then helps with recruiting and sourcing applicants.

Conduct job analysis and create legally defensible job descriptions.   The process of job analysis results in the identification of important information that helps with recruiting and sourcing. Job descriptions communicate in writing the competencies and specifications that define the characteristics of jobs that then may be matched with the KSAOs of candidates to determine fit.

Engage in effective recruiting and selection processes.   Selecting the most appropriate sources for hiring helps increase the number of qualified applicants. The use of social media and other online methods continues to be a primary source for finding talent.

Be able to identify what is important for SCP exam takers.   Senior HR leaders have additional responsibilities that are elevated versions of the day-to-day tasks of a busy talent acquisition team. This includes leading the alignment of strategies and overseeing the recruiting, sourcing, selection, and data collection systems that are inherent to the work of this domain.

Review Questions

1. Which of the following plans is most likely to result in the development of a talent pipeline when properly aligned with organizational strategy?

   A. Succession plan

   B. Talent acquisition plan

   C. Talent needs assessment

   D. Recruitment plan

2. Which of the following M&A strategies is most likely to result in long-term success for the acquiring company?

   A. Divestitures when financially prudent

   B. Larger purchases with maximum shareholder value

   C. Smaller acquisitions over time

   D. Acquisitions of companies whose cultures are most similar

3. You work for a major corporation who has recently partnered with another organization and a major university to focus resources on the development of advanced water technology in third-world countries over the next five years. The partnership resulted in a new corporation. This is the best example of which of the following?

   A. Acquisition

   B. Merger

   C. Strategic alliance

   D. Joint venture

4. Which of the following forces has had the most effect on the need for HR talent teams to invest in upskilling and reskilling efforts for their current workforce?

   A. Political

   B. Economic

   C. Social

   D. Technological

5. The company you work for hired 26 candidates in the first quarter of the fiscal year. The internal costs to hire these candidates was $20,000. The external costs ran an additional $15,000. What is the approximate cost per hire?

   A. $750

   B. $1,200

   C. $1,350

   D. $2,200

6. Which of the following is the best example of a "position" in a salary negotiation?

    A. "I won't pay more than what I started my other engineers at."

    B. "I refuse to work for less than what I am making now."

    C. "We never pay more than the midpoint salary for our market."

    D. All of the above.

7. What is the primary difference between turnover and attrition?

    A. Turnover is objective, whereas attrition is subjective.

    B. Turnover is expressed as a percentage, whereas attrition is not.

    C. Turnover measures all exits, whereas attrition only measures employee-driven exits.

    D. Nothing. Turnover and attrition measure the same thing.

8. What is the most important feature of an applicant tracking system (ATS)?

    A. Its résumé search capabilities

    B. How easily it ties to other HR databases

    C. The candidate experience

    D. The cost to implement

9. The identification of factors such as age, race, and gender are _____ characteristics that help an HR team build _____ to be used in decision-making.

    A. Demographic; reporting

    B. Demographic; analytics

    C. Protected class; reporting

    D. Protected class; analytics

10. A series of preemployment tests designed to help evaluators determine who is ready for employment, training, promotion, or other assignment is the best definition of which of the following?

    A. Talent directory

    B. Assessment centers

    C. Skills inventory

    D. Legally compliant systems

Chapter 7

Employee Engagement and Retention

Exam Notables

Run a simple Internet search on the term "employee engagement," and see how many results are returned. When I did it, I received about 545,000,000. So, when I say that "much has been written about the topic of employee engagement," I am not kidding! But what makes this such a hot topic?

The history of the research is compelling. Many suggest that the concept of employee engagement made its first appearance in a 1990 journal article titled, "Psychological Conditions of Personal Engagement and Disengagement at Work," (doi.org/10.5465/256287) by William Kahn. Since then, engagement has been regarded as the magic bullet of all things in people management, improving outcomes in customer service, retention, employee loyalty, productivity, and more. This shows up in the complexity of SHRM's definition of the topic:

> Employee Engagement & Retention refers to activities aimed at retaining high-performing talent, solidifying and improving the relationship between employees and the organization, creating a thriving and energized workforce, and developing effective strategies to address appropriate performance expectations from employees at all levels.

This chapter serves as a guide through the exam concepts, and it also functions as a look at best practices to help you increase retention through employee engagement efforts.

The SHRM Exam Objectives

SHRM's *Body of Competency and Knowledge (BoCK)* not only summarizes this functional area, but also defines the proficiency indicators and key concepts. No matter your career level, pay special attention to the exam concepts defined "For All HR Professionals" and the "Key Concepts." If seeking the SHRM-SCP designation, you must expand your efforts to include those labeled "For Advanced HR Professionals."

THE SHRM-CP EXAM AND SHRM-SCP EXAM OBJECTIVES COVERED IN THIS CHAPTER INCLUDE THE FOLLOWING:

✓ **For All HR Professionals**

- Designs, administers, analyzes and interprets surveys of employee attitudes (e.g., engagement, job satisfaction) and culture.

- Administers and supports HR and organizational programs designed to improve employee attitudes and culture (e.g., social events, telecommuting policies, recognition, job enlargement/enrichment, workplace flexibility).

- Identifies program opportunities to create more engaging or motivating jobs (e.g., job enrichment/enlargement).

- Monitors changes in turnover and retention metrics, and ensures that leadership is aware of such changes.

- Coaches supervisors on creating positive working relationships with their employees.

- Trains stakeholders on the use of an organization's performance management systems (e.g., how to enter performance goals, make ratings).

- Helps stakeholders understand the elements of satisfactory employee performance and performance management.

- Implements and monitors processes that measure effectiveness of performance management systems.

✓ **For Advanced HR Professionals**

- In collaboration with other leaders, defines an organizational strategy to create an engaged workforce.

- Implements best practices for employee retention in HR programs, practices and policies (e.g., RJP, career development programs, employee socialization).

- Communicates to other senior leaders the results of surveys of employee attitudes and culture.

- Designs and oversees an action plan to address the findings of employee attitude surveys.

- Designs and oversees HR and organizational programs designed to improve employee attitudes (e.g., social events, telecommuting policies, recognition, job enlargement/enrichment, workplace flexibility).

- Holistically monitors the organization's metrics on employee attitudes, turnover and retention, and other information about employee engagement and retention.

- Designs and oversees best practices-based employee performance management systems that meet the organization's talent management needs.

- Designs and oversees processes to measure the effectiveness of performance management systems.

✓ Key Concepts

- Approaches to developing and maintaining a positive organizational culture (e.g., learning strategies, communication strategies, building values).

- Approaches to recognition (e.g., performance or service awards).

- Creation, administration, analysis and interpretation of employee attitude surveys.

- Creation, planning and management of employee engagement activities.

- Employee lifecycle phases (e.g., recruitment, integration, development, departure).

- Employee retention concepts (e.g., causes of turnover) and best practices (e.g., realistic job previews [RJP]).

- Influence of culture on organizational outcomes (e.g., organizational performance, organizational learning, innovation).

- Interventions for improving job attitudes.

- Job attitude theories and basic principles (e.g., engagement, satisfaction, commitment).

- Job enrichment/enlargement principles and techniques.

- Key components of, and best practices associated with, performance management systems.

- Methods for assessing employee attitudes (e.g., focus groups, stay interviews, surveys).

- Principles of effective performance appraisal (e.g., goal setting, giving feedback).

- Retention and turnover metrics (e.g., voluntary turnover rate).

- Types of organizational cultures (e.g., authoritarian, mechanistic, participative, learning, high performance).

- Workplace flexibility programs (e.g., telecommuting, alternative work schedules).

Employee Engagement

The science is clear—employees who are more engaged at work produce better outcomes than those less engaged. *Engagement* is defined as the degree to which an individual has invested their emotional, physical, and mental selves into their role at work. Engaged employees perform better in areas such as productivity, customer service, and safety. Conversely, disengaged workers can be destructive. They are disconnected from their jobs and organizational outcomes, tend to have attendance issues, and in extreme cases, may engage in *counterproductive work behaviors (CWBs)* such as bullying, theft of company property, and substance abuse. CWBs are those activities that actively undermine individual, team, and organizational success.

Research conducted by Gallup in 2020 is not encouraging. This major study found that only 39 percent of the workforce is actively engaged, 49 percent was not engaged at all, and 13 percent was actively disengaged ("Historic Drop in Employee Engagement Follows Record Rise," Jim Harter, Gallup, 2020). This means that 60 percent of the workforce is not connected to their job or organization in a meaningful way! The good news is that there is opportunity for HR teams to have significant impact in this arena.

Organizational Behavior

In the "People" description of the SHRM BoCK, there is a very clear tie between employee engagement and retention. In a 2020 report by Sage Research titled "The Changing Face of HR," 94 percent of respondents noted that titles (and responsibilities) of the HR role are shifting from "Human Resources" to "People." What do the BoCK and Sage Research tell us about both the exams and our roles? The answer lies in the domain of Organizational Behavior.

Organizational Behavior (OB) is the branch of psychological practice that is focused on human behavior at work. Researchers seek to study factors such as human motivation, group behaviors, and leadership theories and apply them to improving employee engagement and, thus, outcomes. Fundamental to this discussion is a thorough understanding of the impact of job attitudes on employee engagement.

Job Attitudes

Employee engagement is a hot topic of study due to its power to drive employee behavior. Referring back to the Gallup study, in a 100-person organization, about 13 employees have a low degree of organizational commitment, lack job satisfaction, and are not invested in the actual work they perform. These are known as the *job attitudes*.

Organizational Commitment

Organizational commitment is the job attitude that reflects loyalty to the organization and is most correlated with the term *retention* or influencing employees to stay with the company. With the average worker holding more than 10 positions in a career, influencing and measuring what retains employees is important.

Stay interviews are structured conversations with current employees to determine what aspect of the job keeps them there. Stay interviews may measure factors such as culture, leadership, the value proposition, and the other job attitudes in an effort to find ways to improve in those areas.

Job Satisfaction   The attitude of *job satisfaction* is defined in OB as how happy an employee is with their job or job experience. Job satisfaction is the most widely studied measure of engagement in OB. Of particular interest is that an employee's sense of *achievement* from work is positively correlated with job satisfaction across cultures, including India, Poland, Australia, Canada, Israel, South Africa, and the United States.

Other factors of job satisfaction are a bit more nuanced because there are job satisfiers and job dissatisfiers. For example, employees may love their coworkers but struggle with the leader. The Job Descriptive Index (JDI) was developed to measure these facets on a scale. Developed at Bowling Green State University, the JDI measures five facets, including satisfaction with coworkers, pay, opportunities for promotion, supervisors, and, of course, the work itself.

Starting in the 1930s, and currently in its second generation, the largest longitudinal study on happiness is being conducted by Harvard University. Influential leaders including John F. Kennedy and Ben Bradlee were participants in this early study, which sought to determine what factors make for a happy life. Is it money, fame, good health, possessions? The findings have held steady over time; what makes for the happiest life is the quality of the connections we have with family, friends, community, and yes, at work. Through this lens, measures of employee engagement must take into account the softer realties of human relations defined with as much precision and with the same degree of importance as we look at productivity or safety measures. Visit the study's home page at www.adultdevelopmentstudy.org or, if you prefer videos, search YouTube for "What makes a good life: Lessons from the longest study on happiness," by Robert Waldinger.

Work Engagement/Job Involvement   The final job attitude is the level of engagement a team member has with the work itself—the actual tasks, duties, and responsibilities of their role. In many cases, the work itself has been found to be more strongly correlated than wages to job satisfaction and, thus, engagement. *Job involvement* is significantly related to employee withdrawal behaviors such as absenteeism and turnover.

Job Characteristics

The way that the work is structured can influence positive outcomes in all three of the employee job attitudes. A seminal work on the study of the job as motivators is Richard Hackman and Greg R. Oldham's *Job Characteristic Model (JCM)*. Their work has served as the benchmark for many theories of motivation related to job structure, with variables based on the JCM's five factors:

Task Identity   The degree to which an employee sees the outcome and purpose of their job. This is directly tied to the cross-cultural satisfier of achievement as a motivator.

Task Significance   Similar to identity, this is the degree to which a task is critical to the organization or consumer. Individuals with a higher sense of purpose have greater degrees of job satisfaction and commitment.

Skill Variety   This is the degree to which an employee is able to use multiple skills on the job. The greater the skill variety, the greater the satisfaction.

Autonomy   Measures of independence is the focus of autonomy. It is an indication of how much independence an employee has to make decisions that are within the scope of the role. Many engaged, productive workers crave a higher degree of autonomy.

Feedback   Performance feedback of the positive and constructive side can increase employee satisfaction. The absence of any feedback, or feedback only when the employee is doing something wrong, has the opposite effect. Feedback is at the core of a company's performance management system.

Work with Purpose

As mentioned in Chapter 6, "Talent Acquisition," the ability of an employer to define a job's purpose is a key indicator of job satisfaction, productivity, and thus, retention, particularly for the millennial generation. By comparison, Sir Christopher Wren's story of a bricklayer illustrates this point.

Wren was a renaissance man with a reputation for fine architecture. In fact, he is credited with being responsible for rebuilding dozens of churches, including St. Paul's Cathedral in London in 1710. With such a responsibility, you can imagine his interest when he came upon three of his bricklayers, the third of whom was working with a fevered sense of purpose and the other two less so. Wren approached the first bricklayer and asked, "What is it that you do?" The worker responded, "Well, I am a bricklayer, I am laying bricks." Wren then approached the second worker and asked the same question and received the response, "I am building a wall." Wren then approached the third bricklayer, the one who was the most productive, and repeated his question. The worker responded, "I am building a cathedral to God."

Which of the three do you believe had the greatest level of job satisfaction? Clearly, it was the one who understood the purpose of his work. HR must investigate and articulate the company's purpose and then communicate to the team why what they contribute is important.

Job rotation is another method used to help improve employee engagement because it allows the individual to work in several positions over time, increasing their skill and value. *Job enlargement* and *job enrichment* are also strategies that use work structures to increase engagement and retention. In job enlargement, the scope of an employee's job is broadened to take on similar tasks, duties, and responsibilities. In job enrichment, depth is added to the employee's responsibilities to develop skills that prepare them for their next role within the organization.

Other developmental activities, such as being selected for special projects and teams, is another way to address engagement levels. Temporary or project assignments can help increase a team member's visibility to management and give them access to other business units with whom they may not otherwise work. Global assignments are of particular interest for those seeking to grow into C-suite roles.

The Role of Culture

The term *culture* in the context of organizational behavior has taken on an outsized level of importance in today's world of work. Going beyond a description of regional patterns of beliefs and behaviors, organizational culture speaks to the identity of the people at the workplace. The type of organizational culture has a direct influence on levels of employee engagement.

Authoritarian cultures are characterized by a power structure where decision-making comes from the top down. The military is an example of this type of culture.

Conversely, participative cultures encourage group problem-solving and feedback at all organizational levels—upward, downward, and peer-to-peer. Global design and invention businesses are built on a participative culture.

Learning cultures take a more holistic, systemwide perspective of engagement, where all employees have a growth mindset—for themselves and others. Startups and tech companies are examples of learning cultures.

A mechanistic culture is one driven by hierarchies and highly structured business units. Straying outside the chain of command is frowned upon. Institutions such as financial, academic, and hospitals tend to be structured in a mechanistic way.

High-performance cultures are characterized by a relentless drive for competitive results. Hedge funds and sports institutions are examples of high-performance cultures that drive organizational patterns of behaviors and beliefs.

More on the different types of cultures can be found in Chapter 4, "The Business Competency Cluster."

Assessing Engagement

Before we can determine the proper intervention related to engagement, it is important to gather data. This ensures that engagement strategies are built to address the correct challenge, not the symptom.

Measuring engagement is often done through employee surveys. The benefits of using surveys are that they help employees feel that their employer cares about what they have to say. Surveys create a direct line of communication to the organizational decision-makers, which increase feelings of empowerment. Anonymous surveys done frequently also prevent turnover, because managers gain insight to current challenges and are able to craft real-time responses.

One HR competency is the knowledge, skill, and ability to identify opportunities to leverage external resources. Purchasing a reliable and valid assessment tool from leading experts, such as the Gallup Q^{12}, is one such opportunity. *12* stands for the number of engagement items being measured through the assessment with outcomes reliably tied to productivity, customer satisfaction, and improved attendance—all potential factors that are positively correlated with improved employee engagement.

Challenges to employee surveys include creating forms that try to measure too much at once. Overall engagement is important to understand on a macro level, but it is the micro data that helps get to the root cause of an issue. Focused surveys target elements such as job satisfaction, organizational commitment, career development, leadership, recognition and rewards systems, and relationships at work. Note that these constructs are all correlated to the reasons why employees leave their job. If we know—through exit interviews or other means—why employees leave, we can get a good sense of what needs to be measured on a deeper level and addressed at an organizational, a departmental, or an individual level. If an employer gathers this data and then fails to respond, employees will stop engaging in a meaningful dialogue, effectively leaving the employer in the dark.

Email and online continues to dominate the methods that employers use to conduct surveys. This approach can be a challenge if the information is not properly secured. HR must also take care to ensure that teams without access to a computer in their work still get their voices heard. This can be done by traditional paper delivery or by scheduling time at company-shared computers to access the form online.

Another method for assessing employee attitudes and engagement is focus groups. HR gathers a select group of individuals and seeks feedback on specific issues. Focus groups are helpful when designing new HR systems, such as benefits or training needs. The focus of these meetings may be strategic, such as bringing teams in to have discussions about product launches or operational in nature, such as how to restructure work to increase efficiencies. When facilitating focus groups, it is important that employees feel safe to share their honest feedback without repercussions. This can occur by firmly establishing the purpose of the group and clearly communicating the parameters around which the group is organizing. In some cases, it is a best practice to have employees write down their responses to focus group questions to increase diversity of thought and to reduce the influence of the more vocal participants.

Positive Engagement Strategies

Many HR thought leaders share the idea that there is no longer such thing as a 20–30-year tenured employee. Yet SHRM's BoCK reflects the demand of employers worldwide that, once key talent is found, we must keep them long enough to earn a return on investment by achieving business goals. The balance can be struck by using positive engagement strategies.

The impact of pay on engagement is an important consideration to teams seeking to build and keep a qualified workforce. One report found that once employees achieve a certain threshold of pay, the money no longer serves as a motivator. Factors such as job security, the work environment, and prospects for promotion all drive engagement beyond hygiene factors such as wages, benefits, or other perks. For this reason, these factors should be measured using surveys and focus groups.

Recognition also has a direct correlation to positive engagement levels. Formal or otherwise, employees that feel appreciated for their contribution report higher levels of job satisfaction and commitment. The closer that HR can align recognition and rewards strategies to employee needs/wants, the more motivating the activity will be. For example, some employees value a title or face time with the CEO, whereas others prefer to be rewarded by more time to work independently on projects about which they are passionate. Some team members are highly motivated by financial rewards and perks, whereas others prefer to be compensated with time off.

Digital badges for service awards are not only effective as motivators, but employees can post news about their employer on their social media accounts, thus increasing brand awareness as an employer of choice. Internally, employees may be assigned as mentors to new hires. Designating the mentors with a digital badge on a company's intranet system helps employees identify the expert on different issues as they navigate a new team or organization.

Once you are successfully certified, you will be able to obtain a digital badge from BadgeCert (badgecert.com) to use on your social media accounts. This will allow you to share your success while giving future employers and others the ability to verify your credential.

Workplace flexibility is another emerging driver of engagement, particularly with the accelerated effect of Covid-19. Seattle-based company Zillow reported that more than 75 percent of those surveyed would prefer to work remotely once the pandemic has passed, predicting a boom for suburban housing markets all over the United States. With larger companies offering telecommuting, doctors increasing telehealth appointments, and markets building grocery delivery services, it is not a stretch to suggest that HR must help employers position their companies to access and retain qualified talent using remote work options. This includes advising management on how to keep a remote workforce engaged.

Engaging a Remote Workforce

In a Harvard Business School podcast, Dr. Marc Harrison, CEO of Intermountain Health-care of Utah, explained how in 2020 they shifted from having approximately 1,000 remote workers to more than 11,000 in just over a week and a half! While their business was already delivering healthcare virtually, he noted that the mechanistic culture of the institution as a whole was resistant to change at the corporate level. Similarly, the stock price of videoconferencing company Zoom grew by more than 100 percent between January and March of that year. Organizations all over the world and in all industries are struggling to shift rapidly to the permanently changed nature of how work should and can get done at all organizational levels.

Post-pandemic, employees will continue to benefit from the virtual work in the form of saved commuting and other work-related costs, such as dry cleaning and eating out every day. Employees are also moving to less expensive areas. Employers will benefit from lower overhead and less need for physical space, not to mention the labor pool that opened up from being able to recruit on a regional, national, or global scale. As the world settles down, a new hybrid workforce has emerged, highlighting the challenges of this work structure.

Remote workers have long had a disadvantage over their on-site peers. The presence of face-time bias, where loyalty is perceived to be strongest among those "seen" at work, existed before the pandemic, and on-site employees enjoyed access to management and strategic projects, easier collaboration, and more social support. Other stressors have become more apparent, such as online meeting fatigue, connectivity frustrations, distractions at home, lack of home office space, and the inability to "turn off" at the end of the day. Women and other minorities have been disproportionately affected by the changed landscape of work. These challenges, along with the new way that work gets done, are demanding that HR help managers learn how to keep a remote workforce engaged, productive, and connected.

Technology is the critical resource to keep teams whole. Creating a centralized source for team resources is much easier through the use of software programs such as Microsoft Teams, Zoom, or Slack. Other techniques to engage a remote workforce include increasing the frequency of employee surveys or using polls to do a daily check-in with the needs of the team. Ask questions related to work burnout and work/life balance strategies, not just about productivity or project status. Some organizations have experimented with "always on" meetings, where a department or team logs onto videoconferencing and stays on camera, just as though they were grouped together in an office. This strategy increases the sense of connectedness and the ability to ask real-time questions over video, as opposed to the more linear text, email, or messaging. The need for "live" human connectedness is just as relevant to remote workers, and it must be planned for and managed.

A mindset shift is required in order to engage remote workers as well. Employers tend to under-estimate their capacity for changes to workplace flexibility. In a traditional 9–5 day, productivity was never at 100 percent—distractions of all sorts existed just as they do in the home office. Team leaders can re-think their expectations and begin to craft jobs that are measured by results as opposed to only time-in-chair. This effort will result in a wider applicant pool and lower brick-and-mortar costs to the business.

Finally, harnessing technology and building relevant competencies is an absolute must for HR leaders of the future. Consider the opportunities that a truly connected workplace offers, from documentation housing to language translation for global teams. Although the pandemic was horrifying on multiple levels, it has forced accelerated change if companies—and HR—want to remain relevant.

Human Resources and the Employee Life Cycle

The employee life cycle is a visual representation of the stages a team member goes through as part of their time with an organization. Although there have been many versions of the life cycle, SHRM describes it as having four phases. As Figure 7.1 illustrates, many opportunities exist for engagement and retention at each stage of the employee life cycle.

Regardless of organizational or job tenure, employees have similar needs that can be addressed through engagement efforts. One way to look at these needs is through the filter of the traditional functions of human resource management.

Recruiting and Selection   As covered in Chapter 6, the employer brand communicates the tangible and intangible, the physical, and the psychological reasons for coming to work for an employer. Engagement activities in this function include the candidate experience while going through the application and selection process. What was communicated? Was the information strictly transactional, or did it speak to the company culture?

Total Rewards   Alternately called Total Rewards and Compensation and Benefits, this is the opportunity for HR to build systems that reward both performance and longevity in order to increase retention. Striking the right balance is key—HR must avoid entitlement pay that only rewards time spent with the employer as opposed to *productive* time spent with the employer. Compensation should be tied to an organization's competitive strategy and include economic, geographic, and industrial factors.

In Total Rewards, there is also the opportunity to use benefits strategically in order to improve engagement. Offering employee assistance programs, for example, can help teams more effectively manage stress. Other programs, such as financial planning services, can help employees see the value of saving for a house, for emergencies, and for retirement (all motivators to stay employed, which equals retention).

FIGURE 7.1   Phases of the employee life cycle

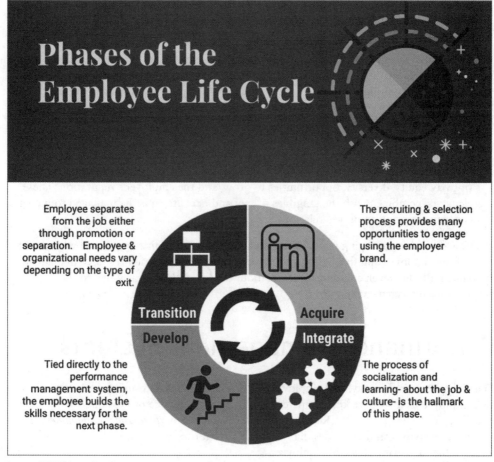

Source: SHRM Learning System

Paid leave programs, such as time to volunteer, adopt a child, or care for an aging parent, are also attractive options that run through Total Rewards. These types of benefits help employees achieve a more satisfying level of work/life balance.

Regardless of the type of reward or recognition, *organizational justice*—the degree of transparency, consistency, and perceived fairness in decision-making—is key to the rewards that create a positive employer/employee relationship.

Learning and Development (L&D)   The Learning and Development (L&D) activities of an HR team are very important to engagement. Our ability to meet the demands of engage-to-retain is grounded in L&D activities. These include tying individual goals based on career pathing to strategic staffing needs of the future.

Employee Relations   "Parties to a contract" is such an intimidating, transactional way to describe the employer/employee relationship! In fact, the use of the word *contract* can negate the at-will nature of employment. However, there is a *psychological* contract that is in play in the employer/employee relationship, and it goes beyond the tangibles of the employer value proposition (EVP). The psychological contract describes the unwritten and less objective expectations that an employee may have of the job and their employer. In exchange, the second party to the contract, the employer, believes that they can rely on the employee to perform to the best of their ability and commit to a long-term stay. Elements of the psychological contract include perceptions of job security, pay equity, diversity, opportunities to grow, and the employer's reputation. These elements, combined with the tangibles of pay and benefits, must be managed to increase engagement using employee relations activities.

HR is critical to managing many of the engagement opportunities presented with the life cycle of the employee and through the traditional functions of human resource management. Fundamentally, however, engagement throughout the life cycle is clearly tied to the performance management system.

Performance Management Systems

The ability to manage individual employee performance and coach supervisors on how to give employee feedback are key competencies for human resource professionals at all stages of their career. The SHRM BoCK's glossary of terms defines *performance management* as the "tools, activities, and processes that an organization uses to manage, maintain, and or/ improve the job performance of employees."

The BoCK references these tools throughout the functional area of engagement in two ways. The first is using the *performance management system* to improve organizational results by maintaining an engaged workforce, and second, to retain top-performing talent.

Figure 7.2 illustrates how a performance management system must be designed to meet organizational goals, job requirements, and individual needs. This kind of alignment requires a system to establish performance standards and measure employee behaviors.

FIGURE 7.2   Aligning individual performance

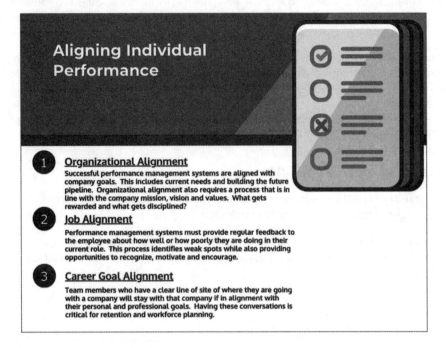

Performance Standards

Writing *performance standards* is different from writing a job description. Performance standards should be related to the tasks, duties, and responsibilities of a job, but they must also be tied to both behaviors and results. One way to do this is to use the SMART goal method. SMART is an acronym used to describe how to write a goal:

Specific: Whether measuring a behavior or a result, the standard should be specific. For a doctor, a poorly written performance standard is "must have a good bedside manner," as opposed to a well-written performance standard of the "doctor demonstrates care and competency when working with patients."

Measurable: Well-written performance standards are measurable and focused on results as opposed to mere quantity (unless piece rate is part of a productivity standard). "Attends monthly safety meeting" does not measure whether or not the employee is actually applying their safety training to their work.

Attainable: HR should coach supervisors to establish standards that measure satisfactory as opposed to highest/lowest performance. These types of standards will highlight above and below average performance for use in designing meaningful feedback.

<u>R</u>elevant: A performance standard should be related to the main responsibilities of the job. For example, it would make sense to have a performance standard to "answer phone professionally within three rings" for a hospital information clerk, but not for a nurse, even if the nurse occasionally answers a phone.

<u>T</u>ime-Based: Finally, strong performance standards establish a time period to increase clarity, often by using words such as "daily, weekly, or monthly" and avoiding words like "always" and "never."

Once the performance standards have been established and clearly communicated, the process of evaluating employee performance can begin.

Evaluating Performance

Many methods are used to evaluate performance, and they generally fall into two distinct groups: category methods and narrative methods.

Category Methods   Category evaluation uses standardized forms and processes to measure employee performance. They are the easiest to develop and use and include the following:

> **Checklist**   A list of statements related to performance are spelled out, and the rater simply checks the box if the employee is demonstrating that behavior.
>
> **Forced Choice Using the Bell Curve**   A comparative method, all team members are mapped on a bell curve. Raters must place employees along the curve, with 10 percent exceeding standards, 10 percent below standards, and 40 percent in the middle as meeting expectations. In between high/low is the rest of the workforce. See Figure 7.3 for an example of a bell curve. In the individual version of forced choice, raters must check a series of statements that describe what the employee is most like and what they are least like.

FIGURE 7.3   Example of a Bell Curve

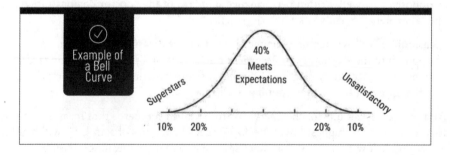

Graphic Rating Using the Likert Scale   The tasks, duties, responsibilities, and other behaviors are categorized by type such as productivity, interpersonal skills, quality, and so on. A scale (developed by Rensis Likert) is used to rate the employee between 1 and 5 (most common), with 1 being unsatisfactory and 5 being above average.

Narrative Methods   Narrative methods are generally more difficult to administer due to the varying degree of the writing skills of managers and the time commitment each involves. The most common narrative methods are as follows:

Behaviorally Anchored Rating Scales (BARS)   Examples of satisfactory and unsatisfactory performance are developed, often again on a scale of 1–5. The rater then selects the rating that is the best example of the employee's actual performance.

Critical Incident   Designed to increase feedback over an entire rating period; the rater documents positive and negative employee performance over time.

Multi-rater or Self-Assessments   Also called a 360-degree review, multi-rater evaluation methods collect data from peers, direct reports, customers, and other stakeholders to gain a clear picture of an employee's entire performance. In a self-assessment, the employee is asked to rate themselves in a set of prescribed categories. Performance feedback is then often focused on gaps between other feedback and the employee's own perception of their skills.

Regardless of the evaluation method selected, they each have pros and cons, as shown in Table 7.1.

TABLE 7.1   Pros and cons of evaluative methods

Method	Pros	Cons
Behaviorally Anchored Rating Scales (BARS)	Provides clear and accurate standards for employee performance.	Complicated to develop and maintain.
Checklist	Easy to develop and use for all levels of management.	May not adequately describe performance standards.
Critical Incident	Provides a thorough review of employee behaviors and results over the entire rating period, thus reducing rater bias.	Are time-consuming and difficult for managers who are less skilled at writing narratives.
Essay	Provides a thorough review of employee behaviors and results.	Similar to critical incident, essays are time-consuming and not appropriate for all levels of management.

TABLE 7.1   Pros and cons of evaluative methods *(continued)*

Method	Pros	Cons
Forced Choice	Provides a data-level look at the team to analyze the performance mix; useful when supervisors must allocate pay increases.	Not all teams have the "proper" mix of high, low, and meets standards employees; employees do not perceive them as fair.
Graphic/Likert scale	Embeds consistency in the process to increase perceptions of organizational justice.	May increase central tendency bias from the rater.
Multi-rater (360 degree)	Provides for meaningful feedback from those affected by the employee's performance.	Not all raters are trained to give feedback.
Self-Assessments	Gives the employee an opportunity to reflect on their own performance.	May result in inflated ratings or low morale if the manager and employee ratings are too far off.

Appraisals

Performance appraisals remain at the top of things employees—and managers—dislike. The traditional annual review has become laborious and compliance-driven, stripping the feedback from significance or as a true driver of behavior. This dissatisfaction is often due to the presence of a variety of rater errors, which include the following:

Central Tendency   The tendency of the rater to rate all employees at the center of a scale, such as "meets expectations" or "3" on a Likert scale. This may occur because the rater wants to appear to be fair.

Halo/Horn Effect   Occurs when the rater benchmarks all ratings around an employee's highest (halo) or lowest (horn) skill set. For example, an employee with excellent quality is rated high in all other categories based on this single performance dimension.

Leniency   The tendency for the rater to give all employees high scores. This occurs for several reasons, one of which is that the rater wants to avoid having difficult conversations.

Strictness   The strictness error comes from raters who make statements such as "Everyone has room for improvement." It may present as a measure of central tendency or as an inflation of task importance to justify a lower score.

Unconscious Bias   Bias is the unconscious tendency to treat people in a certain way based on our unconscious beliefs or values, and all humans do it. This natural tendency to sort and order can result in unfair, discriminatory practices when measuring performance and making other employment-related decisions.

Primacy/Recency/Spillover Effect   These rater errors happen when the rater gives greater weight to earlier (primacy) or later (recency) performance, as opposed to performance over the entire rating period. The spillover effect occurs when a manager continues to measure employee performance against a single incident regardless of performance improvement or failures.

Rater errors are costly. Employees who feel that they are being treated unfairly or that their manager does not care enough to provide adequate feedback that is necessary for success will, at some point, begin looking for another job. HR can help mitigate this by ensuring that all raters are properly trained on how to give legally defensible and meaningful performance feedback on a regular basis (not just once a year) and are trained on how to recognize and avoid the errors discussed here.

Positive Feedback Systems

> Anybody can become angry—that is easy. But to be angry with the right person, and to the right degree, and at the right time, and for the right purpose, and in the right way—that is not within everyone's power and that is not easy . . . .
>
> *Aristotle*

Ultimately, giving performance feedback is one way to ensure that employees have the right amount of information to perform successfully. As the quote by Aristotle demonstrates, it is nearly impossible to use negativity or anger to improve results. In fact, condescension and frustration is one sure way to damage relationships and diminish engagement over time. Positive, encouraging feedback sends a message that the supervisor cares and has the courage to have the difficult but necessary conversations to help the employee succeed. Positive feedback can be the difference between setting an employee on a path to separation and setting the employee on a path to success.

The first step to building a positive feedback system is to increase the frequency of the reviews. Not all performance feedback has to be in the form of an appraisal! It is better to train supervisors on how to provide daily, weekly, and monthly feedback to their teams that recognizes positive behaviors and addresses substandard levels of performance. Another step to consider is unbinding pay from the performance appraisal. This removes the barrier of an employee thinking that every time that they are told "well done," they should expect a pay increase. If that is not an option at your organization, at the very least audit the pay-performance relationship to ensure that what is being rewarded is what *should* be rewarded.

Additionally, companies that rely on innovation and creative problem-solving to survive must recognize that failure is embedded in the process and have language to communicate about it in a positive way. A good example is the company IDEO, who has a motto "fail early and fail often." A positive feedback system is not just about finding and communicating the good stuff, but rather it exists to provide a framework for how to communicate. This framework provides the system necessary to build a culture of innovation that encourages feedback in all directions—not just top-down. This approach increases teamwork and fosters an ownership culture that drives morale and organizational results.

Feedback systems should also take into account cultural norms and personality types. Similar to recognition, motivation is highly individualized, and managers should take the time to get to know their team on a human level to build trust and deliver feedback that hits the target without the unintended consequences of a misplaced/tone-deaf comment.

Evaluating Performance Management Systems

As with all HR systems, the performance management processes should be audited periodically to ensure that they are resulting in the desired outcome. Evaluation can be objective, such as "How many employees have received performance reviews?" and more subjective, such as conducting an employee survey to hear what the teams think about the process.

Feedback should be sought from management to rate their level of satisfaction with the process, and whether or not the performance management system is driving results. Feedback should also be sought from employees. Do they feel the process is fair? Are they getting feedback frequently enough? What other information do they need from their leaders in order to be successful in their role?

SHRM SCP Only

Senior leaders should take a strategic perspective of engagement and retention. We know the following:

- Reality no longer allows for the lifetime worker.
- We must be able to keep qualified talent long enough to achieve goals.
- We have to prepare the workforce to meet future needs.
- We need to craft jobs with purpose.

Working with all other HR functions is necessary to accomplish engagement and retention in the face of all of these factors. For example, HR may need to advocate for a job restructure to include deep learning components. This would be attractive for a college student who needs work experience for a new résumé. With this in mind, HR can engage in replacement planning, knowing that the employee is on deck for only 2–4 years. HR may also design compensation systems that reward loyalty, such as longevity bonuses or benefits vesting schedules that can help HR predict when and where positions will start to shift from filled to unfilled. Learning and development activities should target not only current job tasks, but also those changing as the result of social and technological forces. Doing this will help retain the more seasoned workers needing to gain the technical competencies necessary to meet evolving job requirements. The key is to work with other senior leaders and the management teams to format career development programs at all stages of the employee life cycle, not just at the time of hire.

Businesses with engaged employees are found to outperform those with a disengaged workforce. Therefore, it has been said that the path to becoming a CEO runs straight through first being a successful engagement officer. This includes work far beyond the party planning that many have come to associate with employee socialization efforts. These officers and their teams are responsible for helping employees identify in-house opportunities for growth through career planning and building systems to help them prepare, such as for basic interviewing skills and other development activities. This helps to prepare the current workforce for future needs while increasing retention. Engagement officers are responsible for actively communicating the company mission, vision, and values, along with the employer value proposition to communicate the value of remaining with the employer. This role requires that data be collected to measure employee attitudes and then tying them to improved employee and organizational performance.

As threaded throughout all HR activities, alignment with organizational strategy is key. For this reason, senior leaders are responsible for building HR systems that support higher levels of engagement. This support may include helping to restructure work so that more of it can be done remotely or through job sharing, all the while mitigating the risks associated with such policies.

The SHRM BoCK notes that senior leaders must be able to "holistically monitor" attitudes, turnover, retention, and engagement. In this way, strategic alignment requires that meaningful data be collected, interpreted, and then applied through refinement or development of all HR systems and at all levels of the employee life cycle. Data is often collected through employee attitude or other surveys designed to measure factors of culture, such as coworkers, leadership, diversity, and opportunities for promotion, but also how well each functional area of HR is supporting employee engagement.

Once this data is interpreted, it is up to senior HR leaders to advise C-suite level executives on the interventions necessary in order to improve job attitudes and create a positive organizational culture. These may include several of the strategies mentioned in this chapter, such as job enlargement and enrichment, workplace flexibility, and other ways to influence employee engagement positively.

Closely tied to the job attitudes is the system used to provide employees with meaningful feedback, performance management, and the feedback process. This in turn is tied to the employee life cycle and a team member's career path. In short, a performance management system must be designed to help the employee answer the questions "Where am I now?" and "Where am I going?" This is underscored by a need for an individual purpose that is tied to the organizational purpose. In this way, HR has their finger on the pulse of the talent needs, both as an employee and an employer advocate.

Summary

Employee turnover is a significant challenge for employers to manage. HR supports the retention of talent through employee engagement efforts that seek to (1) increase organizational commitment, (2) improve employee job satisfaction, and (3) engage team members with the work itself. These three elements are called the *job attitudes*.

The first step in the development and management of HR systems is to assess the current state using tools such as focus groups and employee surveys. Once the issues are brought to light, HR will lead the charge to develop positive engagement programs that address the needs of the team.

A particular challenge for employers across the globe is that of engaging a remote workforce. HR is responsible for promoting strategies that optimize the many benefits that virtual work provides for both the employer and the employee.

The life cycle of the employee is a useful tool by which you can identify employee engagement opportunities. These include finding ways to increase engagement before recruiting starts by managing the employer brand and continuing all of the way through to employee separation.

Research shows that one way to improve employee engagement is to offer meaningful and regular feedback to employees. This may be done through a formal feedback system, such as performance appraisals, and through informal systems, including having real-time discussions about employee performance. A performance management system should be tied to clear performance standards so that employees understand what it takes to be successful and to manage risk effectively.

Advanced HR professionals are responsible for designing and overseeing employee engagement and retention activities. This requires that senior leaders have a clear understanding of business strategy. In this way, HR leaders may make recommendations to executives for engagement programs that link strategy to employee needs and then evaluate outcomes for effectiveness.

Key Terms

Employee engagement

Performance appraisal

Performance management

Performance measures

Performance standards

Stay interviews

Talent management

Turnover

Retention

Job satisfaction

Employee surveys

Job enlargement

Job enrichment

Counterproductive work behaviors

Job attitudes

Organizational commitment

Work engagement

Exam Essentials

Understand engagement and retention efforts at all levels of the employee life cycle. With the multiple positive outcomes served by increased employee engagement, HR must find ways to engage through the life cycle of the employee. This includes efforts taken at the acquisition, integration, development, and transition phases of the employee life cycle.

Comprehend and apply theories and models of job attitudes. The three main job attitudes of job satisfaction, organizational commitment, and work engagement form the basis for many theories about engagement. Understanding how individual factors, organizational factors, and the structure of jobs impacts engagement levels will allow HR to craft meaningful interventions.

Understand best practices in developing and applying metrics. Assessing engagement levels using employee surveys and focus groups allows leaders to respond in real time to employee needs. This in turn will increase retention by making employees feel that they are being heard. HR can help manage the challenges that come up with rapid change by increasing the frequency of evaluative techniques and targeting the focus to optimize data.

Be familiar with the performance management process. The performance management process provides many opportunities both to assess and increase employee engagement. Aligning these systems to individual, departmental, and organizational results is important for both the employer and employee.

Be able to identify what is important for SCP exam takers. Senior leaders are called upon to understand the fundamentals of employee engagement and then find ways to elevate the employee experience to increase retention. Taking a holistic approach by crafting engagement strategies at all stages of an employee's career addresses what workers say they need. This includes development opportunities, recognition, finding work with purpose, and rewards and recognition.

Review Questions

1. Which of the following is a positive outcome of high levels of employee engagement?

   A. Safer work practices

   B. Less counterproductive work behaviors

   C. Increased competitive advantage

   D. All of the above

2. Research by Harvard University on Adult Health and Happiness belongs best to which domain of organizational research?

   A. Organizational behavior

   B. Organizational leadership

   C. Human resources

   D. Business management

3. Margaret is an employee who has been with the company for nearly 20 years. She is a high performer who has near perfect attendance and high productivity, and the customers love her! When asked what she loves about the job, she replies that she is "just happy," and that she gets a sense of achievement from her efforts that is very satisfying. Margaret most likely has which of the following job attitudes?

   A. Organizational commitment

   B. Job satisfaction

   C. Work engagement

   D. A positive attitude

4. Every year your organization requires that employees rotate jobs so that they learn and are able to apply new skills. This method of cross-training team members is best represented by which of the factors of job characteristics theory?

   A. Task identity

   B. Task significance

   C. Skill variety

   D. Autonomy

5. Which of the following Total Rewards programs is most likely to increase the retention of a younger workforce?

   A. Paid family leave

   B. Vested retirement benefits

   C. Paid volunteer time

   D. Bonuses

6. What is the primary difference between job enlargement and job enrichment?

   A. Job enlargement adds responsibilities, whereas job enrichment adds different tasks.

   B. Job enlargement adds tasks, whereas job enrichment adds responsibilities.

   C. Job enlargement adds supervisor duties, whereas job enrichment adds development opportunities.

   D. Nothing. They mean the same thing.

7. Which of the following is most positively correlated with increased levels of employee engagement across cultures?

   A. Meaningful work

   B. Pay

   C. Achievement

   D. Job structure

8. At which stage of the employee life cycle does the employer brand support engagement?

   A. Acquire

   B. Integrate

   C. Develop

   D. Transition

9. An employee came to the HR department upset that a coworker got a higher pay increase than she did. Her belief was that the supervisor favored her peer, thus giving him better opportunities to perform, justifying the difference. Which of the following is the best explanation for her complaint?

   A. Unlawful discrimination

   B. Compensation unfairness

   C. Pay equity

   D. Organizational justice

10. The company you work for has decided to leave more than 90 percent of their workforce working remotely. The IT department has the technology in place, and you have written and distributed the telecommuting policy to the affected team members. Management has asked you to prepare a report with recommendations on how the current performance management system should be modified to maintain engagement levels. Of the following questions, which is most important to completing this task?

    A. What are other, similar companies doing?

    B. What do the employees need?

    C. What kind of technology is available for delivery?

    D. What do the managers want to do?

Chapter

8

Learning and Development

Exam Notables

If you've always done it that way, it's probably wrong.

Charles F. Kettering, co-founder of Delco

Strategically, innovation lag has been the doom of many giant brands, including Blockbuster Video, Kodak Film, and Toys "R" Us. Even the popular shoe brand Converse failed to succeed on the strength of their iconic shoe, surviving only because brand giant Nike acquired them. Operationally, the need for innovation and disruption exists in all business units due to the need to balance the demands of time, cost, and quality. In the realm of learning and development (L&D), the need for disruption and change has accelerated over the last several years—and not just because of the pandemic. This accelerated focus was due to the lack of availability of qualified talent, the increasing costs of rising tuition limiting the number of college graduates, and the desire for purpose-driven work. Essentially, SHRM's description of the L&D domain gives us a glimpse of the foundation of this critical HR function:

> Learning & Development activities enhance the knowledge, skills, abilities, and other characteristics (KSAOs) and competencies of the workforce in order to meet the organization's business needs.

The SHRM Exam Objectives

SHRM's BoCK summarizes the functional area and defines the proficiency indicators along with key concepts. No matter your career level, pay special attention to the exam concepts defined "For All HR Professionals" and the "Key Concepts." If seeking the SHRM-SCP designation, you must expand your efforts to include those labeled "For Advanced HR Professionals."

THE SHRM-CP EXAM AND SHRM-SCP EXAM OBJECTIVES COVERED IN THIS CHAPTER INCLUDE THE FOLLOWING:

✓ **For All HR Professionals**

- Uses best practices to evaluate data on gaps in competencies.

- Creates individual development plans (IDPs) in collaboration with supervisors and employees.

- Uses best practices to develop and deliver learning and development activities that close gaps in employees' competencies and skills.

- Uses all available resources (e.g., vendors) to develop and deliver effective learning and development programs.

- Creates internal social networks to facilitate knowledge-sharing among employees.

- Administers and supports programs to promote knowledge transfer.

✓ **For Advanced HR Professionals**

- Designs and oversees efforts to collect data on critical gaps in competencies.

- Provides guidance to identify and develop critical competencies that meet the organization's talent needs.

- Monitors the effectiveness of programs for emerging leaders and leadership development.

- Creates long-term organizational strategies to develop talent.

- Creates strategies to ensure the retention of organizational knowledge.

✓ **Key Concepts**

- Approaches to coaching and mentoring (e.g., formal, informal mentorship programs).

- Career development.

- Developmental assessments (e.g., 360s).

- Knowledge-sharing techniques and facilitation.

- Learning and development approaches and techniques (e.g., eLearning, leader development).

- Learning and development program design and implementation (e.g., ADDIE model).

- **Learning evaluation (e.g., Kirkpatrick 4-level model).**

- **Learning theories (e.g., adult learning theory).**

- **Needs analysis types (e.g., person, organizational, training, cost-benefit) and techniques (e.g., surveys, observations, interviews).**

- **Organizational analysis (e.g., performance analysis).**

- **Techniques for career development (e.g., career pathing, career mapping).**

The Learning and Development System

You may recall from Chapter 5, "Strategic Human Resource Management," that *systems thinking* is the process of how otherwise-independent business units influence the entire organization. In this way, an organization's learning and development (L&D) structure must account for the needs of the whole entity, not just a single part. To understand this in context to our purposes, consider the three main knowledge domains of the exam.

People   It is within this domain that we find the more traditional functions of human resource management, including strategic planning, talent acquisition, employee engagement and retention, and total rewards. L&D activities focus here on the needs of the people who are charged with performing the work of the organization. L&D supports this through technical and skills training initiatives and building programs that increase engagement and retention and by paying attention to adult learning styles. L&D is threaded throughout all these traditional functions by supporting career paths as well.

Organization   This domain covers the competencies related to how an HR department is structured and performs, including organizational development, management of technology and the workforce, and the need to focus developmental efforts on the behaviors that impact relationships at work. Organizational learning refers to a company's ability to adapt to change at an individual, a departmental, and an organizational level. L&D supports these outcomes by aligning training and development programs to organizational strategy, such as reskilling or upskilling teams to respond to growth or divestiture strategies. L&D systems must also identify the skill sets of the current workforce and analyze the gaps in order to ensure that the company is intentionally developing the right knowledge, skills, and abilities in their teams. Technology has changed how work gets done, and not just within a single organization but on a macro scale, such as the availability of a global, virtual worker. L&D activities must continue to keep pace with innovative delivery modes that are engaging and meet team members where they are at logistically and professionally.

Workplace   The functions covered here relate to the climate in which we ask our team to perform. Global workplace factors, diversity and inclusiveness initiatives, risk management, social innovation, and U.S. employment laws (and the compliance training) all must be accounted for in the L&D structure.

Organizations report that they spend the bulk of their training dollars on compliance training. Yet, as you just saw, there are many ways in which HR can help organizations spend their training and development budget to achieve operational and strategic success and meet the professional needs of their team members.

Social Innovation through Learning and Development

Social innovation is the term coined to define companies and people that seek to effect change in unfair systems created by social or environmental barriers. One such issue is the underemployment rates of the formerly incarcerated population. The Prison Policy Initiative notes that recidivism rates significantly go down when the formerly incarcerated find work upon release, and yet this group remains underemployed, with a disproportionate effect on minorities and women. One major barrier is that many of these individuals simply do not have the skill sets necessary to compete, despite having access to time and other resources while incarcerated.

Endovo CEO Brian Hill is seeking to change this. His team has developed a tablet-based learning platform for use in prisons. Content includes teaching skills such as basic reading, writing, and math. The programs also offer support for other opportunities for improvement and life skills through self-help courses, anger management, and how to translate the skills that they used as a criminal to be successful in legitimate work. At the Women's Huron Valley Correctional Facility of Michigan, 900 of the 2,100 women inmates there have signed up for and completed more than 140,000 hours of productive learning on Endovo's platform.

This is not just an example of corporate citizenship. For HR teams tasked with recruiting talent in an ever-shrinking candidate market, finding ways to support the development of these underemployed groups will create the basis for the talent pipeline of the future. Employers can create their own social innovation L&D efforts by identifying internal barriers, such as lack of inclusion and building L&D programs that drive change.

Knowledge Management

The ability of organizations to retain knowledge goes beyond their ability to reduce turnover. *Knowledge management (KM)* programs seek to capture information so that an unexpected employee separation, systems crash, or natural disasters don't completely derail the business.

Knowledge is understood to be either tacit or explicit. *Tacit knowledge* is not just information—it also includes skills and abilities that are gained through work experience. Tacit knowledge is often a hallmark of long-term workers, and it may be tribal—that is, understood collectively by the group but not necessarily formalized. *Explicit knowledge* is easier to quantify and housed in a standard operating procedure (SOP) or database.

Organizations must find ways to retain both types of knowledge through technological databases, such as online reference guides, training videos from employees performing the work, and cross-training so that more than one person knows how to perform tasks. This can be done by designing jobs that rotate employees through tasks, training through job shadowing, and designing work that is collaborative/committee based.

Learning Management Systems

Often tied to a human resource information system (HRIS) or other technological platforms, a *learning management system (LMS)* is the organizational home for L&D activities. At its simplest, an LMS is an easy place to track training documentation for compliance. An LMS is also where participants can sign up for training, document completion, and select from available courses to apply toward career development.

The innovation of LMSs continues to evolve on a regular basis. Integrated systems that go beyond data tracking are developing into full course management. Many systems offer HR the ability to design training using advanced techniques such as simulations, cartoons, and videos. Mobile access makes it easier for individuals to access course content from anywhere. And robust programs utilize engagement strategies such as leader boards, announcements, digital badges, and intranet announcements to keep individuals on track and motivated.

Career Development

Career development is a system of activities that drive the course of an employee's vocation. Taking steps to engage actively in intentional professional activities has benefits for both the team member and the organization. SHRM's glossary of terms defines *career development* as a progression through career stages defined by specific issues and themes. Each stage has different needs that can be targeted within the organization to aid in succession planning and leadership development through career mapping and career planning:

> Career mapping is a visual view of the trajectory a role might take within an organization. It gives employees a clear line of sight of the potential for growth within an organization based on their current role.

> Career planning is working with individuals to identify the process that they will follow and the activities that they will undertake to move into different roles within the organization over time. If an employee understands what they are working toward, and what they need to do to get there, they are much more engaged in their work.

The last several chapters, specifically Chapter 7, "Employee Engagement and Retention," have discussed the importance of purpose to drive employee engagement. Career development has just as much impact on engagement levels, particularly for the younger generation. HR supports this by helping to build a culture that supports growth. From an organizational perspective, this means HR ties career paths to organizational strategy and goals. From an individual perspective, this means that HR helps leaders harness the power of failure toward learning and growth. HR systems also must provide support, such as compensation programs that reward skill acquisition and crafting promotion policies that are skills-based that support equal opportunity for growth. HR must also help build L&D intervention strategies that result in the knowledge transfer necessary to achieve organizational goals.

L&D Intervention Strategies

Intervention is an organizational development term that refers to a structured approach to solve organizational problems or achieve results. Many an HR person has heard from supervisors that an employee " needs training." But the truth is, training and development are not the proper solutions for all things. In fact, investing in L&D solutions that target symptoms as opposed to root causes is one sure way to diminish the power of an overall L&D intervention. To avoid this, HR begins with a needs analysis and then follows through to select the proper L&D intervention strategy.

Needs Analysis

Needs analyses are diagnostic tools designed to assess L&D objectives at an organizational and individual level. There are a few ways to do this, and they include a gap analysis, an organizational analysis, and individual evaluation using developmental assessment techniques.

Gap Analysis

A gap analysis is defined by SHRM as a "method of assessing current state in order to determine what is needed to move to a desired future state." A versatile tool, a gap analysis can be used at a strategic and an operational level, and at a team or an individual level depending on what is being measured.

For training purposes, a gap analysis is used to discover the competency or skills gaps an employee has when compared to a desired state. If the desired state is related to an employee's current job, training would be an appropriate remedy. If the desired state is in the future, a more developmental approach (that may also include training) is appropriate.

Methods to perform these analyses are varied, yet they call upon similar HR competencies to perform. For example, HR could conduct a team survey to discover what training and development needs they believe are necessary to be successful in their roles. Another analysis technique is observation. This is the process of observing an employee at work or asking a supervisor to observe the employee and then make recommendations on how to level up on knowledge, skills, abilities, or competencies.

The Department of Labor's (DOL) website O*Net (www.onetonline.org) exists as a job database that gives us information about job components. O*Net is a resource that can be used to find an accurate definition of the often-confused terms of "skills" and "abilities." O*Net's Job Content Model divides skills into two sets: basic *skills* are the "developed capacities that facilitate learning or the more rapid acquisition of knowledge," and cross-functional skills, which are the "developed capacities that facilitate performance of activities that occur across jobs." An example of a basic skill would be being able to speak English, since that may facilitate learning other skills. An example of a cross-functional skill would be keyboarding, since that is a skill that drives performance. *Abilities* are the "enduring attributes of the individual that influence performance," such as the ability to work with others. And *knowledge* is defined as the "organized sets of principles and facts applying in general domains," such as knowledge of generally accepted accounting principles (GAAP) or SHRM's code of ethics for HR practitioners.

Add depth to your studies by visiting O*Net, and search for the Job Content Model. Click the section titled "Worker Characteristics," as shown in Figure 8.1, for these definitions and more.

FIGURE 8.1   Department of Labor's O*Net Content Model

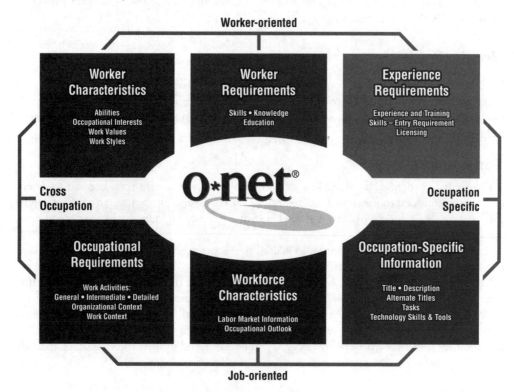

Many organizations call upon their HR leaders to build internal competency models, similar to the one found in the O*Net example. This is an internal database that can help sort and organize employee KSAOs for internal recruitment, career pathing, and replacement planning.

Those who have been in the HR industry for a while know that part of the split between the SHRM exams and the HRCI exams was centered around the need to measure competencies, not just knowledge. Therefore, it seems interesting that O*Net does not give a definition of competencies—only of the singular knowledge, skills, abilities, and other (KSAOs) characteristics necessary for performance. The SHRM glossary fills in this blank, defining competencies as the *collection* of KSAOs that, when working together, drive behavior.

Additionally, an example of a competency model may be found in SHRM's exam BoCK. Look for examples of the knowledge, skills, abilities, and competencies necessary to be a successful HR professional.

Organizational Analysis

An organizational needs analyses is focused on the future: what KSAOs will the employees need to have in order to achieve future results? In this way, organizational analysis must be tied to strategy. Considerations include both training and development activities, as well as acquisition strategies. Will the organizations build the talent necessary to compete from within, or attempt to purchase it externally through sourcing or outsourcing activities? Regardless of the acquisition strategy, jobs will need to be crafted to measure performance effectively.

Organizational analysis may also be done on a single department or business unit. This is appropriate for a department that is experiencing change or high levels of turnover.

Individual Developmental Assessments

Individual assessments are often thought of as part of the formal performance review process, and that is certainly true. However, when an employee has been identified for development, due to lackluster performance or high potential, an assessment, such as a 360-degree or multi-rater review, will help to measure current performance. An individual development plan (IDP) may then be created to document the process of developing the skills necessary for success.

Task Analysis

In this type of assessment, the jobs are analyzed in order to identify the tasks, duties, and responsibilities. This data is then compared to the employee skill sets or future work needs (such as adaptation to technology) to identify deficiencies. From this information, training interventions are designed to increase performance.

Once the needs have been identified through analysis, planned interventions that target desired results are developed. Once again, these can be done at an organizational, departmental, job, and individual level, and they may be designed around development, training, or a blend of both.

Training Interventions and Delivery

Training as an intervention strategy is useful to address several different kinds of employee behaviors. It is different from development in that training focuses on the skills and abilities necessary to support current levels of performance. This includes training for the tasks, duties, and responsibilities of the job, along with technical, basic, and cross-functional skills associated with the work itself.

Soft skills training is focused on the less tangible behaviors that are important for job success. Concepts such as communication, decision-making, and problem-solving all fall under this type of training. One could argue that soft skills training as an intervention is necessary for all employees across all industries. This argument is supported by research that notes that the skills that will be in demand in an automated, digital world are not necessarily technical or easily quantified. Skills that will be in high demand are the ability to communicate, make timely and quality decisions, and solve difficult-to-quantify problems—in short, the human skills that are too complex for robots to navigate easily.

The *Harvard Business Review* published an article with interesting insights related to the soft skills that teams need to succeed in an increasingly digital work world (*The Soft Skills of Great Digital Organizations*, HBR, 2016). They listed the ability to be goal-centric, collaborative, and being able to learn as key to performance, regardless of the technical platform being used. This is more relevant post-pandemic as a hybrid workforce has emerged (part on-site, part virtual). For HR, this tells us that in addition to finding ways to measure these skills during the hiring process, we will need to offer upskilling programs within our L&D systems for our current employees to help manage a new way of doing work.

As discussed in Chapter 6, "Talent Acquisition," the book *Long Life Learning* by Michelle Weise (Wiley, 2021) makes important points about the changing L&D needs of a national and global society. Weise points out that so much of traditional learning is front-loaded to early career and focused on general knowledge. However, research has suggested that most professionally relevant learning occurs over time while on the job. *On-the-job training (OJT)* occurs when a team member is learning the mechanics of their job while performing the tasks, duties, and responsibilities with real-time feedback. OJT techniques may be formal and informal, and they are an excellent lens through which to examine adult learning styles, which include the following:

Visual   OJT often includes written standard operating procedures diagrams, and micro-videos, allowing visual learners to "see" the process before and while performing a task.

Auditory   Real-time, immediate feedback is a hallmark of OJT, providing auditory learners the opportunity to use their preferred sense of hearing to learn and change behaviors.

Tactile   These learners retain information best when they are interacting with the work in a physical way through active practice.

eLearning is a training delivery method where the learners access training content online. In *synchronous training*, the instructor and participants are online at the same time, such as attending live virtual classes or webinars. In an *asynchronous training* setup, participants access the training content independent of the instructor and other classmates, such as with self-directed study. Self-directed study offers adult learners the flexibility to proceed at their own pace and minimizes the need for synchronous instructors. Training materials are standardized for the job, with delivery being done online, at the workstation, in workbooks, and in some courses, still offered through the mail.

Instructor-led training continues to be a popular training delivery method, and it is quite useful when a subject matter expert is required to transfer knowledge or participants need to learn from one another. Although the traditional training room or conference room setup continues to be used, the classroom has also shifted to digital platforms such as WebEx, Teams, and Zoom. Lectures, presentations, readings, and discussion are used in instructor-led training sessions.

Blended learning is another training method that optimizes the learning styles and needs of adults. As the name suggests, this method blends instructor-led, OJT, and self-directed learning. Blended learning allows for the customization of the delivery method that is best suited to the individual learner and circumstances.

These training delivery methods are rapidly changing thanks in large part to technology that harkens back to the quote that opened this chapter. Virtual reality is one example of a disruptor to training delivery, offering simulations that mirror real-life scenarios without the expense or complexity of certain work environments. Technology is also changing the way on-the-job training is done. Many large manufacturing plants are harnessing the power of 5G technology to provide 24/7 access to live, in-house experts to troubleshoot virtually and/ or guide from across time zones.

Instructional Design

Instructional design is both an art and a science that is used to build out training content. On the one hand, there are theories of adult learning that are considered best practices for all training design. On the other hand, every group has different needs that should be accounted for in learning design. For purposes of the exams, the *ADDIE* model for training design continues to be widely used.

Analyze the need.   This first step in instructional design is conducting the needs analysis. As described in an earlier section, a gap analysis is conducted through observation or interviews to determine the KSAOs necessary for successful performance (task analysis) and the skills of the current team members (individual analysis). From this, an HR team first determines if training is the proper intervention strategy (training needs assessment). If the answer is yes, the training targets have been identified.

Design the scope.   A training scope of work details the main points of the intervention strategy. It accounts for the measurable training objectives that will be used in the last step of the ADDIE model—the evaluation stage—answering the question "How do we know that training was successful?"

The scope also must account for how the training will be delivered. In today's era, learning that occurs online through eLearning platforms is important, particularly to reach a geographically dispersed team. Microbursts of training delivered through video is another effective way to deliver content with the added value of being easier to update due to its size. Self-directed, instructor-led, and blended methods are also considered.

Develop the content.   Content building can be done internally, externally, or through modification of off-the-shelf work. For larger organizations, conducting trial sessions is helpful in gathering feedback about the content and delivery, and collecting suggestions on how to make the training more relevant to the objectives or to the team. Adult learning theories should be applied in the design of training content. The science of *andragogy* speaks to how adults learn, versus pedagogy, or how children learn. Malcolm Knowles found there to be key differences between how adults and children learn:

Experience   Adults will filter information through their own experiences to understand.

Motivation   The adult learner must understand why they need to learn and must be intrinsically motivated.

Orientation   The adult learner will orient their attitude toward problem-solving, as opposed to general knowledge gain.

Readiness   Adult learners recognize the importance of learning new behaviors to develop and facilitate their social roles.

Self-Concept   Adults begin to shift from the dependent thinking of children as they age to one that is more self-directed.

Knowles's assumptions give insights into how to design training to maximize the adult learning experience by doing the following:

- Including adults in the planning of the training, from analyzing the needs and defining the objectives to determining the best delivery methods. This can be done by committee for the duration of the design effort or by focus group to refine prior to delivery.

- Anchoring training content to individual, team, and organizational experiences.

- Making the connections between training content and the work.

- Centering the training around problem-solving rather than general or esoteric knowledge.

Implement the training.   Scheduling the sessions, conducting the training, and ensuring the proper documentation for compliance and performance management are all parts of this stage of the ADDIE model.

Keep in mind the adult learning principles as training is delivered! Adults want/need to participate actively in the training. For this reason, a facilitative style has benefits over a traditional, directive style. Facilitation involves a transfer of knowledge by guiding the teams toward new ways of doing and thinking. A directive training style is delivered in the form of a lecture or a demonstration. Regardless, the more active the training session, the more likely the knowledge and behaviors will immediately transfer to the job.

As an HR professional, I spend many hours with adult training participants. Every time I go into a session, I challenge myself to spend only
30 seconds at a time talking. After 30 seconds, I ask a question or start a
discussion with teams. I find that the less I talk, the more I discover the
needs of the people in the room.

This isn't always realistic when the content is complex or I must set up an
activity. But the 30-second rule is a reminder to me that the real transfer
of knowledge for the adult learner happens when they arrive at the proper
conclusion on their own. Often, they lead us exactly to where we needed to
go in order to give them the knowledge and to practice the skills necessary for
success.

Evaluate the outcomes.   For most organizations, HR does not directly generate revenue in the way of production or services. This means that our value may only be measured through the effectiveness of our HR systems. This is important, because the need for senior leaders to understand what HR brings to the table is directly correlated to the value they place on our practice and, thus, our influence.

Measuring the effectiveness of training is key to determining a return on investment (ROI). As noted earlier, many organizations allocate their entire training budgets to compliance training. This is at the expense of the many, many other types of training that can add value. A return-on-investment calculation considers both the objective and the subjective value of training outcomes when compared to the expense.

From there, HR may determine who benefited most from the training and evaluate what changes may need to be made to the training content or mode of delivery. The main purpose of training evaluation, however, is to determine if the training met the original objectives that were written during the design phase. The most widely accepted method to evaluate training is Donald Kirkpatrick's four levels of training evaluation, as shown in Table 8.1.

TABLE 8.1   Kirkpatrick's four levels of training evaluation

Level	Degree	Evaluation methods
Level 1: Reaction	The degree to which the employee enjoyed the training, felt the training was relevant, and was engaged	Post training surveys and questionnaires; interviews
Level 2: Learning	The degree to which the employee learned the knowledge and skills, gained the confidence to perform, and is committed to using the new knowledge and skills on the job	Pre-tests and post-tests during the training session to measure if learning occurred
Level 3: Behavior	The degree to which the participant's behavior changes due to the learning derived from the training and has the systems and processes to support the new behaviors	Simulations, observations, performance appraisals
Level 4: Results	The degree to which the purpose of the training is achieved	Measurement of the leading indicators that suggest the training is headed toward results, which may be done through objective data such as reports on outputs and returns, and through observations

Developmental Interventions

A case continues to be made for the need to develop team members continually, just as organizations focus on the continuous improvement of products or services. Developmental interventions serve organizations by identifying and preparing individuals for future roles, including leadership. Developmental interventions also serve individuals by building the skill sets necessary to activate their potential and grow. As with training interventions, once a need has been identified through analysis, the proper developmental intervention technique may be selected and applied.

Coaching and Mentoring

Coaching and mentoring are programs designed to pair individual employees with someone who can help them grow. The process relies on feedback and support that targets desired outcomes. For this reason, a coaching or mentoring program should have clearly established expectations and goals, with a strong commitment from the employee.

In *coaching*, individual employees meet with their coach on a regular basis. The coach may be someone within the organization or an external resource. This feedback is focused on taking action in real time so that behaviors begin to change. External coaches may also be hired to take the employee through a formal coaching program to target specific skill development.

Mentoring is different from coaching, although the terms are often used interchangeably. The mentor is almost never an immediate supervisor from within the organization, but rather an experienced professional in the area identified for development. The engagement most often has a defined term, and specific goals are established. The mentor/mentee relationship can be a senior-level employee mentoring a junior-level employee or, as is the case with reverse mentoring, a junior mentoring a senior. Informal mentoring often takes shapes organically, where a junior employee seeks the advice of someone they trust or looks up to in order to help the team member navigate the decisions related to their careers. These relationships can go on for a lifetime. Mentoring is a powerful retention tool, but it is also key to developing qualified talent tied to strategic goals.

DeVoe & Company, a consulting agency that supports Registered Investment Advisors, published a report on the need for a "Human Capital Revolution." (`http://www`
`.devoeandcompany.com/our-publications`.) The June 2020 research is telling for all industries needing to transition the next generation of leaders. The report notes that active coaching, career pathing, and leadership planning is key to the development of the next generation of advisors. These activities within a performance feedback system, as described in Chapter 7, "Employee Engagement and Retention," should be developed long before the need arises. And, as the report notes, coaching activities should be part of a continual conversation to engage, retain, and eventually promote individuals.

Apprenticeships

Apprenticeships have been around for hundreds of years, existing as a form of employment contract. The employer, called masters, took responsibility for the welfare and training of a craft in exchange for work for a specific length of time from the apprentice. The structure of the apprenticeships serves as the model for what we know as career mapping today: from apprentice, to journeyman, to master apprentice, who may then train others. Although the terms are certainly outdated, there is much still to be learned from this type of career agreement. Promoted by *Forbes* magazine as "the hot new way to get ahead," many young professionals are seeking a formal development relationship through an apprenticeship. This is the case for many reasons, not the least of which is the rising cost of college, the abundance of jobs in the trades, and the need for employers to achieve a return on investment while stabilizing churn. Building formal apprenticeship programs will require the effort of many more than the HR professionals. U.S. policymakers will need to step in so that these "earn while you learn" programs are built without the exploitative and discriminatory factors that caused apprenticeships to fall out of favor over time.

Job Characteristics

Recall from the last chapter, "Employee Engagement and Retention," the Jobs Characteristic model from Hackman and Oldham. Their model suggests that how a job is structured will drive engagement and motivation through elements such as skill variety, task identity, task significance, autonomy, and feedback. When combined with job enlargement, job enrichment, and job rotation, these same elements may also serve to provide rich developmental opportunities to employees.

Special Assignments

Some employees are highly motivated by exposure to different teams, different locations, and to senior leadership. Offering developmental opportunities by assigning special projects or committee membership is an effective way to meet that need while focusing on other, non-linear projects that come up.

Dual Career Ladders

Dual career ladders exist mostly in the technical, medical, and other professional trades. The name depicts the visual movement that allows for two paths of promotion—one route that demonstrates an upward path by supervising others, and a second ladder depicting movement based on KSAs. This practice is closely tied to an employer's total rewards practices, since this career movement is one way for a team member to increase their compensation through skill or responsibility, as opposed to having to bank on their supervisory skills. HR supports the development of dual career ladders by helping the subject matter experts identify the depth of knowledge, skills, and abilities necessary to achieve a senior-level specialist role. Figure 8.2 shows a simplified version of a dual career ladder.

FIGURE 8.2   Example dual career ladder

Leadership Development

The shortage of future leaders is no secret; it has been this way even before the pandemic spotlighted the dry leadership pipeline. *Leader development* is the HR activity that supports current managers and executives in their roles while preparing them for future roles. It also includes grooming future leaders by helping them develop the appropriate KSAOs related to their career map.

According to research by Zenger and Folkman (`https://zengerfolkman.com/ articles/6-fatal-flaws-that-kill-a-leaders-effectiveness/`), 30 percent of all leaders have at least one "fatal flaw" that will derail their careers—and that's not even the bad news. These fatal flaws are unknown to the leader—blind spots that, unless uncovered, will result in failure. They include the following:

- Inability to inspire and motivate others
- Lack of self-development
- Failure to collaborate

HR must craft leadership development programs that begin with a needs assessment to help identify these and other opportunities for development. Studies have shown that only 30 percent of leadership characteristics are inherited, meaning that 70 percent of leadership behaviors are developed. This demonstrates the importance of organizational leadership development programs.

These studies further suggest that within our teams, we have individuals with the potential to become great leaders if we only activate it! This demonstrates the importance of organizational leadership development programs. This typically takes the form of a leader's self-assessment and gathering perspectives from others using 360-degree feedback. The gaps between how the leader thinks they are doing, and the team's perspective, form the basis of a targeted development plan.

Once the needs have been identified, there are several methods to help leaders develop. Echoing the developmental needs of the entire workforce, leaders must have strong communication skills and the ability to drive results from a workforce that is becoming more and more dispersed.

Leaders that receive coaching and mentoring from senior leaders become organizationally well positioned in that they gain valuable insights into the company culture, organizational challenges, and business strategy. These insights form the backdrop of the leader developing communication, problem-solving, decision-making, and human relations skills, creating a rich depth from which to lead.

Formal leadership development programs are also available for a wide range of topics. There are industry-specific leadership development programs, such as Leadership Development for Physicians from Harvard, as well as general concepts like the Leadership Development Program from the Center for Creative Leadership. HR is tasked with finding an appropriate program and monitoring outcomes to build a pipeline of leaders to meet organizational needs.

SHRM SCP Only

As you read through the exam objectives for advanced HR professionals, you'll see a theme emerge. Senior HR professionals must be able to bridge the gap between the present and future talent needs using the L&D intervention strategies described earlier.

Note that there is also a difference between "doing" and "leading." For example, HR leaders are tasked with designing and overseeing the data analyses techniques. This will involve having an understanding of best practices, but not necessarily doing the work of the task. HR leaders will need to train and mentor HR teams to be able to conduct the gap analyses and interpret results. This applies to all of the L&D competencies described by SHRM's BoCK. In this way, HR leaders should structure the developmental intervention strategies described in an earlier section for their own teams. This includes crafting and offering coaching and mentoring opportunities, creating apprenticeships or offering internships, crafting HR jobs to create depth and learning experiences, finding ways to generate special assignments, and offering dual career ladders for those team members who desire a different path.

The idea of developing future leaders does not just apply within the organizations for whom we work. The practice of human resources is so much about harnessing the power of people. This includes finding ways to support and empower future HR leaders outside of the organization as well. Opportunities for this are vast and rich and include volunteering for local HR chapters, serving on advisory boards for HR curriculum development, and/or teaching courses in HR or exam prep. From our own professional development, these activities help keep us current in the ways our craft is practiced while also engaging in the necessary activities to recertify the SHRM credentials.

As with all advanced HR competencies, a keen understanding of L&D strategies is necessary to achieve alignment with organizational goals. In many ways, HR leaders must be the change champions, intentionally and thoughtfully creating the disruptions that demand innovative solutions in L&D. This need is directly tied to the last objective for the advanced professional, which reads "creates strategies to ensure the retention of organizational knowledge." Although many of the other functions of HR are centered around attracting and retaining the *people*, this objective speaks specifically to retaining the *knowledge*. Paying attention and driving strategies to do so is a key competency of the senior leader. This is done by intentionally scanning the work environment to identify the areas that need a structured knowledge management effort, selling it to senior leaders and department heads, and then leading the way toward the development of KM programs described in the earlier section, "Knowledge Management."

Summary

The need for innovation and disruption in learning and development systems is compelling. Human resources professionals have a significant opportunity to design training and development interventions that drive change and prepare the workforce for the future of work.

It is a best practice within an L&D framework to use analyses to identify needs. From this, targeted development plans are built and resources are identified to bridge the gap between the current and the desired state. This includes administering and supporting knowledge management programs so that key data and skills don't leave if an employee exits.

When properly aligned to organizational strategy, career development is the benchmark from which training and development interventions' efforts are tethered.

Training interventions must account for adult learning styles and relevant training delivery methods to meet the diverse needs of teams and people. Properly designing training around clear training objectives increases the odds that true behavioral changes will transfer to the job. Evaluating training outcomes is necessary to measure the return on investments of the intervention and course-correct where appropriate.

Developmental interventions are focused on future skill sets. Not only do developmental activities prepare an organization's workforce to compete effectively, but multiple studies have shown that developing individuals increases job satisfaction and commitment. It is important to keep in mind that as people achieve the experience level that tenure brings, a dual career ladder may be necessary for those who want to benefit from an increase in responsibilities or pay without necessarily having to manage people.

Leadership development continues to be a real need for organizations around the world. The rapidly changing competitive landscape and the forces that shape organizational strategy (Chapter 5) also are at play in designing leadership development programs, and so this effort, along with all L&D programs, must be agile in order to stay relevant.

Key Terms

Abilities

ADDIE

Asynchronous learning

Blended learning

Knowledge

Coaching

Competencies

Cross-functional skills

Explicit knolwedge

Instructor-led training

Intervention

Knowledge management

Leader development

Learning management system

Mentoring

On-the-job training (OJT)

Skills

Synchronous learning

Tacit knowledge

Exam Essentials

Conduct gap analysis to identify L&D needs and advise leaders. A gap analysis is the critical tool used to identify L&D needs at an individual and an organizational level. Best practices include conducting surveys, observing team members, and conducting interviews with employees and their managers to identity the proper intervention strategy.

Understand learning and development theories to build HR programs. L&D theories are centered around adult learning. This includes the ability to design training programs using systematic structures that meet the needs of adults, while also increasing the successful transfer of knowledge from training to the job. This includes models such as ADDIE and Kirkpatrick's levels of training evaluation.

Other areas where theory should be used to inform practice come from knowledge of developmental techniques and best practices. Understanding techniques for effective coaching and mentoring helps employees to perform and develop the skills necessary for the next step on their career path. HR also should understand how to craft jobs that support on-the-job training (OJT).

Be able to build and utilize L&D structures and techniques that increase retention of both knowledge and talent. Retention is part of the important work of HR practitioners at all levels. Employees who see a clear career path and believe that their employer is invested in their success and in their development are more likely to stay on the job. Retention of knowledge is also part of the structure that must be built. This is to minimize the impact if key talent does exit, or there is a loss of another kind.

Review Questions

1. In which domain of the SHRM exam are you most likely to find L&D activities related to the use of total rewards to incentivize learning?

    A. People

    B. Organization

    C. Workplace

    D. HR competencies

2. Which of the following is the best example of tacit knowledge?

    A. Manager preferences when hiring

    B. General ledger codes for recruiting expenses

    C. How to place an ad online

    D. All of the above

3. As an HR professional for a major manufacturer of microchip technology, you recently discovered that the R&D department operated in independent silos. This meant that there was only one employee trained for each critical departmental function. When you approached the R&D senior leader to discuss why there was no cross-training, he told you that it was to guard the trade secrets of the business. As a strategic partner, this is of concern to you because you know that the loss of even one of these employees would set back the company's ability to meet the needs of a large, global client. Which of the following should you do first?

    A. Go above the senior R&D leader's head to his boss and share your findings.

    B. Conduct further investigation to see if all business units share this philosophy.

    C. Research database knowledge management systems that can be secured.

    D. Encourage the R&D leader to reconsider his position and take action.

4. What is the primary purpose of a career development program?

    A. To attract and retain employees

    B. To align the workforce needs with organizational strategy

    C. To build employee skills and improve their performance

    D. To send a message that the employer cares about the team

5. Which of the following is a more comprehensive view of the activities an employee should take to develop a career over time?

    A. Career map

    B. Career design

    C. Career trajectory

    D. Career plan

6. A supervisor at your organization came to you to express her concern about an employee who had been on the job for approximately two weeks. The employee was not catching on quickly enough, and the supervisor wanted you to start recruiting immediately for a replacement. Which of the following would best help you address the need?

   A. Place a job ad online by end of day.

   B. Assign the new hire to job shadow a more seasoned worker.

   C. Talk to the employee about ways he could improve his performance.

   D. Conduct a gap analysis to identify the correct way forward.

7. According to the U.S. Department of Labor, which of the following is the definition of "basic skills"?

   A. Developed capacities that facilitate learning

   B. Developed capacities that facilitate performance

   C. Developed capacities that influence decision-making

   D. Developed capacities that allow for performance in multiple jobs

8. The director of L&D has asked you to conduct an analysis to determine why the Customer Service department has been experiencing such high levels of turnover in the last six months. What type of analysis should you conduct?

   A. Organizational

   B. Individual

   C. Task

   D. Gap

9. What is the primary difference between synchronous and asynchronous training?

   A. Frequency

   B. Purpose

   C. Timing

   D. Content

10. A normally high-performing team member's behavior has recently changed. She seems bored, and her normal work ethic and "get it done right the first time" attitude has been missing. When discussing the situation with the employee's supervisor, you discovered that the employee had recently been overlooked for a promotion because she "just was not that great with people." The employee felt frustrated and not sure of how she would be able to grow with the company, a sentiment shared by many of her peers who were technically competent. The supervisor is questioning whether this employee is a good fit for the organization considering her attitude in response to not getting the promotion. Before that decision is made, the supervisor is willing to try some intervention strategies, so which of the following should you propose?

    A. Retrain the employee on the minimum standards of job behaviors.

    B. Work with the manager to create a dual career ladder so that the employee may continue to grow.

    C. Ask the employee to job-shadow the worker who did receive the promotion to develop the skills necessary for the next opportunity.

    D. Engage a coach to teach the employee better ways to cope with professional setbacks.

Chapter

9

Total Rewards

Exam Notables

In 1930 in Winter Haven, Florida, George Jenkins opened his first grocery market and named it Publix Food Store. As he grew as a leader and as a supermarket magnate, he sent the message to his employees that "Publix will be a little better— or not quite as good— because of you." Backing this claim with the company's earnings, Jenkins went on to establish one of the largest employee stock ownership plans (ESOPs), with more than 177,000 active account holders to date. Selling the company to employees seems to have paid off; the company has been named the #1 store for customer satisfaction and continues to place on *Fortune*'s "100 Best Companies to Work For" list. Jenkins's success is a powerful example of the impact an employer's total rewards (TR) programs can have. His philosophy proves that compensation and benefits will drive tangible business results if you take care of the employee, as they in turn will take care of the customer. SHRM's definition of this functional area of HR is simple:

> Total Rewards refers to the design and implementation of compensation systems and benefit packages, which employers use to attract and retain employees.

The SHRM Exam Objectives

SHRM's BoCK summarizes the functional area and defines the proficiency indicators along with key concepts. No matter your career level, pay special attention to the exam concepts defined "For All HR Professionals" and the "Key Concepts." If seeking the SHRM-SCP designation, you must expand your efforts to include those labeled "For Advanced HR Professionals."

THE SHRM-CP EXAM AND SHRM-SCP EXAM OBJECTIVES COVERED IN THIS CHAPTER INCLUDE THE FOLLOWING:

✓ **For All HR Professionals**

- Collects, compiles and interprets compensation and benefits data from various sources (e.g., remuneration surveys, labor market trends).

- Implements appropriate pay, benefit, incentive, separation, and severance systems and programs.

- Complies with best practices for and laws and regulations governing compensation and benefits.

- Differentiates between government-mandated, government-provided, and voluntary benefit approaches.

- Performs accurate job evaluations to determine appropriate compensation.

✓ **For Advanced HR Professionals**

- Designs and oversees organizational compensation and benefits philosophies, strategies, and plans that align with the organization's strategic direction and talent needs.

- Designs and oversees executive compensation approaches that directly connect individual performance to organizational success. Ensures the internal equity of compensation systems.

✓ **Key Concepts**

- Approaches to gathering compensation- and benefits-related market and competitive intelligence (e.g., remuneration surveys). Basic accounting and financial knowledge for managing payroll (e.g., total compensation statements). Compensation philosophies.

- Compensation plans for common and special workforce groups (e.g., domestic, global/expatriate, executive, sales).

- Job evaluation for determining compensation and benefits.

- Leave plans and approaches (e.g., vacation, holiday, sick, paid/unpaid leave).

- Other benefits (e.g., disability, unemployment insurance, employee assistance programs, family, flex, wellness programs).

- Other compensation (e.g., deferred compensation, direct/indirect compensation, stock options).

- Pay practices and issues (e.g., pay increases, base pay, pay levels, banding, variable pay).

- Remuneration and labor market data collection and interpretation.

- Remuneration data analysis (e.g., comparable worth, determining compensation, internal alignment, external competitiveness).

- Retirement planning and benefits (e.g., pension plans).

- Total rewards metrics and benchmarks.

Strategic Total Rewards

As demonstrated in Chapter 5, "Strategic Human Resource Management," business strategies drive HR strategies. Like a mission, vision and values statement, and goals, an employer's total rewards strategy is a system built with programs designed to use cash and non-cash (also known as direct and indirect compensation) methods both to attract and retain employees. The foundation of these systems is the organization's *compensation philosophy*. This is the philosophy that describes what the employer believes, driving decisions related to total rewards programs. In many cases, this statement is published on a company web page to communicate to potential employees what values they use to structure compensation and benefits plans. For example, Stanford University's Cardinal at Work website describes their compensation philosophy as follows:

> Stanford is committed to providing a fair and competitive staff compensation program that will attract, retain and reward high-performing employees at all levels. The university is also committed to providing a total staff compensation package tied to the attainment of individual and group results and the achievement of organizational goals.

Stanford's philosophy echoes SHRM's description of what is most important about this functional area of HR, which is using TR programs to attract and keep key talent. It also is a reminder of the importance of a human resource professional's ability to balance the rewards of its team members with business strategy. Although a compensation philosophy will differ based on organizational, industry, and other factors, the statement is the foundation on which the TR programs will be developed.

Building Pay Structures

A *pay structure* is the framework that describes the job categories and pay ranges for all positions within the organization. They are important because, in the absence of a salary structure, pay ranges may not be properly tied to market conditions, pay practices become inconsistent, and employees develop perceptions of unfairness. All three of these reasons lead to employees leaving for other opportunities. From an employer perspective, the absence of a salary structure can also lead to paying too much for talent based on supply and demand as well as pay practices that do not produce a viable return on investment.

Establishing legally defensible and competitive wage ranges is an important task of HR professionals. A *wage band* defines the minimum and maximum pay rate for each position within the organization. Broad-banding is a structure that has no more than five or six wage bands, typically with a spread of between 70 and 100 percent, although that can vary significantly by industry. Figure 9.1 demonstrates a simple salary structure using market data for an HR manager statewide in California.

FIGURE 9.1 Recommended pay range using market data

Position Title:	Market Percentiles		
	25%	**50%**	**75%**
11-3121 Human Resource Managers	$49.01	$66.13	$84.25
	25% of workers earn below this amount	*Mid Point: 50% of workers earn less, 50% earn more.*	*25% of workers earn above this amount*
Recommended Wage Band			
Minimum pay	85% of mid point		$56.21
Maximum pay	115% of mid point		$76.05
Source: California Occupational Employment Statistics			

In their comprehensive work *The Compensation Handbook*, Lance and Dorothy Berger (McGraw-Hill, 1999) share a set of guiding principles for salary structures. They note that salary structures should do the following:

- Provide for competitive pay by using market data
- Strive for the achievement of equity, fairness, consistency, and transparency
- Be flexible to account for market and skill shifts
- Be appropriate for the company culture and needs of the organization

Job Evaluation

The job analysis process described in Chapter 6, "Talent Acquisition," is the process of identifying the tasks, duties, and responsibilities of the job, and the knowledge, skills, and abilities that qualified individuals need to perform the work successfully. This data is important because it serves the *job evaluation* process, which is designed to determine a job's relative value by comparing the job to other jobs within the organization and comparable jobs outside the organization. The comparable factors determine whether HR should use job-based or market-based data for comparison.

Job content methods for job evaluation compares the tasks, duties, and responsibilities of a job in relationship to other jobs within the organization or to the relative market. These evaluations may be quantitative or qualitative.

Quantitative Methods

Quantitative methods for job evaluation are based on objective criteria, which are more easily measured and compared. These include the point-factor method, which identifies the job characteristics that are most important to the work. These are called the *comparable factors*. The comparable factors are further categorized depending on the technique used, which includes the following:

The Hay Plan: Comparable factors are know-how, problem-solving, and accountability.

Factor Evaluation System: Comparable factors include the tasks, duties, and responsibilities of the job and assign points to each based on level of importance; knowledge requirements, such as education and experience; working conditions; physical requirements; and any other factor that should be considered in determining a pay rate.

Pay Factors

Whether or not you are aware of it, you have probably already been using an informal point factor in your company's pay structure! For example, companies that pay an hourly shift differential for swing or night shifts has determined that schedule is a factor that must be accounted for in their pay practice. Many jobs that require an advanced level degree use total rewards packages to attract and retain the talent by offering tenured tracks for university professors. Perhaps your company pays out a retention bonus after the first three years of employment. As you prepare for the exams, engage in critical thinking by looking around your current place of employment and think about what your company is willing to pay for within each job.

Qualitative Methods

Qualitative comparison methods used for job evaluation are also called "whole job" methods. This is because these methods don't break down the job into its parts for comparison, but rather use techniques such as job ranking, where jobs are placed in order based on their level of importance to the organization.

Collecting Compensation Data

By now you will have seen a basic theme emerging with how HR systems are built. The process always starts with assessing organizational needs, then aligning programs with strategies, followed by implementing programs, and lastly evaluating outcomes, with unique stops in between based on the functional area. In total rewards, the collection of data is used during the assessment stage of systems development to identify the types of programs that will best support objectives and align with needs. These outcomes include attracting, retaining, and rewarding team members for performance. This data is collected both externally and internally.

The gathering of competitive intelligence is important to address external parity issues in compensation design. *Remuneration* is the term used to refer to all forms of cash and non-cash compensation, including wages, benefits, bonuses, and incentives. A *remuneration survey* is the instrument used to collect information from the prevailing market to build competitive TR packages.

According to SHRM's glossary of terms, a remuneration survey may look for competitive data for any or all the following:

Base Pay   Expressed as an hourly, weekly, monthly, or annual rate, this is the rate at which an employee is paid and does not include bonuses or benefits.

Pay Ranges and Starting Pay Rates   A pay range is the expression of the minimum and maximum base rate for a position. The starting pay rate describes the rate within the range an employee is paid at the start of employment.

Statutory and Other Cash Payments   Includes pay that is not part of the base wage, such as bonuses, commissions, and overtime.

Paid Time Off (PTO)   A benefit an employee accrues that allows the employee to take time off for personal and other days without losing a day's wage.

Variable Compensation   Variable pay is compensation that is calculated based on performance, such as piece rate or commissions.

Other types of compensation that need to be accounted for include the following:

Deferred Compensation   This is pay and other benefits that are earned but set aside for payment at another time. Deferred plans may be included in executive compensation and retirement planning. A major benefit of deferred compensation plans is that the taxes are deferred as well.

Stock Options   For publicly traded companies, offering employee stock options is a form of equity ownership.

Figure 9.2 shows examples of the components of a total rewards system.

Remuneration surveys seek to collect data about how the relevant market is administering the components of their TR plans. To be relevant to decision-making, HR collects data based on position title, industry, and geographic location of the position. Consider, for example, a mobile phone service provider chain with locations in several cities within multiple states. It may have customer service agents at each location who have the same title and the same tasks, duties, and responsibilities. Even though the jobs are identical, an employer may choose to pay an agent in Rhode Island less than what they would pay an agent in Massachusetts based on the competitive market data for each location.

Part of a compensation strategy is the decision by the employer to lead, lag, or match the market. Employers that choose to lead the market pay above market wages to attract and retain key talent. Employers that choose to lag the market pay less than the midpoint of what the market is paying, usually to preserve cash, or in exchange for some other form of benefit. Matching the market is a strategy that pays like what other employers are offering for similar jobs. Depending on the specific variables based on market conditions of supply and demand, some positions may lead the market, some may lag the market, and some may compensate exactly at 50 percent of market midpoint.

FIGURE 9.2   Total rewards

Total Rewards Programs

Direct

Base Pay
- Wages
- Salaries
- Overtime

Variable Pay
- Commission
- Bonus
- Piece rate
- Shift differential
- Profit sharing

Indirect

Leave
- Volunteer
- Vacation
- Sick
- Other

Perks
- Equipment
- Car allowance
- Travel
- Financial planning

Protection Programs
- Insurance
- Retirement

Benchmarking is an important competency for HR. *Benchmarking* is a process by which HR matches the internal jobs and job descriptions to similar positions in the external market and then compares the compensation levels. From this, HR will see if their pay practices are competitive. Recall from Chapter 8, "Learning and Development," that a competency is a collection of the knowledge, skills, and abilities (KSAs) that a professional must use to achieve a desired behavior. Benchmarking calls on an HR pro's knowledge of data sources, investigative skills, and the ability to interpret large sets of data into the most salient points. In the context of this chapter, benchmarking is used to inform *evidence-based decision-making*, a process that uses data and research to make decisions.

Pay for Social Skills

In 2017, David Deming of Harvard University published a study on the increasing importance of rewarding social skills in the labor market. First, he found that individuals with higher social skills self-select themselves into nonroutine jobs that require more people interaction (sales, consultants, and so on). This is opposed to those with lower social skills who sort themselves into the more routine jobs, such as STEM (science, technology, engineering, and math). Second, he discovered a decline in routine jobs over time and an increase in work requiring social skills such as teamwork, collaboration, and communication. Finally, Deming noted that jobs in all occupations have become less routine over time and that the jobs that remain highly routine are increasingly being computerized. This increased computerization "leads to the reallocation of skilled workers into flexible, team-based settings that facilitate adaptive responses and group problem-solving." For HR pros seeking to reward desired behaviors through their total rewards programs, this means that we must factor in social skills during the job evaluation process and determine the relative worth of those skills when compared to similar jobs within and outside of the organization. Check out the complete report at

```
https://scholar.harvard.edu/files/ddeming/files/deming_
socialskills_aug16.pdf
```

Data Collection Methods

When collecting data internally or externally, you must understand the purpose of the effort. For example, annual wage surveys may be conducted to ensure that wage ranges remain competitive. Or perhaps HR has been tasked with identifying how satisfied team members are with their current levels of pay. Trying to do too much all at once is a daunting task that may yield little information if the data collection methodology fails to have a purpose.

Once the targets have been established, HR may then seek out sources for the information. These sources may include the following:

Professional Compensation Surveys   Purchased surveys are an excellent way to leverage external resources. Offering larger scope and macro data sorted into absorbable pieces, it is well worth the cost if a compensation program is not the retention of qualified talent.

Regional, State, or Local Market Data   This data is usually free of charge and is an excellent baseline to identify market midpoint and establish internal pay scales.

Employee Surveys   Conducting an internal satisfaction survey is useful for identifying how the employees perceive pay practices. As with all surveys, however, take note: asking and then failing to act will undermine the effort and be more destructive than not asking at all.

Industry-Specific Research   Industries such as technology and nonprofits have a whole different baseline of compensation practices. For this reason, it is useful to access specific data related to the industry.

Once the data has been collected, it is up to HR or compensation specialists to advocate for desired changes that are aligned to organizational needs.

Pay Practices

Part of an organizational pay structure is accounting for the many types of pay adjustments and special circumstances that will occur during the life cycle of the employee. The type of adjustment necessary is dependent on the reasons for the adjustment, the most common of which are reviewed next:

Green-Circled/Red-Circled Employees   One of the outcomes of establishing a pay range is the identification of employees who are out of range.

> **Red-Circled Employees**   Employees who are paid above the range maximum are known as *red-circled employees*. This could be the result of tenure or performance-based pay raises that were not aligned with the market.

> **Green-Circled Employees**   Employees who are paid below the range minimum are known as *green-circled employees*. This may occur during salary negotiations, or because they came in with less experience than is required.

HR is tasked with implementing a strategy to address these out-of-range employees. Often, red-circled employees' future pay increases are frozen, or a path is created to identify ways that the employee may take on additional responsibilities for additional pay. For the green-circled employees, a plan is created to increase their pay rate to the minimum, either all at once or phased in over time.

Pay Compression   *Pay compression* occurs when the spread between what the incumbent employee earns and what a new hire for the same position earns is small. This occurs when internal pay increases do not keep pace with market conditions over time. It may also occur when a skill is in high demand and thus the market rate is higher. Pay compression can decrease morale for the incumbent who perceives this condition as unfair, or it devalues the incumbent's loyalty. HR will need to advocate for these workers in order to retain them by reminding senior leaders that part of a strategic pay practice is to understand the cost to replace the team member and negotiate from there.

Sales Compensation   *Commissions* are a common pay practice for sales employees. Of specific note is that even if an employee is earning a full commission, their pay can never go below minimum wage. This requires that HR lead the way to crafting sales pay practices that are legally compliant and that properly incentivize the employee, such as through payment of a draw against future commissions.

Severance Pay   Many HR professionals understand that the termination process is rife with risk. Wrongful discharge claims are based on many reasons, such as unlawful discrimination and violation of the duty of good faith and fair dealing (such as terminating an employee before a bonus is due to be paid out). *Severance agreements* are a risk management tool in which the employer pays the employee a flat amount in exchange for agreeing not to sue. The amount is usually calculated based on years of service, such as weeks' pay for every year of employment.

Severance pay may also be paid to employees who are being laid off. The courts became aware that many older workers were being laid off or otherwise separated and replaced with younger, lower-salaried workers. Employers were using severance agreements to offset the risk of an age discrimination suit. For this reason, severance agreements must meet the requirements of the Older Workers Benefit Protection Act (OWBPA), which established time limits and requires that the employer notify the employee that they may consult with an attorney to review the agreement prior to signing.

Labor Law Compliance

HR professionals must design TR programs that follow state, federal, and local labor laws. These vary tremendously in the areas of overtime requirements, mandatory leave programs, and minimum wage regulations.

Women have historically been underpaid for doing the same or similar work as men. Lilly Ledbetter is a high-profile example of a woman who was paid less than her counterparts at Goodyear Tire Company. Her story resulted in a significant change to the way that claims of pay discrimination are handled (see Chapter 14, "U.S. Employment Laws and Regulations"). Comparable worth is another term that has legal implications regarding pay equity. Comparable worth has been introduced as a remedy to practices of pay disparity. It is a premise that jobs primarily filled by women that require skills, effort, responsibility, and working conditions comparable to similar jobs primarily filled by men should have the same pay classifications and salaries. Pay discrimination is already unlawful. Comparable worth laws seek to call out jobs that are not of the same title or in the same industry, but rather require comparable skill sets. For example, the Markkula Center for Applied Ethics cites findings in Minnesota that compared stress levels, education, training, customer interaction, and responsibilities between registered nurses and vocational education trainers. In this example, registered nurses and vocational educators were found to have comparable factors. Though rated equal, registered nurses—an industry dominated by women—were paid less than the male-dominated vocational educators.

Salary history bans are another emerging issue for HR to manage. Many states are prohibiting employers from asking about previous pay levels. This is because companies use this information to negotiate job offers. Because women have suffered from pay discrimination, asking about salary history and then building an offer from that amount embeds discriminatory practices into the system.

Pay transparency speaks to the degree to which employers are forthcoming with information related to pay practices. In some states, such as California, it is unlawful to prohibit employees from disclosing their pay rates with their peers. Even with states that don't expressly govern this, the National Labor Relations Board protects a worker's right to discuss pay and other working conditions as part of concerted (collective) effort.

According to the Federal Trade Commission (FTC), price fixing occurs any time competitors enter into an agreement that "raises, lowers, or stabilizes prices or competitive terms." This includes employers who collude with their competitors to set wage rates by agreeing not to pay above a set amount. The courts have found this practice to be unlawful because it suppresses the natural market mechanism of supply and demand.

Benefits

A form of indirect compensation, *benefits*, as part of a total rewards package have become an expectation of the workforce. Pressure from the government through mandates as well as the competitive practices of the labor market all have driven employers to be more and more creative with these programs. Mandated benefits are those that are required by federal and state governments, such as Family Medical Leave and the Affordable Care Act. Mandated benefits at the federal level include the following:

- Social Security
- Medicare
- Unemployment
- Military leave
- Time off to vote
- Affordable care (varies)
- Family leave
- Workers' compensation

Note that "mandated" does not equate to "paid." Federally mandated benefits may include wage replacement and/or job protection, or other specific benefits depending on the nature of the regulation. The mandated benefits listed here are covered in more detail in Chapter 14.

Voluntary benefits are those that are required by law. These are programs designed to enhance the employee experience in some way and may include the following:

- Retirement contribution
- Vacation or sick leave
- Time off to volunteer
- Enhanced mental health programs
- Employee assistance programs
- Disability pay or insurance
- Additional insurance, such as life insurance
- Flexible workweeks
- Unlimited paid time off

Note that "voluntary" does not equate to "unregulated." Once an employer chooses to offer retirement benefits, for example, the Employee Retirement Income Security Act is triggered, and the plans must be compliant. Unlimited paid-time-off plans are also affected by labor law, especially in establishing precedent for compliance with laws regulating workers' compensation or disabilities. HR teams must be well versed in the administration of these programs to ensure proper risk management steps are taken.

Employee Mental Health

The Covid-19 pandemic highlighted the gaps in many employers pay and benefits programs. During the pandemic, a survey from World at Work found that nearly 75 percent of the participants reported increased anxiety and nervousness, 66 percent reported increased stress, and 64 percent reported depression or loneliness. However, these issues existed pre-pandemic as well, with World at Work pointing out that 78 percent of employees said they missed work due to mental health issues prior to Covid-19. Despite these high numbers, the use of programs such as an employer's EAP offering is not increasing at a proportionate rate, and many employees do not feel comfortable talking to their managers about their needs. This should be a call to action for employers to note that their employees do not know about the benefits being offered and that they need to educate them on how the program can help.

Employee mental health is also a social issue for the younger generation. In her blog entry "How Gen Z Women Will Reshape the Workplace" (The Women's Network, San Diego State University), Taylor A. Reed notes that the next generation of workers and leaders will place special emphasis on destigmatizing mental illness and stopping the normalization of 60-hour workweeks at the expense of self-care. For HR, this tells us that the hiring and retention of young professionals will be supported through TR programs that offer work/life balance benefits and meaningful mental health assistance.

Compensation Metrics

The administration of total rewards programs does require a baseline understanding of accounting and other financial measures. Many HR teams do not have the luxury of an in-house compensation specialist, and so they must rely on their own competencies to evaluate and communicate the results of TR programs successfully.

Basic accounting practices involves an understanding of reports. These include a company's cash flow statement, which is a snapshot of the company finances showing incoming and outgoing cash and cash reserves in operations, investments, and financing. This statement helps determine if the company can meet its financial obligations, including payroll.

Total compensation statements are a tool used to communicate the value of an employer's total rewards practices to an individual employee. Total compensation statements used to be called "hidden paychecks," and they are a tool used for retention by showing the employee the value of the voluntary and mandated benefits that they receive in addition to their wages.

The evaluation of total rewards systems is important—there is quite a financial outlay in this area of human resources. Here we also find it beneficial to use the categories of quantitative and qualitative methods.

Qualitative methods seek to understand the value of a total rewards program when compared with the desired results. HR leads the way, for example, in accessing utilization data from their insurance programs and surveying the employees to identify which benefits are providing the greatest value and which benefits may be underutilized. Care must be taken not to violate confidentiality laws, but even macro data is useful to understand patterns of use.

Quantitatively, HR should understand the percentage of total compensation costs when compared to other operating costs. This is achieved by adding up all costs associated with total rewards, including direct costs (salaries, overtime, variable pay) and indirect costs (benefits and perks) and then dividing it by the total operating costs.

Understanding total variable versus fixed compensation costs may also serve to inform pay structures.

The *compa-ratio* is another quantitative metric that is used to map individual pay against market or range midpoint. This is calculated by taking the employee pay rate and then dividing it by the pay range midpoint. The number is converted to a percentage by multiplying it by 100.

SHRM SCP Only

The exam requirements for SHRM SCP candidates shows an elevated focus on overseeing the operational practices of total rewards. It begins with advanced HR practitioners leading the charge to identify the company's total rewards strategy and compensation philosophy. In some instances, this may require that HR educate senior leadership on why this practice is important, the purpose, and how it should be used.

SHRM's Education Foundation provides excellent resources for the senior HR leader in this functional area. In their free download "Implementing Total Rewards Strategies" by Robert L. Heneman, they describe the steps to implementing a total rewards strategy as involving the following:

1. **Assessment:** This step identifies what the company needs the total rewards programs to achieve. This includes attracting and retaining key members, and discovering what it is these stakeholders value about total rewards packages.

2. **Design:** From the data collected in step 1, HR leads the way in designing programs that meet the needs of employees and that align with organizational strategies. These include creative components that go beyond base pay, such as flexible work schedules and perks.

3. **Execution:** From here, the programs are properly communicated in advance and then rolled out to the affected team members.

4. **Evaluation:** TR programs must be periodically evaluated to ensure that they are successfully achieving what they were designed to achieve.

Another element of the exam that is reserved for senior leaders is executive compensation. The compensation of chief-level (C-suite) employees is a complex task for which many organizations use compensation committees or a board of directors to build a total rewards package.

One strategy is to use employment contracts that outline the terms and conditions of employment. Employment contracts negate the concept of employment at-will, and thus the employee may only be terminated for cause.

Executive compensation may be a mix of base salary, deferred compensation, stock options, insurance, pension funds, and perks such as housing, company vehicle, and time off, just to name the basics.

The employment contract outlines the components of the executive compensation and includes the "golden" clauses:

Golden Handshake   Outlines the severance amount should the C-level employee involuntarily lose their job. Golden handshakes are controversial; many a C-suite executive who lost their job for negligence or other wrongdoing has received hundreds of thousands of dollars (in some cases, millions) upon exit.

Golden Parachute   Outlines the obligation to the executive should the company be taken over via merger or acquisition. These clauses are used to discourage a hostile takeover due to the exorbitant cost to oust the CEO, for example.

Golden Handcuffs   This clause outlines the financial incentive for a C-level employee to stay in the position, usually through payment of a retention bonus.

Internal equity is another important term to understand for the SHRM exams. This is the "extent to which employees perceive their monetary and other rewards are distributed equally, based on effort/skill and and/or relevant outcomes." *Procedural justice* speaks to the perceived fairness in the process by which decisions are made regarding compensation, benefits, and other rewards. *Distributive justice* relates to perceptions of equity in the distribution of outcomes—a bit of a "who got what and why" employee view. These concepts of justice are key factors in determining whether an employer's pay practices will retain talent.

Summary

The role of total rewards in attracting and retaining talent should not be undervalued. Although much has been written about the impact of noncompensation techniques to increase employee engagement, total rewards still supports basic human needs. It is worth remembering that employees do not work for the money—they work for the things and experiences that money can buy, such as housing, food, college tuition, travel, and staying healthy. It is true that employees seek purpose and identity through their work, and that certainly goes beyond base wages. However, ask any group of employees whether they are paid what they are "worth," and most would answer "of course not." It is nearly an impossible question to answer! For these reasons, it is important that human resource professionals structure pay programs that are based on what the *job* is worth, not what the *person* is worth. This is at the heart of the job evaluation and pay structure processes. That is not to say that other monetary rewards shouldn't be given, especially to align with core values. Corporate savings programs, volunteer pay, and tuition reimbursement are examples of values-driven monetary rewards that do not modify the employee's base pay.

In order to create legally compliant and competitive pay structures, HR leads the collection of internal and external data used to benchmark pay practices. This includes comparing internal jobs with the direct and indirect compensation levels of the competitive market. This data is used to develop the pay structure using market midpoints, the company's total rewards' strategy, and a compensation philosophy to build pay ranges. From this, decisions related to pay adjustments are developed and put into practice.

A key element to attracting and keeping qualified talent is an employer's benefits offerings. The benefits must be robust enough to attract and retain qualified individuals while also managing the cost to the employer. Legal compliance with mandated requirements is also a factor when designing benefits packages.

Key Terms

Benchmarking

Benefits

Commissions

Compensation philosophy

Distributive justice

Green-circled employee

Job evaluation

Pay compression

Pay structure

Procedural justice

Red-circled employee

Severance agreements

Total compensation statements

Wage band

Exam Essentials

Develop an organization's total rewards' strategy and compensation philosophy.   An employer's total rewards' strategy and compensation philosophy establishes the baseline from which an employer will reward employees. It sets the direction of total rewards' practices by defining the employer's commitment.

Understand methods to collect compensation data.   The collection of competitive market intelligence and internal data is used to address issues of equity. This is important in that it allows an employer to offer competitive compensation packages and ensure internal equity.

Build the structures necessary to administer pay programs.   The framework from which pay is delivered must include tools and strategies to address pay delivery and adjustments. These adjustments include giving pay raises and responding to special needs such as pay compression, pay out of range, and executive compensation.

Advise leadership on benefits offerings.   Employer sponsored benefits—whether mandated or voluntary, paid or unpaid—have the power to impact positive organizational results by meeting employee needs. The increasing costs of benefits requires that HR advise employers on benefits strategies that meet the needs and desires of the team while managing such a large employer expense.

Review Questions

1. The company you work for in the highly competitive industry of software development has decided that they want to be "the best paying company in their field." This is an example of which of the following?

   A. Total rewards strategy

   B. Compensation philosophy

   C. Competitive advantage

   D. All the above

2. Of the following, where are you likely to find the minimum and maximum pay rates for a particular job title?

   A. Pay structure

   B. Wage band

   C. Market research

   D. All the above

3. Why is it important to align a salary structure to the company culture?

   A. People will automatically leave if the pay practices do not make them happy.

   B. An inconsistency between pay practices and what the company says they believe could breed a lack of trust overall.

   C. It is the primary way to attract and retain qualified talent.

   D. It is not important to align salary structure with corporate culture.

4. Base pay, statutory payments, and PTO are all components of which of the following instruments?

   A. Remuneration surveys

   B. Mandatory benefits

   C. Benchmarks

   D. Evidence

5. Which of the following problems does the legal concept of comparable worth seek to address?

   A. Severance pay

   B. Pay transparency

   C. Pay equity

   D. Pay compression

6. Apple, Google, Intel, and Adobe were at the heart of a charge of an illegal practice where these tech companies agreed to not "poach" one another's talent—that is, they agreed to not seek to recruit current employees by offering higher salaries or benefits. This resulted in which of the following charges against the companies?

    A. Wage fixing

    B. Antitrust violations

    C. Market suppression

    D. All of the above

7. Which of the following is *not* a mandated benefit of private employers that is governed and administered by the federal government?

    A. Social Security

    B. Workers' compensation

    C. Medicare

    D. None of the above

8. Sam has been a successful nurse practitioner with your organization for 15 years. His pay increases have generally followed the cost-of-living adjustments, and he enjoys working all the overtime that his role requires. Recently, the company hired six new nurse practitioners, and Sam discovered that their starting salary is almost identical to his current salary. He feels discouraged and unrewarded for the time he has worked for the company. This is the best example of which of the following?

    A. Lack of pay equity

    B. Discriminatory behavior

    C. Pay compression

    D. Unfair labor practice

9. Which of the following is true of the golden clauses in executive compensation?

    A. They are used to drive organizational results.

    B. They are usually written into an employment contract.

    C. They always exist to benefit the executive.

    D. They are not enforceable in all states.

10. You have an HR manager who is currently earning $85,000 a year. Calculate the compa-ratio using the market data from Figure 9.1. Which of the following is the compa-ratio for the HR manager?

    A. 62 percent

    B. 65 percent

    C. 72 percent

    D. Not enough information to calculate

The Workplace Knowledge Domain

PART IV

As described in Chapter 1, "The Basics of SHRM Certification," the exam's Body of Competency & Knowledge (BoCK) is organized by three clusters of behavioral competencies and three distinct knowledge domains. The expertise that an HR professional must have to perform well is in the knowledge domains of the People, the Workplace, and the Organization.

Within these chapters, you will learn concepts related to the domain of the Workplace:

Focusing on HR's role in navigating a global workplace

Promoting and designing a workplace that is diverse and inclusive

Assessing exposure to risks while calculating probability of loss

Integrating socially responsible practices that create shared value to stakeholders

Examining concepts related to U.S. employment laws and regulations

SHRM summarizes the domain of the Workplace in the following way:

Foster a diverse and inclusive workforce; manage organizational risks and threats to the safety and security of employees; contribute to the well-being and betterment of the community; and comply with applicable laws and regulations.

The content related to the three clusters of behavioral competencies— Business, Leadership, and Interpersonal—is layered throughout the book. In this part, look for competency highlights related to the Interpersonal behaviors of global and cultural effectiveness and the Leadership competency of ethical practice.

Chapter

10

HR in the Global Context

Exam Notables

In 2015, U.S. retail giant Target closed their 133 stores in Canada. The headline-making liquidation cost the company billions of dollars and affected more than 17,000 workers. Of the top 10 U.S.-based retailers, at least three have failed in an international expansion attempt: Target in Canada, Walmart in Brazil, and Home Depot in China. Conversely, Costco Warehouse, a membership-based organization that is also a top-10 retailer, continues to enjoy the massive success of their global retail warehouses. Tagged the "Costco Craze" by CNBC in 2019, the company operates more than 200 stores in countries such as Japan, Australia, the United Kingdom, and Mexico. As globalization continues to increase, HR professionals will be charged with aligning international teams with operational excellence to deliver organizational results.

Here is the highlight of SHRM's summary of this functional area:

> HR in the Global Context focuses on the role of the HR professional in managing global workforces to achieve organizational objectives.

The SHRM Exam Objectives

SHRM's BoCK not only summarizes this functional area, but also defines the proficiency indicators and key concepts. No matter your career level, pay special attention to the exam concepts defined "For All HR Professionals" and the "Key Concepts." If seeking the SHRM-SCP designation, you must expand your efforts to include those labeled "For Advanced HR Professionals."

THE SHRM-CP EXAM AND SHRM-SCP EXAM OBJECTIVES COVERED IN THIS CHAPTER INCLUDE THE FOLLOWING:

✓ **For All HR Professionals**

- Addresses global issues that influence day-to-day HR activities and makes recommendations for business solutions.

- Maintains up-to-date knowledge of global political, economic, social, technological, legal, and environmental (PESTLE) factors and their influence on the organization's workforce.

- Administers and supports HR activities associated with a global workforce.

- Implements and conducts audits of global HR practices.

- Maintains knowledge of global HR trends and best practices.

- Balances with local needs the organization's desire for standardization of HR programs, practices and policies.

- Builds relationships with global stakeholders.

- Manages the day-to-day activities associated with international (i.e., expatriate) assignments.

✓ **For Advanced HR Professionals**

- Recognizes and responds to global issues that influence the organization's human capital strategy.

- Consults with business leaders on global PESTLE factors and their influence on the organization's workforce.

- Develops a comprehensive organizational strategy that addresses global workforce issues.

- Consults with business leaders to define global competencies and embed them throughout the organization.

- Identifies opportunities to achieve efficiencies and cost savings by moving work (e.g., offshoring, on-shoring, near-shoring).

- Designs and oversees programs for international (i.e., expatriate) assignments that support the organization's human capital strategy.

✓ **Key Concepts**

- Best practices for international assignments (e.g., approaches and trends, effective performance, health and safety, compensation adjustments, employee repatriation, socialization).

- Requirements for moving work (e.g., co-sourcing, near-shoring, offshoring, on-shoring).

Defining Global Strategy

According to Tarique, Briscoe, and Schuler the U.S. economy accounted for more than 50 percent of the global domestic product (GDP) 50 years ago, but today it accounts for less that 20 percent (International Human Resource Management, 2016). The shift to a more globalized market has been happening for decades, and it will continue to grow as more and more countries develop the infrastructure necessary to compete. For example, in 1980 China contributed 5.2 percent to the world's GDP. By the mid-2000s, that number rose to 17.5 percent.

The PESTLE tool introduced in Chapter 5, "Strategic Human Resource Management," continues to be an important filter through which to understand HR and business concepts. PESTLE stands for the political, economic, social, technological, legal, and environmental drivers that shape organizational strategy and identify risk. Examples include the following:

Political   There are many countries where corruption and bribery are the normal ways of doing business. Navigating norms while balancing ethical corporate behavior with profits can be tricky.

Economic   Regional free trade zones that reduce or eliminate tariffs, such as the European Single Market and the modified (albeit controversial) Trans Pacific Partnership (TPP) agreement, exist to encourage trade between countries. This directly affects the cost of conducting international business and increases competition.

Social   Increased travel and migration across the globe, along with affordable costs of living in certain countries, have exposed more individuals to different cultures.

Technological   Competing for global talent will require that businesses create more accessible methods for digitally acquiring and hiring global talent.

Legal   Complying with conflicting tax and labor laws must be regularly addressed to stay in compliance and ensure that employee rights are protected.

Environmental   Deforestation, transportation, potable water, land erosion, and pollution are just a few of the many issues that global organizations will need to address in order to build the infrastructure necessary to do business in certain countries.

One global example of the PESTLE forces at work is the country of Barbados. The government (Political) recognized the increased remote workforce of 2020 (Social) as an opportunity to promote travel to their island. The country created the Barbados "Welcome Stamp," a limited work visa (Legal) that allowed individuals from all over the world to work remotely (Technological). The tourism page of Barbados touts the clean air and sunshine as reasons to consider working on the island for up to 12 months (Environmental). The country charged fees of up to $3,000 for the privilege (Economic).

Multinational Enterprises

A *multinational enterprise (MNE)*, also called a multinational corporation, multinational company, and multinational employer, is a business with operations in more than one country.

As with other home-country operations, the structure of an MNE is critical to achieving organizational aims. Components of structure include home-country headquarters, business units/divisions, company culture, reporting hierarchies, job classifications, and the subsequent tasks related to each role. Systems for knowledge sharing, operations, finance, marketing, R&D, inventory management, and HR must be developed and refined. This applies to all host-country operations, and thus the more countries with entities, the more complex the structure becomes.

Structuring an MNE

There are several ways that an existing organization may choose to enter international markets. They include the following:

- Establish a local presence through a greenfield operation, or building a new facility from scratch on vacant land; a brownfield operation, or by taking over an existing building and renovating it; or a *turnkey operation*—that is, purchasing an existing business and taking over operations.

- Complete a merger and acquisition (M&A). As described in Chapter 5, organizations may engage in various M&A activities, such as creating subsidiaries or entering strategic alliances or joint ventures on an international scale.

- Begin exporting—that is, shipping goods produced in the home country to other countries to test or build market share.

In addition, many U.S.-based organizations choose to offshore or outsource operations. Offshoring or nearshoring is the practice of moving all or part of a business's operations to another country, generally to lower labor and production costs. Companies may choose to offshore the entire operation using one of the market entry methods just listed, or they may offshore only a piece of the business, such as manufacturing or customer service.

Global outsourcing is the practice of contracting with a foreign company for manufacturing or services without taking ownership. The most outsourced business practices are cybersecurity, digital marketing, and customer service. The United States continues to lead global outsourcing, partnering with China for manufactured goods and the Philippines for customer service. India's economic growth is expected to come largely from offering their IT expertise to other nations through outsourcing.

Offshoring and outsourcing are used by companies of all sizes, although it continues to be dominated by larger organizations who can afford to leverage resources. Outsourcing is not only a global practice, but also a staffing strategy. The gig economy has been a source for contracted labor for many years. Reasons for outsourcing are directly related to the challenges that employers have in finding qualified talent and the rising cost of wages and healthcare. Outsourcing helps to address both issues.

HR and Due Diligence

HR supports global operations throughout the life cycle of the business. This includes engaging in the due diligence process when a company pursues global expansion through a merger and acquisition. In addition to the objective data related to pending litigation and finances, HR contributes by searching out HR compatibility factors. These include compatibility of culture, executive decision-making, and information flow. Additionally, HR reviews staffing practices and expectations along with compensation strategies and compares mandatory and voluntary benefits offerings.

HR is also responsible for reviewing existing labor contracts and bargaining agreements. Chapter 18, "Employee and Labor Relations," takes an in-depth look at the relationship between American labor unions and employers. On a global scale, however, this looks quite different. Works councils are defined by SHRM's glossary of terms as "groups that represent employees, generally on a local or organizational level, for the primary purpose of receiving from employers and conveying to employees information about the workplace and the health of the enterprise." Works councils serve as a formal system for employee involvement and allow team members to have a say in issues that affect them, both at home and transnationally.

Integrating and scaling existing HR information systems is another area where HR teams provide support. Factors to consider are the compliance and record-keeping requirements that vary country by country and state by state, along with legal issues such as confidentiality, storage of personnel files, and immigration practices. HR teams should research equivalent laws to all U.S. HR practices and offer insights as part of the due diligence process.

Global Staffing

For global HR leaders, how an international location is staffed is an important consideration with cultural, financial, legal, and operational implications. These factors inform the best method for building global teams. Howard V. Perlmutter, a world authority on globalization, noted that there are four main orientations for building a global workforce. These orientations, or methods, are known by the acronym *EPRG* and include the following:

Ethnocentric   "Ethno" refers to individuals who share a common national origin. In this way, an ethnocentric staffing strategy is one that relies on home-country workers to fill host-country roles.

Polycentric   "Poly" means many, or multiple. In the context of global staffing, it refers to hiring individuals from the host country to manage the day-to-day global operations of an MNE and hiring home-country nationals to manage at headquarters.

Regiocentric   "Regio" refers to a specific region of the world. A regiocentric staffing strategy would focus on hiring individuals that are from a particular region (such as within the European Union), with opportunities for interregional transfers where available.

Geocentric   "Geo" refers to the earth, so a geocentric staffing strategy is one where key employees are chosen regardless of their nationality or where they live.

 Perlmutter's EPRG-typology is a form of qualitative analysis. As a rule, qualitative analysis forms a model or framework from which you can understand and apply HR and business concepts. This is a useful reminder to help you distinguish qualitative from quantitative analyses on exam day.

The most effective international staffing strategies will take into consideration local customs, social mores, and cultural business practices when designing jobs and staffing for MNEs around the world.

It remains to be seen if Perlmutter's typology will continue to be relevant in the new, rapidly evolving markets of global trade. With migration levels growing, automation on the rise, and the increased effectiveness and accessibility of virtual tools, there may be a need to adopt a more unilateral staffing approach. These approaches will consistently focus on fit: person to the job and person to the culture of the organization. This approach will need to account for other variables, such as designing purpose-driven work; establishing and maintaining a positive global reputation; and observing sustainable practices. These are the very same issues driving home-country staffing strategies as well.

Managing Expatriates

Global assignments are a form of professional development that are a lucrative way to fast-track one's career. An expatriate (expat) is a citizen of the home country working on an international assignment. Many companies offer full relocation packages to get the expatriate and their family settled into the host country. This may include costs and activities related to employment visas, flights, housing, freight, and in some cases, storage costs for personal items such as automobiles not shipped. This is just the beginning of addressing the special needs of an expatriate who has accepted or who is considering an international assignment.

Career Development

Although global assignments are considered developmental in nature, long-term assignments can leave an expatriate feeling overlooked for home-quartered opportunities. Job displacement as the result of accepting an international assignment will affect the retention of a qualified, high-performing worker. It is imperative for HR to ensure that the expatriate is notified of headquarters and other location opportunities, and that they have the visibility necessary to be considered for promotion, both during and after the international assignment.

High Turnover

Research by Murat Erogul and Afzalur Rahman (`https://www.researchgate.net/publication/318901116_The_Impact_of_Family_Adjustment_in_Expatriate_Success`) suggests that premature return from an international assignment is between 16–40 percent for assignments in developed countries, and more than 70 percent for assignments in undeveloped countries where cultural behaviors are significantly different. This translates into very real dollars and compromises the morale and professional development of the international assignee over time.

Selecting an employee for an international assignment should be done with care. Personal factors that predict a successful assignment include high levels of stress tolerance, strong communication skills, and above average relational skills. Individuals who speak the language of the host country are also more likely to be successful over time. Having a *global mindset*, defined by SHRM's glossary of terms as "the ability to have an international perspective, inclusive of other cultures' views," is also necessary when selecting for an international assignment. Note that these same personal characteristics will affect the successful adaptation of an expatriate's family as well.

The ability of an MNE to move its employees around the world is the premise of the term and process of *global mobility*. When the process of relocating a team member, and in some cases their family, is efficient, it can increase the odds of a successful assignment. When the process is inefficient, it contributes to a high rate of expat turnover.

Strategies to reduce the turnover of global assignees include the following:

- Offering both short- and long-term assignments based on organizational and employee needs

- Taking control of housing that fixes the cost and considers safety and personal comforts, neutralizing the impact of employee home sales where necessary for relocation

- Offering robust acclimatization programs prior to the assignment for the employee and the family (language, culture, customs, and so on)

- Increasing the focus on the expat experience: benefits, remote options, growth opportunities, and compensation parity

Family adjustment remains a top reason for an international assignment failure. Differences in language, social preferences, food, travel and education, along with a partner's own career needs, all may contribute to lack of expatriate success. HR supports an expatriate's family long before the assignment begins through robust cross-cultural training programs. Ongoing support to navigate the effect of culture shock (differences in values, customs, and attitudes) that set in after the initial novelty wears off should be provided by HR. This includes assigning a host-country mentor and providing for paid trips home to see family and friends, particularly for long-term assignments.

Expatriate Compensation

International compensation strategies must consider several factors. These factors are all related to balancing the needs of the employee with the needs of the organization and the myriad of local legal and customs practices of the host-region.

For the employee, equalizing the cost differences between what they are making and their earnings potential at home with the total rewards package of the international assignment is a key function of expatriate compensation design. For organizations, it is imperative that the return on investment (ROI) of an international assignment be positive. There are several compensation strategies that HR may implement to support the employee and the business.

HR supports international compensation through both policies and practices. One such policy is that of tax equalization. In some cases, expatriates are required to pay host-country taxes, such as in Shanghai, where workers will pay both national and local taxes. A tax equalization policy ensures that the expat's home and host-country taxes do not exceed what they would have paid if not on an international assignment. The company pays any overages.

The U.S. Social Security system covers expatriate workers—those coming in through work visas and those going abroad. The Internal Revenue Service (IRS) has entered into totalization agreements with several countries to help organizations and expatriates avoid double taxation of Social Security and Medicare. These agreements also ensure that expatriates do not have a gap in coverage based on their time earning outside of or within the United States. Figure 10.1 provides examples of countries in which the U.S. has totalization agreements.

FIGURE 10.1   Totalization agreements

Source: U.S. Social Security Administration

Many companies will also offer tax preparation services due to the complicated nature of earning income from more than one country.

For practical purposes, some expatriates may prefer to have their pay split between the home- and host-country currencies. When this occurs, the company may adopt a split pay practice and pay part of the employee's compensation in their currency of choice.

Structuring international assignee compensation is also an important function of HR support. A localization compensation strategy prices jobs based on local labor market factors and pays international workers the same that they would pay a local worker for the same job. This may be combined with additional premium payments such as the following:

Mobility/Foreign Service   A form of allowance that encourages employees to accept an international assignment; about one-half of U.S. companies pay an additional premium to an employee who accepts an international assignment.

Hardship   A premium payment to recognize the difficulties likely to be encountered on a foreign assignment.

Danger   This incentive is paid to encourage assignments in territories that are known to be high risk.

A balance sheet approach is a common method for addressing cost-of-living issues that arise. This is necessary to equalize any cost differences between countries needed to keep the team member whole. In a balance sheet approach, an expatriate is paid under the home-country structure, and allowances are paid to address cost of living and other differentials. International models exist to help employers determine what allowances are necessary. For example, a goods and services allowance may be paid to an expat for the first 90 days as they become more efficient at the buying power of the local currency.

An Efficient Purchaser Index (EPI) is available through many international service providers to help estimate and manage the difference in costs-of-living around the world. These indices include tables comparing cost differences for food, housing, incidentals, and more, and they can ensure that an expatriate is kept whole without overpaying, thereby reducing the overall ROI of a global assignment. For examples of what is included in an EPI, and to learn more about global compensation strategies in general, visit www.imercer.com and search for their global publications.

Repatriation

The final phase of an international assignment is related to bringing the expats back to the headquarters. The repatriation process is the act of reacclimating an expatriate back to their home duties and lifestyle. Assumptions by HR teams or organizational leadership that repatriation is not of great importance is short-sighted. A major benefit of international assignments for organizations is that the expatriate will gain new cultural and operational knowledge to apply once the assignment is complete. The primary challenge to repatriation lies in this acquisition of new knowledge—the team member is not the same person they were when they left. Strategic reintegration through mentoring, clear career paths that utilize the employees newly gained skills, and support of the families are all factors that will ensure a successful return of an international assignee.

Women Expatriates

Many U.S.-based MNEs are established in countries such as Japan, China, and Western European countries. Growing host countries include Mexico, India, the Middle East, and Africa. The cultural values of each of these locations can vary greatly from each other and from U.S. norms. For example, though numbers vary due to the pandemic's disproportionate effect on women in the workplace, a study by Mercer found that only 14 percent of women leaders are serving in expatriate roles. The reasons for the underrepresentation of female expatriates include the following:

- The presence of subconscious bias during the selection process due to stereotypes and other assumptions about women
- Lack of visibility due to not having access to career-building networks
- Lack of women applying for global assignments

The #metoo movement also may have inadvertently stymied female career growth in that many male executives claimed that they were unwilling to take on women as mentees due to potential perception challenges. This is an important reminder that the same systems that keep women from being promoted in home-country jobs are also the same ones that are barriers for global assignments. This means that HR will need to act deliberately in auditing hiring and promotion practices to ensure equal opportunity for global assignments.

Foreign Laws Defense

Employment laws in all countries reflect the cultural values of each society. These values are shaped by religion, customs, history, and the legal system. This means that each country has their own laws governing hiring, separation, wage and hours, time off, and discrimination. In most cases, host-country laws apply to individuals working in another country.

However, a U.S. citizen working overseas for a U.S.-based company is protected by federal antidiscrimination laws such as Title VII of the Civil Rights Act, the Americans with Disabilities Act (ADA), and the Age Discrimination in Employment Act (ADEA). The Equal Employment Opportunity Commission (EEOC) notes that U.S. employers are *not* required to comply with the requirements of these laws if adherence to that requirement would violate a law of the country where the workplace is located. This is the premise of the Foreign Law Defense. Here is an example from the EEOC:

Sarah is a U.S. citizen. She works as an assistant manager for an U.S. employer located in a Middle Eastern country. Sarah applies for the branch manager position. Although Sarah is the most qualified person for the position, the employer informs her that it cannot promote her because that country's laws forbid women from supervising men. Sarah files a charge alleging sex discrimination. The employer would have a "Foreign Laws defense" for its actions if the law does contain that prohibition.

Part of HR's due diligence should be to understand the scope and reach of U.S. labor laws. For more information and guidance from the EEOC, go to eeoc.gov and search for the document "Enforcement Guidance on Application of Title VII and the Americans with Disabilities Act to Conduct Overseas and to Foreign Employers Discriminating in the United States."

SHRM SCP Only

The complexity of human resources in a global context demands much of advanced HR leaders. As strategic business partners, it is necessary for HR to become the expert in the global issues that will affect a global workforce strategy.

The PESTLE tool shows up in the exam body of competency and knowledge several times, and it is a knowledge component of both the CP and SCP exams. For advanced practitioners, the distinction is having the ability to consult with business leaders and influence decision-making. This tells us that HR leaders must have developed business and consultative skills, and that they have built up enough credibility to shape decisions. This may be done by knowledge and expertise in cultural competence of the organization, the home country, and the host countries.

As with all workforce planning strategies, HR leads the way in understanding the trends shaping job behaviors. For example, the mass reshuffling of jobs post Covid-19, dubbed the "Turnover Tsunami" by SHRM'S *HR Magazine*, is one example of a social trend defining organizational competitiveness. HR leaders must help to build global workforce strategies that account for local and global trends and considerations.

In 2018, the Bureau of Economic Analysis found that U.S.-based MNEs accounted for 22 percent of all private industry employment. From this we may infer that MNEs in general are large employers—not in the hundreds, but in multiples of thousands! HR leaders at these organizations can increase the cultural competencies of their workforces around the world. These competencies include developing a global mindset; performing on teams with diverse backgrounds; the ability to operate effectively in a global environment when considering cultural values, norms, and etiquette; and building inclusive practices that improve innovation, creativity, and quality decision-making. These skills will help home-quartered entities as well, since many MNEs have foreign workers employed at company headquarters. HR leaders help to develop these competencies through the operational HR functions, including staffing, performance management, and learning and development.

Going back to the Costco example that opened this chapter, we find HR influence in action. In response to high gas prices in multiple locations, Costco began experimenting with various solutions for this cost to employees by scheduling individuals who live near each other on the same shifts to encourage carpooling, and structuring four 10-hour workdays to reduce commuting costs. Taking these types of regional conditions into account demonstrates cultural awareness that serves the employees and thus delivers valuable organizational results.

Strategically, senior leaders must connect the impact of diversity and inclusiveness and other cultural competencies, demonstrating that leveraging these skills will lead to tangible business results. This means that calculating the ROI of global workforce practices is necessary. For example, HR may provide expertise when calculating the cost of being the employer of record with its added burden of insurance, taxes, and so forth when compared with the cost of an outsourcing or offshoring strategy.

Summary

HR professionals have a significant opportunity to be a true business partner as organizations move more toward a global workforce. This begins by helping leadership shape a competitive international strategy using frameworks such as strengths, weaknesses, opportunities, and threats (SWOT) and PESTLE. Businesses are better able to plan for and manage international issues when they have a deep understanding of the opportunities, threats, and forces that drive operations in host countries.

Moving work away from the main location through offshoring and outsourcing continues to grow in many industries, shifting to countries such as India, China, and the Philippines. Although these practices on a global scale may seem cost-prohibitive to smaller organizations, they can still benefit by outsourcing noncore competencies or by using gig workers.

A multinational enterprise is one that is headquartered in the home country with operations in other nations. HR supports these workforces first by engaging in the due diligence process. HR plays a key role in staffing for global assignments using staffing strategies that are a good fit for the unique circumstances that each country presents.

Regardless of the staffing strategy chosen, managing individuals from the home country who go to work in the host country (expatriates) is key to the successful integration of operations. Issues that must be planned for and addressed include continued professional development, preventing early returns, equitable compensation, and repatriation. Special needs to account for include women expatriates and differing employment laws.

Key Terms

Global mindset   Multinational enterprise
Global mobility   Turnkey operation

Exam Essentials

Support a global business strategy.   Moving operations outside the home country is an effective strategy for employers seeking to lower the costs of production or services. HR competencies such as business acumen and cultural context must be applied.

Develop best practices for managing a global workforce.   HR is responsible for understanding global trends and requirements so that individuals in global assignments are successful. These practices apply to all areas of HR functions, including health and safety, total rewards, and employment laws.

Become a globally competent senior leader.   Advanced HR professionals must partner with all stakeholders within a global organization. This includes developing and maintaining relationships inside and outside of the organization.

Review Questions

1. Which of the following is the primary reason why globalization is growing?

   A. The migration of the workforce

   B. The changing market conditions

   C. The need to remain competitive

   D. The increased interdependency among countries, cultures, and people

2. The Covid-19 pandemic resulted in a hybrid workforce made up of the increasing availability of a qualified, remote, global workforce. This is the *best* example of which of the following PESTLE forces?

   A. Political

   B. Economic

   C. Social

   D. Technological

3. Immigration and tax compliance are both examples of which of the following challenges to managing expatriates?

   A. Political

   B. Social

   C. Legal

   D. Environmental

4. IBM is headquartered in the United States and has more than 300,000 employees working in more than 100 countries. IBM is an example of which of the following?

   A. Applicable large employer

   B. Multinational enterprise

   C. Domestic employer

   D. All the above

5. The international company you work for has plans to expand their financial services operations to Malta. The building being considered for purchase was recently vacated by a gaming company, and it would need moderate improvement. This is the best example of which of the following type of expansion operation?

   A. Outsourcing

   B. Greenfield

   C. Brownfield

   D. Turnkey

6. Under which of the following circumstances is due diligence the *least* important?

    A. In a merger or acquisition

    B. When buying a turnkey operation

    C. When considering parity of country labor laws

    D. When designing expatriate selection criteria

7. Which of the following is a positive outcome of a geocentric staffing strategy?

    A. The availability of the labor market

    B. The cultural compatibility

    C. The common national origin

    D. The ability for near-shore transfers

8. Perlmutter's EPRG model is the best example of which of the following types of analysis?

    A. Quantitative

    B. Qualitative

    C. Regression

    D. Trend

9. Which of the following must be addressed when staffing for international assignments with home-country nationals?

    A. Career development

    B. Repatriation

    C. Cost control

    D. All of the above

10. Fill in the blank: The United States has _____ agreements with multiple countries that serve to avoid the dual taxation of international assignees.

    A. Home-country

    B. Equalization

    C. Totalization

    D. Delta

Chapter 11

Diversity and Inclusion

Exam Notables

In September 1963, Dr. Martin Luther King Jr. published a piece in the New York Times titled, "In a Word—Now." It was delivered in between President John F. Kennedy's June announcement to deliver a Civil Rights Act to Congress, an August rally for equality, a September church bombing that left four little girls dead, and the assassination of JFK in November. The message was simple: the time for change was "now."

The current turbulence and unrest related to race and other forms of discrimination in communities all over the world marks a period in history where once again the time is "now." Although progress has been made in the domain of diversity, equity, and inclusion (DEI), much work remains to be done, particularly with equity in employment and education. The headlines tell the story:

Pregnancy: **"Gap's Athleta Brand Lands Its First Sponsored Athlete. . ."** (**Lauren Thomas, CNBC**)   Olympian Allyson Felix won her 10th medal at the 2021 summer games—this after being offered a 70 percent pay cut in her 2018 contract with Nike just in case her performance declined as the result of pregnancy.

Race: **"Campaign Aims to Liberate Black Women from Student-Debt Burden"** (**Mary Kuhlman, Public News Service, 2021**)   Black women carry more student debt than any other demographic group, furthering systemic economic disparity based on gender and race.

Ageism and Gender: **"PayScale Compares Top Tech Companies"** (`https://www.payscale.com/data-packages/top-tech-companies-compared`)   The median age at large tech companies is under 35 years, and women continue to be underrepresented in tech positions.

Education: **"Class of 2019, College Edition"** (**Elise Gould, Zane Mokhiber, and Julia Wolfe, Economic Policy Institute**)   Only 9.3 percent of young Hispanic high schoolers achieve a college degree compared to Asian American Pacific Islanders at 31 percent and white young adults at 22 percent.

LGBTQ and Religion: **"EEOC Kroger Suit Shows Rift at Border of Religious Rights, Bias"** (**Paige Smith, Bloomberg Law**)   Kroger Grocery Stores was embroiled in a 2020 religious discrimination lawsuit filed by the Equal Employment Opportunity

Commission (EEOC). Two women were fired by the store for refusing to wear aprons with a rainbow heart, as it violated their religious beliefs about homosexuality. In turn, the EEOC is under fire by the LGBTQ community and others for representing the terminated workers, as doing so is said to promote intolerance.

Diversity, equity, and inclusion (DEI) is not just about the legal rights of protected class workers such as those described here. DEI is also about optimizing unique talents to drive results. Organizational benefits include a well-balanced, qualified workforce; increased empathy of the workforce; better representation of the global customer; faster innovation; and creative problem-solving.

Human resource teams have an opportunity to drive collective change throughout their organizations. The SHRM BoCK defines DEI responsibilities to include the following:

> . . .activities that create opportunities for the organization to leverage the unique backgrounds and characteristics of all employees to contribute to its success.

The SHRM Exam Objectives

SHRM's BoCK summarizes the functional area and defines the proficiency indicators along with key concepts. No matter your career level, pay special attention to the exam concepts defined "For All HR Professionals" and the "Key Concepts." If seeking the SHRM-SCP designation, you must expand your efforts to include those labeled "For Advanced HR Professionals."

THE SHRM-CP EXAM AND SHRM-SCP EXAM OBJECTIVES COVERED IN THIS CHAPTER INCLUDE THE FOLLOWING:

✓ **For All HR Professionals**

- **Provides mentoring, training, guidance, and coaching on cultural differences and practices to employees at all levels of the organization.**

- **Consults with managers about distinctions between performance issues and cultural differences.**

- **Develops and maintains knowledge of current trends and HR management best practices relating to D&I.**

- **Contributes to development and maintenance of an organizational culture that values a diverse and inclusive workforce (e.g., conducts diversity training).**

- **Identifies opportunities to enhance the fairness of organizational policies and procedures to all employees (e.g., removes demographic barriers to success).**

- Identifies and implements workplace accommodations.

- Demonstrates support to internal and external stakeholders for the organization's D&I efforts.

✓ **For Advanced HR Professionals**

- Incorporates D&I goals into all HR programs, practices, and policies.

- Advocates for incorporation of diversity goals into the organization's strategic plan.

- Develops, implements, and oversees, in conjunction with other business leaders, enterprise-wide programs, practices, and policies that lead to a diverse workforce.

- Designs and oversees HR programs, practices, and policies supporting the development and maintenance of an organizational culture that values and promotes a diverse and inclusive workforce.

- Designs and oversees HR programs, practices, and policies that encourage employees to take advantage of opportunities for working with those who possess a diverse set of experiences and backgrounds.

- Ensures that HR staff members have up-to-date knowledge of current trends and HR management best practices relating to D&I.

✓ **Key Concepts**

- Approaches to developing an inclusive workplace (e.g., best practices for diversity training).

- Approaches to managing a multi-generational/aging workforce.

- Demographic barriers to success (e.g., glass ceiling).

- Issues related to acceptance of diversity, including international differences (i.e., its acceptance in foreign nations or by employees from foreign nations).

- Workplace accommodations (e.g., disability, religious, transgender, veteran, active-duty military).

Defining Diversity, Equity, and Inclusion

SHRM's glossary of terms defines the term "*diversity*" by building upon the word "differences." Diversity may be surface-level, such as those observable characteristics like race, or deep-level, the unobservable characteristics that include values and beliefs. Examples of differences among people include, age, disability, gender, race, religious beliefs, sexual orientation, socioeconomic status, education, job function, thought processes, personalities, and work styles. The focus of organizational diversity efforts is to integrate these differences in a way that makes organizations and teams stronger.

Leading diversity consultants Lee Gardenswartz and Anita Rowe defined four layers of diversity as they exist in the workplace (`https://www.gardenswartzrowe.com`). These layers include the following:

Organizational Dimensions   Factors such as industry, position, seniority, department, management status, and union affiliation affect belonging and inclusion. Consider that the largest percentage of CEOs within Fortune 500 companies are white males, creating an in-group based on organizational factors.

External Dimensions   Factors such as geographic location, income levels, educational and work experience, and status as a parent. For example, there are in-groups created based on similarity bias, or feeling more connected with those that look like ourselves.

FIGURE 11.1   Four dimensions of a team member

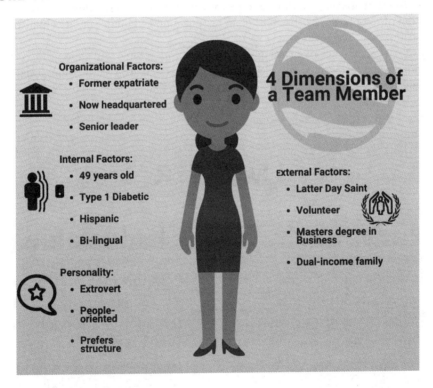

Internal Dimensions   Factors outside of our control, including age, gender, sexual orientation, race, and ethnicity. Generational cohorts with shared attitudes and beliefs are one aspect of this dimension of diversity.

Personality   Perhaps the most personal, these factors represent the hardwired, individual preferences, information processing, and decision-making styles.

Gardenswartz and Rowe's model highlights that there are multiple ways an individual expresses and experiences their identity. These are developed by internal and external factors, as shown in Figure 11.1. Everyone has attitudes, beliefs, and attributes that drive their contributions and create their own unique needs. For many organizations, the question is how to create an environment that takes all these differences and directs them at the same target, making diversity a highly personalized, complex dynamic to manage.

Equity and equal opportunity share common aspects, but they are nonetheless distinct. Equal opportunity is applied within organizations through compliance with antidiscrimination laws that define protected class groups to ensure that they have equal access in employment-related decisions. Employment-related decisions include hiring, promotion, selection for training, compensation, and performance management. Equity focuses on equal distribution of resources. The structure of an organization can inhibit or streamline the equitable distribution of resources.

Inclusion is the practice of ensuring that everyone within the organization can use their unique talents and feel welcomed, celebrated, and valued. Figure 11.2 provides insights from author and researcher Zach Mercurio on key behaviors that support inclusive practices.

FIGURE 11.2   How to create mattering

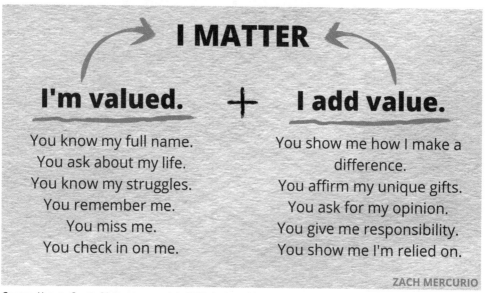

Source: How to Create Mattering, copyright 2021, by Zach Mercurio; used with permission.

For employers, Title VII of the Civil Rights Act of 1964 (introduced by President Kennedy in 1963 and signed into law by President Johnson) is the flagship directive for antidiscrimination and equal employment practices. Originally passed to protect individuals from discrimination based on race, ethnicity, and national origin, the law has been significantly amended and interpreted over the years to address the social disparities of the times. For example, Title VII originally protected a person's gender at birth but now protects the gender with which an individual most identifies. Other protected group characteristics under federal law include the following:

- Race, ethnicity, and national origin
- Individuals over the age of 40
- Sex and gender
- Military
- Religion
- Disability, physical and mental

In the 55+ years since this legislation, the need for employer involvement to protect the rights of these individuals remains an important part of HR responsibilities.

In Figure 11.3, you'll see a snapshot of the labor force population demographics. Pay close attention to the data, and you'll see where the greatest opportunities and challenges lie for HR in managing such a diverse group of individuals.

Focusing on Diversity, Equity, and Inclusion

Organizations that value diversity treat it exactly as they treat other business strategy: by identifying the value and objectives of the effort. Without this clear tie to results, it is easy for DEI initiatives to go off course or be forgotten.

A 2018 report by McKinsey & Company titled, "Delivering Through Diversity" (https://www.mckinsey.com/business-functions/organization/our-insights/delivering-through-diversity found that the more diverse an organization is, the greater its probability of outperforming their less diverse competitors. Both gender and minority representation were positively correlated with company financial performance. As this report demonstrates, there is a case for building a more diverse workplace that goes beyond social justice. Tying organizational results to DEI initiatives begins by having a good strategy that is then supported through operational excellence.

FIGURE 11.3   Demographics of the labor force population

Labor Force
Population

Source: Bureau of Labor Statistics 2019 & 2020*

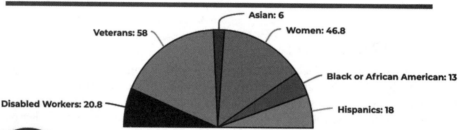

Veterans: 58

Asian: 6

Women: 46.8

Black or African American: 13

Disabled Workers: 20.8

Hispanics: 18

Women at Work	White	Black or African American	Asian	Hispanic or Latino
Sales and office	78.7	12.5	5.1	17.3
Service	72.9	17.0	5.6	25.0
Management, professional, and related	78.7	9.7	8.6	10.4
Production, transportation, and material moving	74.6	16.7	4.8	23.8
Natural resources, construction, and maintenance	86.7	7.5	2.1	31.1

 Baby Boomers- between 57-75 years

 Gen X- between 41-56 years

 Gen Y- between 25-40 years

 Gen Z- between 6-24 years
(Source: Kasasa.com)

Age Data

*NOTE: Estimates for the above race groups (White, Black or African American, and Asian) do not sum to totals because data are not presented for all races. Persons whose ethnicity is identified as Hispanic or Latino may be of any race.

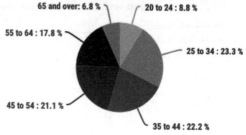

65 and over: 6.8 %

20 to 24 : 8.8 %

55 to 64 : 17.8 %

25 to 34 : 23.3 %

45 to 54 : 21.1 %

35 to 44 : 22.2 %

A Strategic Focus

Strategic barriers to successful DEI initiatives are really the same as those that get in the way of any business strategy. They include a lack of clearly stated, measurable goals and trying to do too many things at once.

Surveying the workplace to understand the current state of DEI is a necessary first step to ensure that a DEI initiative is tailored to the needs of your workgroup, not just a generic off-the-shelf program. Surveys can be done anonymously and through employee focus groups facilitated by an expert in the space to ensure that all voices are being heard and that employees have a safe place to share their concerns. A *diversity council* is a useful way to collect feedback on the issues that need to be addressed, set goals that align with business strategy, and help implement meaningful solutions.

Once the needs have been identified, HR can work with organizational leaders and employees to create strategic initiatives around the need. It is not enough for the senior leaders to create these initiatives; true inclusion efforts will involve those that are affected the most.

Other stakeholder needs should be part of an organization's DEI strategy and exist both internally and externally. Showing support for DEI events within the community signals that the company is committed to contributing to a safe environment at work and in the areas where they operate. Hiring contractors, subcontractors, and supply chain vendors that reflect organizational values is another way to create partnerships that serve more than just profits, which is key to attracting the younger generation as employees and consumers. Contracting with women and other minority-owned businesses is one example of how organizations tangibly commit to supporting DEI within their industries.

Failing to allocate sufficient funds properly to build an effective DEI initiative is another common barrier. Not only does it signal a lack of commitment, but limited budgets also severely inhibit access to the tools and resources necessary to manage change. For example, large organizations willing to spend thousands of dollars to bring in musical guests or high-profile keynote speakers for company events should offer commensurate compensation for guest speakers on issues of DEI. HR leads conversations to make sure that the budget is properly representative of all strategic initiatives.

Company Culture

HR professionals play a key role in creating a culture that supports diversity and inclusion. Drafting a clear purpose statement that proclaims an employer's commitment is one way to launch a DEI initiative. Finding ways to ensure that diverse experiences are contributing in meaningful ways is part of creating a culture that optimizes diversity as a competitive advantage.

This is also an area where many diversity initiatives fail. Lack of cultural awareness, intolerance, groupthink, cliques, and company cultural noise (such as "this is how it's always been done") gets in the way of DEI initiatives being effective. It is one thing to say that a company values all perspectives, and quite another to orient the diversity without some sort of guidance, awareness, and skill building. Competencies for HR to help their teams develop include problem-solving, conflict management, and interpersonal skills that are built from a foundation of respect.

Opportunities for change include how meetings are structured, who is running them, and what voices are heard. Encouraging curiosity and diversity of thought when solving organizational problems encourages diversity of thought, which is one reason diverse teams are more innovative. A culture of DEI is communicated to employees not by what is said, but rather by what gets rewarded and what gets disciplined.

Many organizations are proud of their corporate identity and want their team members to be proud of it as well. Corporate identity is a factor of employee motivation in that employees get a sense of belonging that drives engagement. This can go too far, however, when the company culture demands assimilation over inclusion.

Globalization

For organizations that compete on a global level, key political, legal, and cultural differences exist in diversity and inclusion expectations.

In the United States, the concept of affirmative action is leveling the playing field by setting hiring and other targets for increasing the diversity of the workplace. Affirmative action specifically prohibits the use of quotas, and it is voluntary, unless it is court-ordered to repair past discriminatory practices. Mandated board diversity is gaining popularity in the United States. This is one example of a DEI trend that HR leaders in corporations must watch.

Reservation is the closet global equivalent to affirmative action. Parliaments in many countries have gender quotas that seek equal representation in their legislators. In other countries, the political and cultural rights of women remain subjugated.

Bias remains a factor in globalization DEI as well. This bias may be the result of local or regional beliefs, and thus a global DEI strategy must be custom developed to maximize effectiveness.

Workforce Globalization

The U.S. Department of Labor predicts the need for language translators and interpreters to grow by 20 percent (much faster than average) within this decade (BLS.gov). The key driver of this projected demand? The globalization of the workforce and competitive market.

An example of a potential strategic diversity initiative that delivers on results is the language of the Internet. Data from Web Technology Surveys and Statista show that more than 60 percent of online content is delivered in English but that only 25 percent of all Internet users speak English. That leaves more than 75 percent of the world's population online that speak languages other than English, including Chinese, Arabic, and Spanish.

https://www.statista.com/statistics/262946/
share-of-the-most-common-languages-on-the-internet

https://w3techs.com/technologies/overview/content_language

Organizations are beginning to recognize the need to shape practices that reach this global community of employees and customers. Doing so requires strategic initiatives and operational activities that address the lack of representative practices online.

An Operational Focus

Any strategy is destined to fail without implementation plans and operational support. A key to successful DEI initiatives is the alignment of outcomes to HR operational systems. Opportunities for DEI focus exists in all HR functions, including learning and development, total rewards, performance management, and hiring.

Diversity Training

Most strategic company initiatives require creating some form of training that defines the need for change and building the technical skills necessary to effect the change. Diversity training has been shown to be a key activity in building a culture that supports diversity, equity, and inclusion, and both the content and the quality of facilitation matters.

Awareness is perhaps the most common type of diversity training used by organizations today. Topics covered include reviewing bias and stereotypes and assessing hidden and known values and beliefs. It is important that awareness training delivers on the "why"— why diversity is important to individuals, and how it ties to organizational results and other strategic initiatives.

A skills-based approach to training involves helping employees develop new ways to behave that are aligned with creating a diverse and inclusive workplace. The sidebar gives an example of how virtual and augmented reality training helps employees understand and apply DEI on a more experiential level.

Virtual Reality at Work

Immersive learning experiences are gaining popularity in the space of inclusivity training. Virtual reality (VR) and augmented reality (AR) tools provide trainees with a realistic look at the issues facing their peers. By creating an emotional connection to the experience, change on a deeper level is more likely to happen that will drive new behaviors. STRIVR is a virtual reality training solutions provider. In their eBook *Creating Inclusive Workplaces with Immersive Learning*, they describe what happens to the brain when it experiences a condition called "presence," where the brain does not differentiate between the simulation and real life. When this happens, it is as though the trainee is experiencing a condition first-hand, along with the corresponding physical and emotional responses. For example, in a three-part training session, the employee witnesses an act of microaggression, initiates a microaggression, and is the target of a microaggression. Each scenario highlights a different perspective and reviews effective ways the situation should be handled. Find the eBook and read more about this progressive form of DEI training at `https://www.strivr.com/resources/ebooks/inclusive-workplaces/`.

Best practices for all DEI training include the following:

- Tailor to the specific needs and desired outcome of the company.

- Include a review of the company's commitment to a diverse, equal, and inclusive work-force, along with expected standards of behavior for employees and the consequences for failing to adhere to those standards.

- Mandate attendance by company executives and leaders.

- Coordinate sessions that include diverse participants, including those from different departments.

It is important that employees have a safe place to discover and learn in the training room. Effective facilitators understand the specific issues facing the teams, and they do not have hidden political agendas or personal bias.

Skilled facilitators are credible when they have relevant business acumen and communication skills and are not chosen based on a specific demographic factor only. Co-facilitation is useful to ensure that multiple perspectives are heard and understood. Facilitation techniques should be inclusive and preserve the dignity of all participants while still addressing some of the more complex and sensitive issues, such as transgenderism and religion.

Key to a DEI training initiative is to work with the supervisors. Managers need to learn to recognize behaviors that are out of alignment and understand how to correct them—both in themselves and in others.

HR Systems

HR creates and maintains many of the systems that support company DEI efforts. This means that challenges to DEI also live within the design of HR programs such as performance management, hiring practices, and the design of company DEI policies.

The development of strong DEI policies is an important step that will feed operational practices that support strategic initiatives. Many employers already have antidiscrimination policies that address equal treatment and a zero-tolerance policy for hostile and abusive behaviors. Adding a DEI policy creates a foundation for the initiatives, and it clearly outlines expected standards of behavior and how incidents should be reported and handled.

Helping leaders understand the difference between performance issues and cultural behaviors is necessary to build an inclusive workplace. For example, an individual who cannot work on Sundays due to their religious beliefs should not be penalized or retaliated against. Bias against these individuals in hiring and promotion also exist, as do unfair opinions about their loyalty or commitment. Auditing the performance management process to ensure equity is part of HR support. This is especially important since feedback is tied to pay increases in many organizations. Succession plans and career pathing, plus the identification of "high potential" employees based on multiple factors that consider cultural differences, are also tools that HR uses to ensure fair practices.

Research continues to emerge showing that employer hiring practices are biased, resulting in underrepresentation of the groups described earlier. Examples of lack of equity include unconscious bias, job criteria that disproportionately affect certain groups, and bias around what a professional person should look or sound like. Many states are now banning past salary inquiries during the hiring process. Pay disparity has long been a challenge for protected groups, and making job offers based on previous salary perpetuates this problem.

Eliminating bias in hiring practices begins with the job descriptions to ensure that the education and experience requirements are truly necessary. A review of the essential functions and identifying alternative work methods is useful so that the term "qualified" is more flexible. Using software that delivers blind résumés can help reduce bias that occurs due to ethnic names or pronouns, increasing the likelihood that candidates will be selected for interviews based on their job qualifications. The hiring process is also an excellent place to track metrics to identify potential barriers, such as recruiting sources that do not produce enough diverse candidates.

Pervasiveness in Industries

A *bona fide occupational qualification (BFOQ)* is an exception to the EEO laws enforced by the Equal Employment Opportunity Commission (EEOC). The agency recognizes that under extremely rare circumstances, such as hiring at a religious institution, a person's otherwise protected class characteristic may be necessary for employee performance.

The performance industries have been called out for their lack of DEI practices, among them discrimination in awards, pay disparity based on race, cultural appropriation, and lack of diversity in actors.

In the case of casting, the industry has defended a lack of diversity as a type of BFOQ. Title VII specifically excludes race as a BFOQ, yet casting agents are still able to hire based on physical appearance, height, weight, gender, and similar requirements that would be illegal to consider in most selection processes. Conversely, there is backlash against filmmakers who call for auditions from "nonwhite actors."

There are many industries where DEI is gaining traction. Although the construction industry is still dominated by men, the automated way work is being done is increasing female representation. All industries, from Hollywood to construction sites, have embedded practices that will require specific DEI initiatives to address over time.

Demographic Barriers to Success

In addition to educating and advocating for the industry of human resources, SHRM conducts research designed to drive change. Figure 11.4 shows the key findings of their report on the state of equity and inclusion in the workplace. You'll see that 37 percent of workers are uncomfortable talking about race at work, and more than 65 percent of organizations are not even asking questions about DEI, suggesting that employers are uncertain as well. One of the most compelling challenges that we face as HR professionals is encouraging and facilitating conversations about DEI. It begins by looking at the demographic barriers to success.

FIGURE 11.4   Key findings of SHRM research

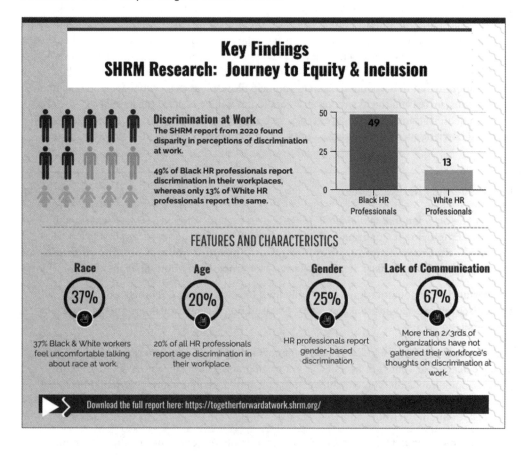

Race, Ethnicity, and National Origin

A main driver of the most recent social justice movement was the killing of George Floyd in 2020. The event gave rise to protests across the United States and highlighted the emotionally charged nature of race relations within society.

Research shows that unlawful discrimination in the workplace continues to be a problem, with certain groups underrepresented in different ways. Pay fairness, access to training, access to the leadership pipeline, and other issues remain firmly out of reach for people of color and other ethnic groups.

There are several possibilities of what gets in the way of meaningful change. These include the following:

- Reluctance or fear to talk about the issues at work
- The lack of promotion of people of color who may serve as role models and mentors for others
- Distrust between different racial groups
- The continued presence of stereotypes
- Lack of diverse recruiting and hiring practices

The presence of unconscious bias and other biological barriers to change may also be responsible for the slow and incremental progress within this domain. The Key Change Institute (KCI) of San Diego is a groundbreaking organization that focuses on training and certifying change leaders to use neuroscience-based models that support their ability to navigate difficult change. The sidebar "Barriers to Change," written by Reut Schwartz-Hebron, a certifying partner at KCI, highlights a few of the biological barriers to DEI initiatives and ways that HR can lead the way to solutions.

Barriers to Change

By Reut Schwartz-Hebron

Three neuro conditions may be responsible for lack of meaningful change through DEI initiatives. They include the following:

1. *Rigidity around our own definition of identity* (which is something in which people are often highly invested). If our identity is tied to practices that are unaligned with DEI practices, and if those practices are highlighted, we are much more likely to try to defend or justify those practices than be open to changing them. HR can help team members overcome this barrier through development of effective response patterns to discomfort. These include building self-awareness and other-awareness competencies using assessments, training, and performance coaching.

2. *Deep split-second activated subconscious biases toward certain identity "categories"* (the speed of the response makes it hard for us to detect it). Recognizing that we are

applying a subconscious bias when that bias is as unnoticeable to us (in the same way that we don't notice the process of air filling our lungs when we breathe or anything else that becomes our default response) takes practice. DEI training related to micro-aggressions and unconscious bias helps team members become more aware of the behaviors that inhibit inclusive practices.

3. *In-group vs. out-group subconscious definitions.* Who we see as part of our in-group, and who we see as part of an out-group, elicits different responses in areas such as showing empathy and giving respect. This is because we actively invest in thinking how those in our in-group feel, or how we would have felt in their place, which is not something we practice for people in our out-group. The good news is that this barrier is easily changed. For example, it can change if we suddenly find ourselves sharing a goal with someone we previously considered in our out-group. HR can facilitate this shift by bringing together employees with different attitudes, behaviors, beliefs, education, and experience and by facilitating discussions, organizing committees, and developing projects that encourage group work.

Women

Several issues are unique to women in the workplace. These include pregnancy, unequal pay (the glass ceiling), misogyny, sexually abusive conduct, and an imbalance of power. These issues minimize and limit the contributions of women, despite their growth in achieving college degrees and equal presence in the workplace.

In 2020, more than 3 million women dropped out of the workforce and 1.6 million have yet to return (CBS News, 2021). This was for a variety of reasons, all related to the Covid-19 pandemic. Women have been historically paid less than men, and thus dual-income families faced with school closures made the decision that mom would stay home with the kids. For essential workers, this was not always the case, and women were left juggling nontraditional working hours and home responsibilities with little time left for self-care. Reports of stress, anxiety, burnout, and substance abuse increased in response to these conditions.

The rise of telemedicine has improved the diversity of mental healthcare. As a case study, Maven Clinic is a telehealth start-up that focuses exclusively on the specific health needs of women, including pregnancy and postpartum depression. In 2020, Maven Clinic saw a 300 percent spike in mental health care use, demonstrating that diverse telehealth options that partner with employer plans can have a strong impact on employee well-being (*Maven Clinic Becomes the First U.S. "Unicorn" Dedicated to Women's and Family Health*, Beth Kowitt, Fortune .com, August 2021). Considering that maternity costs continue to be a large expense for self-funded and sponsored health plans, finding ways to manage the cost while improving care can deliver tangible financial results to a company's bottom line and help retain female employees.

Other challenges for women are centered around their appearance. Makeup, height, and weight requirements, as well as uniform styles in competitive sports, are just a few examples of employment expectations exclusive to women that are unrelated to being qualified for a job. For many years, ethnic hairstyles were stigmatized as being unprofessional, requiring that to fit in, a person's natural appearance had to be altered. In other ways, the only clothing options deemed "professional" for working women were business suits modeled after men's traditional attire. While progress continues to be made, HR professionals can use their voice to educate senior leaders on why these types of employment requirements stigmatize women and how they can work to minimize the bias and stereotypes that limit equity and inclusion in the workplace. HR can also take steps to ensure that women are represented at all levels of the organization, including in the C-suite and the boardroom, through inclusive hiring and promotion practices, covered in an upcoming section.

Ageism

The EEOC protects individuals over the age of 40 from discrimination in all employment practices, details of which are covered in Chapter 14, "U.S. Employment Laws and Regulations." From a DEI perspective, there are several other challenges that HR will use their competencies to help manage.

The age range of employees in the workforce now runs over four generations. One purpose of classifying the workforce into generational cohorts is because these individuals share the social, technological, political, and other experiences that shape collective values, attitudes, beliefs, and behaviors, including the expectations of employment.

As noted in the opening, there is an age gap in the technology industry, with most employees within that sector reported to be under 35 years of age. Many in tech argue that an older workforce is not qualified to perform the work; others say that it is a matter of having equal opportunity to learn. Older workers tend to be better educated, have more work and life experiences, and are staying in the workforce longer than ever before. HR can design programs that support this demographic by focusing their hiring practices on attracting older workers and building training programs that address any skills gaps, such as with technology. Employers that offer part-time work and attractive health benefits will be able to recruit from this qualified workforce to fill open jobs.

When managing a multigenerational workforce, there are also best practices. The first step is to ensure that training and other cultural efforts debunk stereotypes about all generations. This includes the stereotype that millennials "don't want to work" or that older team members "can't handle technology." Offering reverse mentoring and blended problem-solving projects are effective ways to identify and harness the complementary skills of these generations.

Transgenderism

There are an estimated 2 million transgender individuals within the United States today, and they are protected by antidiscrimination laws enforced by the Equal Employment Opportunity Commission (Human Rights Campaign, `https://hrc.org`). Despite this and other protections, there are regular reports of violence against and high suicide rates among this community.

Employers that have a written plan to address transgender needs have more success and offer the greatest protection to their team members. A written plan also should address common issues, including the following:

- Pronoun use

- Restroom access

- Benefits that are available to a transitioning employee

- Zero tolerance for abusive or discriminating behavior

Beyond the written policy, building an inclusive culture will reduce the acts of harm, and this begins within company leaders.

An *empathetic leadership* style is the ability to understand the feelings and needs of others, characterized by compassion and connection. Empathy does not mean feeling sorry for another individual, but rather putting yourself in another person's shoes and understanding how they feel without judgment. Empathic leadership will draw upon SHRM exam competencies such as relationship management, listening, and advocating for a diverse and inclusive workplace. Empathy is also a mark of professional and personal integrity, where in BoCK terms, key behaviors such as respect, openness, and tolerance are fundamental to effective HR leadership.

The topic "Coming of Gender" was the focus of a SHRM conference breakout session delivered by Dawn Kelley in 2021. As the manager of HR for the city of Modesto and mother of a transitioned person, Dawn is uniquely positioned to offer insights into the issues of transgenderism at work. Review the sidebar, where Dawn identifies four other "e" strategies that, in addition to empathy, drives culture-building that is inclusive of transgender and transitioning employees.

Coming of Gender

By Dawn Kelley

There is a lot of talk about diversity, equity, and inclusion (DEI) programs. To me, inclusion must come first. No business can obtain a diverse workforce or equality without ensuring that everyone feels part of the culture and is included—the real kind of "included"—like walking into a room and feeling comfortable in their own skin. As HR professionals, we have an amazing opportunity to get in front of our employees to create this culture by doing the following:

Educate: Provide training on the real information, and use statistics. This is not a one-and-done training or an annual event; it is a dialogue supported by a continuous stream of information.

Enlighten: Use real-life stories to connect your teams to the "why"—why it matters and why it is harmful. Enlighten your senior executives to get their buy-in and participation. True change starts at the top.

Engage: Ask the transgender and transitioning employees how they want to be involved in creating an environment of inclusion. Ask questions such as "Where are the fails?" and "How was the experience when you came on board?" Consider creating a survey to gather data to understand the current thinking of your teams, and then start a committee to discuss.

Energize: Treat all new hires the same, regardless of their differences, by greeting them with a mentor and a sunshine committee, and by scheduling lunch dates with a new-hire ambassador so that they immediately feel welcome. This sets the standard and communicates to all team members that equality and inclusion are action words, not passive promises.

Everyone deserves the right to work in an environment that is free from a judgment of their worth based on gender, relationship status, sexual partner, or clothing. Even well-meaning individuals miss the point when they claim to have "accepted" an individual for who they are. Acceptance is not actually the point of an inclusion initiative, just as we would not check in with a transgender person to signal their acceptance of binary lifestyles. For a workplace to truly embrace DEI, the primary role of all employees is to behave in ways that are welcoming, not hostile and divisive.

Mental Health

The mental health of the general population declined during the Covid-19 pandemic, and substance abuse, including alcohol, increased. Some reports noted that one in three employees admitted to drinking during a remote workday, and the National Safety Council (NSC) reported an increase in deaths from opioid overdoses during the pandemic ("Employers Must Brace for Increased Employee Substance Misuse Due to Pandemic's Impact on Mental Health," June 2020).

Veterans, at more than 50 percent of the workforce population, are also at high risk for mental health issues, including anxiety and post-traumatic stress disorder (PTSD). The U.S. Department of Veteran Affairs states that a relationship between anxiety disorders and homelessness exists for vets:

> Researchers from the VA New England MIRECC and the Yale School of Medicine found that 5.6 percent of more than 300,000 Veterans who were referred to anxiety or PTSD clinics experienced homelessness within the one-year time period of the study. The homelessness rate for the entire Veteran population is about 3.7 percent over a five-year period. (Relationship of PTSD and anxiety disorders to homelessness, Office of Research and Development, https://www.research.va.gov/topics/homelessness.cfm.

Asian Americans suffer from the "model minority" stereotype, which fuels pressure and prejudice. Research shows that this population has elevated depression and suicide rates and are less likely than other groups to seek professional services (Alice W. Cheng, Janet Chang, Janine O'Brien, Marc S. Budgazad, & Jack Tsai, "Model Minority Stereotype: Influence on Perceived Mental Health Needs of Asian Americans," (2017), *Journal of Immigrant and Minority Health*, (19:3): 572–581).

As the previous examples illustrate, mental health in the general population and at work is a complex issue. For this reason, a multifaceted approach is necessary and should be part of an employer's overall health and wellness initiatives.

Susan David makes a compelling case that false positivity is eroding resilience in the workforce. Her work on emotional agility acknowledges that hard things happen to all of us. Labeling sadness, fear, and anger as "bad emotions" sends a message that those emotions should be avoided, or that if you are experiencing them, you must be inadequate (susandavid.com). Helping employees recognize the emotions and validate them, and then teaching them to be more emotionally agile can build the resilience necessary to get through times of difficulty.

Large companies are making headlines with burnout strategies such as permanent work-from-home solutions. The fact of the matter is that remote workers are experiencing burnout as well. Zoom fatigue, isolation, unsafe home conditions, balancing parental responsibilities, and difficulty unplugging exist specifically for virtual workers. Other companies are announcing companywide shutdowns so that their teams can go on vacation, but this is not a practical response for many employers. Truckers, supply chain manufacturers, and healthcare workers do not have the luxury of taking time off or doing their work from home.

HR teams need to normalize conversations around stress, anxiety, and substance abuse, and ask their teams what they need to manage burnout more effectively.

For a review from the front lines of healthcare staffing, read the sidebar interview with Jeffrey Pietrzak. Jeffrey is a member of the Forbes HR Council (https://councils .forbes.com/forbeshumanresourcescouncil) and director of talent development and learning at Trusted Nurse Staffing (www.trustednursestaffing.com). We talked about a few of the mental health issues of the day and what HR can do to address employee needs.

Interview with Jeffrey Pietrzak on the Topic of Mental Health at Work

SR: What are some of the primary issues HR teams are experiencing when it comes to DEI and mental health?

JP: Diversity of thought is an essential aspect of DEI that often feels overlooked. Hiring individuals who are diverse and creative is vital to ensuring the consideration of multiple perspectives. To do this, organizational leaders must create a culture of open-mindedness, where differing opinions are shared freely. It is important to remember that this is a process, not just a single conversation, starting with a company's hiring practices.

There also seems to be a noticeable lack of resilience among employees across industries. Many employees struggle to articulate how the workplace, or how their jobs, are making them feel. This struggle may lead to emotional outbursts, turnover, and a lack of vulnerability to have the necessary conversations to address the cause of a particular challenge. For HR, it's about discovering ways to help employees share their thoughts, opinions, and stressors without fear of punishment.

SR: Smaller employers seem to be less resourced than the organizations making headlines in addressing burnout. What are some things smaller companies can do in the workplace?

JP: We continually look for ways to alleviate burnout, exhaustion, and stress for our staff. Because we work with contract healthcare workers, flexible scheduling and time off between assignments create opportunities to recharge. Our contract healthcare workers are frequently in high-stress situations, with an expectation from facilities that the traveling staff is essentially at a "plug-and-play" experience level. With the expectations very high, we work with our contract staff to support them and act as a sounding board through each assignment, regardless of their experience level.

As a relatively small employer, we also face the challenges created by social media. News of large corporations permanently going remote or thought leaders posting content stating "You're a bad boss if you do this, or don't offer that. . ." are not necessarily connected to the day-to-day reality many businesses face. These posts create an impression of good or bad, lack nuance, and often create stress for employees and employers to meet an unrealistic model for sustainable success.

SR: What do HR professionals need to do to support employee mental health and well-being?

JP: Our traveling healthcare staff work long hours and frequently face stressful situations, often around life and death. We encourage them to take time off and build a network of professional resources designed to help them feel supported. HR in all organizations should build a network of trusted resources to refer team members that are struggling. Some organizations may even benefit from hiring an in-house counselor or partner with a local group to establish a more direct line of access beyond the transactional nature of an employee assistance program.

Ultimately HR teams need to be approachable but must mitigate the prevalence of complicated conversations that take an unexpected turn outside our areas of expertise. Suddenly, we may find ourselves thinking about risk management and where to draw the appropriate line without shutting down a conversation. I find myself in the role of a therapist frequently, which is outside the scope of my skills and expertise. HR teams need expert support and education on how to be most effective in supporting employees, particularly when conversations toe the line between professional coaching and self-help.

Workplace Accommodations

Accommodating individuals with disabilities, including mental health, involves an interactive practice between the employer and the employee. As with many other ways to integrate DEI practices, this process is not a single event—it's a dialogue that evolves as new information is discovered. Often, the individual with a disability does not themselves yet know precisely what they need, and it takes time to land at an accommodation that is effective.

The Americans with Disabilities Act (ADA) has guidelines for employers with 15 or more employees on the interactive process to design reasonable accommodations. Both the employer and employee are required to engage actively in the interactive process to understand what modifications may be necessary for the essential duties of the job. Essential duties should be identified as such within the job description. Examples of accommodations include flexible schedules, modified access to benefits or work practices, job redesign, and reassignment to another position.

Other diverse groups may also need temporary or permanent workplace accommodations. The most common of these are as follows:

Pregnancy   Pregnancy by nature is a temporary condition, and employers are required to reasonably accommodate most requests. A doctor's note can be required. The employer may not treat a pregnant worker differently from any other employee, and they are required to allow nursing mothers additional break time to express breast milk in a designated, private area, other than a toilet stall.

Active-Duty Military   Also required through legislation, employers may not discriminate against active-duty employees such as those in the National Guard. Accommodations include granting additional time off to serve without accruing negative consequences under an employer's normal attendance policy.

Transgender   The Department of Labor issued a best practice guide on restroom use for transgender workers. It states that employees should be allowed to use the restroom that most reflects their gender identity. Employers may designate single occupancy, unisex bathrooms. Many states have other employer requirements for accommodations for this group.

Religion   There are several examples of accommodations that may be required for individuals with a sincerely held religious belief. They include schedule accommodations to observe religious practices, dress code accommodations for religious attire, and job accommodation for those with tasks that are in contradiction to their beliefs (fulfilling birth control prescriptions or manufacturing weaponry as examples).

An employer may claim undue hardship to avoid having to accommodate any of these groups. Here is an example of the guidance from the EEOC (https://eeoc.gov) if accommodating an employee's religious belief is an undue hardship:

> Examples of burdens on business that are more than minimal (or an "undue hardship") include: violating a seniority system; causing a lack of necessary staffing; jeopardizing security or health; or costing the employer more than a minimal amount.

Competency and Knowledge Alignment

SHRM's BoCK describes three main clusters of the knowledge, skills, abilities, and other attributes necessary to perform successfully in HR. They include the Leadership, Interpersonal, and Business competencies from which HR actions are grounded. To pass these exams successfully, candidates must be able to align knowledge with behaviors.

As defined in Chapter 4, "The Business Competency Cluster," each cluster is further expanded into eight competencies. These eight competencies are threaded throughout the knowledge domains of this book in order to align behaviors with the associated technical expertise. A review of the relevant competencies for the structure of the HR function begins here.

Operating in a Diverse Workplace

 SHRM defines the Interpersonal sub-competency of operating in a diverse workplace as demonstrating openness and tolerance when working with people from different cultural traditions.

The interpersonal behavioral competency of operating in a diverse workplace requires knowledge, skill, and self-awareness. Characteristics of an effective HR professional when leading these initiatives include an openness and respect for the individual. Being aware of our own biases is necessary so that they do not create barriers to effective change.

The exam behavioral competencies are closely related, and when operating in a diverse workplace, HR teams will need to call upon the following additional competencies:

Business   HR must align DEI efforts with organizational values and goals, use data to make a business case for diversity, and lead change efforts.

Workplace   DEI initiatives are fundamentally about relationships at work. HR drives efforts by maintaining mutual respect and ensuring that all voices are heard. This includes developing and modeling active listening and facilitation skills.

Leadership   An understanding of the formal and informal work roles that exist within the company is necessary to create the partnerships that will influence DEI efforts. Working with others, HR will help develop and manage the DEI programs, monitor milestones, and evaluate results.

Advocate for Diversity and Inclusion

 SHRM defines the Interpersonal sub-competency of advocating for a diverse and inclusive workplace as designing, implementing, and promoting organizational policies and practices to ensure diversity and inclusion in the workplace.

The development of HR initiatives that support DEI efforts is the focus of this behavioral competency. Best practices are built from the organizational sciences that, when combined with business management principles and other academic domains, result in empirical strategies that will increase the chances of success. To understand the development of a diversity climate through HR systems, we turned to an expert. Pantelis Markou is a corporate executive, industrial-organizational psychologist, and an adjunct professor at the Chicago School of Professional Psychology. Read on for his look at how HR systems support diversity management efforts that succeed.

HR Initiatives for Diversity and Inclusion

By Pantelis Markou, Ph.D.

The essential elements for a diversity management program should be based on an assessment regarding the organization's diversity climate: the degree of individual, group, and organizational diversity factors that are present and understood. For example:

Individual: Employees who are aware of their own identity, and the degree to which they have stereotypes of others

Group: The presence of in-group and out-group bias, such as ethnocentrism (a belief that one's own ethnic group is superior)

Organizational: The presence of bias within HR systems, such as a glass ceiling

Once the climate is understood, an employer can develop a diversity management program that addresses the gaps between the current and the desired state. This is an ongoing process that will need to adapt as the climate changes. HR strategies may include the following:

- Helping senior leaders understand that workforce diversity is a resource that drives organizational performance.

- Implementing diversity committees to assist with the initiatives.

- Changing hiring practices that are biased and/or limiting of minority groups.

- Giving people of minority groups challenging opportunities and assignments so that they can show their value and potential.

- Creating assignments and projects that have budget accountability to create visibility for minority groups in the organizations (Chemers & Murphy, 1995).

- Implementing a solid reward system that includes promotion, salary, and awards (Thomas, 2005).

- Increasing leaders' multicultural competence to help them improve their relationships with their staff. This can be achieved through company-sponsored events and informal gatherings.

- Developing a cross-cultural mentoring program between senior management and minority employees to promote empowerment and the development of meaningful relationships.

Having a diverse workforce doesn't mean that diversity initiatives are automatically successful. Taking steps such as these that are based on the findings of the climate assessment will allow for a functionally diverse workforce.

References

Chemers, M. & Murphy, S. (1995). *Leadership and diversity in groups and organizations.* In M. M. Chemers, S. Oskamp, & M. A. Constanzo (Eds.). *Diversity in organizations: New perspectives for a changing workplace* (pp.157–188). Sage Publications.

Thomas, K. (2005). *Diversity dynamics in the workplace* (pp.148–164). Thomson Wadsworth.

SHRM SCP Only

Human resource leadership in the function of Diversity and Inclusion is pivotal to success. Advanced HR professionals are responsible for incorporating DEI initiatives into all HR programs, practices, and policies. They are also responsible for including enterprisewide practices. The ability to do so is largely dependent on gaining the buy-in of senior leaders.

For this to happen, senior HR teams need to advocate to include DEI as part of the company's business strategy. Using labor force population data, such as that found in Figure 11.3, and statistics, such as those from Web Technology Surveys, found in the earlier section, "A Strategic Focus," are ways to make a business case for DEI. This happens by using this data to show how diversity initiatives can help solve organizational problems and drive growth.

HR will also work with other stakeholders within and outside of the company to build relationships and coordinate efforts that support the employer brand, attract a diverse workforce, and ensure that hiring and other practices are inclusive.

Finally, DEI is an evolving practice that requires HR and their teams to stay up-to-date on best practices. As the organization becomes more diverse, they will also need to adapt existing practices to ensure that they are relevant and continue to achieve the desired results.

Summary

Diversity, equity, and inclusion (DEI) as part of an organizational strategy has been proven to deliver results. Studies have shown that the more diverse a workgroup, the stronger the outcomes are in creativity, problem-solving, innovation, relationships, and financial performance.

Despite these strong reasons for DEI, there are several demographic barriers to success for protected class groups. Underrepresentation of ethnic groups, disparate practices for women, lack of inclusiveness for LGBTQ individuals, ageism, and mental health are all conditions that need to be addressed. HR plays a key role in developing DEI initiatives that resolve these barriers and align success with business results.

HR programs are at the heart of many DEI needs. This includes designing systems that reduce or eliminate bias and promote awareness, such as evaluating hiring, performance, promotion, and compensation systems to ensure that they are fair. Managing workplace accommodations and designing targeted training both contribute to a company culture that is inclusive are part of a full-bodied DEI approach.

Key Terms

Equity	Diversity council
Diversity	Inclusion

Exam Essentials

Align DEI initiatives with organizational strategy.   Diversity, equity, and inclusion have tangible benefits for employees and business success. Human resource teams, especially advanced HR professionals, add value by incorporating DEI into the company's strategic plan.

Understand the best practices for developing a diverse and inclusive workplace.   HR takes the lead for DEI initiatives by working with other department heads to address DEI issues and build a culture that is both diverse and inclusive. This includes understanding how to provide workplace accommodations for protected class groups when necessary.

Address demographic barriers to success.   Research consistently shows that race, ethnicity, national origin, women, age, and the disabled have been disproportionately treated in society and at work. HR leverages their business and HR management capabilities to design systems that eliminate demographic barriers to success.

Review Questions

1. Which of the following is the best definition of inclusion?

   A. Having a diverse workforce with unique education and experience

   B. Hiring individuals regardless of demographic characteristics

   C. Ensuring that all employees can use their unique talents and are welcome

   D. Making sure that HR systems are unbiased

2. Of the following, which group is not offered protection under the original Title VII of the Civil Rights Act of 1964?

   A. Age

   B. Race

   C. Ethnicity

   D. National origin

3. Of the following dimensions of culture, which is most outside of the organization's control?

   A. Union affiliation

   B. Management status

   C. Promotion rates of minorities

   D. Education levels of employees

4. The company that you work for has a high rate of Hispanic employees, but they are concentrated in one specific department and are significantly underrepresented at the management level and above. There are female leads, but they seem hesitant to apply for promotions. Executive management has looked to you to suggest ways to increase this group's representation in leadership. Which of the following DEI strategies should you recommend?

   A. A leadership development initiative for minority groups

   B. Coordinating a diversity council to identify the limitations

   C. Designing training programs to teach English

   D. All of the above

5. The project meetings at your organization are disorganized, unproductive, and quite frankly, exhausting. The sessions are dominated by one department representative, who is convinced that they have the answer to every issue that is brought up. Lately, you have noticed that many meeting attendees have just stopped offering their thoughts, and their body language signals that a different type of groupthink is occurring outside of the meeting room. Of the following strategies, which will result in creating a more inclusive, and thus productive, meeting?

   A. Do not invite the dominating team member to the meetings.

   B. Talk privately with the group members who seem most annoyed about the behavior.

   C. Conduct training on how important diversity of thought is to an inclusive culture.

   D. Establish ground rules for how the meetings will be run.

6. Which of the following DEI training best practices is most likely to result in both increased awareness and behavioral changes?

   A. Mandate management attendance.

   B. Tailor the training to specific organizational challenges.

   C. Include diverse workgroups.

   D. Hire a qualified facilitator.

7. Of the following labor force population, which is the least represented in management positions?

   A. Black or African American women

   B. Asian women

   C. Hispanic women

   D. White women

8. Which of the following elements should be included in a written plan designed to increase inclusivity of transgendered people at work?

   A. Guidelines for restroom access

   B. Guidelines for pronoun use

   C. How to report harassing or abusive conduct

   D. All of the above

9. A female applicant came in and interviewed with a supervisor for a front-desk position at your organization. She had recently been laid off from a similar role due to her former company downsizing. After the interview, the supervisor hesitated to make her a job offer because she was wearing a hijab, and the supervisor was worried that customers coming into the facility would be made uncomfortable. Which of the following statements is true?

   A. The supervisor unlawfully discriminated against the applicant.

   B. The company can claim a BFOQ exists, and thus the applicant is not qualified.

   C. HR should find a different reason why the applicant is not qualified for the role.

   D. HR should coach the leader to understand how stereotypes and concerns about customer preferences is a type of discrimination and not related to the job.

10. Which of the following statements best represents the advocacy role of HR for DEI initiatives?

    A. HR facilitates and leads diversity awareness training.

    B. HR champions the initiatives by working with internal and external stakeholders.

    C. HR ensures that HR systems support company DEI initiatives.

    D. HR models inclusive behaviors to all employees.

Chapter
12

Risk Management

Exam Notables

In 2017, the acting CEO of Samsung was indicted on charges of bribery and embezzlement. In addition to stock price manipulation and auditing irregularities, the filing claimed that the CEO sent millions of dollars to the South Korean president in exchange for a decision approving a company merger. The scandal eventually led to imprisonment of the CEO—and the successful impeachment of the president of South Korea! Comprehensive investigations, fines, jail, a compromised brand, and perceptions of unfair business dealings are just a few of the negative results that occur when an organization fails to manage risk adequately.

The SHRM BoCK notes that organizational risk may come from both internal and external sources, and include financial, operational, health, and safety risks as well as crises related to natural and human-caused situations. It is the responsibility of human resource professionals to help identify risk sources and to work with experts to develop prevention and response strategies. This is reflected in the functional description of the exam domain of Risk Management:

> Risk Management is the identification, assessment and prioritization of risks, and the application of resources to minimize, monitor and control the probability and impact of those risks accordingly.

The SHRM Exam Objectives

SHRM's BoCK not only summarizes this functional area, but also defines the proficiency indicators and key concepts. No matter your career level, pay special attention to the exam concepts defined "For All HR Professionals" and the "Key Concepts." If seeking the SHRM-SCP designation, you must expand your efforts to include those labeled "For Advanced HR Professionals."

THE SHRM-CP EXAM AND SHRM-SCP EXAM OBJECTIVES COVERED IN THIS CHAPTER INCLUDE THE FOLLOWING:

✓ **For All HR Professionals**

- Monitors political, economic, social, technological, legal, and environmental (PESTLE) factors and their influence on the organization.

- Administers and supports HR programs, practices and policies that identify and/or mitigate workplace risk.

- Implements crisis management, contingency and business continuity plans for the HR function and the organization.

- Communicates critical information about risks (e.g., safety and security) and risk mitigation to employees at all levels.

- Conducts due diligence investigations to evaluate risks and ensure legal and regulatory compliance.

- Conducts workplace safety- and health-related investigations (e.g., investigates workplace injuries).

- Audits risk management activities and plans.

- Maintains and ensures accurate reporting of internationally accepted workplace health and safety standards.

- Incorporates into business cases the anticipated level of risk.

✓ **For Advanced HR Professionals**

- Develops, implements and oversees formal and routinized processes for monitoring the organization's internal and external environments, to identify potential risks.

- Monitors and evaluates macro-level labor market, industry, and global trends for their impact on the organization.

- Examines potential threats to the organization and guides senior leadership accordingly.

- Develops, implements and oversees a comprehensive enterprise risk management strategy.

- Develops crisis management, contingency, and business continuity plans for the HR function and the organization.

- Communicates critical information about risks (e.g., safety and security) and risk mitigation to senior-level employees and external stakeholders.

- Ensures that risk management activities and plans are audited and that the results inform risk mitigation strategies.

- Oversees workplace safety- and health-related investigations and reporting.

- Establishes strategies to address workplace retaliation and violence.

- Leads after-action debriefs following significant workplace incidents (e.g., those involving employee safety and security).

- Evaluates the anticipated level of risk associated with strategic opportunities.

✓ Key Concepts

- Approaches to a drug-free workplace (e.g., testing, treatment of substance abuse).

- Approaches to qualitative and quantitative risk assessment (e.g., single loss expectancy, annualized loss expectancy).

- Business recovery and continuity-of-operations planning.

- Emergency and disaster (e.g., communicable disease, natural disaster, severe weather, terrorism) preparation and response planning.

- Enterprise risk management processes and best practices (e.g., understand context, identify risks, analyze risks, prioritize risks) and risk treatments (e.g., avoidance, reduction, sharing, retention).

- Legal and regulatory compliance auditing and investigation techniques.

- Quality assurance techniques and methods.

- Risk sources (e.g., project failures) and types (e.g., hazard, financial, operational, strategic).

- Security concerns (e.g., workplace violence, theft, fraud, corporate espionage, sabotage, kidnapping and ransom) and prevention.

- Workplace/occupational injury and illness prevention (e.g., identification of hazards), investigations and accommodations.

Types of Risk

According to the *Essentials of Financial Risk Management*, by Karen A. Horcher (Wiley, 2005), the terms "risk" and "exposure" are two different things. Although often used interchangeably, risk is defined as the *probability* of loss, whereas exposure refers to the *possibility* of loss. In short, risk exists as the result of exposure. Looking at SHRM's description of this functional area, HR's risk management efforts must be focused on assessing the probability and the possibility of risk and preventing exposure. The BoCK is very specific about the type of risks HR professionals must be able to assess and prevent. Let's focus on those next.

Workplace Safety and Health

The Occupational Safety and Health Administration (OSHA) is explicit in that employers have a general duty to provide employees with a workplace that is free from harm, even if no specific standard exists. When an employee is injured or becomes ill while performing their work, the employer is obligated to return them to their "whole," pre-injured state. If that is not possible, the employer must compensate the injured worker, or in the case of the injured worker's death, the employer must compensate the family. Benefits offered under workers' compensation programs include wage replacement, medical treatment, rehabilitation, disability payments, and survivor benefits. Most private employers in the United States are required to carry workers' compensation insurance; however, the laws vary from state to state. The cost of workers' compensation insurance is 100 percent the responsibility of the employer.

In terms of risk management, the goal of an employer's workplace safety and health program is to communicate hazards to affected employees through written policies, postings, safety training, and prevention efforts. Employers must also provide personal protective equipment (PPE) where necessary. The employee is obligated to follow the code of safe practices and to report injuries, illness, and hazards in a timely manner.

Record-keeping

Record-keeping is another component of complying with OSHA laws. OSHA Form 300/301 must be used by employers to log recordable workplace injuries and illness. Figure 12.1 provides an overview of recordable injuries from Form 300, including the following:

- Death
- Days away from work
- Restricted work or transfer to another job
- Medical treatment beyond first aid
- Loss of consciousness
- A significant injury or illness diagnosed by a physician or other licensed healthcare professional

Figure 12.2 provides the instructions for completing Form 300, which may be done online.

FIGURE 12.1   OSHA's Recordability Criteria

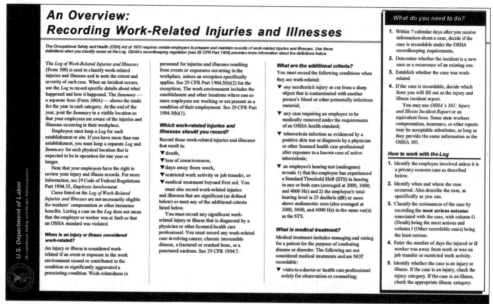

Source: U.S. Department of Labor—Occupational Safety and Health Administration

FIGURE 12.2   OSHA Injury and Illness Log

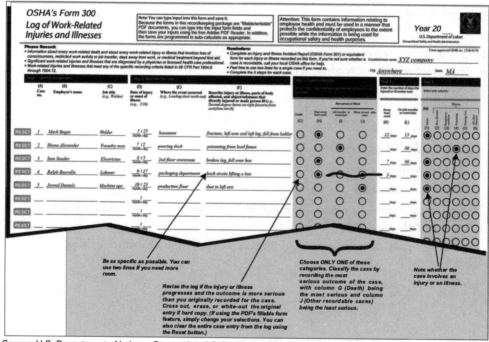

Source: U.S. Department of Labor—Occupational Safety and Health Administration

There are also specific recording criteria for communicable diseases that occurred at work. For the most up-to-date information on the corona virus specifically, visit `https://www.osha.gov/coronavirus/standards`.

Accident and Incident Investigations

Employers seeking to prevent workplace accidents, injuries, and near-miss incidents must conduct investigations. The investigations may lead to disciplinary action of employees for failing to follow safe work rules; however, this is not the main purpose. Discovering the root cause of an incident at work allows the employer to implement measures to prevent a similar incident in the future.

A thorough investigation should be completed for incidents without injury or property damage where there could have been injury or property damage. See the sidebar for an example of a safety incident that did not cause harm and yet still needed to be investigated.

What, Why, and How: OSHA Example of How to Conduct a Root Cause Analysis

A successful root cause analysis identifies all root causes—there are often more than one. Consider the following example:

A worker slips on a puddle of oil on the plant floor and falls.

A traditional investigation may find the cause to be "oil spilled on the floor," with the remedy limited to cleaning up the spill and instructing the worker to be more careful. A root cause analysis would reveal that the oil on the floor was merely a symptom of a more basic or fundamental problem in the workplace.

An employer conducting a root cause analysis to determine if there are systemic reasons for an incident should ask the following:

- Why was the oil on the floor in the first place?
- Were there changes in conditions, processes, or the environment?
- What is the source of the oil?
- What tasks were underway when the oil was spilled?
- Why did the oil remain on the floor?
- Why was it not cleaned up?
- How long had it been there?
- Was the spill reported?

It is important to consider all possible "what," "why," and "how" questions to discover the root cause(s) of an incident.

In this case, a root cause analysis may have revealed that the root cause of the spill was a failure to have an effective mechanical integrity program that includes inspection and repair, which would prevent or detect oil leaks. In contrast, an analysis that focused only on the immediate cause (failure to clean up the spill) would not have prevented future incidents because there was no system to prevent, identify, and correct leaks.

An *investigation* is a fact-finding mission to identify the behavioral or environmental conditions that caused the safety hazard. For this reason, it is important to remain neutral when interviewing involved team members (including witnesses), taking pictures, and documenting other conditions that existed at the time of the accident (such as weather and lighting). Once the data has been collected, it is useful to call together a team of knowledgeable individuals to determine the root cause of the situation. From here, the group can brainstorm about mitigation steps that can be taken to avoid a similar situation in the future.

OSHA gives guidance on how to build an effective incident investigation program so that an employer is prepared for when—not if—an incident occurs. It should include the following:

- How and when management is to be notified of the incident.
- Notifying OSHA, which must comply with these reporting requirements:
  - All work-related fatalities notified within 8 hours.
  - All work-related inpatient hospitalizations, all amputations, and all losses of an eye notified within 24 hours.
- Who is authorized to notify outside agencies (for instance, fire and police)?
- Who will conduct investigations and what training should they receive?
- Timetables for completing the investigation and developing/implementing recommendations.
- Who will receive investigation recommendations?
- Who will be responsible for implementing corrective actions?

Accommodating Injured Workers

When an employee is injured on the job, they may be unable to perform their regular duties. In some cases, the employee may be taken off work completely; in others, the doctor may prescribe modified duty. This is one reason why it is important for HR to work with supervisors in order to ensure that an up-to-date job description exists and that it includes the physical and mental requirements of the job. Doing so allows the medical professionals to make decisions on behalf of employees regarding their abilities. It is a good business practice to offer modified duty. This is because when on modified duty, the employee is paid through the regular payroll. An employee who is taken off of work completely is offered wage replacement through the workers' compensation claim. Because workers' compensation insurance is experience-rated (priced based on usage), paying an injured worker through the payroll will reduce future premium costs.

Security Risks

Seasoned HR professionals have most likely lived through an information breach, financial malfeasance, or aggressive or violent behavior from an employee. These types of security risks must be assessed and treated thoroughly to limit the negative impact on an organization and its stakeholders.

Cybersecurity

Human resources serves as support for all departments, yet HR staff do not have to be subject-matter experts in those business units in order to be effective. This is true even for the IT department, where it seems like a different language is spoken and coding skills are in demand! Cybersecurity exists to protect against threats to a company's intellectual property, guard employee/client confidential information, and safeguard the company's financial resources.

Preventing any sort of threat, whether physical or digital, begins with having standard policies and procedures that define expectations, establish protocols, and ensure compliance. HR also supports IT by engaging resources to keep employees up-to-date on the quickly changing, ever-emerging cyber threats.

 Real World Scenario

Cyberattacks on Global Supply Chains and Institutions

JBS, the world's largest meat packer, located in Brazil, was attacked in the spring 2021 by ransomware. The cyber breach compromised North American and Australian operational systems, disrupting the global supply chain for beef, chicken, and pork (https://cybersecurityworldconference.com/2021/06/01/worlds-biggest-meat-supplier-jbs-suffers-cyber-attack/). The JBS attack occurred just three weeks after a similar attack was made against the Colonial Pipeline. Cybersecurity threats are becoming more and more common, and it is just one example of why organizations need to develop written business continuity and disaster plans, which will be discussed in a later section.

The FBI defines ransomware as "a type of malicious software, or malware, that prevents you from accessing your computer files, systems, or networks and demands you pay a ransom for their return." In order for ransomware and other malware to take root, code must be downloaded. Hackers trick users into loading this code in a variety of ways, including through email, following online links, and on websites commonly visited by employees where the malware is embedded. For this reason, cybersecurity strategies must align closely with the technology policies described in Chapter 19, "Technology Management."

 Real World Scenario

Corporate Espionage or Whistleblowing?

One of the most publicized cases of data theft in history came at the hands of Edward Snowden in 2013, when he exposed the National Security Agency (NSA) for gathering mass intelligence on American citizens—without proper warrants. Snowden smuggled out thousands of confidential documents from the agency on a portable thumb drive, despite NSA's security protocols in place. He later had the files published, claiming whistleblower protection under the Occupational Safety and Health Act (OSHA). Examples such as these highlight the difficulty companies of all sizes face in securing confidential data. HR must lead the charge to establish policies and physical controls to prevent the unauthorized transfer or release of company records.

Workplace Violence

The risk of injuries to employees as a result of workplace violence exists for many reasons. These include violence from coworkers, family members, and disgruntled former employees. Unfortunately, it is difficult to predict workplace violence and thus prevent occurrences of incidents that resulted in more than 450 deaths in 2018. However, taking a look at victim data from the Bureau of Labor Statistics (bls.gov) can help employers hone their prevention efforts:

- 71 percent were female.
- 64 percent were aged 25 to 54.
- 73 percent worked in the healthcare and social assistance industry.

The National Institute for Occupational Safety and Health (NIOSH) is charged with researching all aspects of safety and health—from gathering statistics to recommending PPE. NIOSH reports that workplace violence falls into four main categories:

1. Criminal intent, such as robbery or assault
2. Customer/client, such as with nursing
3. Worker-on-worker, such as fights on the job
4. Personal relationships, which accounts for most of the 71 percent of workplace violence against women

Regardless of the predictability or source of the violence, there are some steps that an employer may take to protect the workforce. This includes training employees on what to do in a violent situation using resources such as local law enforcement and conducting drills for large-scale events such as shootings. Employers may offer hands-on training for women at work, particularly for those in high-risk occupations such as nursing, hospitality, or 24-hour stores, and provide them with emergency equipment where possible. Finally, employers should have a zero-tolerance policy for workplace violence and take immediate action when faced with an issue.

With regard to coworker violence, there are some warning signs that precede violent behaviors. These signs include highly emotional or aggressive reactions to employer feedback, threats, paranoia, and in many cases, drug or alcohol abuse.

Substance Abuse

Using legal or illegal substances, whether at work or not, has an effect on individual performance. These performance challenges include the following:

- Lost time through tardies, absenteeism, and injuries

- Unsafe work behaviors

- Increased healthcare costs

- Lower productivity

- Turnover

- Mood swings and unpredictability

Companies with a comprehensive drug-free workplace program report successful management of substance abuse in the workplace. These programs include written policies, legally compliant drug-testing procedures, and training supervisors to recognize the signs of intoxication and what to do about it. HR also offers support by working with benefits resources to offer counseling and treatment options where appropriate.

Legal substances are a bit trickier to navigate because states and industries have varying regulations. As a general rule, however, an employee has the responsibility to report to work ready for duty. Employers may prohibit employees from reporting to work under the influence of legal substances such as alcohol, prescription drugs that alter consciousness, and marijuana (legal in some states).

The National Safety Council (NSC) has a tool that calculates the costs of substance abuse in your workplace. The calculator is based on research data from the National Survey on Drug Use and Health (NSDUH). For example, a retail employer in Colorado with 50 employees can expect substance abuse in the workplace to cost about $50,000 a year in lost time, turnover, and healthcare costs. This data can be used to make a business case to their leaders on the costs of substance abuse going unchecked at work. Strategies to address the needs include offering better mental health benefits, an employer assistance program, smoking or other gateway-drug cessation programs, and education. Try the NSC calculator using your employer data at www.nsc.org; search for Substance Use Employer Calculator.

Financial Risks

Embezzlement, improper billing, theft, and fraudulent financial statements are just a few examples of the types of financial risks an organization must guard against. However, not all financial risks are to be avoided. Investments, diversifying operations, and capital outlay are strategic risks that can result in significant payoffs. For HR professionals, the goal is to apply risk management techniques to prevent loss while maximizing opportunities.

Effective financial risk management strategies seek to reduce or eliminate uncertainty by introducing controls. Operationally, the Generally Accepted Accounting Principles (GAAP) serve as a guide for the design of finance and accounting responsibilities. Best practices include creating processes that are consistently applied to ensure compliance with regulatory agencies and reduce theft. Segregation of duties (SOD) eliminates the ability of one employee having both authority and access to manage assets. For example, in an accounting department, the responsibility to approve and post journal entries should be separate. SOD may also be applied to IT departments to ensure that no single software engineer has the ability to write and push code into production.

HR's responsibilities include designing jobs that create internal controls to minimize exposure. If roles and responsibilities are not followed, there is an opportunity for collusion, such as between an A/P and A/R employee. HR is often responsible for securing passwords and tracking levels of access within enterprise software. HR is also called upon to lead investigations into fraudulent activity. This includes working with forensic accountants and other experts to objectively review reporting and other sensitive processes that may lead to financial losses.

Enterprise Risk Management

According to the SHRM glossary of terms, organizational effectiveness is the degree to which an organization is able to achieve their strategic objectives. The primary barrier to these accomplishments is risk, including financial or physical loss, compromised operations, and employee health and safety.

The context of the term "enterprise" in business refers to the organization as a whole—all departments and all locations. *Enterprise risk management (ERM)* is the ability to predict and plan for possible exposures at a holistic level, as opposed to only at a business unit level. In a siloed risk management model, an organization relies on unit leaders to manage risks related to their areas of key responsibilities. For example, the chief financial officer (CFO) would be tasked with managing risks related to accounting and finance, the chief technology officer (CTO) responsible for IT risks, and so on. An enterprise approach occurs on a strategic level and trickles down into action plans that occur at the departmental level. This means that the ERM planning process should be built within a strategic framework. This framework begins by analyzing the internal and external threats using tools such as SWOT and PESTLE, covered in greater detail in Chapter 5, "Strategic Human Resource Management."

The Risk Management Process

ERM practices include identifying risks, analyzing the exposure, prioritizing the risks, and then developing treatments on how to best address them. Let's discuss these practices in greater detail next.

Identifying Risk   Similar to the environmental scans that occur when engaged in the organizational strategic planning process, it is necessary for business leaders and their HR departments to consider the internal and external threats to their core business offerings. For most organizations, this will include risks to their human, financial, and physical capital.

The exam calls for a thorough understanding of two specific risk assessment techniques:

Qualitative Risk Assessment   These techniques are usually those that involve consulting with a team of experts. These experts may be found within the organization or located externally. For example, an organization may engage consultants to review the organization and its practices to determine areas of exposure. Internally, HR may lead a safety committee tasked with identifying and abating safety hazards. A hazard exists when a potential for harm has been identified and, if left uncontrolled, can result in damage to a person or property.

Other individuals within the company may be resourced using focus groups, task forces, and individual interviews to determine what types of hazards and other risks employees face on their jobs, the frequency of exposure, and ideas on how to best manage them.

Quantitative Risk Assessment   These techniques are used when there are sufficient objective criteria from which to identify probable risks, along with measures of impact. For example, the insurance industry (workers compensation, business insurance, and vehicle coverage) keeps track of exposures and costs—both hard and soft—associated with injury or damage. This includes information related to major catastrophes all the way down to minor incidents. In addition to the historical view, the insurance industry has impressive predictive models using AI, enabling employers to gather data related to the probability of exposure and degree of vulnerability. From this, the loss ratio may be compared to the costs of taking action.

Quantitative risk assessment tools generally consist of a step-by-step process that begins with the end in mind: what is the primary outcome from a risk scenario? From there, steps are taken to identify the likelihood of a failure/risk occurring, how the risk would be detected, the impact of the risk, possible causes, and finally, the best strategies for prevention. This is often represented through a flowchart, formula, or scorecard.

There are also quantitative tools that calculate loss based on micro data. *Single loss expectancy* is a determination of the monetary loss experienced every time a risk occurs. *Annualized loss expectancy* is the anticipated monetary loss every time a risk occurs over a one-year period.

🌐 Real World Scenario

Cost vs. Benefit to Society

In response to the subcompact automobile craze of the 1970s, Ford Motor Company set out to produce a vehicle that weighed no more than 2,000 pounds and sold for no more than $2,000. Dubbed the *Pinto*, Ford conducted safety testing and discovered a significant issue. The positioning of the gas tank behind the rear axle increased the likelihood of the car catching fire in rear-end collisions—even at low speeds. Ford engineers offered a design solution that would increase the cost of production by $11 per vehicle.

Company leadership got to work conducting a quantitative analysis of risk versus reward. The analysis estimated that leaving the gas tank where it was could result in 180 deaths, 180 burn victims, and 2,100 burned vehicles at an approximate cost of $49.5 million. Making the design changes, however, would increase Pinto production costs by about $137 million. Thus, the company decided that the benefit to society did not outweigh the cost and thus, allowed the car to enter production without change.

By 1978, at least four individuals had died and there were multiple burn victims, prompting Ford to recall 1.9 million vehicles. *Mother Jones* magazine published a scathing indictment of the quantitative cost–benefit analysis used by Ford leaders, and courts concurred, levying punitive damages to victims in the millions of dollars. The cost of Ford's decision far exceeded the original risk assessment of $49.5 million.

The Ford Pinto case demonstrates that where health and safety are concerned, it is not enough to rely on quantitative analysis only. Twenty-first-century businesses must consider not only the financial impact of risk versus reward, but also the impact to employees, their families, the brand reputation, and society as a whole.

Analyzing and Prioritizing Risk Exposure   Once the risk assessment is completed, the evaluation and prioritization processes begin. This includes reviewing the information discovered during the assessment phase. Decisions are made related to which risks pose the greatest threats to organizational heath. From there, the process of prioritizing risk response is put into place. Note that these responses are very rarely a single occurrence. More often than not, a risk management plan must be put into place that includes ongoing assessment, prioritization, and prevention efforts. After the risks have been prioritized, organizational leaders make decisions on how to best treat the risks.

Treating Risk   As a general rule, there are four main methods for treating risk:

Eliminate/Avoid   This approach looks for ways to eliminate the risk completely. Finance departments that follow GAAP by establishing internal controls (such as segregation of duties) are attempting to avoid the risk of fraud and theft.

Transfer/Share   In this strategy, an outside party is engaged to share the risk, such as through insurance. Should exposure occur, the risk is transferred entirely, or it is shared between the insurance company and the employer. This is a common approach in human resources through the purchasing of *employment practices liability insurance (EPLI)*, a plan that will help to offset costs associated with a labor claim.

Mitigate/Reduce   Possibly the most common method of risk management, *mitigation* involves reducing the exposure or impact without eliminating it entirely. Examples include setting up surveillance systems and increasing security for intellectual property as a means to reduce the threat of corporate espionage or sabotage.

Accept   This is the risk management strategy in which an organization accepts the risk as a cost of doing business. An example would be sending employees on global travel to countries where the risk of political violence, kidnapping, and ransom is high.

Note that none of these risk strategies are foolproof. There is the possibility of creating secondary risk that may be more or less acceptable than the risk that is being managed. For example, HR may determine that all new hires should undergo a background investigation prior to starting their first day of work. If the process results in significant underrepresentation of a protected class group, HR creates the risk of engaging in discriminatory hiring practices.

Risk Management Techniques

Most organizational strategic processes begin by assessing the need and end with evaluating the effectiveness of management activities. It is also done this way during the risk management process. Evaluating risk management techniques involves determining if they are achieving the desired result. These results may be in the areas of reduced exposure; compliance with regulations; alignment with corporate mission, vision, and values; or financial gain/prevention of economic losses. Risk management programs should be evaluated on an ongoing basis, as well as any time an exposure comes to light.

In-Process and After-Action Review (AAR)

Nothing is more valuable than human life, and as such, the *U.S. Army Leadership Field Manual* (Center for Army Leadership, 2004) gives an excellent view of the importance of assessing the effectiveness of any strategy with inherent risk. The book describes two types of assessments: in-process and after action. Both methods require clearly defined performance outcomes.

One of the challenges that HR faces with regard to risk management is in the area of quality. Quality defects cost employers significant amounts each year in the form of returned product, waste, warranty work, brand reputation, and liabilities. There is a misperception that quality management is necessary only in manufacturing industries. However, consumers count on both products and services to work as promised and not to cause harm.

Here is a small listing of how significant even a 0.1 percent defect rate can make in different industries.

If 99.9 percent were good enough:

- 500,000 Harry Potter books could have shipped with the wrong covers.
- 16,405 FAA flights could have landed at the wrong airport.
- 420,000 incorrect prescriptions could have been written.
- 234 facelifts could have been done incorrectly.

An in-process review is one tool that is used to prevent quality defects from occurring. In surgery, for example, an in-process review checklist includes the step of a nurse counting sponges before a patient is sewn up in order to ensure that none are inadvertently left behind inside the patient. HR and other leaders determine where there are significant quality risks, and those areas are reviewed constantly to avoid mistakes. When necessary, behaviors are corrected, standards are refined, and the in-process review continues. An in-process review may also be used on a short-term basis. Quality hot spots are identified, the processes/procedures are observed closely, and steps are taken to mitigate exposure when necessary. Sampling products to estimate quality defects is another way to utilize in-process reviews.

An *after-action review (AAR)* also involves evaluation and correcting behavior; however, it is conducted once an event has occurred. An AAR not only focuses on preventing an incident from occurring again, but is also used as a development tool. Once a crisis has passed, a group of involved persons meet to discuss the occurrence and identify the root cause of the issue(s). The employer response is also evaluated to determine what worked and what did not work so that necessary modifications may be made. In football, for example, game tape is reviewed after the game to identify development needs, and a coach or team of experts convenes to create improvement plans.

Stress Tests

"Stressing the system" is a phrase often used to describe the act of putting pressure on a process to see where it bulges or breaks. These pressure points are then evaluated to determine the probability of a break, the impact, and methods of risk treatment. *Stress tests* are dependent on identifying the variables that affect an outcome and then creating scenarios where these variables are manipulated to determine probable results. Stress tests are used in banking and other industries to determine worst-case scenarios using variables such as interest rates, consumer behaviors, economic factors, and so on. Stress and other scenario-based evaluation techniques can be quite complex, and thus these types of tools are often outsourced to industry experts.

Drills

The purpose of *drills* is to give teams the opportunity to practice response behaviors in the event of a crisis or other deviation from normal. They are designed to train team members on what to do in the event of an emergency or other unplanned (but predictable) situation. Perhaps the most widely recognized workplace drill is the fire drill. Drills such as fire, evacuation, and other crisis responses are often required as part of an employer's emergency response plan.

Regulatory Compliance and Audits

For most organizations, HR is not a core competency and thus does not generate direct revenue. One of the ways in which HR provides significant value to their employers is by ensuring that their practices are compliant with the hundreds of labor laws that govern the employment of workers. The costs of employment practice violations can be significant. Engaging the services of a labor attorney who advocates on behalf of employers is one mitigation strategy for these risks, as is the purchase of the EPL insurance discussed earlier. However, the best way to manage compliance risks is to stay in compliance! One way to do this is to schedule regular reviews of required actions. HR compliance audits may include the following:

- Form I-9 files
- Personnel files, including confidential record-keeping practices
- Record retention and destroy practices
- Safety records, such as OSH 300 and 301
- Facility safety walks
- Ergonomic inspections of workspaces
- Payroll, meal/break, and timekeeping records
- Employee classifications
- Mandated posters
- Hiring practices
- Other legal compliance, such as the employee handbook and termination practices

The use of audit checklists is a consistent way to ensure that you are keeping up with the many ways that an HR department can fall out of compliance.

Written Risk Management Plans

Once an employer has identified risks to the company or the employee, it is important that a written plan be created, communicated, and evaluated on a consistent basis. In some cases, a written plan is not just a good business practice—it is required by OSHA. The three most common risk management plans are detailed next.

Business Continuity and Disaster Preparedness Plans

Business continuity plans focus on continuing the essential functions of a business should there be a disruption. For this reason, the first step to developing a plan is to conduct a business impact analysis to identify critical functions. Employers should consider their vulnerability to communicable diseases, natural disasters, severe weather, terrorism, cyberattacks, and fire and chemical exposure, in addition to any risks that are industry-specific (such as mine explosions at mining operations). Once the analysis has been complete, experts should be consulted to develop strategies to protect the critical functions and/or bring them back online as quickly as possible. For example, in the JBS cyberattack discussed earlier, their IT team did not have their digital backup systems connected to the main network. This allowed the company to be back up and running much quicker than if the entire system had been hijacked. Once strategies have been identified, a written plan is developed, and individuals are assigned to implement and monitor it so that the data remains current.

Emergency Response Plans

Prompt warnings to employees to evacuate, shelter, or lock down can be the difference between life and death in the event of any emergency such as a natural disaster, fire, or workplace violence incident. Being prepared for any of these crises is a measure of the duty of care standard described by OSHA, which requires that employers protect their teams from harm.

An *emergency response plan* is a written plan that details the actions necessary to respond to a crisis at work. As such, it begins by conducting a risk assessment to determine potential emergencies. For example, employers in California may include emergency response to earthquakes, whereas an employer in Florida would be better served by having a hurricane response plan. All employers should have plans that focus first and foremost on protecting lives, described by Ready.gov, as orders to do the following:

Evacuate: In the event of a fire or bomb threat

Shelter-in-Place: For situations involving exposure to harm by leaving the building, such as severe weather or chemical release

Lockdown: To protect employees from acts of violence, such as an active shooter

Each of these examples requires that an employer have a warning system in place and that employees are trained to know what to do under each circumstance.

Once protection of life has been established, an emergency response plan should focus on containing the issue. This may include notifying emergency personnel, administering medical treatment, spill control, and firefighting. Many industries have their own, more specific needs for incident control that should be accounted for in a written plan.

Each written plan should have established response protocols, a description of duties and who is responsible for them, a description of personal protection equipment where necessary, and a commitment to conduct various exercises (such as audits, drills, or stress tests) to evaluate efficacy.

Injury and Illness Prevention Plans

OSHA describes injury and illness prevention programs (IIPPs) as a review of processes that focus on identifying hazards and preventing workers from being injured or catching an illness from those hazards. Some states have mandatory requirements that employers of a certain size maintain an IIPP. Common components to these programs include the following:

- Management commitment
- Worker participation
- Hazard identification, assessment, prevention, and control/abatement
- Employee training
- Program/plan evaluation

Regardless of whether or not you work in one of the 34 states that require an IIPP, studies have shown that an active, written injury and illness prevention program reduces worker fatalities, injuries, and diseases and increases employee productivity and morale—all good reasons to have a program in place.

SHRM SCP Only

In 2018, the International Standards Board updated their technical manual titled *ISO 31000:2018: Risk management—Guidelines*. The introduction to the revised edition states near perfectly the role and perspective that senior leaders must have regarding enterprise risk management:

> This document is for use by people who create and protect value in organizations by managing risks, making decisions, setting and achieving objectives and improving performance.

Furthermore, the degree to which an organization is comfortable with uncertainty—another definition of risk—drives the behaviors of senior HR leaders. In some organizations, such as start-ups, risk is inherent and not necessarily a negative thing. For other organizations that are more mechanistic, such as financial institutions, uncertainty is to be avoided, with established practices, rules, and regulations to be followed in order to avoid risks.

Regardless of an organization's risk tolerance, advanced HR teams should focus on risk management techniques that create value and protect stakeholders. This means that risk management practices must be inclusive, holistic, and dynamic—continuously being improved in response to internal and external forces. This concept is reflected in the exam BoCK for SHRM-SCP candidates. The proficiency indicators begin by noting the need to routinize the practice of monitoring the internal and external environments. This may be done formally through the company's strategic planning process using the tools SWOT and PESTLE, described earlier in this chapter. It also requires continuous monitoring of the labor markets where companies compete and understanding industry-specific conditions that will shape risk orientation. Risks may both create opportunities and be viewed as threats; thus, HR professionals must have a strong sense of their organization's risk tolerance, what their competitors are doing, and how well their systems and talent can support strategies for risk treatment.

As with so many other critical HR functions, human resource professionals are called on to gain commitment and buy-in from organizational leaders and individual contributors.

This will require that HR have a deep, objective understanding of the impact of risk treatments, their benefits, and their burdens. Working with internal and external resources, senior HR leaders develop key risk indicators (KRIs) that signal degrees of exposure. These KRIs may be used in creating a persuasive business case that prioritizes actions.

Advanced HR practitioners are responsible for overseeing the cycle of risk management that begins with assessment and ends with monitoring. Risk assessment includes identifying the risks, analyzing probability and possibilities using quantitative and qualitative tools, and designing risk treatments. This includes serving as a liaison to internal and external resources to ensure that the proper data and perspectives are collected. Compliance with regulatory agencies and their standards must be effectively managed through job design, standard operating procedures, audits, and proper record-keeping.

Crisis management is a critical competency for all HR professionals. Senior leaders will oversee the development of business continuity and other emergency response plans that protect team members and the organization from harm. Workplace violence, health and safety, and security from cyber- and other threats all require iterative management efforts. HR will be called upon to effectively lead in-process and after-action debriefs to ensure that quality, safety, and other exposures are addressed.

Advanced HR leaders will need to develop and deploy competencies related to business acumen, leadership, and interpersonal skills. Of equal importance in effective risk management are the sub-competencies of ethical practices, relationship management, communication, and critical evaluation.

Summary

Business leaders from all generations have war stories of how internal and external forces created a chaotic day (or year) at the workplace. Natural disasters, contagious diseases, violence, a stuttering economy, difficulty hiring, regulatory pressures—the list goes on and on.

The variety, complexity, probabilities, and impact of risk to an organization's existence and the health and safety of team members puts HR at the center of the risk management domain. For this reason, HR's influence begins by overseeing the risk analysis process. This includes collecting and analyzing data and making recommendations on the most effective risk treatments.

Many different types of risks must be addressed, including workplace health and safety, threats to security, and substance abuse. Enterprise risk management efforts seek to manage these risks at an organizational level rather than leaving the responsibility to individual departments in a siloed structure.

Not all risks are to be avoided. In fact, many business leaders argue that taking strategic risks allows them to gain a competitive edge in their markets. Strategic HR leaders partner with strategy teams to predict risk and take steps to avoid threats and capitalize on opportunities.

Key Terms

After-action review (AAR)

Annualized loss expectancy

Business continuity plans

Drills

Emergency response plans

Employment practices liability insurance (EPLI)

Enterprise risk management

Investigations

Mitigation

Recordable injuries/diseases

Single loss expectancy

Stress tests

Exam Essentials

Engage in enterprise risk management activities.   The process for managing risks applies to strategic, operational, and financial risks. The risk management process begins by identifying and analyzing exposure and designing methods to treat risks. The risk management process also exists for HR to help advise leadership on when strategic risks are worth taking.

Develop and implement strategies to prevent adverse events.   HR at all levels is responsible for identifying threats to an organization and taking steps through HR systems to manage them. This includes having written policies, designing jobs to minimize exposure, training team members, and complying with regulatory agencies.

Evaluate the effectiveness of risk management techniques.   There are many methods by which to manage risks, including avoid, accept, mitigate, and transfer. These are in addition to in-process and after-action reviews, drills, and stress tests designed to ensure that organizational practices are effective. Evaluating the effectiveness of risk management efforts also includes auditing practices to ensure compliance with regulatory agencies governing health, safety, and financial best practices.

Review Questions

1. Which of the following statements is *false* regarding the primary differences between enterprise and siloed risk management?

    A. Enterprise risk management focuses on the organization as a whole.

    B. Siloed risk management is more effective because it targets specific departmental risks.

    C. Enterprise risk management activities trickle down into individual business units.

    D. Siloed risk management is more narrowly focused.

2. In which step of the risk management process are qualitative or qualitative tools used?

    A. Transferring risk

    B. Mitigating risk

    C. Treating risk

    D. Identifying risk

3. Of the following positive outcomes of effective risk management processes, which is the most important?

    A. Being compliant with regulations

    B. Aligning with organizational strategy

    C. Preventing losses

    D. Reducing workers' compensation costs

4. Every time the network server goes down, it costs the company approximately $300.00. IT estimates that this is likely to happen four times a year. What is the annualized loss expectancy for this risk?

    A. $300.00

    B. $600.00

    C. $1,200.00

    D. $2,400.00

5. Which of the following OSHA standards require that employers protect their workers from harm?

    A. Hazard communication

    B. Duty of good faith and fair dealing

    C. Duty of care

    D. General duty

6. Which of the following is *true* about the employee's responsibility regarding safety and health behaviors?

   A. The employee must report all injuries or illnesses within 24 hours.

   B. The employee must comply with the code of safe practices.

   C. The employee must share part of the cost for their workers' compensation insurance.

   D. All of the above.

7. Which of the following is considered recordable on OSHA's 300 log?

   A. Death

   B. Injury with lost time

   C. Injury with modified duty

   D. All of the above

8. You recently made the recommendation to senior leadership that the company should no longer allow personal visitors on-site, even while employees are on break. Which of the following risks are you most likely taking steps to prevent?

   A. Domestic abuse

   B. Mass shooting

   C. Workplace violence

   D. Corporate espionage

9. What is the first step in developing a business continuity plan?

   A. Communicate with team members.

   B. Identify necessary resources.

   C. Build the plan objectives.

   D. Conduct the risk assessment.

10. You are the HR manager for a large organization with a facility next to a rail spur. You heard a loud collision and upon immediate investigation, you realized that a railcar had tipped over, releasing the chemicals it was carrying. You do not know what chemical was released, but it is spilling fast onto the back property. What should you do first?

   A. Call 911.

   B. Deploy the spill containment team.

   C. Initiate a shelter-in-place for all team members.

   D. Look for hazard signage on the car to identify what kind of chemical had been spilled.

Chapter

13

Corporate Social Responsibility

Exam Notables

The signs are everywhere: having access to the Internet is key to thriving in developed societies. The rise of telehealth, e-commerce, online banking, employment websites, remote learning, social networks, and government services—all are being done through online platforms.

It should come as a surprise, then, that during the Covid-19 pandemic, it was discovered that nearly 17 million children did not have at-home access to the Internet (FCC.gov). In addition to this technological disparity, studies show that minority groups are most likely to suffer from the lack of the knowledge, skills, and infrastructure necessary to utilize these tools. Contributing factors to this digital divide are low education levels, poverty, and geographic location. To combat this social issue, a combination of government intervention, community activism, and resources from organizations such as SpaceX, Google, and Intel have developed targeted initiatives.

Corporate social responsibility is the concept that organizations have a role to play in resolving the social, economic, and environmental issues of today's world.

The following functional area summary tells us how HR drives these efforts:

> Corporate Social Responsibility represents the organization's commitment
> to operate in an ethical and sustainable manner by engaging in activities
> that promote and support philanthropy, transparency, sustainability and
> ethically sound governance practices.

The SHRM Exam Objectives

SHRM's BoCK not only summarizes this functional area, but also defines the proficiency indicators and key concepts. No matter your career level, pay special attention to the exam concepts defined "For All HR Professionals" and the "Key Concepts." If seeking the SHRM-SCP designation, you must expand your efforts to include those labeled "For Advanced HR Professionals."

THE SHRM-CP EXAM AND SHRM-SCP EXAM OBJECTIVES COVERED IN THIS CHAPTER INCLUDE THE FOLLOWING:

✓ **For All HR Professionals**

- Acts as a professional role model and representative of the organization when interacting with the community.

- Engages in community-based volunteer and philanthropic activities.

- Identifies and promotes opportunities for HR and the organization to engage in CSR activities.

- Helps staff at all levels understand the societal impact of business decisions and the role of the organization's CSR activities in improving the community.

- Maintains transparency of HR programs, practices and policies, where appropriate.

- Coaches managers to achieve an appropriate level of transparency in organizational practices and decisions.

- Identifies opportunities for incorporation of environmentally responsible business practices, and shares them with leadership.

✓ **For Advanced HR Professionals**

- Serves as a leader in community-based volunteer and philanthropic organizations.

- Develops CSR strategies that reflect the organization's mission and values.

- Ensures that the organization's CSR programs enhance the employee value proposition and have a beneficial impact on HR programs (e.g., recruitment and retention) and/or contribute to the organization's competitive advantage.

- Creates CSR program activities that engage the organization's workforce and the community at large.

- Coordinates with other business leaders to integrate CSR objectives throughout the organization.

- Coordinates with other business leaders to develop and implement appropriate levels of corporate self-governance and transparency.

- Develops, with other business leaders, strategies that encourage and support environmentally responsible business decisions.

✓ **Key Concepts**

- Approaches to community inclusion and engagement (e.g., representation on community boards, joint community projects, employee volunteerism).

- **Creating shared value (e.g., definition, best practices).**

- **Developing CSR-related volunteer programs (e.g., recruiting and organizing participants).**

- **Organizational philosophies and policies (e.g., development, integration into the organization).**

- **Principles of corporate citizenship and governance.**

- **Steps for corporate philanthropy and charitable giving (e.g., selecting recipients, types, donation amounts).**

Defining Corporate Social Responsibility (CSR)

All ecosystems have some degree of interdependency between the organisms and their environment. Over time, these dependencies create the shared reward of survival. In the context of work, an organization and its partners create similar, deeply rooted stakes of connectedness. SHRM defines stakeholders as "those affected by an organization's social, environmental, and economic impact." These efforts apply to individuals, groups, and the environment on a local and global scale. The human stakeholders are the employees and their families, contractors, and vendors. Communities, shareholders, schools, and volunteers are the group stakeholders affected by corporate practices. Environmental conditions such as air, water, and land are symbiotic partners as well. The health of all stakeholders supports an organization's ability to exist, and companies have the ability to support stakeholder health.

Corporate social responsibility speaks to the role that organizations play in addressing short- and long-term economic, environmental, and social issues. These include small-scale issues, such as driving action on school boards, to the larger, more complex issue of human rights.

CSR efforts require a commitment of company resources to drive change and generate value to all stakeholders. HR has the responsibility to help organizations frame the context of these changes, and it begins by getting the commitment of leadership. This involves aligning CSR initiatives with organizational results.

One example of an environmental issue where leadership is taking action comes from the high-stakes world of asset management. In 2021, CEO Larry Brink of BlackRock published an open letter to his clients. Brink declared that "climate risk is investment risk," neatly tying CSR efforts to results by citing the costs and investment losses from fires, hurricanes, and floods—events often connected to changing climate conditions. Brink tied CSR efforts to financial opportunity as well, noting that "from January through November 2020, investors. . .invested \$288 billion globally in sustainable assets, a 96 percent increase over the whole of 2019" (BlackRock.com). He has since committed BlackRock—the largest asset management corporation in the world—to advance efforts toward climate innovation.

Economic pressures exist for organizations and their stakeholders. Tesla's stock ran up and down based on founder Elon Musk's tweets about Dogecoin, and it is too soon for businesses to know if cryptocurrency is a force to be reckoned with or just a passing fad. GameStop's stock price went up more than 2,000 percent in one month thanks to micro-investors targeting the giant hedge funds of Wall Street. When regulators intervened to address this "activism investment," there were immediate cries on social media of institutional favoritism.

Furthermore, disruptions to the supply chain have had a significant impact on an organization's cost of goods sold, the availability of products, and the resulting price increases that are at the heart of supply and demand. For individuals, if income through wages and other means do not increase at the same rate, consumers are left unable to make ends meet or save for the future. Each of these economic examples affects the ability of an organization and its stakeholders to survive and thrive.

Poverty and the acquisition of sustainable wealth is a factor across the world, including the United States. For example, as shown in Figure 13.1, distribution of wealth in the United States remains top heavy: the top 1 percent of wealth in U.S households is greater than the bottom 50 percent combined.

FIGURE 13.1   Distribution of wealth in the United States

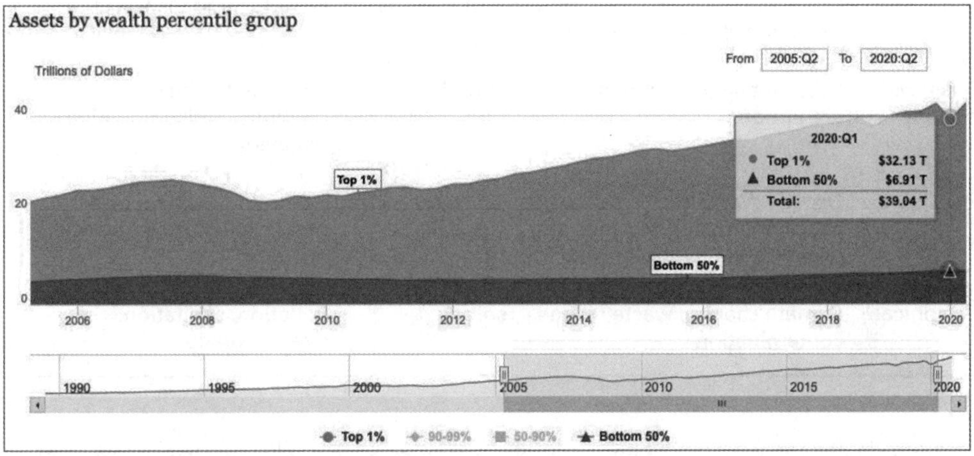

Source: Survey of Consumer Finances and Financial Accounts of the United States

The years 2020 and 2021 were stark reminders of the social issues facing the United States and other countries. In the middle of the Covid-19 pandemic, a civil rights movement arose to fight systemic racism. A political protest at the U.S. Capitol became violent on the day that a peaceful transfer of power was due to occur. The ongoing refugee crisis in Syria and Yemen dominated the headlines. Women left their jobs at a disproportionately higher rate than their male counterparts due to family care and school closures caused by Covid-19.

Diversity, immigration, equal rights, and the availability of half of the qualified workforce are all issues that affect organizational results, and all are addressed through the functions of human resources.

Governments of all sizes are taking steps to address these environmental, economic, and social issues. However, it is not always in society's best interest to wait for the government to dictate right or wrong. This is especially the case when they have a stake in the outcome, such as the ability to raise interest rates on the student loans that the government financed.

Aristotle noted that virtue is character manifested in action. Corporate social responsibility is a strategic organizational commitment to taking action that addresses the economic, social, and environmental challenges facing the world today. Table 13.1 gives examples of the various forces driving CSR strategies on a domestic and international level.

TABLE 13.1 Examples of forces shaping CSR strategies

Force	Developed countries	Emerging countries
Social	Racial discrimination, system inequities (education, digital divide), LGBTQ rights, criminal justice reform	Unskilled workforce, violence against women
Economic	Universal Basic Income (UBI), lack of savings, exorbitant student loan debt	Poverty, food insecurity
Business climate	Labor-management relations, supply chain disruptions	Inhospitable business relations, anticompetitive behavior
Political	Occupy Wall Street, trade agreements, refugee crises, international ocean shipping lane disputes, campaign finance reform	Corruption, violence, lack of infrastructure to attract business
Ecological	Climate change, waste disposal, soil contamination	Pollution, sanitation, overpopulation

Additionally, some issues fall into multiple categories, such as climate change, overpopulation, and infrastructure. These are challenges that consume financial and environmental resources while simultaneously creating social issues. For example:

Climate Change   Extreme weather attributed to climate changes disrupts businesses and displaces employees. Rising temperatures change the natural ecosystems that organisms rely on for survival.

Overpopulation   Countries that are overpopulated struggle to offer services that address basic human needs such as food, water, and shelter. Addressing overpopulation may create harmful environmental practices such as over-farming.

Infrastructure　A lack of infrastructure, such as transportation, power grids, hospitals, and high-speed Internet, drives the ability of cities and countries to compete. Lack of infrastructure also limits commerce and access to the services necessary to be successful in today's world. Developing nongreen infrastructure solutions can negatively affect the environment.

Nongovernment organizations (NGOs) are nonprofit community groups that seek out social, political, and environmental change on a community, national, and global scale. One of the reasons why NGOs exist is to serve as a counterweight to governments that are perceived as (or actually) corrupt, or that are fundamentally unable to address the crises outlined in this chapter. For this reason, most NGOs have systems in place to combat these perceptions.

Many NGOs are well funded, and though not part of the formal government, they still have significant influence on important issues. One example is the Norwegian Refugee Council (NRC), an independent agency started just after the end of World War II. The NRC works under a corporate citizenship model of accountability, transparency, and taking an aggressive stance on corruption such as bribery, kickbacks, embezzlement, and sexual exploitation. The NRC also helps to manage the displacement of refugees forced to flee due to war, violence, and natural disasters. In 2018 alone, the NRC managed to provide support and protection to more than 8 million refugees in more than 30 countries around the world.

Radicalism is a term defined by SHRM as the idea that management-labor conflict is inherent to capitalism. Inequities can only be eliminated by radical change to the economic systems developed and controlled by governments. This concept is tied closely to *social justice*, the view that everyone deserves to be treated fairly in the political, economic, educational, and healthcare systems in society.

Corporate Shared Value

> Not all profit is equal. Profits involving a social purpose represent a higher form of capitalism...
>
> *Michael E. Porter and Mark R. Kramer, Harvard Business School*

In addition to gaining leadership commitment, there are others who must buy into a CSR approach. This may be accomplished by creating and communicating a corporate shared value (CSV) initiative.

Michael E. Porter and Mark R. Kramer of the Harvard Business School define CSV as businesses "generating economic value in a way that also produces value for society by addressing its challenges. A shared value approach reconnects company success with social progress" ("Creating Shared Value," *Harvard Business Review*, 2011). In what is considered to be the seminal article on the drive to create shared value, Porter and Kramer point out that economic, environmental, and social issues are all opportunities to find collaborative success.

CSV is focused on adding value to stakeholders through CSR efforts. This requires a CSR strategy that is aligned with corporate strategy and that takes into account shared rewards. For example, it is reasonable for an organization to want to get the best deal on materials from their supply chain vendors. However, if the supplier is unable to operate due to the pricing demands, they may go out of business. If the supplier goes out of business, then the organization loses a partner that helps them to compete. In CSV, the organization recognizes the supplier as a valued partner and acts accordingly.

One example of how businesses can incorporate CSV into their in the supply chain comes from Ben and Jerry's Ice Cream. CSV is known there as "linked prosperity," and the company commits to this premise by having a set of values that their suppliers must follow. Compliance with these values allows the suppliers to continue working with the giant chain. The ice cream producer is using their buying power to leverage suppliers into addressing the humane treatment of animals and other responsible sourcing practices.

HR leads conversations with each business unit to identify ways in which they may create shared value. Involving organizational leaders and employees ensures that multiple perspectives are considered and will increase ownership over the outcomes.

Benefits of Corporate Social Responsibility

CSR efforts are not only a moral imperative that benefits external groups; there are several tangible and nontangible benefits to integrating CSR efforts into organizational practices.

Research by Nielsen found that in 2018, nearly half of all consumers surveyed were willing to change their behaviors to reduce their impact on the environment. This suggests that these same consumers are willing to pay more for products or services if they know that they are environmentally friendly, a truth demonstrated by the 20 percent growth in sales from companies with products that are organic, sustainable, or clean.

When conceived and implemented properly, CSR efforts yield operational, strategic, and financial results, as demonstrated in Figure 13.2.

Corporate Citizenship

Think for a moment about selecting a physician to treat a sick loved one. Not only would you want them to make your loved one better, but you would also want to ensure that they would not cause further harm. Corporate social responsibility is about doing good for society, whereas *corporate citizenship* is about not harming or contributing to the economic, environmental, and social issues of the day. Two measures of corporate citizenship as they relate to the exams are governance and ethics.

Laws are created to control the behaviors of all citizens, and being responsible corporate citizens requires a good faith effort to comply with the laws of society. *Corporate governance* efforts spring from a commitment to exercise good faith and fiduciary responsibility and to act with transparency and accountability within the bounds of socially responsible behaviors.

FIGURE 13.2   Benefits of CSR efforts

Financial	Strategic	Operational
• Compete in global markets	• Increased brand awareness	• Competitive recruiting
• Create shared value	• Model ethical behaviors	• Contribute to global infrastructure
• Increased sales	• Add to the employee value proposition (EVP)	• Reduced turnover
• Attract specific investors	• Increased consumer trust	• Reduced risk

Benefits of Corporate Social Responsibility

Ethics are a set of behavioral guidelines focused on moral obligations and acting with regard for others. A code of ethics defining employee behaviors is often part of an employee handbook. More and more companies are seeing the value in creating similar standards of behavior for the organization as well.

Integrity is another component of organizational character. The term refers to the commitment of employees, managers, directors, and organizational leaders to act in accordance with ethical and moral principles, and with honesty and consistency, even where there are benefits to acting otherwise.

Corporation vs. Corporate

The term "corporate" is actually, in a way, misleading in that it implies that only businesses that are "incorporated" (translated, large employers) need to engage in CSR, CSV, or governance. The term "corporate" in this chapter is meant to imply "the collective."

This means that it applies to all businesses with stakeholders. The term also speaks to the need to take united action toward radical change, multiplying the efforts through collaboration as opposed only to adding value through independent agency. When there is a corporation with a board of directors, corporate governance has a stricter interpretation that goes beyond the scope of social responsibility.

Sustainable Business Practices

Sustainability is a term generally used to define the need to protect natural resources from depletion. SHRM's definition brings this concept into the business realm. Sustainability is the "practice of purchasing and using resources wisely by balancing economic, social, and environmental concerns toward the goal of preserving present and future generations' interests." This definition was built on the original work of John Elkington in 1997. In his book *Cannibals with Forks: The Triple Bottom Line of 21st Century Business*, (Wiley, 1999), Elkington suggested that a short-term focus on financial profits will be at the expense of long-term, sustainable success. He said that businesses should focus on three main elements, often called the "3 Ps," for Profits, the Planet, and People.

Profit: Sustainable Economic Practices   Private employers exist for many reasons, and one of those is to create profit. *Profit* is a financial measure of the money that is left over after business expenses such as labor or materials are paid. The opposite of profits are losses, which are indicators that a company may be headed for financial trouble unless properly managed. Profit can be reinvested in the business, paid out to *shareholders* (individuals who own stock shares in the corporation) in the form of dividends, invested for future growth, or to complete other, noncore activities. Achieving profit in sustainable ways include acting in good faith on behalf of the organization, providing good stewardship over financial resources and investments, and taking steps to prevent fraud and theft that erodes a business's ability to compete.

Planet: Sustainable Environmental Practices   The factors that have impacted ecological damage include emissions, sourcing, climate change, population growth, and more. These forces have created devastating consequences to the natural resources of land, air, oceans, lakes, and rivers. But who is responsible?

Mark Manson, the author of the blog titled "Life Advice That Does Not Suck," puts it this way (paraphrased): If someone left a baby on your front porch, it may not be your fault, but it is your responsibility. So, it is with the earth. Ultimately, the responsibility lies with governments, corporations, local activist groups, and individual effort. This is done by shaping policies and engaging in practices that attempt to repair existing damage while preventing more.

People: Sustainable Social Practices This form of sustainability focuses on the need to take care of the human stakeholders described in an earlier section. This includes both individuals and groups that are affected by business practices. Social practices that should be planned for and measured include employee health and safety, fair wages, human rights, hazard communication, ethical behaviors, and leadership accountability.

Recycling organization Greenpath Recovery offers an updated view of the triple bottom line that is useful in understanding shared value. The company notes that the 3 Ps should be read as a mathematical formula:

People + Planet = Profit

Only when the first two stakeholders are accounted for will the profits come.

The World Economic Forum launched an initiative in 2021 called The Great Reset. It calls upon its global business partners to lead the effort in building socially responsible industrial practices. Figure 13.3 shows examples of innovative industry efforts striving for change. Partnering with agencies and staying up-to-date with current events is one way that HR may find opportunities to engage their businesses in CSR activities, as is maintaining membership in industry-specific networks. This ability reflects the exam behavioral competencies of relationship building with stakeholders and that of professional integrity by understanding current trends that can affect corporate success.

FIGURE 13.3 Global industry innovation

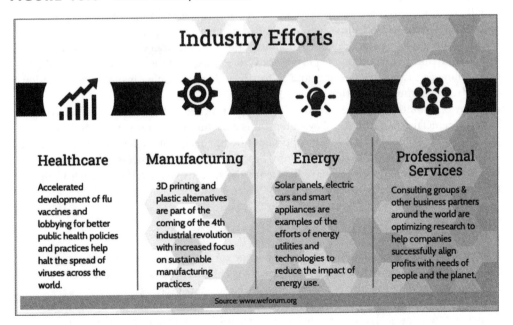

A Global Approach

The Environmental Performance Index (EPI) (`https://epi.yale.edu`) is published by the World Economic Forum (WEF) to rank 180 countries based on their efforts in social responsibility. Areas studied include air quality, sanitation, climate change, biodiversity, and more. In 2020, European countries dominated the top 10 list with their sustainability efforts.

The Role of Human Resources

HR plays a significant role in developing systems that help organizations achieve the benefits of strategic CSR management. It is useful to view these benefits through the functions of an HR department.

Business Strategy

The effective alignment of CSR choices with organizational needs will create profit and value. Value is defined in this context as something of worth that is reciprocal and beyond only monetary gain.

HR contributes to this area by shaping the organizational philosophy statement and policies related to the CSR initiatives. Also called a policy statement, its purpose is to outline how CSR programs will be developed and integrated into the organization. A strong philosophy statement will outline the purpose of CSR efforts, the pillars of the program (clean energy, hunger, sustainable farming, and so forth), and the reasoning behind these selections as they relate to the organization's core competencies.

Many organizations choose to show their support through philanthropy with charitable aid and financial donations. A policy statement is a useful tool to frame these philanthropic guidelines. This should include a description of how the recipients will be selected, describe what type of aid is available, and define any program limits. This process helps to minimize frustration from employees who have different values, needs, or opinions, and who help hold organizations accountable.

Talent Acquisition

Finding qualified talent continues to be a challenge for most industries and employers. Numerous studies show that the employer brand is enhanced, consumer trust is increased, and individuals want to work for companies with a social conscience.

The 2018 Nielsen report referenced earlier also found that younger professionals are 75 percent twice as likely to frame their consumer behaviors around sustainability. In Chapter 6, "Talent Acquisition," we learned that these same young individuals also have a desire to work for companies that put purpose over profit. This matters as millennials currently make up the largest workforce population. HR teams may optimize these generational trends by effectively communicating their social responsibility efforts through their employer's brand. HR also plays an integral part in crafting jobs with meaning and developing systems that support these values.

Social media can be used to great effect by organizations to communicate the employee value proposition—the monetary and nonmonetary reasons why someone should come work with the team.

For more insights on the report from Nielsen, look at the summary titled "Was 2018 the Year of the Influential Sustainable Consumer?" at www .nielseniq.com.

Risk Management

Taking steps to address the economic, social, and environmental issues that directly affect the business is a strategic way to manage risk. For example, a clothing retailer that takes steps to monitor and address human rights issues within their supply chain avoids the risk of an abuse scandal that could compromise the brand and resulting profits.

Part of the HR exams requires that leaders be able to show employees the value of engaging with the company's CSR efforts. Employee health and safety provides the perfect forum for doing so, offering the important perspective of "What's in it for me?" Table 13.2 provides examples of health and safety threats facing different professionals and how their employer can mitigate those threats through CSR efforts.

TABLE 13.2   Employee benefits of CSR health and safety initiatives

Worker	CSR effort
Medical professionals	Employer advocates for vaccination education to prevent contagious diseases.
Firefighters	Unions support research groups seeking to find safer ways to respond to terrorist or chemical attacks.
Power Crews	Utilities commit resources toward addressing climate change that contributes to hurricanes, tsunamis, and other natural disasters.

Consider the industry where you practice HR. What are the social, economic, and environmental threats facing your teams? In what ways can your organization contribute to mitigating these threats?

One challenge facing employers is that some of the threats to their teams are the exact reason why they are in business! Strategically, this can create a conflict of interest in that the elimination of the threat could compromise their profitability, employee job security, and other desired outcomes. A conflict of interest is a situation in which participation in an activity for the benefit of one party may conflict with or have direct or an indirect negative impact on the employment relationship or outcomes.

There are also times when addressing one issue inadvertently creates another. For example, in 2016 California became the first state to ban the use of plastic shopping bags due to their lack of biodegradability; shoppers had to bring their own reusable bags to stores. In 2020, when the Covid-19 pandemic was in full swing, reusable bags presented a health risk to retail workers, prompting the governor of California to issue an executive order allowing single-use bags again.

When building a CSR strategy, organizations of all sizes need to consider the opposing view to ensure that they are not shaping practices that increase harm to other stakeholders.

Total Rewards

The political debates over paying a living wage and universal basic income (UBI) share one thing in common—the need for individuals to earn enough to meet their fundamental needs: healthcare, housing, and food. An employer's total rewards practices can address these elements by paying fair wages and offering benefits that support a healthy lifestyle.

The savings crisis in America is another opportunity for compensation specialists to craft financial wellness programs. In addition to the traditional retirement savings accounts, employers are beginning to encourage cash savings. Employees may elect to auto-contribute an amount from their paycheck each month, and the employer matches up to 100 percent of that amount.

Mental health is another area where there seems to be growing disparity, and which should be of concern to HR teams. Many employee volunteer initiatives focus on the benefits to external stakeholders such as community groups. However, there are several well-documented studies showing that acts of service provide a significant mental health boost to the volunteer. A study by United Healthcare reported that employees who volunteered over the previous 12 months felt healthier, were in better moods, and experienced less stress. These efforts also increase an employee's sense of worth, happiness, and even career development due to their exposure to group or task leadership opportunities. Physical activity, a sense of purpose, and the collective action characteristic of many volunteer projects can also help individuals who suffer from depression.

HR strategies that support volunteer initiatives include crafting leave policies that offer additional time off to volunteer in their communities. HR teams may also partner with local groups to coordinate fundraising, organize food drives, or help out in an emergency.

HR is expected to champion volunteerism by communicating the benefits and applying their human relations skills to recruit team members. This includes organizing the teams in ways that optimize the individual and complementary skills and abilities. All volunteers should be strong company ambassadors by being positive representatives of the organization and the initiative(s).

Learning and Development

Coaching is a critical function of an HR department's learning and development (L&D) activities. In corporate social responsibility, this includes helping managers achieve the right degree of transparency without compromising confidentiality. Transparency speaks to organizational leaders being open about their policies and practices, and it is a major factor in building and maintaining trust. HR professionals must model the desired behaviors for leaders, employees, and the communities where they operate.

Carl Jung, the famous Swiss psychoanalyst, coined the term "the collective unconscious" to describe how a group's shared beliefs, attitudes, and opinions form a legacy bank from which humans unconsciously draw. This happens to all cultural groups to varying degrees, including organizational cultures. It could explain why individuals have such difficulty with change, despite compelling rational and emotional reasons for the change. Overcoming systemic barriers is necessary to truly effect change, and that requires changing human behavior. For example, a diversity initiative may require leaders to draw from many domains, including:

Psychology: Training teams to understand, recognize, and overcome unconscious bias

Neuroscience: Training teams in methods to unlearn behaviors in order to remove barriers to relearning new behaviors

Organizational behavior: Developing global leaders in the cultural competencies necessary to be effective in diverse societies

Transparency, role modeling, coaching leaders, and using academic principles to drive change all help teams to develop a more holistic mindset in order to understand the impact of and encourage engagement in organizational CSR initiatives.

SHRM SCP Only

None of the issues described thus far come with easy solutions. It may be tempting for organizations to turn the other way and just focus on their own survival and their employee's needs. This is especially true for small businesses that simply don't have a lot of resources to spare. Advanced HR leaders can use their influence to develop CSR strategies that are aligned with organizational results and the company's mission and values. This includes building a compelling business case using tools such as environmental scanning to identify opportunities and threats. Senior leaders may also need to become well versed in risk management practices to identify opportunities to mitigate risk to their teams and the organization while at the same time contributing to CSR efforts.

The employee value proposition (EVP) mentioned in the "Talent Acquisition" section earlier has both strategic and operational impact in that it serves to attract and retain qualified talent. When employees are given a voice in deciding how the organization may contribute to addressing social, environmental, and economic issues, it can enhance the EVP. Senior leaders use focus groups and/or committees to gather feedback to use when designing CSR programs that are beneficial to the organization and the EVP. This will require that HR develop the listening competencies described in SHRM's BoCK, where upward communication is encouraged and the feedback systems trusted.

Using the philosophy and policy statements as the foundation for CSR initiatives is another way that HR leaders may apply their skills. These tools outline the commitment that an organization makes and helps HR hold the company accountable to positive outcomes. Transparency when measuring promised efforts is key and a measure of organizational character.

The role of human resources described in this chapter is the responsibility of advanced HR leaders. This means that they need to stay up-to-date on programs that promote well-being, fair wages, skills development, and ethical business practices, and then advocate for their integration into the organization.

Relationship-building is another core competency that will be utilized to affect positive change. For the purposes of the SCP, this includes coordinating with other business leaders, inside and outside of the company. For HR teams to be trusted, they must model behaviors that they seek in others by volunteering in the community and leading strategy sessions to identify relevant CSR initiatives.

Summary

Corporate social responsibility is defined as a set of initiatives designed to address the social, economic, and environmental needs of organizational stakeholders. These stakeholders include the individuals, groups, and ecosystem factors that drive joint survival.

Integrating CSR into business practices will be most successful when the initiatives align with organizational results. The benefits of CSR activities may be strategic, operational, or financial, and they may present as monetary (increased sales) or nonmonetary (enhanced employee value proposition) rewards. In addition to communicating the benefits of CSR, crafting programs that link prosperity and provide shared value is another way to engage organizational leaders and teams successfully.

The need for individual and corporate ethical behavior cannot be underestimated. This functional area addresses stakeholders that are most at risk and thus requires champions with character. Sustainable business practices, for example, should be focused on not just profit, but on people and the planet as well.

HR has an important opportunity to influence these initiatives throughout many of their systems, including business strategy, talent acquisition, risk management, total rewards, and learning and development.

Key Terms

Corporate citizenship

Corporate governance

Profits

Shareholders

Social justice

Exam Essentials

Understand key CSR issues and benefits.   Issues of corporate social responsibility exist at local, national, and global levels. HR must understand the scope and impact of these issues in order to engage leaders and employees in implementing the CSR initiatives. This includes deputizing employees as volunteers to represent the organization in community events.

Differentiate between corporate social responsibility, corporate citizenship, and corporate shared value.   Corporate social responsibility initiatives exist to take care of, and in some cases repair, harm that has occurred to stakeholders. Corporate citizenship is a commitment to behave in a manner that does not cause harm. Corporate shared value is the premise that CSR issues are opportunities to link company success with social progress.

Be able to guide your teams toward sustainable business practices.   Sustainability is the idea of building business practices that can be maintained over time and to preserve the availability of resources. HR is responsible for identifying and promoting opportunities to engage in responsible business practices to sustain profits, people, and the planet.

Review Questions

1. Fill in the blank: The more _____ an organization is with its stakeholders, the more likely they will need to depend on each other's success for mutual survival.
   - **A.** Divided
   - **B.** Connected
   - **C.** Engaged
   - **D.** Entrenched

2. In order to achieve the success of CSR initiatives, gaining the commitment of resources is most likely necessary from which of the following organizational members?
   - **A.** Leadership
   - **B.** Government
   - **C.** Communities
   - **D.** Employees

3. Which of the following is the *best* example of a force that affects all industries in all nations?
   - **A.** UBI
   - **B.** Violence against women
   - **C.** Poverty
   - **D.** Climate change

4. Which of the following may be *best* interpreted as an economic, social, and environmental challenge facing businesses today?
   - **A.** Lack of infrastructure
   - **B.** Infectious disease
   - **C.** Overpopulation
   - **D.** All of the above

5. The primary difference between CSR and corporate citizenship is which of the following?
   - **A.** CSR is focused on social, economic, and environmental issues, and citizenship is focused on compliance.
   - **B.** CSR is focused on social issues, whereas citizenship is focused on environmental issues.
   - **C.** CSR is focused on environmental issues, whereas citizenship is focused on ethical issues.
   - **D.** There is no real distinction between CSR and citizenship.

6. Which of the following strategies may be used by HR to support sustainable people practices?
   - **A.** Hazard communication
   - **B.** Paying fair wages
   - **C.** Human rights activism
   - **D.** All of the above

7. Why is it important for organizations to align business strategy with CSR strategies?

   A. To be good stewards of resources

   B. To drive profit and value

   C. To convince leaders to engage

   D. To address unfair systems

8. You recently began a project designed to define, refine, or add tasks that are sustainable to each organizational job. Doing so will allow you to reduce the consumption of resources over time. The project has required that you collaborate with other business leaders, and in some cases, shift job responsibilities between employees to ensure that all roles share a focus on sustainable business practices. Which of the following is most likely your highest priority?

   A. Reduce costs

   B. Protect organizational assets

   C. Enhance the EVP

   D. Restructure work

9. Increased brand awareness, modeled ethical behaviors, and an improved EVP are all examples of what type of organizational benefit to corporate social responsibility efforts?

   A. Strategic

   B. Operational

   C. Financial

   D. All of the above

10. Which of the following is an expected standard of behavior for a human resource professional when undertaking a volunteerism initiative?

   A. Recruit volunteers.

   B. Take a leadership role in the community.

   C. Communicate the mental health benefits of service work.

   D. All of the above.

Chapter 14

U.S. Employment Laws and Regulations

Exam Notables

It seems that every day brings a new challenge when it comes to navigating the hundreds of laws that apply to the workplace. The U.S. courts offer insights into the legal trends that affect the workplace today. Consider that Civil Rights filings rose by 7 percent, lawsuits for violations of the Americans with Disabilities Act (ADA) increased by 28 percent, and defendants charged with marijuana offenses dropped by 26 percent (Federal Judicial Caseload Statistics, 2019). This does not reflect numbers at a state level. These examples demonstrate that *compliance* drives HR efforts in the areas of compensation, employee relations, safety and health, equal employment opportunity, leave and benefits, and general risk management practices. This could be why SHRM's BoCK summarizes this functional area as follows:

> . . .the knowledge and application of all relevant laws and regulations
> in the United States relating to employment—provisions that set
> the parameters and limitations for each HR functional area and for
> organizations overall.

This chapter serves as a guide to understanding the key components of the major employment-related labor laws.

The SHRM Exam Objectives

SHRM's Body of Competency and Knowledge (BoCK) not only summarizes this functional area, but also defines the proficiency indicators and key concepts. No matter your career level, pay special attention to the exam concepts defined "For All HR Professionals" and the "Key Concepts." If seeking the SHRM-SCP designation, you must expand your efforts to include those labeled "For Advanced HR Professionals."

THE SHRM-CP EXAM AND SHRM-SCP EXAM OBJECTIVES COVERED IN THIS CHAPTER INCLUDE THE FOLLOWING:

✓ **For All HR Professionals**

- Maintains a current working knowledge of relevant domestic and global employment laws.

- Ensures that HR programs, practices, and policies align and comply with laws and regulations.

- Coaches employees at all levels in understanding and avoiding illegal and noncompliant HR-related behaviors (e.g., illegal terminations or discipline, unfair labor practices).

- Brokers internal or external legal services for interpretation of employment laws.

✓ **For Advanced HR Professionals**

- Maintains current, expert knowledge of relevant domestic and global employment laws.

- Establishes and monitors criteria for organizational compliance with laws and regulations.

- Educates and advises senior leadership on HR-related legal and regulatory compliance issues.

- Oversees fulfillment of compliance requirements for HR programs, practices, and policies.

- Ensures that HR technologies facilitate compliance and reporting requirements (e.g., tracking employee accidents, safety reports).

✓ **Key Concepts**

- Compensation

    - EXAMPLES

        - Employee Retirement Income Security Act of 1974 (ERISA); Fair Labor Standards Act of 1938 (FLSA; Wage-Hour Bill; Wagner-Connery Wages and Hours Act and amendments;

        - Equal Pay Act of 1963 (amending FLSA);

        - Lilly Ledbetter Fair Pay Act of 2009; Ledbetter v. Goodyear Tire & Rubber Co. (2007).

- **Employee Relations**

  - **EXAMPLES**

    - **Labor Management Relations Act of 1947 (LMRA);**

    - **Taft- Hartley Act;**

    - **National Labor Relations Act of 1935 (NLRA); Wagner Act; Wagner-Connery Labor Relations Act;**

    - **NLRB v. Weingarten (1975);**

    - **Lechmere, Inc. v. NLRB (1992).**

- **Job Safety and Health**

  - **EXAMPLES**

    - **Drug-Free Workplace Act of 1988;**

    - **Guidelines on Sexual Harassment;**

    - **Occupational Safety and Health Act of 1970;**

    - **Equal Employment Opportunity.**

  - **EXAMPLES**

    - **Age Discrimination in Employment Act of 1967 (ADEA) and amendments;**

    - **Americans with Disabilities Act of 1990 (ADA) and amendments;**

    - **Civil Rights Acts;**

    - **Equal Employment Opportunity Act of 1972;**

    - **Uniform Guidelines on Employee Selection Procedures (1978) (29 CFR Part 1607);**

    - **Griggs v. Duke Power Co. (1971);**

    - **Phillips v. Martin Marietta Corp. (1971).**

- **Leave and Benefits**

  - **EXAMPLES**

    - **Family and Medical Leave Act of 1993 (FMLA; expanded 2008, 2010);**

    - **Patient Protection and Affordable Care Act (ACA; "Obamacare");**

    - **National Federation of Independent Business v. Sebelius (2012);**

    - **Miscellaneous Protection Laws.**

- **EXAMPLES**

  - **Employee Polygraph Protection Act of 1988;**

  - **Genetic Information Nondiscrimination Act of 2008 (GINA).**

The Regulatory Environment

> Democracy cannot work unless it is honored in the factory as well as the
> polling booth; men cannot truly be free in body and spirit unless their
> freedom extends into places where they earn their daily bread.
>
> *Senator Robert Wagner as he introduced*
> *the National Labor Relations Act (NLRA) of 1935*

As the quote implies, politics and the rule of law have been partners with industry for
many years. Just as a society develops standards of conduct related to governing a body,
it stands to reason that social movements will also drive change to the workplace where
so many Americans spend their waking hours. In fact, understanding the context of the
social movements of the time bills were introduced gives us a key perspective on the intent
behind the rule.

We are living history right now as the social climate drives even more change at work. In
this way, we can anticipate governance over safely working at home, or increasing diversity
by requiring women to serve on boards of directors and many other social forces that will
drive policymaking.

These changes through regulation may come about in multiple ways:

Administrative Regulations   These are created and enforced by regulatory
agencies, such as the Equal Employment Opportunity Commission or the Internal
Revenue Service.

Common/Case Law   Case law are rules that are established through the judicial
system and based on a judge's interpretation and application of existing laws. An
example is *Griggs vs. Duke Power*, which established that all preemployment tests,
including the high school diploma requirement, must be job-related and nondiscriminatory in both intent and effect.

Executive Orders   These are regulations signed into law by the president of the United
States without explicit approval from Congress. Executive Orders apply only to federal workers, such as Executive Order 11246, which prohibits federal contractors with
contracts over $10,000 from discriminatory hiring practices. This order also requires
affected contractors to take affirmative action.

Federal Laws   These are regulations passed by Congress and signed by the president of
the United States. Federal laws apply to all 50 states, and can apply to federal workers

or private employers, publicly traded companies, or those with just one employee. These include the major labor laws such as Title VII of the Civil Rights Act of 1964, the Fair Labor Standards Act, and The Americans with Disabilities Act.

State Laws   Statutes passed by state legislatures apply only within the state borders. State laws must meet or exceed the federal equivalent when one exists. The U.S. Constitution grants supremacy to federal law—that is, federal law supersedes the states. However, state laws all must meet or exceed federal requirements. If there is conflict, it is a best practice to err on the side that gives greater protection to the employee.

HR practices have evolved to keep pace with the regulatory environment. It is not enough simply to understand the mechanics of the law; HR professionals must be able to advise organizations on the risk of taking or not taking action.

Human resources is often called upon to train team members and supervisors on appropriate behaviors so that violations do not occur. This training is especially important for supervisors and managers who are considered agents acting on behalf of the company. This applies any time a supervisor is making an *employment-related decision* such as hiring, firing, promoting, making decisions about pay, or selecting who receives training opportunities.

Firing employees comes with particular risks for unlawful or wrongful termination. The Equal Employment Opportunity Commission (EEOC) gives several reasons that an employee termination may be deemed "unlawful":

Violation of Employment Contract   The common-law doctrine of at-will employment states that in an employment relationship, either party can terminate the agreement at any time and for any reason, with or without notice to each other. Employment-at-will does not apply when there is an express, written employment contract that outlines the terms and conditions of employment, including reasons for termination. In addition to a written contract, there are other exceptions to the doctrine of at-will employment:

Implied Contract   The employee had reason to believe they could only be terminated for cause, such as a record of positive performance reviews or statements from supervisors.

Public Policy   The at-will doctrine does not apply if an employee is exercising a right under the law, such as taking time off to vote or refusing to break the law on behalf of the employer.

Covenant of Good Faith and Fair Dealing   This exception speaks to the expectation that employees should be treated fairly in employment. An employer may violate this covenant if they fire a salesperson to avoid paying a large commission or terminating an employee to avoid fully vesting in a retirement account.

Termination as a Form of Revenge or Retaliation   Charges of retaliation remain high on the list of most charges filed with the EEOC against an employer. The law finds that employees have the right to talk about their dissatisfaction with an employer. If an employee complains about wages or is a *whistleblower* (reports employer wrongdoing) and is terminated as a result, they will have a claim of wrongful termination based on retaliatory practices.

Termination as a Result of Harassment   The EEOC enforces several labor laws that guarantee employees the right to a workplace that is free from harassing and abusive behaviors. Reporting the harassment or being pressured to quit (constructive discharge) is a form of unlawful termination.

Workplace Discrimination Leading to Wrongful Termination   Labor law is also clear that employment-related decisions cannot be made on the basis of protected class conditions, such as race, age, or sexual orientation. If an employee is terminated because of these protected class characteristics, they would have a legitimate claim of wrongful termination.

HR professionals should take steps to ensure that all supervisors and team members receive training on these concepts. HR must then support a culture that holds team members accountable for their behaviors through coaching, discipline, demotion, or termination when appropriate.

With more than 80 percent of U.S. businesses having less than 100 employees (sbecouncil.org), it is possible that you are reading this as an HR department of one. For this reason, you will need to develop external resources, preferably the labor attorney who will be called in to act on your organization's behalf when (not if) the need arises.

Laws Enforced by the Equal Employment Opportunity Commission

The *U.S. Equal Employment Opportunity Commission (EEOC)* is responsible for enforcing federal laws that make it illegal to discriminate against a job applicant or an employee because of the person's race, color, religion, sex (including pregnancy, transgender status, and sexual orientation), national origin, age (40 or older), disability, or genetic information.

Most employers with at least 15 employees are covered by EEOC laws (20 employees in age discrimination cases). Most labor unions and employment agencies are also covered.

The laws apply to all types of work situations and employment-related decisions, including hiring, firing, promotions, training, wages, and benefits.

Americans with Disabilities Act

Employer Size: 15 or more employees

Disability discrimination occurs when an employer or other entity covered by Title 1 of the Americans with Disabilities Act treats a qualified individual with a disability who is an employee or applicant unfavorably because they have a disability. Disability discrimination also occurs when an applicant or employee is treated less favorably because they have a history of a disability (such as a past history of cancer), is perceived to have a physical or mental impairment, or is believed to have a transitory condition, one not expected to last 6 months.

The law requires an employer to provide *reasonable workplace accommodation* to an employee or job applicant with a disability, unless doing so would cause *undue hardship*—that is, significant difficulty or expense.

The law also protects people from discrimination based on their relationship with a person with a disability. For example, it is illegal to discriminate against someone because their child has a disability that may require care.

Federal employees and applicants are covered by the Rehabilitation Act of 1973 rather than the Americans with Disabilities Act. The protections, however, are the same.

Civil Rights Act of 1964

Employer Size: 15 or more employees

Title VII of the Civil Rights Act was passed to provide equal opportunity in the work-place. This law is considered to be the foundation from which all other antidiscrimination laws are built. It is unlawful to discriminate against any employee or applicant for employment because of race or color, religion, sex, national origin, and most recently, sexual orientation. This applies to any employment-related decision such as hiring, termination, or promotion. Title VII also prohibits employment decisions based on stereotypes and assumptions about abilities, traits, or the performance of individuals of certain racial groups.

Title VII prohibits both intentional discrimination and neutral job policies that disproportionately exclude protected-class groups and that are not job-related. The *Uniform Guidelines on Employee Selection Procedures (UGESP)* were created to help employers develop selection tests that are *reliable* (consistent over time) and *valid* (predict what the tests say it will predict) predictors of success on the job. It is a useful resource for employers that can be found at uniformguidelines.com.

The original text of Title VII did not explicitly prohibit discrimination on the basis of age or pregnancy. For these reasons, Title VII was amended by the following acts:

Age Discrimination in Employment Act

Employer Size: 20 or more employees

The Age Discrimination in Employment Act (ADEA) prohibits treating an applicant or employee less favorably because they are over the age of 40. It is not illegal for an employer to favor an older worker over a younger one, even if both workers are age 40 or older.

Pregnancy Discrimination Act

Employer Size: 15 or more employees

The Pregnancy Discrimination Act (PDA) forbids discrimination based on pregnancy when it comes to any aspect of employment, including hiring; firing; pay; job assignments; promotions; layoff; training; fringe benefits, such as leaves of absence and health insurance; and any other term or condition of employment. The PDA requires parity, meaning that an employer does not have to offer more to a pregnant worker; rather, the employer simply must offer the same as how other, similarly situated employees are treated.

When making a decision such as hiring, selection for training, promotion, or benefits, consider the "but for" doctrine—that is, would a protected class worker be treated differently "but for" the condition? If the answer is yes, an employer should reconsider the action.

Genetic Information Nondiscrimination Act

Employer Size: 15 or more employees

The *Genetic Information Nondiscrimination Act (GINA)* prohibits the use of genetic information in making employment decisions and restricts employers from requesting, requiring, or purchasing genetic information. It also requires that employers who do receive or have access to this information follow strict confidentiality rules.

(

Laws Enforced/Administered by the Occupational Safety and Health Administration

The Occupational Safety and Health Administration (OSHA) is responsible for enforcing the safety standards of the Occupational Safety and Health Act (OSHA), which exists to accomplish the following:

> . . .assure safe and healthful working conditions for working men and women; by authorizing enforcement of the standards developed under the Act; by assisting and encouraging the States in their efforts to assure safe and healthful working conditions; by providing for research, information, education, and training in the field of occupational safety and health; and for other purposes.

The Occupational Safety and Health Act created the Occupational Safety and Health Administration and the National Institute for Occupational Safety and Health (NIOSH).

Occupational Safety and Health Act

Employer Size: All employers

OSHA standards fall into four categories: General Industry, Construction, Maritime, and Agriculture. OSHA issues standards for a wide variety of workplace hazards. Where there are no specific OSHA standards, employers must comply with the General Duty clause, which states that all employers have a general duty to provide a workplace free from hazards—even if an OSHA standard does not exist for that hazard.

The most frequently cited OSHA violations continue to be the following:

- Fall Protection (Construction standards)
- Hazard Communication (General Industry standards)
- Scaffolding (Construction standards)
- Lockout/TagOut (General Industry standards)
- Respiratory Protection (General Industry standards)
- Ladder Safety (Construction standards)
- Powered Industrial Trucks (General Industry standards)
- Fall Protection (General Industry standards)
- Machinery/Machine Guards (General Industry standards)
- Eye & Face Protection (General Industry standards)

Regardless of which standards apply to you, compliance with OSHA always begins by having a written plan, such as an Injury and Illness Prevention plan, an Emergency Response plan, or a Hazard Communication plan. Although fundamentally about preventing injuries, accidents, and near-miss incidents, requirements for all OSHA mandated plans include educating employees through training, hazard identification, hazard abatement, and prompt investigations.

National Institute for Occupational Safety and Health

Employer Size: N/A

The *National Institute for Occupational Safety and Health* is considered a nonregulatory agency that was created by the Occupational Safety and Health Act but administered through the Centers for Disease Control. Their mission is as follows:

> To develop new knowledge in the field of occupational safety and health and to transfer that knowledge into practice.

NIOSH has three main goals:

- Conducting research to reduce worker illness and injury and to advance worker well-being.

- Promoting safe and healthy workers through interventions, recommendations, and capacity building

- Enhancing worker safety and health through global collaborations

NIOSH has data available on the efficacy of back braces, minimum standards for safety footwear, best practices on how to prevent needlestick injuries in a healthcare setting, how to properly select and fit respiratory devices, and so forth. The list is comprehensive and, thus, an excellent resource for HR professionals that can be found at https://www.cdc.gov/niosh/index.htm.

Whistleblower Protection

Employer Size: All employers

The Occupational Safety and Health Administration is also charged with enforcing *whistleblower* protections. These protections prohibit retaliation against employees who complain about unsafe or unhealthful conditions or exercise other rights under the Occupational Safety and Health Act. Each law has a filing deadline, varying from 30 days to 180 days, which starts when the retaliatory action occurs.

A whistleblower complaint must have four key elements:

- The employee engaged in activity protected by the whistleblower protection law(s) (such as reporting a violation of law).

- The employer knew about, or suspected, that the employee engaged in the protected activity.

- The employer took an adverse action against the employee.

- The employee's protected activity motivated or contributed to the adverse action.

Laws Administered by the Office of Workers' Compensation Programs

The Office of Workers' Compensation Programs (OWCP) exists to administer claims under the Federal Employees' Compensation Act and the Longshore and Harbor Workers' Compensation Act. They provide benefits to employees who have been injured on the job.

Federal Employees' Compensation Act

Applies to: All federal employees
  The Federal Employees' Compensation Act (FECA) made comprehensive workers' compensation benefits under this act available to federal employees, the Peace Corps, and AmeriCorps VISTA volunteers.
  Benefits available under FECA include wage replacement for permanent or partial disability, medical costs for care, and vocational rehabilitation/training.

Longshore and Harbor Workers' Compensation Act

Applies to: All maritime workers and non-maritime workers if they perform their work on navigable water and their injuries occur there
  The *Longshore and Harbor Workers' Compensation Act* provides for compensation and medical care to certain maritime employees (including longshore workers and harbor workers, such as ship repairers, shipbuilders, and shipbreakers) as well as to qualified survivors should their work result in the death of a worker.

Laws Administered by the National Labor Relations Board and the Office of Labor-Management Standards

The United States has a long and troubled history with organized labor, although it certainly has evolved over time to be more productive in certain industries. The development of works councils and *labor cooperatives* have made great strides in developing mutually beneficial agreements to ensure the health of both employers and covered members.
  The relationship between the employer and the union, and the union and its members, are covered by the trifecta of labor relations laws: the National Labor Relations Act (NLRA), the Labor Management Relations Act (LMRA), and the Labor Management Reporting and Disclosure Act (LMRDA).

National Labor Relations Act

Employer Size: Most private sector employers

Also known as the Wagner Act, the National Labor Relations Act (NLRA) was enacted by Congress to protect the rights of employees and to encourage collective bargaining. In short, the NLRA established a worker's right to form a labor/trade union. An employer violates these rights by committing an *unfair labor practice (ULP)*, which includes the following:

- Interference, restraint, or coercion to vote against union representation
- Employer domination or support of a labor organization
- Discrimination on the basis of labor activity
- Retaliation for exercising rights to organize
- Refusal to bargain in good faith

The acronym TIPS is an easy way to remember ULPs. When there is union activity, employers should not do the following:

- **T**hreaten
- **I**nterrogate
- **P**romise
- **S**py

The NLRA also established the workers right to *strike*, which is a work stoppage used to put pressure on the employer to make a change or concession. Strikes are a form of concerted (collective) protected activity.

The lawfulness of a strike may depend on the object, purpose, timing, or conduct of strikers.

Employees who strike for a lawful object may be considered economic strikers or unfair labor practices strikers. Both keep their status as employees, however, with differing reinstatement rights.

Economic strikers exist when they are striking higher wages, shorter hours, or better working conditions. Economic strikers can be replaced by their employer if the employer has hired bona fide permanent replacements who are filling their jobs.

Employees who strike to protest an unfair labor practice committed by their employer are called unfair labor practice strikers. Such strikers cannot be fired or permanently replaced.

Labor Management Relations Act

Applies to: Most private sector employers

Also known as the Taft-Hartley Act, the Labor Management Relations Act (LMRA) was passed as an amendment to the NLRA. Its purpose was to balance the rights of employers with the rights granted by the NLRA to unions.

There are several key terms for the exam that can be explored through the filter of the LMRA:

Closed Shop   Employees are required to join a union as a condition of employment/continued employment. Closed shops were declared illegal under the LMRA.

Union Shop   A union shop is one where the employer signs an agreement allowing unions to require union membership after the 30th day of employment. Union shops remain lawful under the LMRA.

Featherbedding   A security practice, featherbedding occurs when employers are required to pay for work/workers that are unnecessary or redundant. This practice was declared unlawful under the LMRA.

Secondary Boycotts   Occurs as a form of solidarity where a union that has a primary dispute with one employer pressures a neutral employer to stop doing business with the first employer. Secondary boycotts were also declared unlawful.

Additionally, supervisors were excluded from bargaining units, and unions were prohibited from charging exorbitant initiation fees and membership dues.

Just as employers may commit an unfair labor practice, so too may a union. Examples of union ULPs include the following:

- Mass picketing in such numbers that nonstriking employees are physically barred from entering the facility
- Acts of force or violence on the picket line or in connection with a strike
- Threats to do bodily injury to nonstriking employees
- Threats to employees that they will lose their jobs unless they support the union's activities
- Statement to employees who oppose the union that the employees will lose their jobs if the union wins a majority
- Fining or expelling members for crossing a picket line that is unlawful under the act or that violates a no-strike agreement

The National Labor Relations Board is responsible for enforcing the NLRA and its amendment, the LMRA. Employees may file a ULP charge with the NLRB against the employer or the union.

The Office of Labor-Management Standards (OMS) will investigate criminal and civil complaints filed by members against their unions under the Labor-Management Reporting and Disclosure Act (LMRDA).

Labor-Management Reporting and Disclosure Act

Applies to: Unions except those solely representing state, county, and municipal employees

Also known as the Landrum-Griffin Act, the Labor-Management Reporting and Disclosure Act (LMRDA) addresses the relationship between a union and its members. Fundamentally, the LMRDA established a bill of rights for union members as follows:

- Union members have equal rights to nominate candidates for union office, vote in union elections, and participate in union meetings. They may also meet with other members and express any opinions.

- Unions may impose assessments and raise dues only by democratic procedures.

- Unions must afford members a full and fair hearing of charges against them.

- Unions must inform their members about the provisions of the LMRDA.

- Members may enforce rights through a private suit against the union but may be required to exhaust internal union remedies for up to 4 months before filing suit.

- Union members and nonunion employees may receive and inspect collective bargaining agreements. This right may be enforced by the individual or by the Secretary of Labor.

The LMRDA also protects union funds from embezzlement and requires labor organizations to file annual financial and other accountability reports.

 The three labor laws related to unions were written for a very specific reason:

NLRA: Gave employees the rights to form unions; first passed in 1935.

LMRA: Balanced the rights of employers with the rights of unions; passed as an amendment to the NLRA in 1947.

LMRDA: Protected union members from corrupt union practices, passed in 1959.

In addition to the trilogy of laws listed above, there have also been significant court cases involving the NLRB. For the exams, you should be familiar with the findings of *Lechmere, Inc. v. NLRB* and *National Labor Relations Board v. J. Weingarten, Inc.*

Lechmere, Inc. v. NLRB

At issue in the Lechmere, Inc. v. NLRB case was whether or not a large retail employer committed an unfair labor practice by not allowing a union to organize on company property. The union argued that the employees were not accessible any other way because they lived over a large metropolitan area, and, the employer was therefore violating their right to organize by not giving the union access to them while at work (specifically, the parking lot owned in part by the store). The NLRB originally ruled against the employer. The Supreme Court, on appeal, overturned the NLRB's decision, noting that the NLRA protects an employee's right to organize, not the unions' right to violate trespassing laws, and that the union failed to demonstrate that the employees could not be contacted any way other than on company/private property.

National Labor Relations Board v. J. Weingarten, Inc.

The NLRB had established in previous cases that union workers had a right to representation from their union in any situation that could lead to discipline. Weingarten, a food service business, had recently hired an investigator to determine if a store employee had stolen a box of chicken. During the investigation, the employee requested union representation several times and was denied. Although eventually cleared of any wrongdoing, the employee filed a grievance with the union, who then filed a ULP against Weingarten. In NLRB v. J. Weingarten, Inc., the Supreme Court found for the NLRB, noting that any inquiry into employee behavior could have a collective impact, and thus union representation should be present.

For a time, the right to representation at a meeting that may lead to discipline or termination was extended to all employees, whether or not their employer was unionized. The NLRB has since reversed itself on this, and only unionized workers maintain this right. Nevertheless, it is an issue for HR pros to keep track of.

Laws Administered by the Wage and Hour Division

The U.S. Department of Labor (DOL) has several branches responsible for the administration of labor laws. The Wage and Hour Division (WHD) is dedicated strictly to interpreting and enforcing laws related to compensation. Wages are considered a fundamental right of workers, and so it is no surprise that the administration of wages and benefits is highly regulated.

Figures 14.1, 14.2, and 14.3 are examples from the WHD's Twitter feed of the types of enforcement actions and costs employers face for violations.

FIGURE 14.1   WHD Overtime Violations

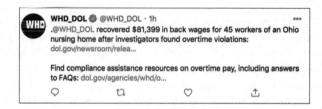

FIGURE 14.2   WHD FLSA Violations

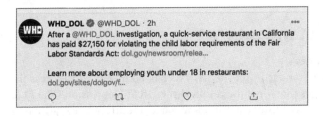

FIGURE 14.3   WHD Prevailing Wage Violations

Davis-Bacon Act

Employer Size: N/A

Contractors and subcontractors with federally funded/assisted contracts in excess of $2,000 must pay workers at least the local prevailing wages. This applies to projects involving the construction, alteration, or repair (including painting and decorating) of public buildings or public works.

Prevailing wage is the combination of the basic hourly rate and any fringe benefits that are listed in the wage determination included in the contract. The prevailing wage may be paid as cash wages or by a combination of cash wages and employer-provided bona fide fringe benefits. Prevailing wages, including fringe benefits, must be paid on all hours worked on the site of the work.

A *wage determination* is the listing of wage rates and fringe benefit rates for each classification of laborers and mechanics in a geographic area for a particular type of construction such as building, heavy, highway, or residential.

Employees who believe their employer has not paid them in accordance with the requirements of the Davis Bacon Act would generally file a whistleblower claim under the False Claims Act.

Employee Polygraph Protection Act

Employer Size: All employers

The Employee Polygraph Protection Act (EPPA) bars most employers from using lie detectors on employees, but it permits polygraph tests in limited circumstances. These circumstances include using polygraph tests for security roles and jobs where drugs are being handled (such as cannabis shops). Employees must be given written notice at least 48 hours in advance and be notified of why they are being asked to submit to questioning.

Fair Labor Standards Act

Employer Size: Varies

The Fair Labor Standards Act (FLSA) was passed in 1938 to address the social and economic challenges that were the result of the Great Depression. The FLSA addressed three major issues: establishing a minimum wage, requiring overtime pay, and regulating child labor.

Employers covered by the FLSA may be determined in two different ways:

1. **Enterprise Coverage**

   Employees who work for certain "enterprises" are covered by the FLSA. These enterprises, which must have at least two employees, are:

   a. those that have an annual dollar volume of sales or business done of at least $500,000

   b. hospitals, businesses providing medical or nursing care for residents, schools and preschools, and government agencies

2. **Individual Coverage**

   Even when there is no enterprise coverage, employees are protected by the FLSA if their work regularly involves commerce between states (interstate commerce).

For non-exempt workers, covered employers must pay at least the federal minimum wage and overtime pay of one-and-one-half-times the regular rate of pay for any hours worked over 40 in one week.

 The federal minimum wage has remained flat at $7.25 since 2009, and thus many states have established their own minimum wage requirements. Currently, the highest state wage is about $15.00 an hour. In 2021, the "Raise the Wage Act" was introduced to gradually increase the federal minimum wage to $15.00 by 2025. Written as an amendment to the FLSA, the bill was not passed by Congress in 2021.

For nonagricultural operations, the FLSA restricts the hours that children under age 16 can work and forbids the employment of children under age 18 in certain jobs. For agricultural operations, it prohibits the employment of children under age 16 during school hours and in certain jobs deemed too dangerous.

The FLSA has had several amendments over the years, the most relevant for our purposes being the Equal Pay Act of 1963 and the Portal-to-Portal Act.

Equal Pay Act

Employer Size: All employers

The Equal Pay Act (EPA) requires that men and women in the same workplace be given equal pay for equal work. The jobs need not be identical, but they must be substantially equal. Job responsibilities (not titles) determine whether jobs are substantially equal. All forms of pay are covered by this law, including wages, benefits, overtime, bonuses, stock options, profit sharing and bonus plans, life insurance, vacation and holiday pay, allowances, and travel expenses. If there is an inequality in wages between men and women, employers may not reduce the wages of either sex to equalize their pay.

An individual alleging a violation of the EPA may go directly to court and is not required to file an EEOC charge beforehand.

Portal-to-Portal Act

Employer Size: Virtually all employers

The Portal-to-Portal Act amended the FLSA specifically to clarify the definition of a "compensable workday." Generally, commute time is not compensable, but travel time on behalf of the employer is compensable. This includes traveling from one place of work to a secondary location—from one portal to the next portal. Time spent changing into a mandatory work uniform is compensable, although other preliminary activities may not be. Travel time to attend voluntary training is not compensable.

Family and Medical Leave Act

Employer Size: 50 or more employees

The *Family and Medical Leave Act (FMLA)* entitles eligible employees of covered employers to take unpaid, job-protected leave for up to 12 weeks. Qualifying events include the following:

- The birth of a child and to care for the newborn child within one year of birth
- The placement with the employee of a child for adoption or foster care, and to care for the newly placed child within one year of placement
- To care for the employee's spouse, child, or parent who has a serious health condition
- A serious health condition that makes the employee unable to perform the essential functions of their job
- Any qualifying exigency arising out of the fact that the employee's spouse, son, daughter, or parent is a covered military member on "covered active duty"
- 26 workweeks of leave during a single 12-month period to care for a covered service member with a serious injury or illness if the eligible employee is the service member's spouse, son, daughter, parent, or next of kin (military caregiver leave)

Covered employees are also entitled to the continuation of group health insurance coverage under the same terms and conditions as if the employee had not taken leave.

The FMLA only applies to employers that meet certain criteria. A covered employer must meet one of these criteria:

- Private sector employer with 50 or more employees in 20 or more workweeks in the current or preceding calendar year, including a joint employer or successor in interest to a covered employer

- Public agency, including a local, state, or federal government agency, regardless of the number of employees it employs

- Public or private elementary or secondary school, regardless of the number of employees it employs

Only eligible employees are entitled to take FMLA leave. An eligible employee is one who meets all of the following criteria:

- Works for a covered employer

- Has worked for the employer for at least 12 months

- Has at least 1,250 hours of service for the employer during the 12-month period immediately preceding the leave

- Works at a location where the employer has at least 50 employees within 75 miles

In addition to the federally mandated protections offered by the FMLA, five states have short-term disability requirements that run concurrently with FMLA time off. These states are California, Hawaii, New Jersey, New York, and Rhode Island.

Walsh–Healey Public Contracts Act

Employer Size: N/A

The Walsh–Healey Public Contracts Act has similar provisions as the FLSA, and it applies to companies that work on contracts in excess of $15,000.

The act requires payment of minimum wages that equals the prevailing wage, set standards for overtime compensation, restricts the employment of minors, and creates additional safety and health standards.

Laws Administered by the Mine Safety and Health Administration

As of 2019, there were more than 650,000 mine workers in the United States, all working under highly hazardous conditions. As depicted in Figure 14.4, a 1968 mine explosion in Farmington, West Virginia prompted the federal government to step in and establish the *Mine Safety and Health Administration (MSHA)*. Its purpose is as follows:

> . . . to prevent death, illness, and injury from mining and promote safe and healthful workplaces for U.S. miners.

MSHA enforces safety and health requirements at more than 13,000 mines, investigates mine accidents, and offers mine operators training, technical and compliance assistance.

FIGURE 14.4   1968 mine explosion

Source: The United States Department of Labor

Federal Mine Safety and Health Act

Employer Size: All Mine Operators

The Federal Mine Safety and Health Act holds mine operators responsible for the safety and health of miners. It provides for the setting of mandatory safety and health standards, mandates miners' training requirements, prescribes penalties for violations, and enables inspectors to close dangerous mines. The safety and health standards address several hazardous conditions, including explosive gases, fire, equipment, airborne contaminants, and roof falls, just to name a few.

MSHA also established requirements to address the high incidence of the occupational disease of black lung.

The Mine Improvement and New Emergency Response Act

Employer Size: All Mine Operators

In 2006, another piece of major legislation, the Mine Improvement and New Emergency Response (MINER) Act, was passed in order to expand protections to covered workers. The new regulations cover the following:

- Requires each underground coal mine operator to develop and continuously update a written emergency response plan

- Promotes use of equipment and technology that is currently commercially available

- Requires each mine's emergency response plan to be continuously reviewed, updated, and recertified by MSHA every six months

- Directs the Secretary of Labor to require wireless two-way communications and an electronic tracking system , permitting those on the surface to locate persons trapped underground

- Requires each underground coal mine operator to make available to each mine two experienced mine rescue teams capable of a one-hour response time

- Requires mine operators to notify MSHA within 15 minutes of a death at the mine, or an injury or entrapment at the mine that has a reasonable potential to cause death, and establishes a civil penalty of $5,000 to $60,000 for mine operators who fail to do so

- Requires MSHA to finalize mandatory health and safety standards relating to the sealing of abandoned areas in underground mines

- Requires NIOSH to establish an interagency working group to share technology and technological research and developments that could be used to enhance mine safety and accident response

- Raises the maximum criminal penalty to $250,000 for first offenses and $500,000 for second offenses, and establishes a maximum civil penalty of $220,000 for flagrant violations

- Establishes a Technical Study Panel on the use of belt air and fire-retardant belt materials in underground coal mines

- Gives MSHA the authority to obtain an injunction (shutting down a mine) in cases where the mine operator has refused to pay a final civil penalty assessment

Laws Administered by the Employee Benefits Security Administration

The Employee Benefits Security Administration (EBSA) offers information and assistance on employer-sponsored retirement benefit and health benefit plans. They are responsible for enforcing and educating employers and covered individuals on matters related to the administration of the Employee Retirement Income Security Act.

Employee Retirement Income Security Act

Employer Size: All employers
Employers are not obligated under the law to offer retirement plans; it remains a voluntary benefit. However, once a plan is offered, it is regulated by the Employee Retirement Income Security Act (ERISA). ERISA requires disclosures and other reports to plan members about the details of their plan, in addition to establishing fiduciary responsibility for those who plan and control assets, which can include human resource professionals. A plan fiduciary must act for the well-being of the beneficiary.

ERISA has had two significant amendments: the Consolidated Omnibus Budget Reconciliation Act (COBRA) and the Health Insurance Portability and Accountability Act (HIPAA).

Consolidated Omnibus Budget Reconciliation Act

Employer Size: 20 or more employees
The Consolidated Omnibus Budget Reconciliation Act (COBRA) grants covered employees the right to continue their health insurance coverage after a qualifying event for a limited period of time. A qualifying event includes separation (for any reason other than gross misconduct), reduced hours, death, divorce, and other life events. Employees who elect COBRA coverage are responsible for the entire plan premium and may be charged a 2 percent administrative fee.

Time limits are a critical factor when administering COBRA. The covered employee and eligible dependents must be given at least 60 days to elect coverage. COBRA requires that continuation coverage extend from the date of the qualifying event for a limited period of 18 or 36 months. The length of time depends on the type of qualifying A plan; however, it may provide longer periods of coverage beyond the maximum period required by law.

When the qualifying event is the covered employee's termination of employment or reduction in hours of employment, qualified beneficiaries are entitled to 18 months of continuation coverage. If a qualified beneficiary is eligible for a disability extension, they may be covered for 29 months. Dependents may be granted an 18-month extension (for a total of 36 months) if a secondary qualifying event occurs, such as the death of a covered employee.

Health Insurance Portability and Accountability Act

Employer Size: N/A
The primary function of the Health Insurance Portability and Accountability Act (HIPAA) is to allow employees who change jobs to obtain health insurance even if they or a family member has a preexisting health condition or is pregnant. It does so by prohibiting plans from denying coverage or charging higher premiums to affected individuals. Covered entities include health plans, healthcare clearinghouses, and healthcare providers that electronically transmit health data. Employers must protect the confidentiality of any information gathered from a covered entity.

Patient Protection and Affordable Care Act

Employer Size: 50 or more employees

In 2010, President Barack Obama undertook a healthcare initiative to ensure that all Americans had access to affordable health care. Although the initiative did include provisions for government-subsidized health insurance through state trading centers, it placed a burden on employers to offer affordable health care insurance. The result was the Patient Protection and Affordable Care Act (PPACA), also known as the *ACA* and *Obamacare*.

In addition to requiring that affected employers offer affordable health insurance plans to employees, the PPACA extended the age a dependent could remain on a healthcare plan to age 26 regardless of marital status, prohibited preexisting condition exclusions for children under the age of 19, and required more easy-to-understand summary plan descriptions (SPDs).

Applicable large employers face penalties for failing to provide any insurance at all, and if an offered plan does not provide minimum value (being offered to at least 95 percent of the workforce).

Affected employers must file an annual return with the IRS that describes their healthcare offerings along with other employee data.

Small employers who choose to offer health insurance to their teams may be eligible for a tax credit for up to two years.

Laws Administered by the Department of Homeland Security or the Department of Justice

Complying with immigration laws is a complex task, with multiple enforcement agencies. For example, the Department of Homeland Security (DHS) provides oversight to the U.S. Citizen and Immigration Services (USCIS), the agency responsible for enforcing many immigration laws. The Department of Justice's Civil Rights Division (DJCRD) covers civil rights for immigrants, and the Wage and Hour Division of the Department of Labor investigates and enforces visa classification claims. The laws they share responsibility for are listed next.

H2A Temporary Agricultural Workers

Employer Size: N/A; employers must apply and be approved
  Enforced by the U.S .Citizen and Immigration Services

The Immigration and Nationality Act (INA) regulates the admission of foreign workers into the United States. Under certain conditions, agricultural employers may also be allowed to bring nonimmigrant foreign workers to the United States to perform agricultural labor or services of a temporary or seasonal nature.

Employers must file Form I-129, Petition for a Nonimmigrant Worker, on a prospective worker's behalf.

Immigration and Nationality Act

Employer Size: All employers
   Enforced by Department of Justice
   The Immigration and Nationality Act (INA) requires that employers only hire individuals authorized to work in the United States. INA also prohibits discrimination against those same individuals. Generally, employers are not allowed to treat individuals differently in hiring, firing, or recruitment because of their citizenship status. Citizenship status includes a person's current or prior immigration status. U.S. citizens, U.S. nationals, asylees, refugees, and recent lawful permanent residents are protected class workers under these provisions.
   All employers must verify an employee's employment authorization and identity by completing Form I-9. During the Form I-9 process, a worker must show documentation establishing the worker's identity and permission to work in the United States.

USCIS publishes the M-274 Handbook for Employers. This 51-page document explains the ins and outs of completing Form I-9. The M-274 was last updated in April 2020, and a summary of those revisions can be found in Appendix B.

www.uscis.gov/i-9-central/form-i-9-resources/
handbook-for-employers-m-274/handbook-for-employers-m-274

Employers are not allowed to request more or different documents than are required by law to verify employment eligibility, reject reasonably genuine-looking documents, or specify certain documents over others based on citizenship status or national origin.
   Note that the Wage and Hour Division of the Department of Labor enforces actions related to compliance with the employment obligations of a specific visa classification.
   E-Verify is a government program that verifies a worker's employment eligibility electronically, using information from Form I-9. Sometimes E-Verify does not verify a worker's employment eligibility right away and issues a "tentative non-confirmation" (TNC). If a worker decides to take action in response to a TNC, E-Verify prohibits employers from firing, delaying the employment of, or taking any adverse action against, employees because they are contesting their TNCs.
   Employers sometimes receive notice that an employee's name and Social Security number (SSN) do not match the records on file with either the Social Security Administration or an outside entity drawing on publicly available Social Security number data. SSN no-matches can happen for a number of reasons, including an unreported name change, typos, or inaccurate employer records. Employers should not use the mismatch by itself as a reason for taking any adverse employment action against any worker.

The Immigration Reform and Control Act (IRCA) signed by President Ronald Reagan amended INA, and it created penalties for employers who knowingly hire those who are not authorized to work in the United States.

Miscellaneous Laws and Concepts

In addition to the major federal labor laws listed so far, there are other ancillary components to compliance. In many cases, the following topics are prohibited or regulated through multiple labor laws, executive order, or precedent set through the courts.

Drug Free Workplace Act

Employer Size: N/A

The Drug-Free Workplace Act requires federal agency contractors and grantees to certify that they will provide a drug-free workplace as a pre-condition of receiving a contract or a grant from a federal agency. It is enforced by the agency that awarded the contract. Compliance includes having a written policy, encouraging treatment and recovery of users, and having a system for drug screening.

Garnishment of Wages

Employer Size: N/A

Garnishment of employee wages by employers is regulated under the Consumer Credit Protection Act (CCPA), which is administered by the Wage and Hour Division. A wage garnishment is a court-ordered withholding of an employee's pay to satisfy a debt. These debts may include back taxes, child support, and student loan arrears. Note that in response to the economic challenges caused by the Covid-19 pandemic, the federal government paused any garnishing of wages for student loans that were in collections. Garnishments are enforced by various federal and state agencies.

Harassment

Employer Size: 15 or more employees under Title VII and the ADA; 20 or more employees under the ADEA

Harassment is a form of employment discrimination that violates Title VII of the Civil Rights Act of 1964, the Age Discrimination in Employment Act of 1967 (ADEA), and the Americans with Disabilities Act of 1990 (ADA).

Harassment is unwelcome conduct that is based on race, color, religion, sex (including pregnancy, sexual orientation, and sexual identity), national origin, age (40 or older), disability, or genetic information. Harassment becomes unlawful where (1) enduring the offensive conduct becomes a condition of continued employment or (2) the conduct is severe or pervasive enough to create a work environment that a reasonable person would consider intimidating, hostile, or abusive.

Annoying or obnoxious team members, or single occurrences (unless extremely serious) do not typically rise to the level of harassment under the law. To be unlawful, the conduct must create a work environment that would be intimidating, hostile, or offensive to reasonable people.

Offensive conduct may include, but is not limited to, offensive jokes, slurs, epithets or name calling, physical assaults or threats, intimidation, ridicule or mockery, insults or put-downs, offensive objects or pictures, and interference with work performance. Note the following about harassment:

- The harasser can be the victim's supervisor, a supervisor in another area, an agent of the employer, a coworker, or a non-employee.

- The victim does not have to be the person harassed but can be anyone, such as an observer, affected by the offensive conduct.

- Unlawful harassment may occur without tangible loss, such as loss of wages or termination.

Prevention is the best tool to eliminate harassment in the workplace. Employers are encouraged to take appropriate steps to prevent and correct unlawful harassment. They should clearly communicate to employees that unwelcome harassing conduct will not be tolerated. They can do this by establishing an effective complaint or grievance process, providing anti-harassment training to their managers and employees, and taking immediate and appropriate action when an employee complains. Employers should strive to create an environment in which employees feel free to raise concerns and are confident that those concerns will be addressed and have a zero-tolerance policy for retaliation.

Employees are encouraged to inform the harasser directly that the conduct is unwelcome and must stop. Employees should also report harassment to management at an early stage to prevent its escalation.

Lilly Ledbetter Fair Pay Act

Employer Size: N/A

The Lilly Ledbetter Fair Pay Act was the first bill signed into law by President Barack Obama. Lilly Ledbetter was a manager at Goodyear Tire and Rubber Company who experienced pay discrimination—male executives were paid more for the same work based on gender. When she filed a pay discrimination charge with the EEOC, she lost because she was outside the 180-day statute of limitations. The Lilly Ledbetter Fair Pay of 2009 amended the time restrictions by establishing a reset—the 180-day statute of limitations resets at the end of every pay period.

LGBTQ Sex-Based Discrimination

Employer Size: 15 or more employees

Title VII of the Civil Rights Act of 1964 prohibits discrimination because of an "individual's race, color, religion, sex, and national origin." Sex discrimination involves treating someone (an applicant or employee) unfavorably because of that person's sex. Sex discrimination against an individual includes treatment based on gender identity or transgender status, or because of sexual orientation.

In *Bostock v. Clayton County, Georgia*, the Supreme Court held that firing individuals because of their sexual orientation or transgender status violates Title VII's prohibition on discrimination because of sex. As the Court explained, "Discrimination based on homosexuality or transgender status necessarily entails discrimination based on sex; the first cannot happen without the second."

For example, if an employer fires an employee because she is a woman who is married to a woman but would not do the same to a man married to a woman, the employer is taking an action because of the employee's sex. Similarly, if an employer fires an employee because that person was identified as male at birth but uses feminine pronouns and identifies as a female, the employer is taking action against the individual because of sex since the action would not have been taken but for the fact the employee was originally identified as male.

Many states have enacted their own provisions related to LGBTQ discrimination.

Retaliation

Employer Size: 15 or more employees under Title VII and the ADA; 20 or more employees under the ADEA

EEO laws prohibit punishing job applicants or employees for engaging in protected activity. It is unlawful to retaliate against applicants or employees for the following reasons:

- Filing or being a witness in an EEO charge, complaint, investigation, or lawsuit
- Communicating with a supervisor or manager about employment discrimination, including harassment
- Answering questions during an employer investigation of alleged harassment
- Refusing to follow orders that would result in discrimination
- Resisting sexual advances, or intervening to protect others
- Participating in a complaint process
- Requesting accommodation of a disability or for a religious practice
- Asking managers or coworkers about salary information to uncover potentially discriminatory wages

In addition, an employer is not allowed to respond to a complaint in any manner that could discourage someone from resisting or complaining about future discrimination. This includes if an employer does any of the following:

- Reprimands the employee or gives a performance evaluation that is lower than it should be
- Transfers the employee to a less desirable position
- Engages in verbal or physical abuse
- Threatens to make, or actually makes, reports to authorities (such as reporting immigration status or contacting the police)
- Increases scrutiny
- Spreads false rumors; treats a family member negatively
- Makes the person's work more difficult (for example, punishing an employee for an EEO complaint by purposefully changing their work schedule to conflict with family responsibilities)

Sexual Harassment

Employer Size: 15 or more employees

Similar to what was described in the earlier section on LGBTQ rights, it is unlawful to harass a person (an applicant or employee) because of that person's sex.

Harassment can include "sexual harassment" or unwelcome sexual advances, requests for sexual favors, and other verbal or physical harassment of a sexual nature.

Harassment does not have to be of a sexual nature, however, and can include offensive remarks about a person's sex. For example, it is illegal to harass a woman by making offensive comments about female stereotypes.

Both victim and the harasser can be either a woman or a man, and the victim and harasser can be the same sex.

Although the law doesn't prohibit simple teasing, offhand comments, or isolated incidents that are more obnoxious than serious, harassment is illegal when it is so frequent or severe that it creates a hostile or offensive work environment, or when it results in an adverse employment decision (such as the victim being fired or demoted).

The harasser can be the victim's supervisor, a supervisor in another area, a coworker, or someone who is not an employee of the employer, such as a customer, contractor, or vendor.

Worker Adjustment and Retraining Notification Act

Employer Size: 100 or more employees

Although more than half a dozen states have their own requirements for employee notification of mass layoffs, all were based on the federal Workers Adjustment and Retraining Notification Act (WARN). Covered employers are required to provide at least 60 calendar days' advance written notice of a plant closing and mass layoff affecting 50 or more employees at a single site of employment. Unforeseeable business circumstances, failing companies, and natural disasters provide exception under WARN. WARN violations are enforced by private action in the federal courts.

Retention of Documents

A component for compliance with all labor laws is how long relevant documents should be retained. This is the case so that a record of the actions taken can be used should there be a future dispute and so that employers don't retain a record for too long (when mistakes could then be used against them in future cases).

Table 14.1 takes an at-a-glance look at the major requirements by law. The shortest record retention requirement is one year, and OSHA has the longest employee exposure records of 30 years.

TABLE 14.1   Record-keeping and retention

Regulation	Type of record(s)
Americans with Disabilities Act	Personnel files, including application forms, promotion, involuntary termination, transfers, termination, employment tests, training, rates of pay, and requests for reasonable accommodations, must be kept for at least one year from the date after the record is created or the action described is taken, whichever occurs later.
	All personnel records relating to a charge filed with the EEOC must be retained until disposition of the action.
	Covered employers must always keep a copy of the most recent Form EEO-1 at each unit or headquarters.
Age Discrimination in Employment Act	Employers must keep records containing an employee's name, address, date of birth, occupation, rate of pay, and compensation earned per week. The records must be kept for at least three years from the date of entry.
	The records must be kept for one year after the record is made or the personnel action described is taken, whichever is later.
	Personnel records for persons in temporary positions may only be kept for 90 days after the personnel action.
	If enforcement action is brought against an employer, records must be kept until the final disposition of the action. This includes:
	Records used in hiring (for example, applications, résumés, and responses to job ads).
	Records pertaining to employment decisions (for example, termination, demotion, promotion, transfer, layoff, recall, and selection for training).
	Results from employment tests, job advertisements, training records, and physical exams in connection with any personnel action.
	Benefit plans, written seniority systems, and written merit plans or a written summary of the system must be kept for one year longer than the duration of the plan.

Regulation	Type of record(s)
Davis-Bacon Act	Covered contractors must maintain payroll and basic records for all covered laborers and mechanics during the course of the work and for a period of three years. Records to be maintained include name, address, and Social Security number of each worker.
Employee Polygraph Protection Act	Records related to the event for a minimum of three years from the date the polygraph examination is conducted or from the date the examination is requested if no examination is conducted.
Employee Retirement Income and Security Act	Plan documents, contracts and agreements, participant notices, and compliance documents for at least six years from the date the report was filed.
	Participant-level benefit determinations until the plan has paid all benefits and enough time has passed that the plan won't be audited.
Equal Pay Act	Records of wages, wage rates, job classifications, and other terms and conditions of employment for three years.
Fair Labor Standards Act	Three years for payroll records, collective bargaining agreements, sales, and purchase records.
	Records on which wage computations are based should be retained for two years; for example, timecards and piecework tickets, wage rate tables, work and time schedules, and records of additions to or deductions from wages.
Family Medical Leave Act	Basic payroll and identifying employee data, dates, hours, and documents describing employer policies and employee benefits at the time leave was taken for three years.
GINA	All personnel and employment records made or used, including, but not limited to, requests for reasonable accommodation; application forms submitted by applicants; and records dealing with hiring, promotion, demotion, transfer, layoff or termination, rates of pay, compensation, tenure, selection for training or apprenticeship, or other terms of employment for one year from the date of making the record.
	When an employee is fired, the personnel records must be kept for at least one year from the date of termination.
IRCA	Completed Form I-9 for three years from the date of hire or one year after termination, whichever is later.
LMRDA	Basic information and data, including vouchers, worksheets, receipts, and applicable resolutions five years after the filing of the documents.

TABLE 14.1   Record-keeping and retention *(continued)*

Regulation	Type of record(s)
OSHA	The OSHA 300 Log, the annual summary, and the OSHA Incident Report forms must be retained by employers for five years following the end of the calendar year that these records cover. Employers must retain employee exposure records for the duration of employment plus 30 years. Training records must be retained for three years from the date on which the training occurred, although it is advisable to retain training records for the duration of employment.
Title VII of the Civil Rights Act of 1964	All personnel and employment records made or used, including, but not limited to, requests for reasonable accommodation; application forms submitted by applicants; and records dealing with hiring, promotion, demotion, transfer, layoff or termination, rates of pay, compensation, tenure, selection for training or apprenticeship, or other terms of employment for one year from the date of making the record. When an employee is fired, the personnel records must be kept for at least one year from the date of termination.

SHRM-SCP Only

In addition to understanding all of the laws we have discussed from an operational perspective, senior leaders will be called on to take an elevated *risk management* approach. This includes overseeing the systems to ensure compliance with the least disruption to organizational competitiveness. Planning is one way to do this. For example, www.ready.gov has business continuity plan templates to plan for a disaster or emergency.

Conducting regular HR audits is a method used to manage legal risks. For compliance purposes, an HR audit helps reduce liability. From an effectiveness perspective, an HR audit ensures that the compliance systems are not placing an undue burden on processes, or that policies are not so onerous as to diminish impact. For example, one company had an elevated approval system for employee disciplinary action. The process required that the manager complete the written warning and then send it to corporate HR for review and approval. With more than 500 employees, HR was running about three weeks behind on their review, making the process completely ineffective. A senior leader would understand that training managers on how to take legally compliant disciplinary action, and then spot-auditing documentation, is a much more effective practice. SHRM has an excellent resource on how to conduct HR audits:

www.shrm.org/resourcesandtools/tools-and-samples/toolkits/pages/humanresourceaudits.aspx

Senior HR leaders will also need to take point when a charge is made with a regulatory agency. In some cases, charges come in litigated, meaning that an employee bypassed filing a complaint with a state or federal agency and went straight to a labor attorney. Leaders must monitor progress and engage legal resources to ensure a favorable—or at least less costly—action. This includes modifying current practices to prevent similar issues from happening again.

Many Human Resource Information Systems (HRIS) systems have built-in features for record-keeping. Senior HR leaders should take steps to activate these modules, train all leaders to use them, and then audit for compliance on a periodic basis. For example, documentation of safety training and accidents/incidents is a component of compliance with OSHA laws. Effective HRIS systems have features to log training and upload documentation for easy access should the need arise.

Lobbying is a form of political activism designed to influence government behaviors toward a group's interest. The largest lobbying group on behalf of the practice of human resources is SHRM. They continue to take steps to influence labor laws in the area of overtime, diversity, immigration, and pay equity. HR practitioners may choose to get involved at a local or a regional level.

Summary

Navigating labor laws that originate through the courts or Congress, executive order, or state laws is an important part of an HR professional's day-to-day risk management activities. These activities include training employees and managers, building HR systems that are compliant with all applicable laws, and staying current as laws change and new laws are passed.

Key components to compliance are understanding which laws apply to your organization, which is typically based on employer size. HR must also rely on external resources, such as a labor attorney, and know which agencies to contact should they need more information about compliance and enforcement.

Document retention is another hot spot for compliance in the areas of collection, reporting, and analysis. Knowing how long to retain certain documents, as well as how to destroy documents, is another facet of complying with U.S. employment laws and regulations.

Key Terms

Compliance

Disability

Employment-related decision

Equal employment oportunity commission

Prevailing wage

Reliable

Risk Management

Strike

Undue hardship

Unfair labor practice (ULP)

Uniform Guidelines on Employee Selection Procedures

Validity

Wage determination

Whistleblower

Reasonable workplace accommodation

Exam Essentials

Understand compliance with the major wage and hour, leave, and benefits laws.   Compensation and benefits are a critical HR function that serve to motivate and reward team members. Complying with the onerous labor laws, such as the FLSA and the FMLA, is a key responsibility of HR personnel and systems.

Navigate the regulations related to employee relations.   There are multiple relationships at work that HR is responsible for influencing, and this includes the relationship between an employer, a union, and its members. Understanding the ins and outs of the NLRA, LMRA, and the LMRDA ensures that no unfair labor practices or other violations occur.

Maintain compliance with safety and health standards.   Reporting to a safe and healthy workplace is a fundamental right of all workers. OSHA, both the act and the administration, along with resources provided by NIOSH, provide rules and tools to help employers stay in compliance with safety and health standards.

Develop equal employment opportunity policies to comply with the law.   Cultivating diversity and inclusiveness at work is not just an employment best practice, but an ethical and legal responsibility as well. Title VII of the Civil Rights Act of 1964 provides a strong foundation to prevent unlawful discrimination against protected class groups. These groups include race, national origin, age, sex, pregnancy, sexual orientation, disability, religion, and military service.

Educate leaders and employees on the legality of certain behaviors. Implementing policies, procedures, and rules to comply with the major labor laws will not be enough to protect a company from a claim under federal labor laws. Companies must be able to show that employees were aware of these requirements through training and documentation, and that HR takes actions toward those who fail to comply.

Maintain an appropriate record-keeping system. As the old HR saying goes, "If it isn't documented, it never happened." Keeping accurate records that are available upon demand is a large part of HR administrative tasks. It is necessary to balance the need for records without keeping items for too long, or improperly storing said records. A comprehensive record-keeping system to ensure compliance with the various record-keeping and retention requirements is necessary to manage risk properly.

Review Questions

1. An employee at a fast-food restaurant with a large birthmark on her face was not allowed to work in client-facing positions, because management believed her birthmark would make some customers uncomfortable. This is an example of what type of discrimination under the Americans with Disabilities Act?

   A. Discrimination against a qualified individual with a disability.

   B. Discrimination based on being perceived as having a disability.

   C. Discrimination based on having a record of a disability.

   D. This was not discrimination since she was not disabled.

2. An electrical contractor in Florida built a bona fide piece-rate payment system under which their electricians were paid. Despite this, the company was forced to pay back wages in the amount of $173,851. Which of the following FLSA requirements was most likely violated?

   A. Minimum age requirements

   B. Travel time

   C. Compensable time

   D. Overtime

3. Which of the following statements under the Federal Employee Compensation Act (FECA) is true?

   A. Only federal employees are covered under FECA.

   B. FECA is an exclusive workers' compensation program.

   C. FECA will pay for vocational rehabilitation.

   D. All of the above.

4. During the Covid-19 pandemic, a union filed a lawsuit against the Department of Labor (DOL) and the Mine Safety and Health Administration (MSHA) regarding regulations for social distancing. At issue was the elevator that took miners down into the mines, packing them in so that "people's faces are literally inches away from each other." Which of the following was most likely the complaint of the union?

   A. The need for an emergency standard

   B. A violation of infectious disease controls

   C. A violation of confined space standards

   D. A failure of general duty

5. Which of the following was an amendment to ERISA?

   A. The Portal-to-Portal Act

   B. The Equal Pay Act

   C. The Consolidated Omnibus Budget Reconciliation Act

   D. The Age Discrimination in Employment Act

6. How many hours does an employer have to obtain a completed Form I-9?

    A. Before an employee's first day of work for wages

    B. 24 hours

    C. 48 hours

    D. 72 hours

7. The H2A visa program applies to which of the following groups?

    A. Agricultural workers

    B. Nurses

    C. Information technology workers

    D. All foreign workers

8. What is the primary factor in determining whether unlawful harassment has occurred?

    A. The conduct was violent.

    B. The conduct was unwelcome.

    C. The conduct resulted in a tangible employment action.

    D. All of the above.

9. According to the UGESPs, all employment tests must be _____ predictors of future success on the job.

    A. Valid

    B. Legal

    C. Equitable

    D. Tangible

10. How long must OSHA Log 300 be retained by an employer?

    A. 1 year

    B. 5 years

    C. 10 years

    D. 30 years

The Organization Knowledge Domain

As described in Chapter 1, "The Basics of SHRM Certification," the exam's Body of Competency & Knowledge (BoCK) is organized by three clusters of behavioral competencies and three distinct knowledge domains. The expertise that an HR professional must have to perform well is in the knowledge domains of the People, the Workplace, and the Organization.

Within these chapters, you will learn concepts related to the Organization:

Structuring an HR department to meet the unique needs of the organization

Understanding the key activities related to developing and maintaining organizational effectiveness

Integrating HR practices that contribute to meaningful workforce management

Approaching the terms and conditions that guide the relationship between an employee and labor groups

Managing the dynamic use of technology in human resources

SHRM summarizes the Organization domain in the following way:

Create an effective HR function fully aligned to organizational strategy; enhance the effectiveness of the organization at large; ensure that the organization's talent pool has the skills and capabilities to achieve organizational goals; promote positive relationships with employees; and leverage technology to improve HR functioning.

NOTE The content related to the three clusters of behavioral competencies— Business, Leadership, and Interpersonal—is layered throughout the book. In this part, look for competency highlights of leadership and interpersonal behaviors.

Chapter 15

Structure of the HR Function

Exam Notables

The July–August 2021 edition of *Harvard Business Review* contained an interesting article titled, "Why Do So Many Strategies Fail?" The author, David J. Collis, noted that the primary reason why so many strategies fail is that leaders focus on the parts of strategies instead of the whole—that is, on a single strategy at the expense of the system.

This is certainly understandable when, in HR departments for example, the immediate demands are important. It may be necessary to push hard in recruiting because teams can't find qualified people or target the design of incentives to help bring employees back from hybrid work schedules. If an HR team's attention remains too narrow, however, it distracts from the other strategic elements, reducing value.

HR departments need to spend time building the foundational systems necessary for long-term departmental and organizational success. This includes finding ways to deliver and sustain value, prepare the workforce for the future, and be properly integrated into other business units. This is reflected in SHRM's definition of this functional area:

> Structure of the HR function encompasses the people, processes, theories and activities involved in the delivery of HR-related services that create and drive organizational effectiveness.

The SHRM Exam Objectives

SHRM's BoCK summarizes the functional area and defines the proficiency indicators along with key concepts. No matter your career level, pay special attention to the exam concepts defined "For All HR Professionals" and the "Key Concepts." If seeking the SHRM-SCP designation, you must expand your efforts to include those labeled "For Advanced HR Professionals."

THE SHRM-CP EXAM AND SHRM-SCP EXAM OBJECTIVES COVERED IN THIS CHAPTER INCLUDE THE FOLLOWING:

✓ For All HR Professionals

- Adapts work style to fit the organization's HR service model (e.g., centralized vs. decentralized), to ensure timely and consistent delivery of services to stakeholders.

- Seeks feedback from stakeholders to identify opportunities for HR function improvements.

- Acts as HR point-of-service contact for key stakeholders within a division or group.

- Provides consultation on HR issues to all levels of leadership and Management. This goes with the above bullet.

- Coordinates with other HR functions to ensure timely and consistent delivery of services to stakeholders. This goes with the above bullet.

- Ensures that outsourced and/or automated HR functions are integrated with other HR activities.

- Analyzes and interprets key performance indicators to understand the effectiveness of the HR function.

✓ For Advanced HR Professionals

- Designs and implements the appropriate HR service model for the organization (e.g., centralized vs. decentralized), to ensure efficient and effective delivery of services to stakeholders.

- Creates long-term goals that address feedback from stakeholders identifying opportunities for HR function improvements.

- Ensures that all elements of the HR function (e.g., recruiting, talent management, compensation and benefits, learning and development) are aligned and integrated, and provide timely and consistent delivery of services to stakeholders.

- Identifies opportunities to improve HR operations by outsourcing work or implementing technologies that automate HR functions (e.g., time, payroll). This goes with the above bullet.

- Designs and oversees programs to collect, analyze, and interpret key performance indicators (e.g., balanced scorecard) to evaluate the effectiveness of HR activities in supporting organizational success. This goes with the above bullet.

✓ Key Concepts

- Approaches to HR operational integration (i.e., how HR structures work together).

- Approaches to HR function/service models (e.g., centralized vs. decentralized).

- Approaches to HR structural models (e.g., center of excellence [COE], shared services).

- Elements of the HR function (e.g. recruiting, talent management, compensation, benefits).

- HR-function metrics (e.g., HR staff per fulltime employee, customer satisfaction, key performance indicators, balanced scorecard).

- HR staff roles, responsibilities and functions (e.g., generalists, specialists, HR business partners).

- Outsourcing of HR functions.

Human Resources as a Core Competency

A *core competency* is defined as a unique capability that differentiates a business from its competitors, often expressed as an organization's strength. When a core competency and strategy are aligned, organizational results will follow. For example, the fast-food restaurant chain In-N-Out Burger's core competencies are quality, cleanliness, and service. This shows up in their business operations in multiple ways:

In-N-Out Burger's Core Competencies:

Quality: All burgers are cooked fresh to order.

Operations: There are no microwaves or freezers at their restaurants.

Supply Chain: Their partners select premium cattle for In-N-Out Burger and commit to humane practices.

Human Resources: The company pays above average wages and benefits to their team members; they also use the arrow in their logo to communicate the company culture: "The arrow points to pride."

Strategy: The company limits their menu to four main items.

Research & Development: The founder designed a two-way intercom (the precursor to the modern drive-through) so that customers did not have to get out of their cars to order.

Marketing: The company has a secret menu (with a large cult following), demonstrating how brand awareness can drive consumer behavior.

Source: www.in-n-out.com

Many organizations are beginning to see that the characteristic that truly differentiates them from their competitors is their human resources—the people, processes, and practices. HR as a core competency can support other core organizational strengths such as the following:

Knowledge   When an organization chooses to differentiate themselves from their competitors using specialized expertise, the HR practices of selection and career pathing are important. These efforts focus on subject matter expertise, giving the organization a knowledge-based strategic advantage. A financial services company that specializes in the needs of the young professional is an example of a knowledge-based differentiation strategy. HR also leads the process of ensuring that knowledge is properly documented and stored so that knowledge is not lost if an employee exits.

Quality   A quality strategy that focuses on people as a competitive advantage requires clearly defined performance outcomes and an organizational structure that puts quality before cost or time. This translates into HR activities such as paying for results and training.

Productivity   An HR competitive advantage may also be achieved with productivity as the pull factor, such as in the manufacturing industry. HR activities to support this strategy include job design, safe work practices, alternate shifts, and attendance incentives.

Often, HR team roles are developed based on the traditional model of HR functions, such as HR strategic planning, talent acquisition, employee engagement and retention, learning and development, and total rewards. Focusing on these areas does not diminish the need for HR professionals to be strategic business partners; it provides a framework that allows for clearly defined roles and responsibilities. Doing so helps to avoid work redundancies, establishes clear performance standards, increases accountability, and provides the opportunity to incorporate strategy through all HR functions.

The Role of Human Resources

The Standard Industrial Classification (SIC) system was designed in the 1930s in response to the growing U.S economy. Its purpose, according to the North American Industry Classification System (NAICS) Association, was to "classify establishments by the type of activity in which they are primarily engaged and to promote the comparability of establishment data describing various facets of the U.S. economy." This process resulted in a large database of economic and industry-specific data, including the classification of employers by size.

Figure 15.1 shows that the vast majority of all businesses in the United States have fewer than 100 employees (NAICS.com). Consider this data alongside the research conducted by a leading outsourcing resource, ADP Payroll Processing. Their studies found that 70 percent of smaller companies have ad hoc HR management practices (aHRM), where HR responsibilities are managed by non-HR people. This includes individuals with no formal training, as shown in Figure 15.2.

FIGURE 15.1   Statistics: U.S. employer size

Counts by Total Employees (Updated October 2021)	
Total Employees	**Number of Businesses**
1 - 4 employees	12,412,906
5 - 9 employees	1,857,439
10 - 19 employees	804,251
20 - 49 employees	406,032
50 - 99 employees	149,646
100 - 249 employees	87,931
250 - 499 employees	33,310
500 - 999 employees	18,932
1,000+ employees	23,865
Uncoded records	1,749,400
Grand Total	17,543,712

Because of the risks inherent within the employment relationship, even a single harassment or wrongful termination lawsuit is enough to justify the salary of an HR team member when you factor in penalties, judgments, and labor attorney fees. Additionally, a focus on business strategy, sales, or finance is diluted when the leaders of these organizations must manage the daily needs of personnel.

A question that has received much debate is, "At what point should an organization bring in a formal HR team? "

The correct ratio of HR to FTEs (full-time employees) is still somewhat fluid; however, a study published by SHRM in 2016 offers a few insights ("How Organizational Staff Size Influences HR Metrics," SHRM.org). Figure 15.3 shows that smaller organizations have a higher HR-to-FTE ratio than their larger counterparts. This is because it takes a minimum number of HR employees to administer core services, regardless of headcount. Once that number is achieved, it is not necessary to increase the number of HR staff at the same rate as that of new hires.

FIGURE 15.2   aHRM data from ADP

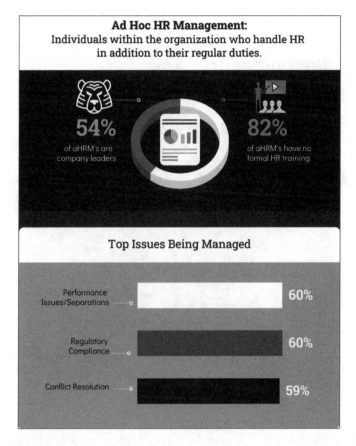

The HR-to-FTE ratio metric is calculated by dividing the number of full-time employees by the total number of HR staff members and then converting it to a percentage by multiplying it by 100.

Here is an example for an organization with 300 FTEs and 4 HR team members:
4/300 = 0.0133 × 100 = 1.3 HR team members for every 100 employees.

In order to benefit from the economies of scale described in the SHRM study, an HR department must be structured to maximize efficiencies while delivering timely and consistent services to the stakeholders.

HR's Job

Many employers are frustrated by the lack of qualified human resource professionals with experience; new HR pros are frustrated because they cannot gain the required experience unless they are hired. This unproductive cycle will only end when businesses, HR teams, and educators are in alignment with the knowledge, skills, abilities, and other attributes (KSAOs) necessary to be effective.

FIGURE 15.3   HR Support by Employer Size

The *Association to Advance Collegiate Schools of Business (AACSB)* is a global nonprofit that seeks to support the next generation of business leaders. They advance this aim by viewing both students and businesses as stakeholders of the educational system. In the SHRM publication *SHRM Human Resource Curriculum* (SHRM.org, 2018), the AACSB executive vice president and chief strategy and innovation officer Daniel R. LeClair, Ph.D. began the foreword with the following:

> Driven by powerful changes in the business environment, organizations of all types—from start-ups to multinationals, not-for-profit to governmental, local to global—are demanding strategic leadership from HR professionals. Today, the breadth and depth of business knowledge, as well as the mastery of management skills required of HR professionals are unprecedented.

Many universities are now adopting SHRM'S guidelines for HR curriculum. The benefits include standardization of HR knowledge for college graduates, informing HR program curriculum to reflect the field, bridging the gap between education and experience, and ensuring that a business perspective is taught. SHRM supports this approach by ensuring that successful CP and SCP candidates are well versed in the behavioral competencies related to business (see Chapter 4, "The Business Competency Cluster").

An *internship* is one method that helps an HR professional transition from school to an entry-level role in HR. An internship must be structured so that the intern is learning a skill set that is complementary to their studies. An HR team that may already be stretched too thin can benefit from the hiring of an intern. Properly designing the job can take an administrative burden off HR's desk so that they are free to work on the more strategic or people-oriented tasks of the job.

A *human resource business partner (HRBP)* is defined by the exam's glossary of terms as "an HR professional who advises an organization's leaders in developing and implementing a human capital strategy that closely aligns with overall mission, vision, and goals." A human capital strategy is a term that feels vague (and is not explicitly defined in the exam's glossary of terms). However, as a general rule, a *human capital strategy* is one that defines the HR objectives within each functional area to drive organizational goals. Tracking the results of a human capital strategy may be done using a balanced scorecard. See the section "Measuring Human Resource Contributions," later in this chapter, for more on this tool.

An HRBP does not have to be a senior leader—HRBPs exist at all stages of a career, whether as a generalist serving multiple HR functions or a specialist focused on one or two. Regardless of the career level of an HR professional, they can add value by focusing on the alignment of HR initiatives and behaviors with organizational governing statements such as the mission, vision values, and strategic goals.

Table 15.1 gives examples of HR job titles and a description from the Department of Labor's job database.

TABLE 15.1 Sample job titles for HR by career level

	Sample titles	Summary description
Manager and above	Human resource managers	Plan, direct, or coordinate human resources activities and staff of an organization.
	Industrial-organizational psychologists	Apply principles of psychology to human resources, administration, management, sales, and marketing problems. Activities may include policy planning; employee testing and selection, training, and development; and organizational development and analysis. May work with management to organize the work setting to improve worker productivity.
	Chief diversity officer (CDO) or Chief human resource officer (CHRO) or Chief talent officer (CTO)	Determine and formulate policies and provide overall direction of companies or private and public sector organizations within guidelines set up by a board of directors or similar governing body. Plan, direct, or coordinate operational activities at the highest level of management with the help of subordinate executives and staff managers.

TABLE 15.1   Sample job titles for HR by career level *(continued)*

	Sample titles	Summary description
Mid-level	Human resource specialists	Recruit, screen, interview, or place individuals within an organization. May perform other activities in multiple human resources areas.
	Compensation, Benefits and Job Analysis Specialists	Conduct programs of compensation and benefits and job analysis for employer. May specialize in specific areas, such as position classification and pension programs.
Entry-level	Human resource assistants, except payroll and timekeeping	Compile and keep personnel records. Record data for each employee, such as address, weekly earnings, absences, amount of sales or production, supervisory reports, and date of and reason for termination. May prepare reports for employment records, file employment records, or search employee files and furnish information to authorized persons.

Source: Department of Labor O*Net Job Database www.onetonline.org

Typically, each HR position will fall within the roles and responsibilities that are tied directly to the traditional, functional areas of a human resource department.

Integrating Human Resources

Achieving a strategy that puts HR as a core competency requires deep integration of human resources practices with other operational activities.

Finance and Accounting

Finance and accounting are often used interchangeably to describe the function of managing an organization's financial resources. However, they are separate activities. *Finance* professionals take a more strategic view of how to best manage assets and risk, including investments, loans, cash, and capital. The *accounting* function is operationally responsible for transaction management. This includes posting credits, paying receivables, and reporting on the company financials. HR works closely with these departments to help manage risk, design payroll practices, and address tax regulations.

Information Technology

The *information technology (IT)* group is responsible for managing the digital resources—hardware and software—of an organization. These include the platforms from which an organization processes financial transactions, purchases raw materials, manages inventory levels, and manages customer service. These activities are often delivered through an enterprise resource planning (ERP) system. The IT department also is responsible for protecting company, customer, and employee confidential and propriety information and building firewalls to keep out threats. HR supports IT by partnering with them to establish policies and practices that govern the use of these systems. HR may also help to select qualified team members and identify training resources to keep IT teams up-to-date on the swiftly changing technology environment.

Research & Development (R&D)

The *research & development (R&D)* function is responsible for developing the products and services that an organization delivers to its customers. This function may redesign existing products or innovate new ones to drive future revenue. Innovation and creativity are key aspects of R&D. HR supports these characteristics by making sure that a diverse workgroup is selected in order to ensure that multiple perspectives and talents are considered, especially ones that reflect the target market. HR may also offer support by guiding project management efforts, collaborating with other leaders to access funding through grants, and protecting intellectual and other property rights through trademarks, copyrights, and patents.

Marketing and Sales

The *marketing* function of an organization is responsible for positioning a company's product or services for sale by creating need or desire. This is usually done through the four Ps: product, price, promotion, and placement. Behaviors include conducting market research to inform R&D product development efforts, providing competitive intelligence to price the products properly, using channels such as social media and trade shows to promote the products and services, and identifying the best placement of their product to maximize sales.

Sales is responsible for generating the revenue of an organization by selling the products and services and building relationships with distributors or the direct customer.

HR supports both marketing and sales in multiple ways, such as using the gig economy to source graphic designers. HR is also responsible for designing commission-based pay structures that encourage results without compromising ethics. HR partners with marketing to utilize online "career" portals, either to attract new candidates or to communicate with existing employees. Both tasks represent the opportunity to communicate the employer brand utilizing videos and other digital tools to HR's customers.

Operations

Operations is the function that includes how the organization's products and services are produced and delivered. This includes managing the supply chain from purchase to finished goods and facilities management. Operations also refers to the delivery of services to customers. HR partners with operations teams to address health and safety needs and conduct workforce planning to ensure that qualified talent is available and to help forecast and manage labor costs by conducting pay surveys.

The goal of successfully integrating HR practices into the functions just listed is to maximize the impact of human resources as a core competency on any scale. Functions such as recruiting, performance management, compensation systems, safety, and security are critical to achieving optimal results. Note also what HR integration is not: taking on the work of other departments. True integration occurs when HR competencies are used to move the company forward.

HR acts as the point of contact for all employees, and it serves as an adviser to leaders of each business unit. For example, if an employee has a question about their health insurance, an HR team member would need to respond in a timely fashion in order to ensure that the employee's rights are protected, but also so that the team member feels as though the HR crew genuinely cares about their employment experience. This will aid in retention.

Human Resource Service Models

The "approach to structuring and delivering an organization's HR services to support organizational success" is the definition of an *HR shared service model*. The proper method for delivering HR services is dependent on many factors, including the following:

1. Operational structure:

    ▪   The number of locations and employees

    ▪   Global facilities

    ▪   Availability of HR talent and expertise

2. Strategic goals:

    ▪   Employee acquisition targets

    ▪   New market entry

    ▪   Risk management, threats, and opportunities

Once these factors are known, HR takes the lead on how best to design the HR delivery structure.

Centralized/Decentralized HR Structures

The size of the organization makes a difference when it comes to selecting the best structure of the HR function. For smaller, one-location employers, a *centralized structure*—that is, having all HR staff housed in one location—makes the most sense. In some cases, it's more beneficial to maintain a *decentralized structure*, or one where HR is performed within each business unit, at individual locations, or within multiple countries. Centralized structures allow for standardization of HR practices, along with consistent application of organizational policies, procedures, and rules. Decentralized structures provide more autonomy to each business unit or location, allowing for more control and alignment with local or regional practices.

In a decentralized HR structure, headquartered HR may still exist to drive the more strategic purpose of the HR function. One way to achieve this is through an HR *center of excellence (COE)*. A COE is defined by SHRM as "a team or structure that provides expertise, best practices, support and or knowledge transfer in a focused area." For example, for the human resource function, HR teams act as consultants and account managers to the internal stakeholders, providing expertise within their specialty function. A COE may have advisers that focus on compensation and benefits, risk management, employment law, or employee relations. Time zone may be a special consideration, requiring HR teams to adapt their schedules in order to be available for their customers.

The rise of remote work has created another opportunity for organizations to structure their HR service operations. Virtual HR teams may be built with employees, consultants, and project-contract workers, the last two of these being a form of outsourcing.

Outsourcing

HR professionals at mid- to advanced-career levels are finding more and more success as contract workers. HR consultants offer support for organizations as generalists in a few or many of the HR functional areas, or they may specialize, such as with executive recruiting.

You may recall from Chapter 10, "HR in the Global Context," the concept of *outsourcing*, which is the process of contracting with third-party vendors to take over an entire business unit, such as manufacturing; a particular function, such as COBRA administration; or to work on projects, such as specialized training. In the context of the structure of an HR department, outsourcing may be viewed as an external resource to support HRBPs and organizational outcomes.

Outsourcing is particularly valuable for the "HR department of one" to help shift some of the more time-intensive processes such as recruiting. Outsourcing is useful for the processes or programs that require extensive compliance, or subject matter expertise, such as with benefits administration. As companies begin to increasingly rely on their HR teams as business partners, outsourcing the more tactical HR processes frees up HR to do the strategic work. A disadvantage of outsourcing is that HR loses control over the process. For example, if the payroll function is outsourced and an error is made, employees may not receive the kind of response from the contracted agency that the company desires. Another disadvantage is that outsourcing tends to be expensive depending on the services provided.

In addition to recruiting, benefits administration, and payroll, other commonly outsourced HR activities include the following:

- Using a labor attorney to write the employee handbook
- Contracting with staffing agencies to fill open positions
- Utilizing third-party vendors to deliver employee recognition programs
- Hiring external coaches to develop team members
- Working with certified safety professionals to identify hazards

Legally, an organization does not avoid liability for the outsourced HR functions. As the employer of record, at minimum, and under certain circumstances, the company will share joint liability if the vendor violates an employee's rights (see Chapter 18, "Employee and Labor Relations," for more on joint liability). Following an established process when selecting a vendor may help mitigate this risk. The process should begin by analyzing the needs of the department and the organization and researching solutions.

Other factors that must be considered when designing an outsourcing solution is the budget. This will require that HR understand the cost of completing the activity in-house. For example, if the HR leader is considering outsourcing all staffing to agencies, data related to recruiting costs (advertising and labor), cost per hire, and turnover rates by source should be collected. This number may then be compared to the cost of outsourcing the staffing function to a contractor. HR should also factor in the lost productivity of a position being open too long. If the labor market for a particular talent is tight, it may be in the organization's best interest to pay a higher agency fee to leverage their connections, rather than stumble through operating without the talent for an extended period of time.

Finally, just as with outsourcing any part of the business, the process within an HR department should include completing a request for proposal, making the selection, and then regularly evaluating the new vendor to ensure that desired outcomes are being achieved.

Measuring Human Resource Contributions

The use of *key performance indicators (KPIs)* is defined by SHRM as the "quantifiable measures of performance that gauge an organization's progress toward strategic objectives or other agreed-upon performance standards." KPIs may be made up of hard or soft data, and they are used as the basis for analysis and decision-making.

A key performance indicator is a collection of information. Analysis and decision-making are the actions taken using the KPIs as a basis. This is an example of the relationship between SHRM's knowledge and behavioral competencies.

HR leaders are responsible for establishing HR performance targets that are aligned with organizational targets. Regularly measuring performance allows for real-time adjustments to HR initiatives in order to ensure that organizational goals are achieved. HR KPIs exist for all HR functions; here are a few of the most common department level measures:

HR Expense–to-Revenue Ratio   *HR Expense divided by revenue*

The purpose of this measurement is to develop an HR department's budget, and it should account for all HR expenses, including outsourcing and other external resource use.

HR Expense–to–Operating Expense Ratio   *HR expense divided by operating expense*

The purpose of this metric is to understand the proportionate amount of money the company invests in its HR function. The formula should include all costs associated with the HR department without duplication. For example, if labor calculation is included in the total operating expense, it should not be included in HR's total expense.

This formula may also be used to evaluate specific HR functions. For example, calculating all training expenses and dividing it by FTE or operating expense identifies the investment per team member or overall function. A higher ratio indicates greater investment, and it may be used to communicate the employee value proposition or in hidden paychecks (concepts explored in more detail in Chapter 6, "Talent Acquisition," and Chapter 9, "Total Rewards").

Revenue per FTE   *Total revenue divided by the number of full-time employees (FTEs)*

The purpose of this metric is to understand organizational efficiencies. It is useful on a department level as well, such as in marketing in order to understand how much revenue may be generated by a new hire when compared to the salary. For example, if the CEO wants to hire a graphic designer at $80,000 per year, knowing the department's revenue per FTE can help anticipate the return on investment (ROI) or the break-even point of that hire.

For a comprehensive look at other HR metrics, download SHRM's 2019 publication *SHRM HR Metrics* from www.shrm.org. The data shows the different kinds of metrics that may be used in each functional area. Beyond preparing for the exam, it is a valuable resource to have in your practice toolbox.

Balanced Scorecard   A *balanced scorecard* is the tool of choice to use when seeking integrated metrics. It is an organizational performance management tool that measures outcomes compared to goals. The balanced scorecard uses terms such as leading indicators and lagging indicators, described in Chapter 5, "Strategic Human Resource Management." As a refresher, a *leading indicator* is one that may affect future performance, whereas a *lagging indicator* looks at past performance. When applied to human resource activities, it is a full-picture look at how well an HR team is supporting its stakeholders and achieving their human capital strategy. In short, did HR effort directly result in organizational outcomes?

The Balanced Scorecard Institute defines four key perspectives. Through an HR department lens, they are as follows, including examples:

- **Customers (employees, other business units):** Support all departments in the performance management process.

- **Financial:** Develop strategies to improve company financials, such as managing the cost of employee health insurance.

- **Internal Business Processes:** Use social media and other methods to drive employer brand awareness and recruiting.

- **Learning and Growth:** Design career paths that improve employee satisfaction and increase the skill set of the workforce.

  Just as with an organizational scorecard, an HR review should be clearly defined by objective criteria that is distinctly tied to company strategic goals. The metrics should focus on results, not just data.

Competency and Knowledge Alignment

SHRM's BoCK describes three main clusters of the knowledge, skills, abilities, and other attributes necessary to perform successfully in HR. They include the Leadership competencies, Interpersonal competencies, and Business competencies from which HR actions are grounded. In order to pass these exams, candidates must be able to align knowledge with behaviors.

As defined in Chapter 4, each cluster is further expanded into eight competencies. These eight competencies are threaded throughout the knowledge domains of this book in order to align behaviors with the associated technical expertise. A review of the relevant competencies for the structure of the HR function begins here.

Delivering Messages

SHRM defines the Interpersonal sub-competency of delivering messages as action taken to develop and deliver, to a variety of audiences, communications that are clear, persuasive, and appropriate to the topic and situation.

Knowing what information to deliver, and to whom it should go, takes critical thinking skills. If you have ever been trapped in an email string or group IM, a response of "Reply all" can really hijack an inbox! Additionally, language affects the clarity of the messages. Too much technical jargon will be lost on new hires, whereas a lack of use of business language diminishes credibility and creates misunderstandings.

Using the appropriate medium to deliver messages can help minimize these challenges. For difficult conversations, it is generally best to engage face-to-face, where body language and other cues can shape the dialogue. When compliance is a priority, email and other written communication is best, as the date and time of delivery will be documented.

Presentation skills are another competency that individuals in HR must master. This competency goes beyond the bulleted PowerPoint presentation; HR personnel are called upon to share information virtually, so platform skills such as Zoom, WebEx, and Slack are necessary.

The use of emoticons and emojis has increased over the last several years, becoming much more widely accepted. This could be because the increased use of technology has "flattened" context by removing emotion from the exchange. Studies have shown that the majority of emoji/emoticon users do so to increase the positivity of the message. HR should align their use of social trends with the company culture and then model behaviors.

At mid-career, HR professionals are likely to be called upon to communicate more complex topics such as giving performance feedback and facilitating focus groups.

Exchanging Organizational Information

 SHRM defines the Interpersonal sub-competency of exchanging organizational information as the KSAOs necessary to translate and communicate messages effectively among organizational levels or units.

HR functions and their corresponding policies, procedures, and rules are a complex, dynamic system that can be intimidating. For example, the employee handbook is supposed to be a communication tool to share information about the rights and responsibilities of the employee and what they can expect from employment with the organization. Because of the litigious nature of the employment relationship, the handbooks have become riddled with "legal-ease" phrases that the average professional may not be skilled enough to understand unless they have an MBA or have graduated from law school. For this reason, HR talent should take care to communicate HR-related data in ways that are appropriate for the targeted audience.

> Don't adapt to the energy in the room; influence the energy in the room.
>
> *Unknown*

Another opportunity for HR to develop their communication competencies is by having a positive, solution-oriented energy when communicating, even if they don't necessarily agree. Many situations and circumstances are not so easy to unravel, and leaders are left with selecting the solution that "sucks the least." This is not to say that HR should go along with unethical or harmful decisions. They should, however, ensure that they voice the proper attitude of support for organizational initiatives where appropriate and refrain from contributing to negativity.

Listening

 SHRM defines the Interpersonal sub-competency of listening as the ability to understand information provided by others.

Communication has three subjects: the sender, the receiver, and the message. The humans involved in this triage must develop proper listening skills if the message is to be properly understood.

In the technical world, it is all too easy for HR and other leaders to give direction via email. Doing so, however, does not provide an opportunity for the receiver to ask clarifying questions in the moment, or to demonstrate understanding through physical cues such as eye contact, head nodding, and facial expressions. Asking questions and reading body language are both functions of *active listening*, which is the ability to fully engage with the speaker, understand their message, and respond with relevance.

Additionally, the idea of conflict has a negative connotation, and this is certainly true when conflict is destructive. However, the ability to listen to opposing views, and encourage others to do so as well, is key to quality problem-solving, decision-making, and innovation. HR leads this effort by ensuring a respectful exchange of opinions that are focused on ideas and problem-solving, not on the personal characteristics of the individuals involved.

It is in this same spirit that HR must develop the final listening sub-competency described by the exam BoCK, that of soliciting feedback from other business units about the effectiveness of the HR department. It is very easy to fall into the habit of thinking only about the barriers of being effective HR pros—long hours, difficult personalities, regulatory vortexes, lack of resources, external economic forces. . .truly the list is very long. However, the function of HR has never been static—we have always been called upon to evolve so that we parallel the changing needs of our stakeholders. Regularly seeking out feedback about the ways that an HR department could be better business partners normalizes this behavior. Doing so allows for a proactive, solution-oriented response, as opposed to reacting when HR makes a mistake or is misperceived.

HR's ability to communicate has a major impact on the nature of the relationships that exist in the workforce in spite of the continued rise of automated work practices. The nature of the Interpersonal competency of relationship management is geared toward what robots cannot do, which is manage the complexity of relationships between humans. This is left strictly up to leaders, including HR teams, to manage.

Networking

 SHRM defines the Interpersonal sub-competency of networking as the ability to effectively build a network of professional contacts both within and outside of the organization.

SHRM makes special note that the behavioral competencies are all about taking action. The act of *networking* serves to build the connections necessary to identify internal and external resources with shared interests. Not just a social game, an HR network finds ways to create value for stakeholders. This means contacts should be both within an HR community but also serve in other, non-HR roles as well.

The benefits of doing this are many. For HR professionals, it is helpful to have a community of like-minded individuals to learn from and provide support, especially for those nuanced issues that are keeping them up at night. HR, of course, is bound by confidentiality. A network, however, can be an insightful source to point them in the right direction. Building relationships with local SHRM chapters, staffing vendors, insurance agencies, training professionals, and other subject-matter experts creates partnerships that add value.

Networking through social media is also an effective and low-cost way to get the word out about job opportunities and share the reasons why teams should come to work with you, or to find third-party contractors where necessary. For this reason, an online network should be built up with both HR and industry-specific professionals.

Relationship Building

 SHRM defines the Interpersonal sub-competency of relationship building as effectively building and maintaining relationships both within and outside of the organization.

SHRM's definition of the behavioral competency of relationship building is very similar to their definition of networking. The key distinction is that once a network has been established, HR professionals must take action to invest in those relationships in order to optimize the connections. This is done primarily through the application of human relations principles designed to build trust.

Trust is developed over time. It takes a concerted effort that includes showing authentic concern for the well-being of others throughout all HR activities, even the difficult ones such as discipline. HR becomes a trusted influence when they are honest, respectful, and responsive to the needs of leaders and employees. Relationship building also includes listening to different perspectives and advocating where necessary to ensure that HR practices meet the needs of all stakeholders, not just the vocal few.

There are many rewards of building strong relationships, and HR is tasked with influencing the dynamics of the many different types of relationships at work. The behavioral sciences produce study after study that show a positive relationship between an employee and a supervisor increases productivity and retention. Strong relationships between coworkers contribute to a cohesive organizational team and reduce the risk of a hostile work environment or unlawful discrimination.

Finally, networking and relationship building have another element in common—they are designed to be reciprocal. Individuals in human resources should make a conscious effort to support their networks and in-house teams and call upon their expertise when necessary. This shows regard for others' talents and ensures that the organization's best interests are served by guarding and accessing qualified resources.

SHRM SCP Only

Senior HR teams members need to understand all of these concepts because they are the primary point of contact to design and manage these systems. System design includes collecting data to understand the leading and lagging indicators that demonstrate HR service success. When HR is not performing, advanced HR professionals take the lead to understand the barriers and recommend solutions, including restructuring service delivery where necessary.

Staffing an HR team properly is one way that an advanced HRBP is able to ensure that the department functions are delivered correctly and in a timely manner. When services are compromised for any reason, HR must respond quickly to find alternatives using metrics such as HR-to-FTE. Depending on the need, HR may staff with interns, add HR headcount, seek to automate processes through employee self-service models, and partner with IT to identify hardware and software options or outsource.

HR leaders are long-range thinkers. They are able to understand the current state and look ahead to anticipate future needs and lay the foundation to build upon as the organization defines and refines strategy. This strategic ability is partly hardwired—some people just are able to think more holistically—but it may also be learned through experience and by asking for meaningful feedback from all stakeholders. Developing and nourishing a network of HR and non-HR people also helps HR stay attuned to the trends and changes that will need to be accounted for when designing initiatives and advising other leaders.

The communication competencies described in an earlier section are also elevated for seasoned professionals. They must be fluent in the business language of executives and be able to present complex information concisely. One busy CEO once advised their consultant to "be brief, be brilliant, and be gone." Other communication competencies for senior leaders include the ability to communicate the company mission, vision and values, and how HR initiatives are aligned with strategic goals. Giving and receiving feedback and communicating difficult messages with respect while being open to alternative views is also important. HR is responsible for using their influence to positively communicate the company vision and create *buy-in*, a "process by which a person or group provides a sustained commitment in support of a decision, approach, solution or course of action" (SHRM *Glossary of Terms*, www.shrm.org).

Once HR has identified a need using KPIs, feedback, and their own skill sets, they will need to make a *business case* to leaders for its implementation. A business case is "a tool or document that defines a specific problem, proposes a solution, and provides justification for the proposal in terms of time, cost efficiency, and probability of success."

Summary

In order to be strong business partners, human resource teams must have their own department in order. There are many ways that this is accomplished.

The structure of the human resource department may inhibit service delivery or make it more efficient. Service models to consider include centralization, decentralization, or outsourcing. All three have advantages and disadvantages that are dependent on strategic and operational factors. Knowing how to structure the department involves using communication skills to solicit feedback, listen, and design solutions to ensure that the needs of organizational stakeholders are met.

Staffing the HR department is another factor that drives HR service levels. Developing strong social networks with local colleges helps to establish a pipeline from which to attract qualified managers, generalists, specialists, and the entry-level professional.

Aligning HR initiatives with organizational core competencies is a critical way for HR to demonstrate their value. Positioning human resources as a core competency in and of itself helps to integrate HR practices within other business units. Measuring these outcomes is achieved through the use of KPIs, data used to identify opportunities for improvement.

Key Terms

Active listening

Balanced scorecard

Business case

Buy-in

Centralized structure

Core competency

Decentralized structure

Exam Essentials

Build human resources into a core competency. A core competency is the competitive advantage of an organization—how the business differentiates itself in their market. When people are part of the core competency, the human resource department has the opportunity to influence the success of an organization directly through their practices.

Design HR departments and understand job roles. Companies that view HR as strategic business partners understand the value in the department's work. Serving teams through job design, recruiting, compensation, training, risk management, and more is the job of HR generalists and specialists that are supported by HR managers and other organizational leaders.

Deliver HR through models that maximize service. HR service models are highly dependent on other organizational factors such as size, location, and strategic goals. Centralized and decentralized structures have their advantages and disadvantages, as does outsourcing certain parts of the HR work.

Communicate to leaders the value of HR activities. Measuring the value of HR is important so that HR and the leaders understand what is working and what needs improvement. Actively seeking out this feedback is necessary so that HR initiatives are truly aligned with business goals and results.

Translate HR knowledge into behavioral competencies. The knowledge of human resource practices must be applied in order for HR to make a difference and remain relevant. This includes communicating effectively, building relationships, and positively influencing company stakeholders.

Elevate the work as an advanced HR professional. Senior HR professionals are responsible for "all of the above." It is not enough simply to have the knowledge; HR leaders must be able to analyze data, make recommendations, design solutions, and be long-range thinkers.

Review Questions

1. You are currently the HR director for an internationally recognized university system with 500 FTEs. The HR department includes you, an HR manager, two generalists, and one training specialist. Payroll is handled through the accounting department. Leadership has just announced that the next fiscal year's strategic plan is focused on building diversity, equity, and inclusion (DEI). Their top two goals are to promote innovation in research by enhancing creativity through diversity and to create a culture of inclusivity and respect within the university and among the student body. Which of the following should the HR team tackle first?

   A. Look for an intern from the local university who understands DEI.

   B. Check in with the leaders of all current research projects to analyze the diversity of their teams and address gaps.

   C. Begin to craft a job description for a chief diversity officer.

   D. Design employee training to teach them how to identify bias and learn about stereotypes.

2. Using the scenario from question 1, what is the current HR to FTE ratio?

   A. 0.1

   B. 1

   C. 1.2

   D. None of the above

3. Which of the following is the most important skill for an HRBP to have in order to be effective?

   A. Business acumen

   B. Recruiting

   C. Data analysis

   D. A positive attitude

4. Which of the following positions are responsible for ensuring that HR initiatives help the company achieve its goals?

   A. HR manager

   B. HR generalists

   C. Training specialists

   D. All of the above

5. Which of the following is the best example of integrating human resources into other business operations?

   A. Outsourcing staffing to an agency

   B. Hiring a second-shift HRBP to work directly with the employees on swing shift

   C. Being the point of contact for IT services because the company does not have a formal IT department

   D. Processing payroll

6. Which of the following is an advantage of centralized HR service delivery?

    A. Centralized HR structures reduce the cost-of-service delivery.

    B. Centralized HR structures provide for higher levels of business unit autonomy.

    C. Centralized HR structures create consistency in HR service delivery.

    D. Centralized HR structures allow for regional alignment where appropriate.

7. A performance-based pay system is most likely to strengthen an organization's competitive position in which of the following core competencies?

    A. HR

    B. Quality

    C. Knowledge

    D. Supply chain

8. Which of the following leading performance indicators (LPIs) is most effective if you want to understand organizational efficiencies?

    A. HR expense to revenue

    B. The balanced scorecard

    C. HR expense to operating expense

    D. Revenue per FTE

9. Which of the following competencies require that HR professionals partner with internal and external resources?

    A. Listening

    B. Exchanging organizational information

    C. Networking

    D. Delivering messages

10. The message, the sender, and the receiver are elements of which of the following interpersonal competencies?

    A. Listening

    B. Exchanging organizational information

    C. Networking

    D. All of the above

Chapter 16

Organizational Effectiveness and Development

Exam Notables

There is much to be curious about regarding *social yawning*, a phenomenon with no clear cause. Some studies suggest that contagious yawning is a form of group behavior, an unconscious show of empathy for others. Others note that the copycat behavior may be a form of social bonding—a way to connect. Neuroscientists have discovered the "mirror neuron," a bit of brain energy that fires when a behavior, such as yawning, is observed in others, triggering a similar reaction.

Although social yawning seems a rather benign influence on relational behaviors, what if the issue were more disruptive, such as contagious aggressiveness? Is it possible that the mirror neuron is responsible for escalated behaviors in a workgroup, both positive and negative? Does the science of neurology and other "-ologies" (psych, bio, type, socio, and so on) hold answers on how to manage conflict, change, and teams—the major intervention activities of organizational effectiveness and development? These concepts are examples of competencies that HR must develop using multiple resources to align the workforce with the workplace so that organizational results are achieved.

SHRM summarizes this functional area as follows:

> Organizational Effectiveness & Development concerns the overall structure and functionality of the organization and involves measurement of long- and short-term effectiveness and growth of people and processes, and implementation of necessary organizational change initiatives.

The SHRM Exam Objectives

SHRM's BoCK not only summarizes this functional area, but also defines the proficiency indicators and key concepts. No matter your career level, pay special attention to the exam concepts defined "For All HR Professionals" and the "Key Concepts." If seeking the SHRM-SCP designation, you must expand your efforts to include those labeled "For Advanced HR Professionals."

THE SHRM-CP EXAM AND SHRM-SCP EXAM OBJECTIVES COVERED IN THIS CHAPTER INCLUDE THE FOLLOWING:

✓ **For All HR Professionals**

- Ensures that key documents and systems (e.g., job postings and descriptions, performance management systems) accurately reflect workforce activities.

- Supports change initiatives to increase the effectiveness of HR systems and processes.

- Identifies areas in the organization's structures, processes, and procedures that need change.

- Provides recommendations for eliminating barriers to organizational effectiveness and development.

- Collects and analyzes data on the value of HR initiatives to the organization.

✓ **For Advanced HR Professionals**

- Aligns HR's strategy and activities with the organization's mission, vision, values, and strategy.

- Regularly monitors results against performance standards and goals in support of the organization's strategy.

- Establishes measurable goals and objectives to create a culture of accountability.

- Consults on, plans and designs organizational structures that align with the effective delivery of activities in support of the organization's strategy.

- Assesses organizational needs to identify critical competencies for operational effectiveness.

- Designs and oversees change initiatives to increase the effectiveness of HR systems and processes.

- Ensures that HR initiatives demonstrate measurable value to the organization.

✓ **Key Concepts**

- Application of behavioral assessments (e.g., personality assessments).

- Intergroup dynamics (e.g., intergroup conflict).

- Intragroup dynamics (e.g., group formation, identity, cohesion, structure, influence on behavior).

- Organizational design structures and approaches (e.g., customer, functional, geographic, matrix, program).

- Organizational performance theories, structures, and approaches.

Organizational Effectiveness and Development Defined

> Our history books have shown us that the systems we use to organize our lives have an enormous impact on our collective reality. This knowledge makes it imperative to innovate systems that serve us intelligently. . .not only creating models that fit new realities, but continually updating old models to keep them viable in a rapidly changing culture.

> Wheels of Life, *Judith Anodea, PhD, Llewellyn Publications, 1999*

Many strategic partners confuse the terms *organizational design* and *organizational development*. Organizational design relates to the structure of an organization; organizational development refers to the processes and systems that drive performance within that structure. It may surprise you to know that the quote above, which so perfectly captures the essence of organizational effectiveness and development (OED), came from a book on how to balance *chakras*, the human body's energy centers. The parallel is useful.

All human bodies share similar design components—there is a skeletal structure, specific organs such as the heart, the central nervous system, brain synapses, and so forth. These elements exist in all human beings regardless of gender, race, country of origin, profession, marital status, or religion. How the body develops is a function of maintenance—exercise, nutrition, stress management, social connectedness, and institutional access. When any of these systems are internally or externally out of balance, an intervention becomes necessary.

Organizational effectiveness is defined by SHRM as the "degree to which an organization is successful in executing the strategic objectives and mission." Organizational development is the planned effort to address barriers to organizational effectiveness using *interventions*, or planned disruptions orchestrated to effect change.

Proactive interventions are those that seek to anticipate problems before they arise. One example of this approach is in risk management, where data is analyzed for the possibility and probability of risk, and steps are taken to manage the exposure properly. Remedial interventions are those that are taken when a condition changes or a problem has been identified. For HR, an important competency is the ability to collect and analyze data related to the effectiveness of HR initiatives to influence company, individual, and group behaviors.

Effective interventions are those that are designed specifically to achieve company goals or address barriers. Strategically, an organization may use brainstorming to identify intervention targets. Questions such as "What gets in the way of increased sales?" or "How can we increase the diversity of our teams?" are used to align interventions with measurable results.

Questions are an important part of identifying the barriers to effective results. Take, for example, an organization that is experiencing higher than average turnover. An HR team may ask questions such as the following:

- Why are the employees leaving?
- What is the tenure of the exiting employees?
- What do the exit interviews say?

For example, if the answers show that most of the separations occur in the first 30 days of employment, they didn't receive enough training, and the pay was too low, HR may recommend process interventions. This could be designing a new hire onboarding program, conducting stay interviews to identify strengths, or implementing a sign-on bonus that pays out after the first six months of employment. When considering process interventions, think through the filter of the exam knowledge domains for solutions (Total Rewards, Talent Acquisition, Learning and Development, and so on).

Asking questions is an easy way to start identifying the root cause of an issue. True development interventions require a deeper look into the people, process, or structural barriers to organizational effectiveness.

Exercise 16.1

Challenge yourself using our example of organizational turnover. Using the knowledge domains of the CP and SCP exams, think through other possible solutions that target the root cause(s) of the turnover. For example, in what ways could you design an intervention using the principles of Employee Engagement and Retention (Functional Area 3 of the exam BoCK; refer to Chapter 7, "Employee Engagement and Retention")?

People Interventions

Interventions involving people are incredibly complex since many factors drive performance. These factors include personal characteristics, group dynamics, leadership abilities, and the quality of conflict, all of which are of equal importance when designing change.

Individual Behaviors

The academic domain of industrial-organizational (I-O) psychology is structured to examine the application of psychological principles within the workplace. This includes studying how individual attitudes and beliefs drive performance and the use of psychological assessments to match people to jobs.

Personality Assessments

Chapter 14, "U.S. Employment Laws and Regulations," provided the legal perspective of using any type of preemployment test, specifically when complying with the Uniform Guidelines on Employee Selection Procedures (UGESPs). When using a behavioral assessment, including personality tests, it is important first to identify what performance the assessment is measuring. Some personality tests are designed to be predictive, whereas other are not.

Nonpredictive assessments, such as the Myers–Briggs Type Indicator (MBTI), are useful in individual and team performance coaching and to increase self-awareness. *Predictive assessments* are used in selection for training, promotion, and hiring by identifying characteristics related to energy orientation, social skills, motivators, work styles, and other traits. To be legally defensible, predictive assessments must be reliable and valid. This means that the assessment consistently predicts what it says will occur over time.

Table 16.1 reviews four of the most common personality assessments being used by employers, along with their advantages and disadvantages.

TABLE 16.1 Top personality tests in use by employers

Assessment	Advantages	Disadvantages
Myers–Briggs Type Indicator (MBTI) Forced choice assessment used to identify preferences related to energy orientation, information processing, decision-making, and organization.	Based on positive psychology; all types are considered healthy. Enhances understanding of the hardwiring that drives behaviors.	Not designed to be predictive. Can be misunderstood and misused.
DISC Identifies traits of dominance, influence, steadiness, and compliance.	Uses a common language to improve team performance and increase self-awareness.	Requires specialized training to administer. Reports are 20+ pages long and it may be difficult for some HR professionals to apply results to the job.
SHL Occupational Personality Questionnaire Measures the behavioral styles of emotions, thinking, and feelings, and relationships with people.	Useful in job placement activities, such as hiring and promotion, because it is designed to be predictive. Is available in more than 30 languages.	If not properly aligned with the KSAOs of the job, qualified candidates may be overlooked.
Big 5 Measures the degrees of openness, conscientiousness, extroversion, agreeableness, and neuroticism (OCEAN).	Considers environmental and biological factors that influence performance.	The trait of "neuroticism" may be perceived as negative.

When deciding about using personality assessments at work, HR should consider multiple factors. This includes making sure that the assessment meets the requirements of the UGESPs. Other considerations include how easy the assessment is to administer, if the tool is customizable, whether the test is available in multiple languages, and the degree of support available for interpretation and application of the results.

Performance Management

Managing individual performance may be done through formal and informal channels. Technically, performance management is a process intervention, illustrating that many OED efforts require a hybrid approach. However, feedback of any kind remains one of the top methods used to motivate employees. The performance process may be broken and in need of intervention if the following occurs:

- It over-relies on the annual appraisal as the only form of feedback an employee receives.

- Supervisors are not trained on rater bias.

- Feedback is not focused on behaviors, but rather on personal characteristics.

- The employees value the process only to get a pay increase.

- The process is aligned with individual performance but not with group and organizational results.

Group and Team Dynamics

Google's *re:Work* (`https://rework.withgoogle.com`) dedicates an entire section to the study of teams, noting that:

> Teams are often where real production happens and where employees experience most of their work. Understanding team effectiveness involves looking at complex dynamics and demographics.

One of the challenges laid out in a case study by re:Work is that many HR systems are designed to manage individual performance—not group performance. A key concept of OED is the ability for HR to help manage the intergroup dynamics of teams.

re:Work is a website that gives free access to many case studies that are relevant to the exams. This is important, because the exams require the ability to apply concepts to the workplace. Whenever possible, support your preparation by accessing real-world examples of knowledge in action. Find the teams case study that explores the data solutions company return path here:

`https://rework.withgoogle.com/case-studies/`
`return-path-team-effectiveness/`

Defining Groups and Teams

I-O psychology defines teams/groups as a collection of individuals with shared goals. Shoppers at a mall, for example, would not be considered a group since they do not share responsibilities—they are simply assembled at the same place at the same time. If, however, there is a fire at the mall, and the group begins to work together to help evacuate people, call 911, or aid the elderly, they become a team.

Formal groups are those that are organized by the company, such as work units or committees. The team purpose is outlined through a charter, and clear roles, responsibilities, and hierarchies are established. Informal groups are those that are more social in nature, such as employees that regularly take walks or eat lunch together. Both are important to organizational performance. Formal groups direct their efforts toward a shared target; informal groups provide the social connectedness that drives a sense of belonging and esteem.

Virtual teams must also be designed to achieve results and offer the connectedness that individuals need. This can be tricky. This and other challenges to managing a remote team are discussed in more detail in Chapter 7. For purposes of this exam domain, the focus is on how groups are developed and managed.

Group Development

The work of Bruce Tuckman in the 1960s remains the most cited research relating to how groups come together. Tuckman's theory found that there are five stages of group development. These stages are necessary for a group to become productive and are characterized by both harmony and conflict, as shown in Figure 16.1.

Tuckman's theory has been expanded upon over time. No group is exactly alike, which means that each team may spend more time in one stage than in another, with some never making it out of the storming stage. Some teams may move back and forth between stages, particularly as new group members are added or the team purpose changes. Some groups may go through a period of inactivity that changes only as the deadline gets closer.

As an example, a high school drama teacher was tasked with organizing the annual school play to be performed in May. The script was selected at the beginning of the school year, and tryouts were completed by August. Parts were assigned in early September to give the group time to memorize lines, build sets, design costumes, and stage rehearsals. The team met weekly, and the drama teacher spent a lot of unproductive time on what she referred to in private as "babysitting." Over the years, she noticed something: most of the productive outcomes occurred about a month before show time, regardless of how much time she spent on the traditional management efforts of directing, organizing, controlling, and managing.

The next year, she decided to try something different. In September, she selected the script, held auditions, and worked with the students to build the plan for stage props. After that, they met only once a month to socialize, play improvisation games, and work on small tasks. In January, the teacher picked up the pace and rehearsals started, costume fittings began, and the stage started to take shape. Daily rehearsals began two weeks before show time and the students nailed the first performance!

What this wise drama teacher discovered was the phenomenon of punctuated equilibrium—that is, the idea that groups go through various phases of productivity that accelerate gradually, spiking right before a deadline.

HR Alignment

The question that comes up around Tuckman's theory, punctuated equilibrium, or the neuroscience ideas that opened this chapter is: just what is HR supposed to do with them? The answer is to align knowledge with behaviors. These exams are experienced-based and require the ability to apply these concepts to the work environment.

FIGURE 16.1   Tuckman's five stages of group development

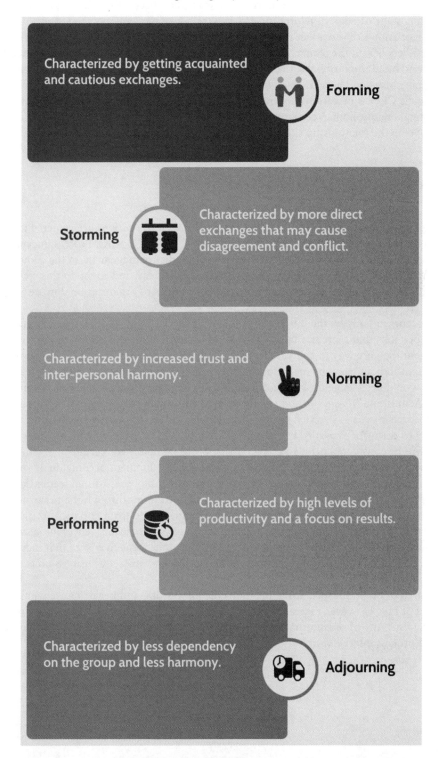

For example, HR may share Tuckman's model with a team leader and facilitate a discussion about what stage the group is in and what their needs are at that moment. During the forming stage of team development, HR can train group members on emotional intelligence, negotiation skills, conflict resolution, and the need for constructive conflict. HR also helps members design the team charter, create the individual roles and responsibilities documents, and build the processes for the team activities, including who will be responsible for assigning tasks and how decisions will be made. HR may use punctuated equilibrium to help manage CEO expectations, following up at the right time to ensure that productivity is accelerating. Finally, human resource professionals should be the go-to resource that helps teams develop the relationship skills necessary for performance.

Process Interventions

For purposes of this functional area of the exam, *process interventions* are centered on the need for HR to support "key documents and systems" (SHRM BoCK). Process interventions are more commonly understood through the lens of quality management, in the context of business strategy, workforce management, risk management, and so on. In this section, however, it is important to understand how HR contributes to organizational processes to improve results.

This occurs initially by the job posting process. It can be easy to forget when recruiting for open jobs that there is a talented group of in-house individuals. It is shortsighted to assume that the only way to source talent is from outside the organization. In some cases, an internal candidate may be ready for the next role right away; in most cases the team member would need some upskilling or reskilling to be ready for a change (see Chapter 6, "Talent Acquisition"). A *job posting* is the internal equivalent of an external recruiting ad. It is a document used to describe the position details, and the knowledge, skills, and abilities necessary to perform. Typically, HR will establish a timeframe from which only internal candidates will be considered prior to going outside of the company to recruit.

The performance management process supports the development of individuals within an organization. In addition to the performance appraisal and other formal feedback systems, HR may cultivate learning and development opportunities through the performance management process by encouraging projects that contribute to team and organizational cohesiveness. The performance management process also serves inclusiveness initiatives. It is not enough only to hire a diverse workgroup; HR must take steps to ensure that individual voices are heard by supporting exposure to different leaders, projects, business units, and developmental roles.

This area of the exam specifically mentions the job posting and performance management processes of HR. However, take a moment and look back at Chapter 15, "Structure of the HR Function." Any of the internal systems that are under the purview of HR teams may require a process intervention if they do not support measurable results.

International Organization for Standardization

The International Organization for Standardization (ISO) is a valuable resource when it comes to understanding best practices in business processes. ISO is a nongovernmental agency that seeks to establish common ground for industry practices across the world; its American equivalent is American National Standards Institute (ANSI). Documents are developed by a team of international experts that agree upon best practices. HR may use these standards to help guide process interventions in the areas such as quality management, information security management, and occupational health and safety.

For the HR department, there are currently 24 published ISO standards that define human resource excellence and another 8 under development as of 2021. They include standards related to knowledge management, HR vocabulary, leadership, occupational safety and health, metrics, human governance, recruitment, and workforce planning. The 2021 releases include standards related to workplace diversity. As a process intervention, the standards may be used informally within organizations to develop a common language and practices, or a business may choose to become certified. The certification is not done by ISO, but by external providers that follow the ISO best practices for a certifying agency. Successful certification from a credible provider offers customers and other stakeholders the assurance that a company's internal processes are compliant with quality, safety, ethics, and other benchmarks. More information is found on ISO's website at www.iso.org.

Structural Interventions

How an organization is structured serves many outcomes. Communication flows within the organizational framework, upward, downward, and side to side. Systems are designed to assist the workflow, and hierarchies of authority identify the chain of command. Factors such as accountability, informing, and authorizing changes all must be supported through the formal and informal structures of the workplace. The exam is specific about the types of structures with which you must be familiar on exam day.

Customer or Product

For businesses with multiple product lines or distinct customer groups, this organizational structure allows for the concentration of resources. This decentralized format means that each product or customer unit will have its own support staff, including R&D, finance, customer service, and marketing. In this setup, a specific strategy may be developed to drive growth through branding, innovation, and production using a more specific workforce plan to address nuances within the labor force population or industry. For example, a large real estate firm may have an international, residential, and commercial division.

Functional

A functional structure is one that groups employees into business units organized by similar skills or roles. This is the familiar structure that defines departments by job roles and skill sets, such as marketing, finance, human resources, production, research and development, and so forth.

Geographic

Geographic structures are organized by location. This can be at a state, regional, national, or international level. Like the product/customer structure, this is a decentralized operation, with each business unit having its own support resources.

Matrix

A matrix structure is a hybrid blend of function and product/customer. Employees serve on cross-functional teams, which are groups of employees from different divisions using their talents toward a shared outcome. This means that they will report to their functional "boss," but also to various project manager(s).

Human resources supports these structures by ensuring that clear roles and responsibilities documents exist. In some cases, the roles and responsibilities documents will read as a job description. Other roles require a more detailed view, such as outlining who is responsible for each function and describing the communication channels necessary to meet outcomes (customer needs, system requirements, financial transparency, and so on).

Managing Change

The knowledge domains of HR are a good place to start when identifying the challenges that often become the barriers to organizational effectiveness. Employee satisfaction is a knowledge competency tied to employee engagement and retention, job design, leadership effectiveness, corporate social responsibility, and a company's mission and values. These are all factors that are addressed through a cultural intervention.

For example, consider a common job posting process where the company requires an internal candidate to get a recommendation from their current supervisor. In theory, this makes sense—the supervisor can speak to the strengths and opportunities for improvement that the individual would bring to the desired role. In a dysfunctional work culture, this practice is unlikely to be effective. If the employee is a good worker, the supervisor may not want to lose them, and so plays down their talents. If the employee is not a good worker, the supervisor may be keen to make them someone else's problem instead of addressing the performance deficiency head on. When the culture is not conducive to organizational results, a change initiative is necessary.

According to the SHRM glossary, change management refers to the principles and practices for managing a change initiative so that it is accepted. Change management is also the practice of identifying and providing the necessary resources (people, financial, tools/equipment) so that the initiative will be successful. A change initiative is described as a transition in an organization's technology, culture, or behavior of any team member. HR technicians are often designated as the change agent—that is, the individual responsible for helping teams accept the changes and embrace the new behaviors.

When initiating change, it is not enough simply to give directives, write new standard operating procedures, or rely on a chain of command to change employee behaviors. Adult performers need to understand "the why." Additionally, if an organization does not have a clearly defined outcome for a change effort, the change initiative is likely to fall short. For these reasons, it is important to effectively diagnose the gap between current and desired performance. Reviewing current versus desired state is a key activity of the strategic planning process using tools such as strengths, weaknesses, opportunities, and threats (SWOT) or gap analyses. In other cases, change declares itself when a new condition arises. For example, when hurricanes Harvey and Irma hit the United States' southern coastline within two weeks of each other, fuel and other commodities were left in short supply or quickly became cost prohibitive to obtain. This and other conditions required businesses to adapt quickly using remedial intervention strategies while remaining aligned with their mission, vision, and values.

 Real World Scenario

Business Practices and Corporate Social Responsibility

Price gouging is the practice of raising prices before, during, or after a state of emergency has been declared; price gouging is illegal in most states. In anticipation of Hurricane Irma, residents of the Florida coast were buying up essentials such as plywood and bottles of water, leaving shelves bare and many without. Those in direct line of Irma's landfall began moving inland, staying with friends or families, or booking hotels. Some local businesses sought to take advantage of the circumstances by raising the price of these essentials to an "unconscionable" degree. The Florida Office of the State Attorney reported one such case where a local motel admitted to increasing the nightly rate of a room by 138 percent in the days leading up to the hurricane (https://keyssao.org). The owners were eventually prosecuted. This example speaks to the ethics of business practices in general, and it links to the exam competencies of personal and professional integrity and the knowledge competency of corporate social responsibility.

Whether designing a people, process, or structural intervention, managing change is a key competency for HR professionals.

Competency and Knowledge Alignment

SHRM's BoCK describes three main clusters of the knowledge, skills, abilities, and other attributes necessary to perform successfully in HR. They include the Leadership competencies, Interpersonal competencies, and Business competencies from which HR actions are grounded. In order to pass these exams, candidates must be able to align knowledge with behaviors.

As defined in Chapter 4, each cluster is further expanded into eight competencies. These eight competencies are threaded throughout the knowledge domains of this book in order to align behaviors with the associated technical expertise. A review of the relevant competencies for Organizational Effectiveness and Development begins here.

Teamwork

 SHRM defines the Interpersonal sub-competency of teamwork as the ability to participate as an effective team member, and to build, promote, and lead effective teams.

Managing teams requires interpersonal knowledge, skills, and abilities specifically in emotional intelligence (EI). EI is an individual's ability to recognize and control their own emotions and read the emotions of others. Teams with participants that have high levels of EI tend to outperform those with low degrees of EI. Teams with low EI levels are likely to lack problem-solving skills, have poor relationships with their teammates and other departments, and have low productivity. Additionally, when a team member with high EI is surrounded with members with low EI, it can decrease morale. This imbalance may even begin to lead the employee with high EI to behave in ways in which they would not normally engage to fit in or simply to get by. HR teams help team members increase self-awareness using people interventions (such as personality assessments) and then coaching to build trust. *Coaching* is a form of direct communication that targets specific individual behaviors and is an effective positive intervention strategy.

Team-oriented assessments are another method that HR can use to develop groups. Regardless of the tool, HR should begin with very clear outcomes so that progress can be measured and real-time changes made as necessary. One way to do this is for HR professionals to participate in team projects that are not HR-related. Having access to others helps HR learn about the business and get to know the team members that are HR's customers.

HR systems must be structured in a way that supports group results. Once again, the exam knowledge domain provides a filter to generate ideas on how to do this. In Total Rewards, HR would design pay systems that reward team performance. In Employee Engagement and Retention, a multi-rater system would be the most effective way to deliver meaningful feedback. Talent Acquisition activities would be highly task-focused, helping teams to source new talent that will add value to the group dynamic and results.

Conflict Management

SHRM defines the Interpersonal sub-competency of conflict management as the ability to manage and resolve conflicts by identifying areas of common interest among the parties in conflict.

Many types of conflict occur at work. Disagreements about the work itself and interpersonal challenges are the most common. Constructive conflict has been found to increase innovation and lead to improved quality decision-making. HR should not seek to eliminate conflict in the workplace, but rather to help leaders and team members get better at understanding and working with it.

As shown in Figure 16.2, management expert and consultant Patrick Lencioni describes conflict on a continuum. Conflict that is personal or aggressive is dysfunctional and destructive, eroding trust and contributing to a toxic culture. Teams that *lack* conflict are likely stagnant or working hard but with very little meaningful results. Effective teams are those that are honest and that act with transparency so that all perspectives are considered, even when things get a little heated. When this happens, the quality of the recovery will be the difference maker. This is where HR may shine!

Training employees to understand the root cause of conflict, and coaching leaders on how to guide their teams through conflict is part of the competency of conflict management. This includes maintaining respect for all employees involved without compromising company values, a focus on problem-solving, and holding employees accountable to productive standards of behavior. HR must also model the appropriate conflict management techniques, both personally and within their own teams.

FIGURE 16.2   The Conflict Continuum

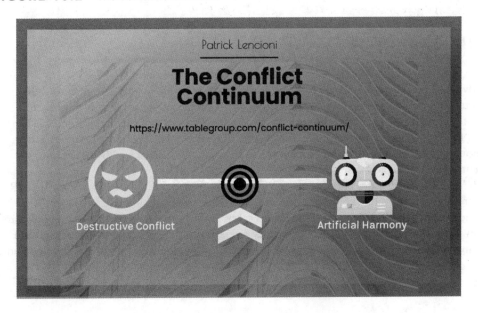

A practical model for how to develop conflict resolution skills was developed by Robert Blake and Jane Mouton. Their tactics include five basic modes of conflict resolution:

Accommodate   The leader values harmony over disagreement. This is appropriate when the issue has little impact on results.

Assert   The leader uses their authority to resolve the conflict. This is useful when a decision must be made quickly, or the situation calls for the leader's particular level of expertise.

Avoid   The leader chooses to not get involved. Like the accommodate method of conflict management, avoiding a disagreement or staying out of a dispute is useful when the issue has little value, or when the team members are appropriately handling the resolution process themselves.

Collaborate   The leader looks for what William Ury calls "the third side" (*The Walk from No to Yes*, https://www.youtube.com/watch?v=Hc6yi_FtoNo, 2010). The third side helps teams to focus on the issue(s), not on individual positions. This approach is useful to begin to get to the root of the conflict and develops team members to focus on shared interests rather than power. This conflict management approach ties directly into SHRM's competency definition of Conflict Management (see the topic heading earlier).

Compromise   The leader relies on an iterative process in which each party to the conflict relinquishes something they value. This exchange goes on until agreement is found. Compromising is necessary when individuals are fully vested in their point of view, however, this may not result in the "best" solution. Compromise is likely to be ineffective if the disagreement is about personal values.

SHRM SCP Only

Advanced HR professionals are first and foremost responsible for the alignment of HR strategy to organizational results. If the company is underperforming in a certain area, it is up to HR first to look at the HR systems that support results and then ask questions such as "In what ways can HR improve organizational results?" For this reason, senior leaders should look within the HR department to identify people, process, or HR structural intervention needs and address them.

An HR team that does not get along well creates more than just a headache for the HR manager. HR teams lose credibility and influence when they are not able to model the concepts and develop the competencies necessary for change. The chapter opening illustrates how important it is for senior leaders to pay attention to the sciences and encourage their teams to become experts in emotional intelligence, conflict management, team development, and change. HR effectiveness flows from this expertise and allows for maximum support when other departments are challenged with similar issues.

Measuring results is an imperative for HR leaders in all functional areas. In OED, this requires the ability to establish the metrics to be measured and to find ways to collect and interpret the data intelligently. From this, HR makes recommendations on how to improve the critical competencies that drive organizational effectiveness. These competencies may be developed through people, process, or structural interventions using change management principles.

Summary

Organizational effectiveness is directly measured by the ability of a company to achieve results. When there are barriers to effectiveness, proactive or remedial development interventions are designed and delivered. Human resource teams are called upon to support these initiatives through conflict management, change management, and team management efforts. Interventions may be designed at an individual team or an organizational level, and they must be aligned to business strategy and the mission, vision, and values of the organization.

Individual interventions are those that seek to improve employee behaviors. The use of legally compliant personality assessments is useful in coaching and development, and to make selection decisions for hire, promotion, and training. The performance management system is a process intervention that targets individual behaviors.

Group interventions are designed to improve the collective results of a team. These interventions may be necessary at the forming, storming, norming, performing, and adjourning stages of Tuckman's group development theory.

Process interventions seek to address lack of consistency and other barriers to effectiveness. Depending on the nature of the barrier, HR may lead interventions in quality management, risk management, and technology management. HR must also pay special attention to the HR processes to ensure that they support the productivity of other departments. This applies to all HR systems, easily understood through the filter of the exam knowledge domains.

Structural interventions target the framework of the organization. Organizational restructuring may be necessary when there is poor communication, customer dissatisfaction, or when business strategy changes.

All types of interventions require that HR teams be comfortable with leading change initiatives. This necessitates competency development in areas such as teamwork and conflict management.

Senior leaders are required to manage and measure the effectiveness of intervention efforts and be the voice for ethical change when necessary.

Key Terms

Interventions

Job posting

Nonpredictive assessments

Organizational development

Predictive assessments

Process interventions

Uniform Guidelines on Employee Selection Procedures

Exam Essentials

Apply organizational effectiveness and development principles to the workplace.   Human resource practitioners must be able to apply OED principles to their own departments and support OED initiatives throughout other business units. This requires a thorough understanding of the principles of OED.

Understand the different types of interventions.   Once an area of improvement has been identified, HR leads the way in designing, implementing, and measuring people, process, or structural interventions. Tools that may be used include behavioral assessments, models of team development, and knowledge of various structures designed to improve efficiencies and address stakeholder needs.

Align behavioral competencies with knowledge competencies.   The exams note that there are certain behavioral competencies that support all the knowledge domains of human resources. For purposes of OED, HR must develop, apply, and model the competencies of teamwork and conflict management to support HR and other organizational results effectively.

Review Questions

1. The primary goal of the function of organizational effectiveness and development (OED) is which of the following?

   A. To improve the performance of employees

   B. To increase organizational process efficiencies

   C. To improve a company's competitive advantage using restructuring where necessary

   D. To measure effectiveness and intervene when improvement is necessary

2. Fill in the blanks: Organizational effectiveness is to _____ as organizational development is to _____.

   A. Results; conflict

   B. Team performance; individual performance

   C. Overcoming barriers; developing solutions

   D. Interventions; design

3. The organization you work for has several open, critical positions. Your team is actively recruiting and finding qualified candidates, but by the time an offer is made, the candidate has usually found something else or simply does not respond to your calls and emails. Company leaders are looking at the HR team to come up with solutions to convert more job offers to hires. Which of the following should you do first?

   A. Call the candidates who are rejecting the offers to find out why.

   B. Review the HR practices for where they may be falling short.

   C. Tell the managers that they must make their hiring decisions more quickly.

   D. Increase the pay rates across the board for all open positions.

4. The study of how individual attitudes, beliefs, and values drive performance at work is the primary focus of which of the following academic domains?

   A. Personality assessments

   B. Sociology

   C. I-O psychology

   D. Neuroscience

5. Which of the following personality assessments is not designed to be predictive and thus should not be used in employee selection procedures?

   A. MBTI

   B. DISC

   C. SHL

   D. Big Five

6. Which of the following is the *best* example of an organizational team?

   A. A group of people who are in the same department

   B. A group of people who work in the same building

   C. A group of people who are working on a shared project

   D. All the above

7. Which of the following is the internal equivalent of an external recruiting ad?

   A. Job description

   B. Roles and responsibilities document

   C. Job interest card

   D. Job posting

8. Which organizational structure exists for the following business: a major auction house has locations across the globe? Each location has its own profit and loss statements and is managed at a local level using local talent.

   A. Customer

   B. Functional

   C. Matrix

   D. Geographic

9. What is the main difference between change management and a change initiative?

   A. Change management is the intervention, whereas the initiative is the disruption.

   B. Change management is the solution, whereas an initiative is the problem.

   C. Change management is the process, whereas an initiative is the objective.

   D. Change management is the system, whereas an initiative is intervention.

10. A cross-functional team within your organization is underperforming. The manager has confided in you that the team meetings are highly unproductive and extremely boring, and lack any innovative problem-solving. The groups seem to work together fine, and this is evident in the employee engagement survey that you recently completed. Where is this team likely to be on the conflict continuum?

   A. Artificial harmony

   B. Constructive conflict

   C. Destructive conflict

   D. None of the above

Chapter

17

Workforce Management

Exam Notables

The Wall Street Journal reported that, in July 2021, companies had more than 9 million jobs available. Oddly enough, the article also reported that more than 9 million Americans were looking for work but could not find jobs ("Job Openings Are at Record Highs. Why Aren't Unemployed Americans Filling Them?" *The Wall Street Journal*, July 9, 2021). The article went on to discuss the various ways that the pandemic has rapidly changed the way work gets done, including the attractiveness of remote work and the "great reset" as employees switched jobs in record-breaking numbers.

In response, companies launched HR pilot programs designed to manage and even capitalize on these conditions. The popular video app TikTok made headlines by encouraging applicants to record video résumés and send them directly to partners such as Target, NASCAR, and Shopify (#TikTokResumes, #CareerTok). Dropbox completely redesigned their brick-and-mortar workplaces, seeking to combine the best of working from home with working in a collaborative environment. They renamed their workspaces "Dropbox Studios" (https://techcrunch.com). McDonald's raised hourly pay to $18.00 in some locations (www.sltrib.com). Facebook, Amazon, and Microsoft announced that the work-from-home (WFH) option was permanent (https://startuptalky.com). These are all examples of how organizations relied on their HR systems to manage the workforce under short- and long-term conditions.

SHRM defines this knowledge domain as follows:

> Workforce Management refers to HR practices and initiatives that allow the organization to meet its talent needs (e.g., workforce planning, succession planning) and close critical gaps in competencies.

The SHRM Exam Objectives

SHRM's BoCK summarizes this functional area and defines the proficiency indicators, along with key concepts. No matter your career level, pay special attention to the exam concepts defined "For All HR Professionals" and the "Key Concepts." If seeking the SHRM-SCP designation, you must expand your efforts to include those labeled "For Advanced HR Professionals."

THE SHRM-CP EXAM AND SHRM-SCP EXAM OBJECTIVES COVERED IN THIS CHAPTER INCLUDE THE FOLLOWING:

✓ **For All HR Professionals**

- Identifies gaps in workforce competencies and misalignment of staffing levels.

- Implements approaches (e.g., buy or build) to ensure that appropriate workforce staffing levels and competencies exist to meet the organization's goals and objectives.

- Plans short-term strategies to develop workforce competencies that support the organization's goals and objectives.

- Administers and supports approaches (e.g., succession plans, high potential development programs) to ensure that the organization's leadership needs are met.

- Supports strategies for restructuring the organization's workforce (e.g., mergers and acquisitions, downsizing).

✓ **For Advanced HR Professionals**

- Evaluates how the organization's strategy and goals align with future and current staffing levels and workforce competencies.

- Develops strategies to maintain a robust workforce that has the talent to carry out the organization's current and future strategy and goals.

- Coordinates with business leaders to create strategies (e.g., succession planning, leadership development, training) that address the organization's leadership needs.

- Develops strategies for restructuring the organization's workforce (e.g., mergers and acquisitions, downsizing).

✓ **Key Concepts**

- Analysis of labor supply and demand.

- Approaches to restructuring (e.g., mergers and acquisitions, downsizing).

- Best practices and techniques for knowledge management, retention and transfer.

- Leadership development and planning (e.g., high-potential development programs).

- Succession planning programs and techniques.

- Techniques for organizational need-gap analysis (e.g., examination of HR records, interviews, focusgroups).

- Workforce planning approaches, techniques, and analyses (e.g., attrition, gap and solution, implementation and evaluation, reduction in force, supply and demand, workforce profile).

Integrating Workforce Management

> Workforce planning is the process that provides strategic direction to
> talent management activities to ensure an organization has the right people
> in the right place at the right time and at the right cost to execute its
> business strategy.
>
> *Lance and Dorothy Berger,* Talent Management Handbook,
> *McGraw Hill, 2010.*

If a common thread exists throughout the knowledge and competencies domains, it is this: HR practices must be in alignment with the internal and external conditions that drive strategy and growth. In this functional area of the exam, *Workforce Management*, the integration that occurs is between talent management and business strategy. This includes a review of the PESTLE forces that are driving the way that the workforce is managed.

The concept of supply and demand is rooted in economics. It is the idea that the scarcer the resource, the more valuable it becomes. Labor supply and demand is broadly measured by the unemployment rates published by regional, state, and national governments. When the unemployment rate is high, there is an abundance of qualified workers. This is because many workers are not working and thus collecting unemployment pay. When the unemployment rate is low, there is a scarcity of talent. This is because many individuals are working, and thus they are not collecting unemployment. The goal of workforce management is to optimize staffing levels to balance the availability of qualified employees with the needs of the company. To do this, organizations will need to take a more detailed look at the supply and demand factors that drive workforce plans.

Workforce Planning

Workforce planning is the process of continually evaluating the current workforce and its ability to achieve organizational goals. This process uses both a short-term and a long-term planning horizon.

Labor supply and demand analyses are conducted to collect and interpret data related to internal and external talent availability (supply) and the future staffing needs of the organization (demand). When there is a disparity, plans are made to bridge the gap.

Demand Analysis

The Office of Human Resources Health has a high calling: to recruit and staff a highly diverse workforce for The National Institutes of Health (NIH), one of the world's leading medical research companies. The NIH played an important role in Covid-19 research and has contributed to understanding diseases such as melanoma and migraines. In addition to their research in medicine, the NIH has a series of best practice guides for many areas of business, including human resources. For example, they published a guide on the practical application of demand analysis in labor analysis (https://hr.nih.gov/workforce/

workforce-planning/demand-analysis). The purpose of a *demand analysis* is to understand current conditions and what might change to project talent needs properly. Questions that the NIH recommends to truly understand the conditions that affect the need for staff include the following:

- What percentage of an FTE's time is required to deliver a service/product?

- Are there anticipated changes in technology, policies, regulations, or customer base that would affect workload demand?

- What opportunities are there to leverage resources with other departments?

This last question is important, because HR professionals are tasked with addressing any misalignment of staffing levels, such as one business unit laying off employees while another is recruiting. Other variables that affect staffing levels include gross sales, new customer acquisition, organizational restructuring, natural attrition, and the introduction of efficiency technology.

The Parking Lot Exercise

I realize that the short-term goal of reading this book is to pass your exam. As with workforce plans, however, a long-term, professional focus is also necessary. For this reason, I have sought in each chapter to identify resources that give you tools to apply these concepts at work. The Office of Human Resources Health mentioned earlier has a practical tool called the *Parking Lot Exercise*. The purpose of this tool is to organize and prioritize projects in order to help anticipate resource needs. Part of the Parking Lot Exercise is to sort the workload into five categories:

- Projects to keep

- Projects to parking lot

- Projects to discontinue

- Projects to improve

- Projects to add

Facilitating these types of exercises with company leaders is a critical competency for HR teams to have while navigating the workforce planning process. Take a look at the entire exercise guide here:

https://hr.nih.gov/sites/default/files/public/documents/2020-06/
Parking%20Lot%20Exercise.pdf

Statistical Forecasts

Statistical forecasts are another method used to analyze demand. These forecasts rely on objective, measurable data so that reasonably accurate projections may be made to anticipate future staffing needs.

In regression analysis, past variables are used to predict future demand. In simple linear regression analysis, a single variable related to employment is used to project future needs. In multiple linear regression analysis, several variables are used to make the same projection. The goal is to discover whether a correlation exists between variables that may be used to project demand.

In simulations, an employer establishes scenarios to be used in planning. For example, if sales grow by 15 percent in the summertime, the employer may need to hire temporary workers or extend operating hours to maintain production levels. Simulations are also used in risk management scenario planning to create business continuity and other types of disaster plans.

Judgmental Forecasts

A judge in a courtroom is considered an expert, and their opinions are, quite literally, law. Judgmental forecasts rely on the use of experts and best practices to make decisions about conditions that will affect future staffing needs. Experts may come from outside the organization, such as when HR uses a labor attorney to anticipate how employment law may change in the future. Experts may also come from within the company, such as interviewing managers to get their input on what changes or challenges they are experiencing within their business units.

A *rule of thumb* is a type of forecast that uses generalities as a guide. One such estimate from the U.S. Small Business Administration is that the cost of an employee is typically 1.25 to 1.4 times the base salary (https://www.sba.gov/blog/ how-much-does-employee-cost-you). HR may use this rule of thumb to forecast labor costs if certain employment variables change, such as payroll taxes or workers' compensation insurance costs. Note that this example uses a rule-of-thumb estimate in a simulated "if this, then that" forecast.

Supply Analysis

A *supply analysis* reviews the labor force population to identify the KSAOs and demographics of the available workforce, also called a workforce profile. Externally, this is done in many ways, including by contacting regional occupational resources through the local government or groups such as the chamber of commerce. Analysis should include unemployment statistics, percentage of service workers versus blue-collar workers, and industry prevalence by region.

Intuitively, an organization seeking to expand their tech business may think first of Silicon Valley, California, even though other areas such as New York, Utah, and Texas are all growing in the tech sector. For example, Empire State Development reports that New York is ranked #1 in the Northeast for science, technology, engineering, and mathematics (STEM) graduates, #2 in the nation for the highest number of residents who are scientists and engineers, and #3 in the country for high-tech employment (https://esd.ny.gov/

esd-media-center). Because many regions offer incentives, such as tax breaks to attract businesses to their area, HR professionals should include in their research a review of offerings, including those for subsidized training. Finding these incentives is one way that HR teams can add value to the bottom line.

Trend analysis is another qualitative analysis method, and it is an opportunity for HR teams to get creative in their research. For example, in addition to being the largest online job posting website, Indeed.com tracks employment data. In June 2021, the Indeed Insights team noticed a spike in job postings marked "urgent" or "immediate hire." Although news outlets were reporting the shortages of talent in the food, retail, and tourism sectors, Indeed's research showed similar upticks in sectors such as personal care and home health, childcare, nursing, and cleaning and sanitation (https://www.indeed.com/lead/urgent-job-postings-on-the-rise?hl=en&co=US). If you are an HR professional recruiting for these industries, you will need to prepare management and budgets for longer time-to-hire metrics, increased costs of recruiting, and the potential to have to increase base pay or incentives to attract talent. Reading these trends allows for a more proactive planning approach.

Identify Gaps and Plan Action

In addition, HR is responsible for analyzing the internal skill sets of current employees. Gaps that may be discovered include the KSAOs to perform but also gaps in diversity, challenges with retention, time-to-fill obstacles, and a lack of a leadership pipeline. These are the issues that need to be managed through the BoCK knowledge responsibility to understand "approaches (e.g., buy or build) to ensure that appropriate workforce staffing levels and competencies exist to meet the organization's goals and objectives."

The phrase "build or buy" refers to whether the business should build the competencies within the existing workforce or buy the talent from the external labor market. In some cases, short-term strategies such as purchasing talent from a staffing agency may be necessary. In other cases, companies take a longer-term approach and restructure their staffing and retention methods where appropriate.

For high HR achievers, this next phrase may be difficult to hear: you do not have to have all the answers. If fact, accessing in-house experts through focus groups and employee interviews will give the HR practitioner insights that they may not have otherwise considered. Asking team members and managers about their needs and the needs of the department is an effective way to ensure that any gap management intervention technique is targeting the right organizational challenges, whether through people, process, or organization (see Chapter 16, "Organizational Effectiveness and Development," for a refresher on interventions).

Planned exits such as natural attrition and reductions-in-force will also need to be accounted for in the workforce plan. Planned exits are a gift to human resources! It gives them time to address the specific task of managing the knowledge of the workforce.

Knowledge Management

Absolute statements are very rarely accurate, particularly in business. And yet knowledge management is a practice that affects every organization in every industry and within every department.

For HR, *knowledge management* is achieved by using several of the exam knowledge competencies, including technology management, strategic planning, and risk management.

Knowledge Management

Knowledge management is an iterative process—one that begins by defining the boundaries encompassing the subject matter at hand. For example, an exam Body of Knowledge (BoK) or Body of Competency and Knowledge (BoCK) is a tool used to define the framework that defines the knowledge and competencies necessary for the HR profession. The result is a guiding document used to engage in a continuous process of updating the scope as new information or best practices become available. The BoCK is also used to train and evaluate the KSAOs necessary to be certified successfully as a subject matter expert.

Tech industry giant IBM defines knowledge management (KM) as:

> . . . the process of identifying, organizing, storing and disseminating information within an organization. . .A knowledge management system (KMS) harnesses the collective knowledge of the organization, leading to better operational efficiencies.

Using a technology expert to define KM for purposes of exam preparation is intentional, because so much of how knowledge is created, retained, transferred, and protected occurs using technology. Productivity software, personal computing, mobile devices, and the countless systems discussed throughout this book (customer relationship management [CRM], HRI [Human Resource Information], and enterprise resource planning [ERP], for example) all are attempts to manage the staggering amount of information that is generated through work and within HR departments throughout the life cycle of the employee.

Failing to manage knowledge properly creates several challenges. When knowledge is not shared, redundancies of efforts occur, resulting in lost productivity and increased costs of activities. In business strategy Six Sigma/Lean terminology, redundancies of effort would be considered a form of waste—something the customer is not willing to pay for. Knowledge management systems also streamline communication flow and address the risk of knowledge loss that can occur when a critical employee leaves an organization.

Another aspect of knowledge management is the existence of *knowledge workers*, a term first created by management expert Peter Drucker in the 1950s. The date is significant because the nature of work was drastically changing from production output to knowledge work. This parallels the times in which we are living now, as illustrated in the chapter opening, which demands a change in how workforces are managed. Drucker defined knowledge workers as those who apply high-level knowledge obtained through education and experience to achieve outcomes, and they exist in all industries. The term is the equivalent of the "white-collar worker" still in use by statistical agencies when discussing administrative and other nonmanual laborers. Drucker coined the term because, for the first time in history, information workers were growing faster than their blue-collar counterparts (`www.corporatefinanceinstitute.com`). HR teams support these knowledge workers through learning and development efforts. HR also encourages diversity to ensure that not only those who have received formal education receive development opportunities. In a virtual world, HR must also help to secure knowledge and protect data from unauthorized access, concepts discussed in more detail in Chapter 19, "Technology Management."

Functionally, human resource teams can use knowledge management systems to great effect in training and development activities. Using videos to develop micro-learning databases is growing in popularity, as is designing self-service knowledge databases for employees. High-potential employees may be called upon to develop standard operating procedures or reference guides as part of their development in their career plan.

Finally, HR is tasked with creating a culture that encourages transparency. This includes helping to create a learning organization, one where knowledge and ideas are freely shared, constructive disagreements are welcomed and rewarded, and written materials are created and updated to ensure consistency, efficiencies, and equitable performance management.

Leadership Development

In 2016, a major study by SHRM, in partnership with the Network of Corporate Academies, sought to review the perceptions of human resource individuals on 10 separate leadership dimensions. Not surprising to the experienced HR professional, most participants agreed that leadership development was critical to their organizations. *Leadership development* is defined by SHRM in their glossary as a "professional program that helps management and executive-level employees develop knowledge, skills, abilities, and other characteristics (KSAOs) related to leadership."

The top two barriers to effective leadership development programs in the study were budget and time, followed closely by lack of support and engagement with the process:

```
https://www.shrm.org/hr-today/trends-and-forecasting/
research-and-surveys/Documents/
Leadership-Development-The-Path-to-Greater-Effectiveness.pdf
```

As with any HR initiative, human resources must get stronger at building a business case by demonstrating how leadership development activities will help an organization achieve its results. For this reason, leadership development must be tied to corporate strategy.

The Leadership Gap

As discussed in Chapter 11, "Diversity and Inclusion," diversity leads to better organizational outcomes, including creative problem-solving, innovation, and customer loyalty. As documented in the 2020 report on leadership statistics conducted by CompareCamp (https://comparecamp.com/leadership-statistics/#1), demographics matter. Consider the following issues facing leadership development efforts today:

- Baby boomers are at various stages of their phased organizational exits, with 10,000 of them reaching the retirement age of 65 every day.

- Millennials make up most of the workforce, yet 63 percent of those surveyed do not feel ready to lead.

- Women hold 22 percent of seats on boards of directors, and only 24 of the Fortune 500 companies had female CEOs in 2019.

- African Americans hold fewer than 8 percent of all leadership positions; Asians fewer than 4 percent.

There is real opportunity for HR to align their diversity efforts with corporate strategy, specifically in leadership development.

Succession Plans and High-Potential Employees

One way for HR to increase the diversity and tie leadership development efforts to organizational results is through the design and implementation of *succession plans*. These plans are defined by SHRM as a "process of implementing a talent management strategy to identify and foster the development of high-potential employees or other job candidates who, over time, may move into leadership positions of increased responsibility." Note that the exam focuses these plans on preparing high-potential employees for future leadership roles. Determining what "high potential" means is a function of selection criteria.

The succession plan process begins by properly selecting the individuals to develop. Many employees have the talent necessary to manage, direct, and even lead others. When selecting employees to put into the leadership pipeline, it is important to consider the "other" aspect of KSAOs. HR should pay attention to those who may need development in other, more basic skills. Take, for example, an employee for whom English is their second language. If they have a high level of emotional intelligence, verbal communication, and other leadership competencies but need additional support in written business communications, they should be considered as having high potential. In all succession plans, a customized development approach is necessary to ensure that the leadership pipeline is filled with a diverse group and that employees receive exactly what they need to be successful.

In addition to the standard KSAs, selection for leadership development programs should include criteria such as life experiences, informal education and volunteerism, motivation and drive, interpersonal influence, empathy, managerial courage, and the ability to manage change and conflict.

Measurement tools such as Korn Ferry's Assessment of Leadership Potential (KFALP) (https://www.kornferry.com/content/dam/kornferry/docs/article-migration/KFALP_Technical_Manual_final.pdf) are a useful way to assess aptitude. HR should rely on tools that measure for language, customs, and other differences when selecting assessments. This is key to supporting corporate diversity, equity, and inclusion (DEI) initiatives so that data (and decisions based on that data) are not lost in cultural translation.

Replacement plans are different from succession plans in that they have a shorter planning window of 12 months or less. Candidates are selected based on current skill sets as opposed to potential alone.

Leadership Theories and Styles

Traditional theories of leadership focus on traits, behaviors, and contingencies. *Trait-based theories* are those that seek to understand the personal characteristics that make a person a leader. Factors such as gender, intelligence, and social skills dominate these theories.

Behavioral theories suggest that effective leadership is less a function of how a person is biologically wired, but rather how that person acts. For example, an introverted, intuitive person may successfully use their insights to understand the needs of their team and be an effective leader. Some studies show that extroverts have greater self-efficacy and thus also make excellent leaders. The energy-orientation traits (introversion and extroversion) in these examples do not drive success; it is how the person uses their natural wiring that matters.

Contingency theories propose that it is the situation under which a leader must perform that determines effectiveness, as well as the nature of the work. Leaders emerged in rapid rates in the immediate aftermath of the 9/11 attacks on the World Trade Center in New York. Title, pay rate, and group belonging were not the drivers for these informal leaders to act.

The interest in discovering what makes leaders tick is certainly not new; it has been studied as far back as Lao Tzu's advice on governing in the Tao Te Ching. This is because leadership effectiveness drives positive outcomes in problem-solving, productivity, organizational effectiveness, employee retention, culture, employee morale, and much, much more. With the challenges facing organizations today in workforce management, having strong leaders is rapidly becoming a critical competency that HR helps to manage. For this reason, it is important to understand leadership theories and styles.

Inclusive Leadership

A *Harvard Business Review* article by Juliet Bourke and Andrea Titus, "The Key to Inclusive Leadership" (2020), noted that inclusive leadership is a critical capability, both for leaders and their organizations. The authors found that what leaders say and do makes up to a 70 percent difference as to whether someone feels included. The authors identified six traits of inclusive leaders:

- **Bias Awareness:** Understands bias, explicit and unconscious, and takes steps to reduce it in themselves and others
- **Collaboration:** Empowers others and focuses on psychological safety
- **Cultural Intelligence:** Attentive to and embraces other cultures, adapting where necessary
- **Curiosity about Others:** Shows genuine interest and open mindset
- **Humility:** Creates space for others to contribute and succeed
- **Visible Commitment:** Authentically communicates a desire to be inclusive

HR supports inclusive leadership by crafting hiring practices that seek to measure these traits, rewarding inclusive leadership behaviors, training leaders on what makes for inclusive leadership, and measuring inclusiveness within the workforce, specifically related to individual leadership practices. HR also leads discussions with leaders and their teams on the effectiveness of the company—and the leaders'—inclusive efforts. For this, leaders must be open to feedback and committed to the process.

Path-Goal Theory of Leadership

The *path-goal theory of leadership* suggests that when the path toward achieving a goal is clear, motivation is generated. In this theory, the leader defines the goals, clarifies, addresses barriers, and provides ongoing support (*Leadership: Theory and Practice*, Peter G. Northouse, Sage Publications, 2016).

The path-goal theory also illustrates the people management techniques of the Leadership competency in the exam BoCK. For the path-goal style to be effective, the leader must act in both a directive and a supportive role, behaviors that are natural opposites. Whether a leader should be more directive or more supportive depends on the followers' needs. To be effective, leadership competencies must be developed to understand the followers' individual characteristics and act with patience, a plan, and a purpose.

In addition to the leader and the follower, the task is relevant in path-goal theory. This occurs within the scope of participative leadership. In participative leadership, the leader encourages active involvement from the follower (leadership behaviors). This works for a follower who is self-directed and desires autonomy (follower characteristics). Participative leadership is particularly important when a task is unclear or has not been done before (task characteristics). Understanding the relationship between the leader, the follower, and the task is necessary to achieve results. Figure 17.1 illustrates the major components of this theory.

FIGURE 17.1   Components of the path-goal theory

As a style of leadership, participative management is built on the firm foundation of employee involvement. This requires that the leaders develop competencies for coaching and mentoring and use delegation to develop their team. Delegation has many benefits to the leader, to the team member, and to the organization. For the leader, it frees time up to work on the important activities that often get overlooked at the expense of the urgent ones. For team members, delegation is the opportunity to learn new skills or work across teams as part of a career path. Upskilling and reskilling is highly desired by the younger generation, and it is necessary for the more mature workforce as the nature of work changes. From an organizational perspective, the benefit is that these types of developmental activities build a pipeline that may be used for succession and replacement planning and to better manage organizational knowledge.

Situational Leadership

In *situational leadership*, emphasis is placed on the circumstances under which a leader must act, as opposed to the trait-based theories that rely on individual characteristics. In the situational approach, a leader adapts their style to the task at hand and assesses the ability of the team to achieve results. The leader then makes decisions about how to move forward. The key components of situational leadership are delegating, participating, selling, and telling. For example, a leader will need to engage in more telling behaviors for a low-performing employee, whereas the leader should delegate more to their high performers.

 Originally developed by Paul Hersey and Kenneth H. Blanchard in 1969, the situational approach is now being more thoroughly researched and expanded by the Center for Leadership Studies (https://situational .com). As of 2019, The Ken Blanchard Companies focus on the Situational Leadership II (SLII) model (www.kenblanchard.com).

Transformational Leadership

Transformational leadership theory was one of the first to begin to look at the relationship dynamics between leaders and followers. Its premise is that the quality of the relationship between the leader and the follower creates shared success. The reciprocity of this theory is that when leaders do *not* act in their own self-interest, both the leader and the follower are transformed and are better positioned to achieve results.

Transformational leaders can influence others, often using their natural charisma or the ability to make others want to follow them. Transformational leaders stimulate the thinking of their teams, harnessing the power of new perspectives to improve problem-solving and build trust. These leaders are adept at customizing their leadership style to meet the needs of the people charged in their care.

The opposite of transformational leadership is *transactional leadership*. This leadership style relies on an exchange—a "this for that" approach such as "you will get paid if you take out the garbage." The emphasis is on reward and punishment as opposed to the growth-and-development emphasis of transformational leaders.

The empirical research on transformational leadership has supported the basic premises put forth by Bernard Bass and James Burns over 25 years ago. Specifically, transformational leaders are different from transactional leaders in terms of their personalities, moral perspectives, values attitudes, and behaviors. Transformational leadership also has generally been shown to have a more positive impact on motivation and performance. Finally, we also have evidence that this style of leadership is not born into leaders, but rather it can be developed over time.

Leader-member exchange (LMX) also relies on the leader-follower relationship. The target of these studies is the nature and quality of the energy of the interactions between the leader and follower (the dyadic, a whole made of two, or dyad). In this theory, followers are grouped as "in-group" or "out-group." This does not mean that employees are treated unfairly; however, in-group followers involve themselves more with the leader, take ownership of tasks and duties, and, as a result, are given more responsibility.

LMX theory represents one of the most researched leadership topics over the past two decades. The LMX scale in its various forms has been correlated with a broad range of variables, including follower satisfaction, performance, and turnover, at both the individual and group levels of analysis. However, researchers have debated whether LMX theory creates inequities or even injustices in organizations based on its assumption that leaders create in-groups and out-groups.

Table 17.1 shows a list of these major leadership elements and their advantages and disadvantages.

TABLE 17.1   Leadership theories and styles: advantages and disadvantages

Theory	Advantages	Disadvantages
Inclusive	Achieves meaningful results in an organization's DEI initiative.	May take time to implement for maximum effectiveness; current practices will have to be scoured to uncover the root cause(s) of any lack of inclusivity.
Participative	Empowers employees to take ownership in their role and their contributions.	Not all employees want to be actively involved or they do not have the skills to participate at the same rates as other team members. This could result in a lack of inclusivity.
Path-Goal	Follower performance and satisfaction are increased when the leader focuses on motivation.	May be difficult for leaders to understand and adapt to all types of employee motivators, especially when managing large groups.
Situational	Followers feel supported when the leader adapts their style to the followers' needs.	May result in perceived favoritism and inconsistency in applied style.
Transformational	Has positive benefits for the leader, the follower, and the organization (increased productivity, morale, and motivation).	May sacrifice short-term needs for long-term gains. Can lead to over-reliance on the leader.

Competency and Knowledge Alignment

SHRM's BoCK describes three main clusters of the knowledge, skills, abilities, and other attributes necessary to perform successfully in HR. They include the Leadership competencies, Interpersonal competencies, and Business competencies from which HR actions are grounded. To pass these exams successfully, candidates must be able to align knowledge with behaviors.

Each cluster is expanded into eight competencies. These eight competencies are threaded throughout the knowledge domains of this book to align behaviors with the associated technical expertise. A review of the relevant competencies for the Organizational Effectiveness and Development competency begins here.

Navigating the Organization

SHRM defines the Leadership sub-competency of navigating the organization as the ability to work within the parameters of the organization's hierarchy, processes, systems, and policies.

Disruptive politics and divisive silos at work are exhausting and unproductive, and yet they remain firmly embedded within our institutions. This means that HR and other leaders must become adept at navigating the pitfalls and seeking to form productive alliances that are not rooted in self-interest.

The Lominger Sort Card assessment tool (as described in *FYI: For Your Improvement, A Development and Coaching Guide*, by Michael Lombardo and Robert Eichinger, 2014) describes the competency of "political savvy" as a form of organizational positioning. This competency is characterized by being sensitive to how organizations and people function, having a mindset that organizational politics are necessary, and being a "maze-bright" person. This definition aligns with SHRM's description of HR's need to understand the hierarchies, formal and informal work roles, and relationship dynamics between workers. *Formal structures* are those that are systematic and known; *informal structures* are more loosely aligned and often work underground. In formal structures, communication flows through specific channels such as meetings and emails. In less formal structures, HR will need to tap into the meeting-that-happens-after-the meeting in order to get a pulse on a situation.

Understanding these dynamics is the knowledge competency and addressing them in healthy functional ways is the behavior. Savvy HR teams are responsible for facilitating conversations between individuals and teams, using their influence to drive the achievement of company goals. In some cases, the same applies to pushing forward with HR initiatives that are necessary to manage the workforce successfully.

Workforce management is accomplished through the use of allies—that is, individuals within the organization who help drive organizational and HR initiatives. Strong allies are those with a deep understanding of the organizational dynamics outside of the formal structures, who share the vision, and who are willing to act outside of their own self-interests.

HR should use its influence and credibility to encourage a more transparent organization where employees feel psychologically safe to speak freely and where constructive conflict is welcome and managed at all levels of the organization.

Vision

SHRM defines the Leadership sub-competency of vision as the ability to define and support a coherent vision and long-term goals for HR that support the strategic direction of the organization.

A vision is naturally part of an organization's governing directives, along with the company mission and values. Developing and communicating a company or HR vision helps employees understand their purpose. When communicated well, employees have a clear line of sight as to how they contribute to organizational effectiveness. This is key to active engagement and job satisfaction, both factors of employee retention.

Also consider the barriers to vision. Organizations with an identity crisis will struggle to articulate why the company exists and where it is going. Negative politics, poor hiring practices, and entrenched teams—these are all barriers to organizational effectiveness that are addressed through the HR department. HR helps teams focus on behaviors that drive the achievement of organizational outcomes. This can be done by facilitating brainstorming sessions and guiding leaders toward a clear picture of where the company is going. From this, action plans may be developed, implemented, and evaluated.

Managing HR Initiatives

SHRM defines the Leadership sub-competency of managing HR initiatives as the execution, implementation, and management of HR projects or initiatives that support HR and organizational objectives.

Closely tied to the concepts covered in Chapter 15, "Structure of the HR Function," managing HR initiatives is the ability to develop HR programs that drive organizational effectiveness. These programs are framed by the knowledge domains, such as Total Rewards and Learning and Development.

Managing HR initiatives requires HR professionals to develop and draw on the other exam behavioral competencies. HR professionals should lead their organization and teams to achieve results using their business acumen to ensure that HR programs are relevant to business strategy.

HR experts must act with personal and professional integrity and ethics to ensure that no conflicts of interests exist when making decisions about HR programs and activities. These business partners provide consultation to managers and senior leaders on departmental and organizational behaviors that are compliant with labor laws and use their critical evaluation skills to understand risk and then design HR initiatives to manage exposure. These and other outcomes require that HR develop strong interpersonal and relational skills to work with others in order to maximize performance and drive change.

HR people also need to communicate effectively to all stakeholders when conducting a needs assessment to design HR projects. These skills come in handy when reporting on the progress of the initiatives and are tied closely to the need to be agile when making real-time changes as the HR project progresses.

Finally, many HR initiatives should be aligned with the organizational interventions discussed in Chapter 16, "Organziational Effectiveness and Development," Individual interventions may be required for high-potential employees as part of developmental activities. Process interventions may be required to manage successfully the technical systems necessary for effective knowledge management. An organization with an M&A or downsizing strategy will require HR to lead interventions designed to restructure the way work gets done and manage the personnel systems to do so.

Influence

 SHRM defines the Leadership sub-competency of influence as inspiring colleagues to understand and pursue the strategic vision and goals of HR and the organization.

The sub-competency of influence is another that is threaded throughout HR behaviors. If an HR professional lacks influence, they will be unable to drive the performance changes that are necessary at individual, departmental, and organizational levels. Influence is not task-oriented; influence is one of the softer sciences and, as Dale Carnegie said:

> When dealing with people, let us remember we are not dealing with creatures of logic. We are dealing with creatures of emotion....

> How to Win Friends and Influence People,
> *Dale Carnegie & Associates, 1936*

This can be a challenge for the more transactional of leaders, and if an HR person is too transactional, overly focused on compliance, or narrow-minded, HR will be perceived as being "the one that says no all of the time." This leads directly to lack of influence, and HR will no longer have a seat at the table, which in turn, creates more challenges for HR to manage down the line. When this happens too often, HR is viewed as being ineffective.

Influence involves developing the relational skills necessary to motivate others and advocate for the proper course of action. HR can gain influence by being credible subject matter experts both in HR and the business. Influence is cultivated by developing strong listening skills and staying open-minded to new ideas. It is helpful to remember that there are often multiple ways to achieve goals; being flexible in one situation gives you space to negotiate on the challenges that are less tractable.

SHRM SCP Only

Many of the preceding chapters have focused on the rapid evolution of the way work gets done and the need for HR leaders to keep up. At very few other times in history has there been such a concentrated call to action that the Covid-19 pandemic accelerated.

Even before the pandemic, changes were happening through technology, organizational restructuring, and developing trends in work-from-home, working across cultures, and managing multiple generations in the workplace. Senior HR leaders are tasked with evaluating how well or poorly their teams are aligning staffing levels with current work and future strategies.

This evaluation is done in several ways, and the first is through the lens of inclusiveness; HR leaders being viewed as business partners. Long has the need for HR to "have a seat at the table" been discussed. This phrase refers to advanced HR professionals being involved in the development of organizational strategies and then contributing by aligning HR initiatives with business goals. HR leaders need to make the business case that *people* are the critical competencies and thus HR systems are necessary to support strategic outcomes. For some companies, this is already the case. For other, smaller organizations, this may take more influence.

Senior leaders should encourage their HR teams to become professionally certified in human resources and/or in industry-specific standards, because part of a credible HR team is their ability to speak the language of business (see the communication sub-competency in the exam BoCK).

HR teams also support workforce development strategies to build a pipeline of workers. These workers may need to be reskilled, upskilled, or developed from within to perform. Building a leadership pipeline is also important using succession and replacement planning tools. Advanced HR professionals are responsible for identifying the employees who have the potential to succeed their leaders. HR must also design the leadership training and development programs to ensure that a diverse, qualified group of individuals is given the opportunity to lead.

Summary

Workforce management is the planned effort to integrate HR practices and initiatives within the organization to help meet current and future staffing needs. This integration is accomplished by engaging in the workforce planning process that analyzes supply and demand. Once a gap has been identified, HR leads the effort to optimize staffing levels using practices within the HR functional areas.

When gaps exist between the necessary knowledge competencies of teams, HR leads the effort to engage in knowledge management practices. This effort includes capturing knowledge when and where it originates, storing it, and retaining it for future use. The effort is often closely aligned with the technology management practices covered in Chapter 19.

Gaps may also exist at a leadership level. When this is the case, HR leads efforts to create bench depth (talent downstream), selecting high-potential employees for development efforts through career planning, succession planning, and replacement planning. Knowledge of general leadership theories, principles, and styles allows HR to coach and mentor, as well as model appropriate leadership behaviors to maximize influence and effectively navigate the formal and informal organizational systems.

Advanced HR professionals are sought out as leaders of the workforce management efforts including evaluating the analysis methods being used and then making recommendations on the findings to optimize staffing levels and avoid misalignment. Senior leaders should also cultivate any strategic insights to align HR practices with intervention plans at the individual, process, or structural level.

Key Terms

Behavioral theories	Rule of thumb
Contingency theories	Situational leadership
Demand analysis	Statistical forecast
Knowledge management	Succession planning
Knowledge workers	Supply analysis
Leadership development	Trait-based theory
Leader-member exchange (LMX) theory	Transactional leadership
Replacement plans	Transformational leadership

Exam Essentials

Understand how to integrate workforce management practices with business strategy.　Human resource teams must be able to balance workforce staffing needs with current and future business strategy. This is done by designing and integrating workforce management practices that balance staffing levels with organizational strategies.

Conduct supply-and-demand analysis to identify competency gaps and create a workforce plan.　HR is responsible for analyzing labor force supply and demand as part of a workforce plan. Asking questions, using statistical forecasts, and using gap analysis tools ensure that HR creates short- and long-term strategies to optimize staffing levels and avoid misalignment.

Develop competencies to manage organizational knowledge effectively.   HR professionals are key to helping organizations manage, retain, and transfer knowledge, often using digital tools. Recruiting for knowledge workers and then managing them within the framework of organizational effectiveness and development is also the role of HR teams.

Be familiar with and apply principles of leadership.   The shortage of qualified workers exists at all organizational levels, including leadership. HR aligns leadership development efforts with career pathing for high-potential workers, succession, and replacement planning, and with DEI initiatives to ensure that the selection criteria do not unintentionally exclude a diverse workgroup.

Develop leadership and interpersonal competencies necessary to be effective.   The ability to navigate the organization, align efforts with the company vision, and use their influence is necessary to manage HR initiatives. HR initiatives are interventions designed to support organizational outcomes and respond to planned and unforeseen workforce management needs that drive success.

Review Questions

1. Of the following human resource functions, which one is most closely aligned with the practice of workforce management?

    A. Learning and Development

    B. Total Rewards

    C. Talent Planning and Acquisition

    D. Employee Engagement and Retention

2. As an HR generalist for a high-tech company based in Salt Lake City, Utah, John realizes that the local labor supply will not have the talent available to meet organizational hiring needs over the next three years. Which of the following strategies should he consider?

    A. Analyze specific skills shortages to design training programs that reskill or upskill current workers.

    B. Make a business case to senior leaders for wage increases to match the competitive market.

    C. Research options for a satellite office in New York, where there is an abundance of technical talent.

    D. All of the above.

3. Which of the following terms describes the process of creating different versions of knowledge management programs to remain relevant?

    A. Continuous improvement

    B. Iterative

    C. Managed

    D. Designed

4. Which of the following is the major focus for knowledge management programs?

    A. Retention and transfer

    B. Compliance with regulatory agencies

    C. Securing the data

    D. Technological integration

5. Part of your role as a senior generalist is to interview managers to assess their staffing needs. In one of the interviews, the manager told you that they like to hire one customer service representative for every 100 customers. This supervisor is using what type of forecast?

    A. Situational

    B. Demand

    C. Statistical

    D. Rule of thumb

6. Which of the following is a major barrier to leadership development programs today?

    A. Budget

    B. Time

    C. Availability of talent

    (D.) All the above

7. Which of the following leadership theories relies on characteristics of the leader, the follower, and the task?

    (A.) Path-goal

    B. Situational

    C. Transformational

    D. LMX

8. What is the primary difference between succession and replacement plans?

    A. The quality of candidate

    B. The nature of the work

    C. The planning horizon

    (D.) The urgency of need

9. Why is the sub-competency of navigating the organization considered a form of political savvy rather than strictly an interpersonal skill?

    A. Because navigating the organization does not require interpersonal skills.

    (B.) Because it requires HR individuals to be skilled in both the formal and informal organizational systems.

    C. Navigating the organization is transactional as opposed to relational.

    D. All the above.

10. Which of the following requires an alignment with other governing documents and organizational beliefs?

    (A.) Vision

    B. Influence

    C. Navigating the organization

    D. Interpersonal skills

Chapter

18

Employee and Labor Relations

Exam Notables

"Please tell me you're Republicans" quipped President Ronald Reagan to the hospital staff charged with his care after an assassination attempt left him with a life-threatening gunshot wound. Five months later, the president was back at work as the commander-in-chief, this time battling a dispute between the federal government and their employees—the air traffic controllers. Despite the presence of a collective bargaining agreement, Reagan demanded that the 11,000 striking workers return to their jobs or face being fired (https://millercenter.org/president/ronald-reagan/key-events). Watch the President's speech and justification for the threats of firing at https://millercenter.org/reagan-vs-air-traffic-controllers.

This event illustrates the contentious history of the relationship between unions, union members, and employers. It also makes light of the influence that party politics has on government decision-making, such as regulating the terms and conditions of union and non-union employment. Whether leading negotiations, shaping policies, or interpreting employment rights, HR teams are a resource for employees and an adviser for employers. This is summarized by SHRM's definition of this functional area:

> Employee & Labor Relations refers to any dealings between the organization and its employees regarding the terms and conditions of employment.

The SHRM Exam Objectives

SHRM's *Body of Competency and Knowledge (BoCK)* not only summarizes this functional area, but also defines the proficiency indicators and key concepts. No matter your career level, pay special attention to the exam concepts defined "For All HR Professionals" and the "Key Concepts." If seeking the SHRM-SCP designation, you must expand your efforts to include those labeled "For Advanced HR Professionals."

THE SHRM-CP EXAM AND SHRM-SCP EXAM OBJECTIVES COVERED IN THIS CHAPTER INCLUDE THE FOLLOWING:

✓ **For All HR Professionals**

- Supports interactions with union and other employee representatives.

- Supports the organization's interests in union-management activities.

- Assists and supports the organization in the collective bargaining process.

- Participates in or facilitates ADR processes (e.g., arbitration, mediation).

- Makes recommendations for addressing other types of employee representation (e.g., governmental, legal).

- Develops and implements workplace policies, handbooks, and codes of conduct.

- Provides guidance to employees on the terms and implications of their employment agreement and the organization's policies and procedures (e.g., employee handbook).

- Consults managers on how to supervise difficult employees, handle disruptive behaviors, and respond with the appropriate level of corrective action.

- Conducts investigations into employee misconduct and suggests disciplinary action when necessary.

- Manages employee grievance and discipline processes.

- Resolves workplace labor disputes internally.

✓ **For Advanced HR Professionals**

- Manages interactions and negotiations with union and other employee representatives (e.g., governmental, legal).

- Serves as the primary representative of the organization's interests in union-management activities (e.g., negotiations, dispute resolution).

- Manages the collective bargaining process.

- Consults on and develops an effective organized labor strategy (e.g., avoidance, acceptance, adaptation) to achieve the organization's desired impact on itself and its workforce.

- Educates employees, managers, and leaders at all levels about the organization's labor strategy (e.g., avoidance, acceptance, adaptation) and its impact on the achievement of goals and objectives.

- Educates employees at all levels about changes in the organization's policies.

- Coaches and counsels managers on how to operate within the parameters of organizational policy, labor agreements, and employment agreements.

- Oversees employee investigations and discipline.

✓ **Key Concepts**

- Approaches to retaliation prevention.

- Approaches to union-organization relations (e.g., collective bargaining, contract negotiation, contract administration process).

- Causes of and methods for preventing and addressing strikes, boycotts, and work stoppages.

- Disciplinary procedures and approaches.

- Employment rights, standards, and concepts (e.g., labor rights, living wage and fair wage concepts, standard workday), according to the International Labor Organization (ILO).

- Techniques for disciplinary investigations.

- Techniques for grievance and complaint resolution.

- Types and development of compliance and ethics programs (e.g., design, implementation, performance measures).

- Types and structures of organized labor (e.g., unions, works councils, trade union federations, other employee collectives).

- Types of alternative dispute resolution (ADR) (e.g., mediation, arbitration) and their advantages and disadvantages.

- Unfair labor practices, according to the ILO.

- Unionization approaches, methods, and management (e.g., acceptance, avoidance strategies).

Employment Rights and Responsibilities

Employee and labor relations is like the exam content of U.S. employment law in that it is heavily oriented toward employment rights and responsibilities. Rights and responsibilities exist for employees, and employers have certain rights and responsibilities as well. When a union is present, they are responsible for establishing rights that go beyond the regulatory protections already in place.

Employees are defined by SHRM as "persons who exchange their work for wages or salary." The *employer of record* is the entity that is responsible for the health and welfare of the employee and who may set the conditions of employment, including wages, work schedule, time off, and benefits.

In 2020, the Department of Labor (DOL) issued updated regulations to the Fair Labor Standards Act (FLSA) regarding *joint employers*. An employee may have "one or more joint employers. . .any additional 'person' (that is, an individual or entity) who is jointly and severally liable with the employer for the employee's wages." The DOL identified the factors that determine if there may be joint employment—if the entity or individual:

- Benefits from the work of the employee

- Hires or fires the employee

- Supervises and controls the employee's work schedule or conditions of employment to a substantial degree

- Determines the employee's rate and method of payment

- Maintains the employee's employment records

The DOL updates also identified factors that, when present, do not automatically assume joint liability. They include the following:

- Operating as a franchisor or entering into a brand and supply agreement, or using a similar business model

- The potential joint employer's contractual agreements with the employer requiring the employer to comply with its legal obligations or to meet certain standards to protect the health or safety of its employees or the public

- The potential joint employer's contractual agreements with the employer requiring quality control standards to ensure the consistent quality of the work product, brand, or business reputation

- The potential joint employer's practice of providing the employer with a sample employee handbook or other forms, allowing the employer to operate a business on its premises (including "store within a store" arrangements), offering an association health plan or association retirement plan to the employer or participating in such a plan with the employer, jointly participating in an apprenticeship program with the employer, or any other similar business practice

Human resources are responsible for managing these factors to ensure that employees are properly classified and to protect the employer from unnecessary litigation.

Employment Agreements

In addition to the individual employment contracts covered in Chapter 6, "Talent Acquisition," and the collective employment contracts of unions, there are other types of agreements that explain or limit an employee's rights.

Noncompete Agreements

Noncompete agreements (NCAs) are those that restrict an employee's ability to work in the same/similar space as their employer upon separation, or to go to work for a competitor. A noncompete outlines for how long the individual must refrain from competing with their former employer or client. Noncompete agreements are not enforceable in many states, since no entity has full discretion over someone's right to earn a living. For example, in 2016, Jimmy John's sandwich shop was sued by New York and Illinois due to their noncompete agreements that prohibited sandwich makers from working at competitors within a 3-mile radius of *any Jimmy John's in the country*. The plaintiffs won. In 2021, President Biden proposed new rules that limit the ability of an NCA to infringe on a person's right to earn a living ("Biden Moves to Restrict Noncompete Agreements, Saying They're Bad for Workers," by Andrea Hsu, NPR.org). This move is part of a larger attempt to eliminate the competitive barriers that keep people from economic independence.

Nondisclosure Agreements

Nondisclosure agreements (NDAs) seek to restrict an employee's ability to disclose company trade secrets and other confidential information, including customer lists, trade secrets, and research data. Social media creates the risk of unintentional disclosure of company information. For example, one employee took a selfie while at work, not realizing that pallets of brand-new, unlaunched products were serving as the backdrop. When they posted it to their social media accounts, they inadvertently shared confidential, competitive information. HR helps employers navigate these types of situations using NDAs and through policies addressing social media use. These and other policies are distributed through the employee handbook.

Employee Handbooks

A *policy* is a statement of expectation for employee and employer behavior, and it is used to outline rights and responsibilities. Many employers use an *employee handbook* to document and communicate the policies, procedures, and rules that govern employment.

An employee handbook is not required by law. However, compliance with many employment regulations require that an employer have a written policy in place. For example, when complying with harassment prevention laws, the first step is to have a written policy that prohibits harassing and other abusive behaviors at work. A written policy, training of supervisors and employees, prohibition of retaliation, and prompt investigation all help the employer to establish an "affirmative defense" against a charge of unlawful harassment.

Employers must take care not to have overly broad policies that restrict an employee's rights or that get in the way of attracting and retaining workers. For example, *moonlighting* is a term used to describe a worker who has a second job. In a gig economy (an increase in self-employment through contract work, often called "gigs"), this is not uncommon. A policy that prohibits moonlighting may keep an otherwise qualified worker from staying in their position, or from accepting a job offer in the first place, because it overly restricts their right to earn a living. However, a moonlighting policy is appropriate when there is a conflict of interest or a safety hazard due to fatigue.

Employee Code of Conduct

Whereas a policy is a statement that outlines employee and employer rights and responsibilities, a code of conduct is specifically addressed toward employee behavior. A safety code of conduct, also called code of safe practices, serves to outline what are safe and unsafe behaviors.

Employment Disputes

As with any agreement between two or more parties, it is likely that a dispute over behaviors will arise. These disputes occur when an employee violates a policy, or when an employer violates an employee's rights. Prior to disciplining an employee or resolving a complaint through a third party, HR leads an investigation to gather facts and decide the proper course of action.

Under certain circumstances, a third party may be hired to investigate. This is often done in conjunction with another stakeholder, such as a workers' compensation insurance company that has a financial obligation to pay out benefits. In many cases, however, it is up to HR to conduct an impartial investigation into the circumstances surrounding the employee complaint.

"I need to talk to you, but. . .um. . .I don't want you to say anything." So begins many difficult conversations with employees who need to talk to HR about a complaint! The truth is, HR cannot guarantee confidentiality. As a neutral party, HR gathers the information necessary to ensure that an investigation is fair to all involved, and that includes talking to others who have information about the event(s). HR must still act with discretion and only engage with individuals who "need to know," or who can provide clarity. HR should take good care to document the findings using neutral, fact-based language that avoids emotional claims or personal opinions.

It is also important that HR ask the complainant what an ideal outcome would be. If HR immediately acts by reassigning an employee while an investigation is being conducted, it could be viewed as retaliation. More than half of all complaints filed with the Equal Employment Opportunity Commission (www.eeoc.gov) are a charge of retaliation, punishing an employee for exercising their rights under a law. Although HR cannot stop an employee from filing a complaint, they can present an affirmative defense.

NOTE   Retaliation is prohibited by all nondiscrimination laws, and it is covered in more detail in Chapter 14, "U.S. Employment Laws and Regulations."

Employee Discipline

It is an unfortunate reality that part of the duties of HR is to discipline employees who are not performing.

A positive discipline strategy is always preferred to its more authoritarian, disciplinary counterpart, progressive discipline. Positive discipline is characterized by a focus on coaching and mentoring to success. A written action plan, such as a performance improvement plan (PIP), is often used to ensure follow-up and accountability.

Progressive discipline strategies are those that have specific steps that are followed. These steps typically follow a procedure such as the following:

First step: Verbal warning

Second step: Written warning

Third step: Final written warning

Fourth step: Termination

One challenge to progressive discipline policies is that they can create an implied contract, meaning that the employee has a reasonable expectation that these steps will be followed regardless of the severity of the behavior. HR addresses this by having strong statements of at-will within their policies and clearly stating the right to proceed directly to termination where appropriate.

Figure 18.1 identifies the pros and cons of positive versus progressive discipline procedures.

FIGURE 18.1 Positive vs. progressive discipline

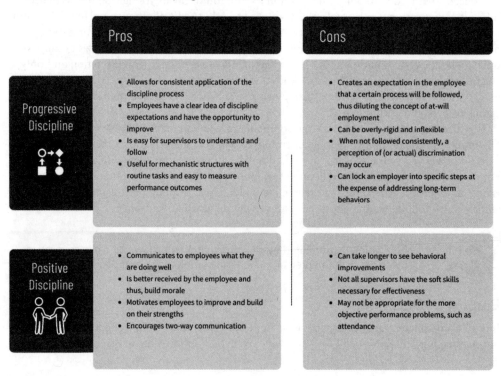

Regardless of the approach, care should be taken to focus on the behavior, not on the person. HR supports the process by training supervisors, participating in the discipline sessions, and documenting for compliance purposes to manage the risk of a wrongful discharge or wrongful termination claim effectively.

Alternative Dispute Resolution

When an employee violates an employment agreement of any sort, a dispute may occur. This requires an investigation to determine the facts of the matter.

HR plays an important role in helping supervisors and leaders handle disputes internally. Failure to do so means that the dispute may be escalated to an outside party. When that outside party is the labor board, the Equal Employment Opportunity Commission, or a labor attorney, the risk of a costly dispute resolution exponentially increases. For this reason, if an organization and their HR team is unable to resolve the complaint internally, the next best practice approach is the use of alternative methods, agreed to in writing, usually at the time of hire.

Alternative dispute resolution (ADR) is an "umbrella term used for the various approaches and techniques, other than litigation, that can be used to resolve a dispute" (SHRM Glossary of Terms). As the definition suggests, ADR methods are not only useful when resolving employee grievances, they may also be used to handle any disagreement between an employer and an employee (or a trade union, when present).

The most common ADR methods, and their definitions from the exam glossary of terms, are as follows:

Arbitration: Disputing parties agree to be bound by the decision of one more impartial person to whom they submit their dispute for final determination. An arbitrator's decisions may be binding or nonbinding, depending on the agreement.

Mediation & Conciliation: Methods of nonbinding ADR by which a neutral third party tries to help disputing parties reach a mutually agreeable decision. The mediator or conciliator acts as a facilitator and is not authorized to make any binding decisions.

Ombuds: An ombuds representative from within or outside of the organization may be designated as a third-party, neutral investigator. They retain no disciplinary or decision-making authority. An ombud may refer the issue to one of the previous methods of ADR.

Peer Review: A panel of employees agrees to hear the details of a dispute and offer their perspective for resolution. Peer reviews are not binding, and HR supports the panel by acting as a facilitator and training panel members on active listening and other skills to facilitate a positive experience.

ADR methods are used to reduce the cost of employment lawsuits that arise out of employee disputes. Whether binding or not, the use of third parties offers a neutral perspective that may lead to successful outcomes. Many employers require that employees sign ADR agreements as part of their new hire paperwork; individual states vary in the criteria, application, and enforceability of such agreements.

The Economic Policy Institute

A study by the Economic Policy Institute updated in 2018 had some interesting findings ("The Growing Use of Mandatory Arbitration," by Alexander J. S. Colvin, https://www.epi.org/publication/the-growing-use-of-mandatory-arbitration).The findings included the following:

- More than half—53.9 percent—of nonunion private-sector employers have mandatory arbitration procedures. Among companies with 1,000 or more employees, 65.1 percent have mandatory arbitration procedures.

- Mandatory arbitration is more common in low-wage workplaces. It is also more common in industries that are disproportionately composed of female workers and in industries that are disproportionately composed of African American workers.

- Among the states, mandatory arbitration is especially widespread in California and Texas, border states with a heavily populated immigrant workforce.

It will be interesting to see if the Supreme Court backtracks on any of its previous rulings related to the enforceability of arbitration agreements, particularly if they are found to be part of systemic inequalities that are being more closely scrutinized.

Intellectual Property Rights

Plagiarizing poets and food chef egos form the backdrop for the birth of intellectual property rights (*The Genesis of American Patent and Copyright Laws*, Bruce W. Bugbee, 1967, Public Affairs Press). Poems and recipes are considered intellectual property (IP), a thought-asset of the original creator. When that work is created on behalf of an employer, a question of ownership can occur. Generally, creative work that originates while in the employ of a company belongs to the employer—the employee has no claim unless there was an agreement in place defining ownership. The U.S. Patent and Trademark Office (USPTO) notes that trademarks, patents, copyrights, domain names, and business name registrations are all different, and care should be taken to ensure that the business registers for the proper protection.

Patents

A patent protects an invention, granting an individual or entity exclusive rights to monetize their original process, design, or other invention for a specified period. There are three types of patents:

Plant   Granted for 20 years, these patents apply to seed and other original plants that have not been for sale in the country for more than one year. Applications for cannabis plant patents have been steadily rising as laws are changed and commercial growers gain popularity.

Utility   Also granted for 20 years, a utility patent focuses on the specific, original, non-obvious function of a process or invention. These are the most common type of patent filing. Walmart filed for a utility patent on robotic bees, remote-controlled drones that can detect pollen.

Design   Protection is granted for design patents for 15 years. Design patents cover a unique visual element, such as appearance or ornament. The original iMac, for example, first had a design patent, since it did not qualify for a utility patent because computers were not an original work.

Copyrights

A copyright protects an original artistic or literary work, including computer software, books, and music. For HR, this is relevant when purchasing and reproducing training material from a third party. Organizationally, securing rights to copy is a form of risk management when a product or service is the competitive advantage.

Trademarks

The USPTO notes a key distinction between a trademark and a business name. A trademark typically protects brand names and logos used on goods and services. Use of a business name does not necessarily qualify as trademark use, though other use might qualify it as both a business name and a trademark.

Domain Names

A domain name is part of a web address that links to the Internet protocol address (IP address) of a particular website. From the USPTO website (`www.uspto.gov`), a domain name is registered "with an accredited domain name registrar, not through the USPTO. A domain name and a trademark differ. A trademark identifies goods or services as being from a particular source. Use of a domain name only as part of a web address does not qualify as source-indicating trademark use, though other prominent use apart from the web address may qualify as trademark use."

Trade Unions

A trade union, also called a labor union, is defined by SHRM's glossary of terms as "a group of workers who formally organize and coordinate their activities to achieve common goals in their relationship with an employer or group of employers." Unions are organized by industry, such as ironworkers, carpenters, nurses, and truck drivers. Being organized by trade allows labor unions to address the specific and unique needs of these employees. Shared interests include wages, working conditions, hours, retirement, training, and safety.

Real World Scenario

Sports Federations

Federations are formed when nongovernment bodies join to oversee their area of responsibility. Many unions are part of federations, such as the AFL-CIO, formed when two independent trade unions joined together to advocate on behalf of their members' shared interests.

Another area where federations are common are in international sports, such as the International Swimming Federation and the International Skating Union. Social justice and social responsibility are beginning to change how these federations must operate. For example, an issue emerged at the 2021 Summer Olympics in Tokyo when the International Handball Federation (IFH) fined the Norway team for improper clothing because they wore shorts instead of the required bikini bottoms—despite the fact that their male counterparts were allowed to wear shorts. Singer Pink took to social media to criticize the IFH for its "very sexist rules" ("Pink Offers to Pay Fine Handed to Norway's Beach Handball Team after They Refused to Wear Bikini Bottoms," by Christopher Brito, www.CBSnews.com, 2021). Germany also made headlines at the event by debuting full-body leotards for their gymnasts. It is clear from these social markers that nongovernment governing agencies, such as federations, will need to adapt to changing social norms, or be held accountable, just like employers.

Fundamental to a union's purpose is concerted activity, taking collective action to influence work-related issues. Examples of this type of activity from the National Labor Relations Board (NLRB) include "talking with one or more coworkers about your wages and benefits or other working conditions, circulating a petition asking for better hours, participating in a concerted refusal to work in unsafe conditions, openly talking about your pay and benefits…." The employee has the right to talk collectively directly with the employer and the media, report to a government agency, or meet with a union representative to talk about how a union may help with these grievances.

If an employer fires, disciplines, or threatens to do either, they have committed an unfair labor practice (ULP), even if the union has not yet been elected to represent the employee. Review Chapter 14 for more information on ULPs, strikes, and boycotts, and the three major laws governing labor relations.

⊕ Real World Scenario

Apprentice Shoemakers Strike for Higher Wages

The first effort to organize in the United States was made by apprentice shoemakers in the late 18th century:

> In 1794, numerous journeymen shoemakers in Philadelphia formed the Federal Society of Journeymen Cordwainers with the goal of protecting their wages. During the next several years, they called several "turn-outs,". . .during which the society's members tried to prevent all journeymen from working for less than standard wages.

As a result of these turnouts (strikes), charges were filed against several shoemakers for conspiracy to raise their wages; all were found guilty (Philadelphia Cordwainers Trial of 1806, `https://philadelphiaencyclopedia.org/archive/cordwainers-trial-of-1806`) beyond custom work and single locations, creating a need to reduce production expenses. To maintain profits, the craftspeople began to lower apprentice wages.

The beginning of unions occurred during a time when a new nation was politically, economically, socially, and industrially structured. The two-party system that emerged after George Washington had very different ideas of how the country should be run; at issue were national versus states' rights, work for wages versus the master/apprentice structure, and the use of slave labor. The contentious relationship between politics and labor relations is part of the foundation of the United States.

Works Councils

The desire for collective action also exists on a global level. Works councils are defined by the SHRM glossary as "groups that represent employees, generally on a local or organizational level, for the primary purpose of receiving from employers and conveying to employees information about the workforce and the health of the enterprise."

Works councils may be sanctioned by governments, meaning that employers of a certain size are required to have this type of permanent employee representation. Members of councils are elected and may include both management and employees, employees only, or employees with management oversight. The primary purpose is to cooperate with management because of the interdependencies between the employer and the employee. If the company succeeds, the employees have relative job security. If employee health and safety is improved, the company saves money and employee health is protected. The premise of this view of works councils is very similar to the corporate shared value (CSV) concept described in Chapter 13, "Corporate Social Responsibility." However, not all works councils are welcome. In some industries, a works council is seen as a competitive force that a union must oppose.

A major difference between labor unions and works councils is that works councils do not negotiate bargaining agreements. Works councils do not exist in the United States because company-dominated unions are a violation of the National Labor Relations Act.

In co-determination, employees on a works council participate in organizational decision-making about wages, safety, hours, and other terms and conditions of employment. This is achieved with a dual board structure: a management board and an employee board. In other structures, there is a single management board, and employees may serve as members or nonvoting advisers.

Collective Bargaining

Employees, employers, and joint employment represent the relationship between an individual and the entity that benefits from their work. In the absence of an employment contract, the relationship is said to be at-will (described in more detail in Chapter 14). When a collective bargaining agreement exists, the relationship between the employer and the employer is covered under a group employment contract. The groups are sorted into bargaining units.

Bargaining units are formed by members within a community of interest, or a group of employees with shared interests in wages, job duties, hours, and other conditions of employment. Properly sorting members into bargaining units is an important distinction, because unions only have the right to negotiate terms and conditions of employment for the bargaining unit that certifies their representation, a process that begins with the union organizing process.

The collective bargaining process is shaped by several factors. These include following the law so that a unfair labor practices do not occur. The NLRB also requires that both the employer and the union bargain in good faith, meaning that they send representatives who are authorized to act on behalf of their stakeholders. Another factor influencing the collective bargaining process are the precedents set by previous agreements. This can become a problem when previous concessions set the bargaining bar too low or create a less desirable outcome. For example, when contract-costing an agreement, many employers prefer to pay wage increases in one lump sum, as opposed to increasing the hourly rate. Doing so is attractive to the members, because they receive a perceived windfall. In the long term, however, their overall earnings are reduced. This is because overtime pay and retirement benefits are calculated based on the hourly wage. HR supports the collective bargaining process by gathering required information to cost a contract properly, guide and advise organizational leaders when negotiating, and analyze language to ensure that it protects the organization while encouraging transparency so that the administration of the contract is not adversarial.

Contract Administration

As with any governing document that pertains to employees, HR has the responsibility to participate actively in the contract administration process. This involves acting with integrity to ensure that both the employer's and employees' rights are protected in accordance with the contract. HR may need to educate themselves on the issues that pertain to the contract and call upon external resources, such as a specialized attorney, to properly manage risk.

One way to think about HR's role in contract negotiations and administration is once again to use the functional areas of the exam as a filter. When negotiating a contract, HR will need to consider organizational strategy and values. Wages, time off, and employee health benefits are bargaining issues that must be addressed. Training supervisors on the proper conduct during union organizing and how to work in a productive way with union representatives all fall within HR's responsibilities.

Employee Grievances

During the contract period, it is likely that employee grievances will arise. A *grievance* is a formal complaint against the organization by a union member. A grievance procedure is included in a collective bargaining agreement and must be followed by all parties to the contract. A general grievance process focuses on the reporting chain of command and responsiveness. For example, a typical process would be that the employee first reports a grievance to their immediate supervisor, either verbally or in writing. The supervisor will work with the employee and the union representative to resolve the issue. If the union representative is not satisfied, the complaint is escalated. If the grievance is still not resolved, it runs up the chain of command until it reached the final stage, the use of an outside party to weigh in.

Union members have the right to be represented during any investigatory meeting that may lead to disciplinary action. These are known as Weingarten rights due to their establishment during the court case of *NLRB vs. J. Weingarten, Inc.* For this reason, HR should ensure—and coach leaders—that if a protected member requests representation, their Weingarten rights are not violated.

Union Strategies

Ask HR professionals about unions, and many of them will have the perspective that they are "bad"—something to be avoided. And for organizations seeking to retain a direct relationship with the employee, this is true. In other cases, it is best for the organization simply to accept the presence of unions, similar to the risk management strategy of the same name. A union acceptance strategy seeks to create a positive impact for all stakeholders: the organization, the employees, and the union.

On the flip side, other organizations choose to avoid union organizing within their facility or industry. The employer does so by taking active measures to communicate with employees the benefits of remaining union-free. This is much easier before a union begins organizing, since the employer has much more freedom to say what they would like to say without fear of a ULP charge. HR supports an avoidance strategy by engaging in positive employee relations strategies, building a healthy organizational culture, and training supervisors to recognize organizing behaviors.

Larger organizations often employ third-party union avoidance resources, and/or have dedicated internal resources to proactively avoid an organizing campaign from getting started.

International Labor Relations

As discussed in the earlier section "Works Councils," employee organization and the need for labor standards exists on a global scale, often sanctioned, or standardized by governments or nongovernment organizations. One such example is that of the International Labour Organization (ILO). Established in 1919 as part of the Treaty of Versailles that ended World War I, the ILO operates on the premise that social justice is the only way that sustainable world peace will be achieved. These ideals are shared by the more than 180 member states, with a goal to establish standards related to labor rights, living wages, fair wages, and standard workdays. Recently, the ILO has made a special effort to advance ethical standards (www .ilo.org). The following is a list of some of the content areas addressed by the ILO:

- Freedom of association and collective bargaining
- Elimination of child labor
- Equal opportunity and treatment
- Vocational guidance and training
- Employment security
- Wages

The ILO is a tripartite body, meaning that the standards are developed in partnership with the governments, employers, and workers. These experts have identified a series of unfair labor practices, which include acts of discrimination, manipulation, and interference (similar to the TIPS acronym of threaten, interrogate, promise, or spy) described in Chapter 14. The ILO serves as an educational resource. For example, take a look at their video that describes ULPs against trade unions and workers:
https://www.youtube.com/watch?v=fAx4Gil-Y50

Competency and Knowledge Alignment

SHRM's BoCK describes three main clusters of the knowledge, skills, abilities, and other attributes necessary to perform successfully in HR. They include the Leadership, Interpersonal, and Business competencies from which HR actions are grounded. To pass these exams, candidates must be able to align knowledge with behaviors.

As defined in Chapter 4, "The Business Competency Cluster," each cluster is further expanded into eight sub-competencies. These sub-competencies are threaded throughout the knowledge domains of this book in order to align behaviors with the associated technical expertise. A review of the relevant sub-competencies for Organizational Effectiveness and Development begins here.

Negotiation

SHRM defines the Interpersonal sub-competency of negotiation as the ability to reach mutually acceptable agreements with negotiating parties within and outside of the organization.

Pluralism is defined by SHRM's glossary of terms as a "type of a labor environment in which multiple forces are at work in an organization, each with its own agenda, and in which conflict is overcome through negotiation." It is built on the principle that a common good can and should be found when negotiating. This holds with SHRM's definition of the behavioral competency of negotiation described earlier, and it means that HR is not neutral in negotiations but rather focused on shared interests. Issues to be negotiated revolve around needs, interests, and power.

Behaviors associated with these goals include maintaining a professional demeanor during negotiation discussions. The term "professional" has come under fire recently in that it can refer to outdated expectations of how businesspeople should "look." This includes a person's hair, clothing, head coverings, and jewelry, items most often associated with a person's race, religion, or ethnicity. HR must take care not to use the term to stereotype or marginalize others.

In some cases, an impasse may occur that stalls further discussion. This often happens when values are at stake or emotions involved. When this occurs, HR is responsible for helping to move the negotiations along, offering or asking for concessions, and keeping parties focused on the task, not the position.

In many cases, formal negotiations, such as those that take place during the collective-bargaining process, must adhere to governing laws from the National Labor Relations Board. Section 8 of the NLRB requires both parties to bargain in good faith, which "encompasses many obligations, including a duty not to make certain changes without bargaining with the union and not to bypass the union and deal directly with employees it represents. These examples barely scratch the surface" (www.nlrb.gov). Diving deeper, the NLRB goes on to give several examples of what this means:

- Make changes in wages, hours, working conditions, or other mandatory subjects of bargaining before negotiating with the union to agreement or overall impasse, unless (1) the union prevents the parties from reaching agreement or impasse; (2) economic exigencies compel prompt action; or (3) the proposed change concerns a discrete, recurring event scheduled to recur in the midst of bargaining (such as an annual merit-wage review), and you give the union notice and opportunity to bargain over that matter.

- Fail to meet with the union at reasonable times and reasonable intervals.

- Fail to bargain in good faith concerning mandatory subjects of bargaining.

- Refuse to furnish information the union requests that is relevant to the bargaining process or to the employees' terms or conditions of employment.

- Refuse to sign a writing that incorporates a collective bargaining agreement you have reached with the union.

SHRM SCP Only

Senior HR leaders often walk a tight line between being an advocate for the employer and the employee. When a union is present, the union assumes the role of employee advocate. This does not mean that HR stops serving the employees, but rather that they assume the responsibility of representing the organization's interests when negotiating a collective bargaining agreement.

When an employment dispute comes into litigation, it will generally land on the desk of the advanced HR professional. These leaders are expected to respond to and interact with the agencies and employee representatives (such as union stewards and attorneys) in a way that manages risk. Fundamental to this is overseeing the disciplinary and grievance processes to ensure that no employment rights are violated in the first place. HR achieves this by training managers and supervisors, writing legally compliant policies, monitoring employee investigations, and proactively auditing these practices to adapt where necessary.

Strategically, advanced HR teams help their employer adapt a union strategy. These strategies include avoidance, acceptance, or adapting to the new relational structure that union representation brings. Advanced HR teams should focus on a positive employer-labor relationship, regardless of union strategy. Participative management techniques that include all stakeholders in decision-making is one way to ensure that the employer-employee relationship serves the common interests and avoids being out of balance. Doing so improves employee morale, productivity, job satisfaction, and retention.

HR's ability to communicate through written tools can be severely strained under the weight of legal jargon. Employee handbooks, collective bargaining agreements, conduct codes, and ethics policies can all be rendered ineffective if the team members cannot understand them. It is the responsibility of HR leaders to put these tools in place to manage risk effectively, and also to improve communication with those affected. This requires operating with integrity and transparency when training or advising all organizational members. It also will call upon HR's ability to coach, develop, and influence others so that organizational results are achieved.

Summary

The functional area of Employee and Labor Relations relies heavily on the fundamentals of the employee-employer relationship. From a strictly transactional perspective, this exam domain explores the terms and conditions of employment and begins by defining the employer of record. In some cases, a trade union exists to act on behalf of its members. When this is the case, the standards of employment are negotiated through the collective bargaining process. These standards may be built on previous employee agreements, or they may be developed in partnership with a federation of unions, the government, and preferably, in an amicable way with the employer.

When disputes arise, it is beneficial for the employer to seek alternatives to litigation using methods such as arbitration, mediation, conciliation, and peer-review panels to ensure that a fair outcome is achieved.

HR helps employers avoid disputes using many tools, including properly conducting investigations and developing employment agreements and policies, procedures, and rules contained within an employee handbook. When an employee violates one of these standards, the discipline or separation process begins.

The behavioral competency of negotiation toward a common interest is critical for HR teams to influence fair outcomes that positively contribute to the employer-employee relationship.

Key Terms

Arbitration

Bargaining unit   Mediation

Conciliation   Moonlighting

Employee handbook   Negotiation

Employer of record   Ombuds

Grievance

Exam Essentials

Support and lead the efforts of employee and labor relations.   When a union represents employees, human resources must take the lead in the formal and informal actions that shape the relationship. This includes participating in the collective bargaining process and protecting employment rights.

Ensure positive employee-organization relationships.   Employment rights and responsibilities exists for both employers and employees. Human resources is responsible for ensuring that both the employer and the employee have what they need to ensure that a positive relationship exists that protects shared interests.

Develop workplace policies, handbooks, code of conduct, and other agreements that outline the terms and conditions of employment.   The employer-employee relationship is an agreement to exchange work for wages and other benefits. Properly outlining these terms and conditions communicate the expectations of both parties.

Understand the principles of negotiation and when they are governed.   The behavioral competency of negotiation involves the ability to reach mutually acceptable agreements on many subjects, including when negotiating with a union to establish the collective bargaining employment agreement. The National Labor Relations Board requires that the employer and union bargain in good faith.

Review Questions

1. Which of the following is the *best* way to prevent retaliation from occurring at work?
   - **A.** Train managers and supervisors.
   - **B.** Promote a culture of dignity and respect.
   - **C.** Discipline employees that exhibit retaliatory behaviors.
   - **D.** None of the above.

2. You are an HR department of one working for a manufacturing organization with 100 FTEs and a seasonal workforce placed through a staffing agency. Which of the following is responsible for the employment rights of the workers?
   - **A.** Your company
   - **B.** The staffing agency
   - **C.** A union (if present)
   - **D.** All of the above

3. Which of the following is *not* a factor from the DOL used to determine if joint employment exists?
   - **A.** Has the ability to hire or fire employees
   - **B.** Maintains employment records
   - **C.** Operates as a franchisor
   - **D.** Sets employee work schedules

4. Wages, working conditions, and health benefits are all examples of which of the following?
   - **A.** Bargaining subjects
   - **B.** Bargaining units
   - **C.** Concerted protected activity
   - **D.** Vocational guidance

5. Which of the following make up the tripartite nature of the ILO?
   - **A.** Employers, workers, unions
   - **B.** Government, employers, unions
   - **C.** Government, employers, workers
   - **D.** Employers, nongovernmental organizations, and governments

6. Which of the following describes the process of arbitration?
   - **A.** A legally binding decision by a neutral third party in an employment dispute
   - **B.** A method to resolve employee grievances when there is a collective bargaining agreement in place
   - **C.** A dispute management resource that is often quicker than going through litigation
   - **D.** All the above

7. Of the following reasons, why might an employer choose to ask new hires to sign ADR agreements?

   A. To encourage safe work practices

   B. To limit the ability of an employee to file a claim of employment discrimination

   C. To mitigate the cost of employment disputes

   D. All of the above

8. Which of the following employment agreements has a particular challenge with enforceability?

   A. NDA

   B. NCA

   C. IP

   D. Code of conduct

9. Which of the following is the agency that enforces section 8 of the National Labor Relations Act?

   A. NLRB

   B. EEOC

   C. DOL

   D. USPTO

10. You work for a large organization that uses a participative approach in meetings that discuss wages, working conditions, and other terms and conditions of employment. It includes members of management as well as union and nonunion members. This ensures that all voices are heard, that true needs are identified, and that quality decisions affecting workers are made. This is the best example of which type of environment?

    A. Federation

    B. Pluralism

    C. Democratic

    D. Conservative

Chapter

19

Technology Management

Exam Notables

The world is changing and it's a technology revolution. An interview with AT&T Senior Vice President of Infrastructure and Build, Mo Katibeh describes the impact of 5G and the explosion of the Internet of Things (IOT) phenomenon (Harvard Business School podcast, February 19, 2021, `https://www.hbs.edu/managing-the-future-of-work/podcast/Pages/podcast-details.aspx?episode=17891183`). Katibeh shares that AT&T already has 70 million connected IOT devices on their network, including cars, pet callers, and smart bicycles. In response, industries are rapidly innovating practices to leverage 5G capabilities. In the wine industry, for example, connected sensors placed in the soil are used to monitor water levels. Doing so allows grape producers to try to re-create conditions that could lead to replication of a vintage reserve. Katibeh describes the impact of technology on business competitiveness, costs, safety, quality, training, and job crafting—all areas of influence for today's HR teams. It begins with HR's ability to incorporate technology into the department's own processes and practices, as demonstrated by SHRM's functional description:

> Technology Management involves the use of existing, new and emerging technologies to support the HR function, and the development and implementation of policies and procedures governing the use of technologies in the workplace.

The SHRM Exam Objectives

SHRM's BoCK summarizes the functional area and defines the proficiency indicators along with key concepts. No matter your career level, pay special attention to the exam concepts defined "For All HR Professionals" and the "Key Concepts." If seeking the SHRM-SCP designation, you must expand your efforts to include those labeled "For Advanced HR Professionals."

THE SHRM-CP EXAM AND SHRM-SCP EXAM OBJECTIVES COVERED IN THIS CHAPTER INCLUDE THE FOLLOWING:

✓ **For All HR Professionals**

- Implements and uses technology solutions that support or facilitate delivery of effective HR services and storage of critical employee data.

- Implements HRIS that integrate with and complement other enterprise information systems.

- Develops and implements organizational standards and policies for maintaining confidentiality of employee data.

- Uses technologies in a manner that protects workforce data.

- Provides guidance to stakeholders on effective standards and policies for use of technologies in the workplace (e.g., social media, corporate and personal e-mail, internet messaging).

- Coordinates and manages vendors implementing HR technology solutions.

- Uses technologies that collect, access, and analyze data and information, in order to understand business challenges and recommend evidence-based solutions.

✓ **For Advanced HR Professionals**

- Evaluates and implements technology solutions that support the achievement of HR's strategic direction, vision, and goals.

- Evaluates and selects vendors to provide HR technology solutions.

- Designs and implements technology systems that optimize and integrate HR functional areas.

- Develops and implements technology-driven self-service approaches that enable managers and employees to perform basic people-related transactions (e.g., scheduling, timekeeping, compensation administration, benefit enrollment, information changes).

✓ **Key Concepts**

- Approaches to electronic self-service for basic HR and people management functions (e.g., scheduling, timekeeping, benefit enrollment).

- Data and information management (e.g., data integrity, confidentiality, security, disclosure).

- HRIS capabilities and use.

- Policies and procedures for procurement.

- **Policies and practices for technology and social media use (e.g., bring-your-own-device, websites, computers for personal activity).**

- **Software for recruiting and applicant tracking.**

Impact of Technology on HR Management

With so many small businesses and thus small HR departments in the United States, it is easy to overlook the value of "big" technology. Challenges include technology being too expensive, too comprehensive for needs, or too difficult to learn. However, technology's ability to increase efficiency makes it well worth a look at how to leverage it throughout the HR department systems.

Leading research company Sage commissioned a 2020 independent study of senior HR leaders in 500 midsized organizations across five different countries and multiple industries (`https://www.sage.com/en-gb/blog/the-changing-face-of-hr/`). The focus was to review their technology platforms and intentions. Researchers found that more than 80 percent of HR leaders are making changes to how their HR systems are delivered. See Figure 19.1 for an illustration of the findings.

FIGURE 19.1   Rates of technology adoption in HR

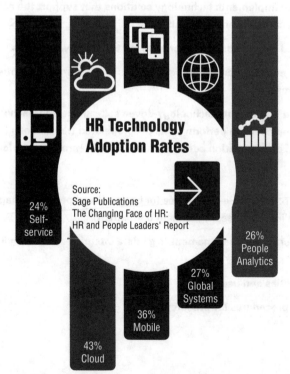

Technology and General HR Practices

Technology has had an impact on every part of the practice of human resources. As you can see in Figure 19.1, cloud computing is the number one technology being adopted by HR teams in recent years. *Cloud computing* is the delivery of services through the Internet. Data is housed in physical or remote servers that do not require a full, on-premises infrastructure. Benefits include lower IT costs, on-demand access, and the ability to administer HR practices via *employee self-service (ESS)*. ESS is embedded within most *human resource information systems (HRISs)*. SHRM defines an HRIS as the "IT framework and tools for gathering, storing, maintaining, retrieving, revising and reporting relevant HR data." ESS and HRIS systems grant employees access through an online portal to do several things, including the following:

▪ Make changes to their schedule or request time off.

▪ Update personal data, such as addresses and phone numbers.

▪ Enroll in benefits during open enrollment periods.

A look back at the challenges of older iterations of HRI systems is helpful. A 2016 SHRM article notes that dysfunctional HRI systems were challenged by "disparate systems, redundancies, data all over the place and no reporting" ("5 Steps to Managing an HRIS Implementation," by Aloah D. Wright at https://www.shrm.org/resourcesandtools/hr-topics/technology/pages/5-steps-to-managing-an-hris-implementation.aspx). It makes sense, then, that current HRI systems are focused on integrating with other *enterprise management systems (EMSs)*, software, and other platforms used to manage business operations. For example, many distribution facilities operate on a warehouse management system that drives inbound and outbound product. This includes modules for inventory management, return merchandise authorizations (RMAs), scheduling, load schematics, and so forth. When a case is picked and loaded, a scan makes an adjustment to several parts of the system. If the scanned case comes back for any reason, it is re-scanned into the system as customer returned, damaged, mis-picked, and so on. An HRI system that is integrated will be able to cull valuable information used to manage performance, calculate labor cost per case picked, reveal quality trends, and more.

Automation

Automation continues to be a priority for many industries and business units. The challenges for HR are very similar to the challenges for customer service centers that seek to automate customer responses to improve efficiencies. The employees are HR's customers, and when a team member has a question or a challenge, being able to respond to it in a timely fashion and resolve the issue is important. A high-profile example of the troubles of automation happened at Amazon, early on during the Covid-19 crisis of 2020. An article from BenefitsPro.com in June 2020 highlighted the challenges for employees and an HR team at what was just the beginning of the pandemic ("Amazon's Automated HR Systems Leave Workers Frustrated," by Matt Day at https://www.benefitspro.com/2020/06/08/

amazons-automated-hr-system-leaves-workers-frustrated/). Amazon reportedly added 2,500 additional HR staff to respond to the global challenge, and yet employees still reported hour-long wait times, erroneous automated termination letters, and calls to global service centers with staff poorly equipped to answer questions.

Part of the challenge was that Amazon had recently taken back the automated HR function from a third-party vendor and thus was not yet fully back up and running with their in-house processes. Although this example is from an intense time in history, much can be learned from the employee experience with automation at Amazon. HR must take care to build automated processes that have exit points to live support. When contracting out to third parties, HR must measure and address the employee experience quickly to minimize the loss of (or reduced) service. The technological framework from which automation occurs must have enough bandwidth (capacity) and latency (lag time between the request and the automated response) to handle high volumes without compromising levels of service. Just as customers will leave companies due to poor service, so too will employees leave organizations when HR service levels are not running at optimal levels.

Third-Party Vendor Management

For a small HR department tasked with technology management, the use of third-party vendors, or contractors, makes perfect sense. Even for larger HR teams, it is usually necessary to have technology-support vendors in some capacity, such as for the learning management systems described in Chapter 8, "Learning and Development," or the HRIS services described in this chapter. An important HR competency is the ability to procure and effectively manage these vendors.

A *request for proposal (RFP)* or *request for quote (RFQ)* is a document used to capture the scope, purpose, requirements, and budget for a technology project where appropriate. This document is then shared with a third-party vendor, asking them to respond with their capabilities, cost to implement, and timeline. From this, the process of selecting the right partner begins.

Technology Policies

Human resources have long been tasked with the development and implementation of company policies, procedures, and rules. The increased use of technology—both personal and company owned—has created an environment that can be risky and that can drive down productivity if not properly managed. This management process begins with a written policy that establishes expectations. Figure 19.2 shows the top technical productivity destroyers. It demonstrates the type of tech issues that should be addressed through policies, as will be reviewed next.

FIGURE 19.2   Top technology distractors at work

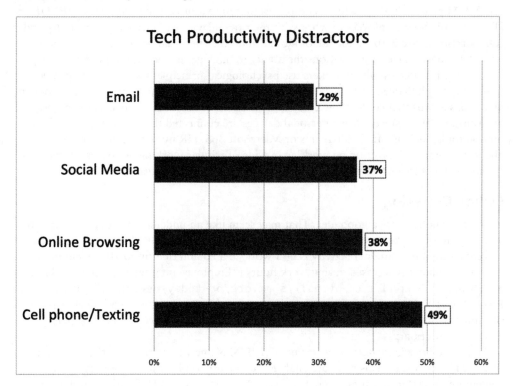

Mobile Phones and Devices

In 2021 Pew Researchers found that the majority of Americans have mobile devices and that more than 85 percent of those devices are smartphones ("Demographics of Mobile Device Ownership Adoption in the United States" at https://www.pewresearch.org/internet/fact-sheet/mobile/). It is not a stretch to say that most employees have a mobile device that they bring to work, affecting productivity, privacy, security, and more. Many HR professionals decide that there is no way to manage device use while on the clock. Although inevitability is certainly a factor, certain best practices can limit the negative impact that mobile device use has in the workplace.

Mobile device management (MDM) is the process of monitoring, managing, and securing mobile devices in the workplace. It includes establishing a policy of when and where the devices may be used; what content may be accessed and published, such as taking pictures at work with a mobile device's camera; and distinguishing policies between a personal and a company-owned device.

Bring Your Own Device

The MDM process is also useful in companies that have a *bring-their-own-device (BYOD)* IT policy. Allowing employees to work with their own device can increase productivity and collaboration. Systematizing the use of mobile and other personal devices is important for several reasons. It gives organizations the ability to manage the security risks of *social engineering*, the practice by which hackers use psychological principles to manipulate people on technological platforms. These techniques include malware, phishing scams, and methods to obtain passwords that could allow entry into an entire network. HR supports the process of ensuring that employees using personal devices are connected through company collaboration tools, such as Microsoft Teams or Microsoft 365. HR must remind team members about the company's position on working outside of regular working hours. Issues may arise for hourly workers related to overtime and for all workers with work/life balance.

Online Browsing

Internet use policies are a good idea. That may seem like an understatement, considering the vast amount of risk that online browsing by employees creates. SHRM reports that up to 40 percent of employee Internet activity is non-work-related and that up to 70 percent of pornographic content is accessed during work hours ("Employee Internet Management: Now an HR Issue," by Erin Patrick, `https://shrm.org/hr-today/news/hr-magazine/Pages/cms:006514.aspx`). From accessing inappropriate content on work devices to theft of company time by employees shopping online, HR must be proactive and anticipate what guidance is necessary.

   Employee Internet management software (EIMS) is one way to monitor the use of the Internet by employees. This software enables a company to block inappropriate website content and social media sites where necessary. A key feature of EIMS is the ability to customize access for employees who are responsible for surfing the web or managing company social media sites.

Social Media

The National Labor Relations Board has extended the definition of "workplace" to social media sites. This means that employees have the right to engage in concerted protected activity online, such as complaining about a boss or posting dissatisfaction with their pay. However, this protection does not extend to the right to harass other workers online, reveal trade secrets, or violate the privacy of others. A robust social media policy goes beyond limiting access during working hours. The policy must clearly define the expected standards of behavior without infringing on an employee's rights. HR is well advised to make sure that its social media and other Internet-related polices are properly vetted by labor counsel.

   Part of the exam requirements for both the CP and SCP reminds us that a key part of technology management is integration. HRIS must integrate with EMS, which must also tie MDM and EIMS systems. They must work together in a way that is effective and efficient, with minimal redundancies and workarounds.

Employee Monitoring

Employers in the United States are allowed to monitor company-owned devices. This includes monitoring emails, keystrokes, screen content, active/idle time, and Internet activities as well as other productivity- or work-related content.

Employees, however, do have the right to a reasonable expectation of privacy, especially when it comes to personal information or other non-work-related issues. For this reason, policies must be clear about the company's monitoring practices of both company-owned devices and BYODs, including how data will be reset or cleaned upon separation.

When writing and enforcing policy, remember that the laws vary from state to state, so HR must be current on federal law as well as state laws. As a general rule, a monitoring policy should do the following:

- Clarify that there is little expectation of privacy when using a company-owned computer or working through the company network.
- Clearly define the expected standards of equipment and network use.
- Explicitly outline the ways in which the employee will be monitored.
- Clearly state that personal data and other non- work-related information will not be gathered.
- Require an employee's signed acknowledgment of the policy.

Productivity software is useful when creating a systems solution that is consistent.

Risk Management

As mentioned earlier, the use of technology in the workplace comes with some form of risk for the employee, for the customer, and for the organization as a whole. HR typically will partner with the internal IT department or external service provider to initiate techniques to manage these risks.

Compliance is a major driver of data integrity and security. This is, in part, because an organization's ability to provide records in labor disputes is often key to an effective response. The electronic storage of records has only in the last several years been accepted in most HR practices. Because employee records include confidential information, such as Social Security numbers, immigration status, and medical records, digital storage must provide for adequate security. Digital storage security includes limiting who has access to files, on-demand retrieval (with backup), and controlling the type of information shown, such as displaying only the last four digits of a Social Security number.

In an era where Zoom and other online meeting software has proliferated, so too have the risks associated with use, such as unauthorized access. HR can help teams securely navigate a virtual room by training meeting organizers to take a few precautions such as the following:

- Setting up passcodes for meeting admittance
- Using authority hierarchies for any shared documents (read-only, edit)
- Ensuring that document sharing is secure to avoid sharing confidential content

Anyone who has failed to save a document and then experienced a system crash knows how frustrating it is to lose work. When the failure is systemwide due to a natural disaster or other catastrophic event, the entire set of operations of an organization is severely debilitated. The Department of Labor's site at www.ready.gov is an excellent place to begin building an IT recovery plan. The content there includes instructions on conducting a business impact analysis for critical processes, putting into place recovery strategies, and developing the full plan and methods to conduct drills to assess readiness.

SHRM SCP Only

Advanced HR professionals must understand all the elements we've covered related to using technology platforms to deliver HR services. Where the difference between generalist and senior levels lies is in the specific competency of *evaluation*—from technology selection to the effectiveness of the program.

Similar to the HR department, IT plays a support role concerning the companies' core competency. The effectiveness of HR technology, then, must be evaluated based on how well—or how poorly—it supports the company's core competency. If the company's core competency is service through people, then HR deliverables through platforms must be in alignment with employee engagement and satisfaction efforts. If the company's core competency is manufactured goods, then HR technology should integrate with other operating systems to measure labor inputs and outputs.

From a practical point of view, all technology solutions should seek to reduce costs through improved efficiencies and to increase productivity where possible. In an HR department, this can occur through the reduction of HR head count by implementing employee self-service programs. Senior leaders will need to make sure that all employees have equal access to these self-service options and that employees have the necessary skill sets to navigate the programs in a way that is user-friendly.

Summary

The technology revolution has affected all the ways in which a business operates, including within the HR department. In addition to using technology to automate processes and streamline reporting, there are opportunities throughout all of the HR functions to leverage the benefits of platform solutions. These opportunities must be managed through HR activities that begin by sourcing the proper technology solutions through the RFP process.

Bringing technology solutions into the HR department is the goal of many HR leaders, regardless of the number of employees. This is because of the improved efficiencies that cloud computing and integrated HR information systems can offer. Ultimately, any technological solution must align with the organization's core competency and the strategic direction that the company is taking. Technology may also be used to enhance the forces shaping the way that work gets done, such as with the hybrid on-site/virtual workforce that emerged after the beginning of the Covid-19 pandemic in 2020. These real-time issues may drive short-term strategies, such as implementing mobile timekeeping systems, adding in productivity trackers, and accounting for business continuity should the systems be disrupted.

HR is also responsible for managing the inherent risks associated with the use of the Internet, BYOD practices, social media use, data integrity, and privacy.

Key Terms

Cloud computing

Employee Internet management software (EIMS)

Employee self-service

Enterprise management system (EMS)

Human resource information system (HRIS)

Information management

Mobile device management (MDM)

Social engineering

Exam Essentials

Know how to implement technology solutions that support the HR function.   The major functions of human resource management, such as Recruiting, Total Rewards, and Learning and Development, may all be supported through technology. These activities are typically organized within a human resource information system (HRIS) that is integrated with other enterprise software.

Be able to use technology to increase employee self-service for basic functions.   Administrative activities such as changing an employee's address are easily automated. Doing so frees up HR departments to focus at operational and strategic levels and to service employees in a more impactful way.

Know how to manage the risks associated with technology applications.   As with most other areas, HR is responsible for drafting policies that limit the risks associated with a practice. As a first step, technological risks require written policies that outline expected standards of behavior. For advanced professionals, the ability to evaluate these policies in order to ensure that they stay up-to-date with emerging issues is a key competency.

Be able to name the key distinctions between a generalist and a senior-level role.   Advanced HR professionals are called upon to oversee the implementation and evaluation of technology solutions. This includes evaluating the effectiveness of technology specifically designed to improve HR efficiencies.

Review Questions

1. Which of the following is the most critical element when selecting a human resource information system (HRIS)?

    A. Ability to integrate with other programs

    B. The cost of implementation

    C. The program's capabilities

    D. Delivery through the cloud

2. Which of the following were found to be reasons HRIS programs were found not to be useful?

    A. Redundancies

    B. Lack of coherent systems

    C. Lack of reporting

    D. All of the above

3. Which of the following must be considered when determining a technological platform's ability to handle high-volume activities?

    A. Documentation and storage

    B. Bandwidth and latency

    C. Employee self-service and enterprise management

    D. Employee experience and HR capacity

4. Acme Insurance is an employer with 60 regular employees and 10 independent contractors, with a strategy to grow by 20 percent over the next fiscal year. This strategy will require that you become more involved with business strategy and aligning HR systems to the growth plan, such as building a performance management system and conducting wage surveys for the new hires outside the area. The HR department that you manage, consisting of two employees besides yourself, is already struggling to keep up with the demands of the organization. In addition to the regular HR responsibilities, your team is responsible for the IT tasks of setting up email, troubleshooting computer problems, monitoring smartphone use, tracking laptops, and dealing with server issues. Which of the following intervention strategies would be the most effective?

    A. Hire another HR generalist with IT experience.

    B. Hire an IT specialist.

    C. Offshore the IT tasks.

    D. Research and engage a third-party vendor.

5. Starting with the scenario from Question 4, what should be your first step in making a selection for IT support?

   A. Put together a scope of work.

   B. Create an RFP.

   C. Decide on who the resource will be.

   D. Scan social media for any information on the resource(s).

6. Which of the following should be included in an MDM policy?

   A. A prohibition about using a mobile phone camera in employee locker rooms

   B. A reminder that employees are never allowed to use mobile phones while on the clock

   C. A list of options available for company-sponsored smartphone models

   D. All of the above

7. Which of the following is the most accurate phrase that describes the activities of social engineering?

   A. Phishing schemes

   B. Psychological manipulation

   C. Unlawful activity

   D. All of the above

8. Which of the following types of software is most likely to prevent access to prohibited websites on the Internet?

   A. MDM

   B. ESS

   C. EIM

   D. EMS

9. Which of the following is *false* regarding monitoring employee activity on company-owned equipment?

   A. An employer may take screenshots of employees' monitors while they are on the clock.

   B. An employer must have written authorization from employees to monitor their online activity.

   C. An employer may not explicitly monitor employee personal information, even if they are on a company-owned device.

   D. An employer may not prohibit an employee from discussing their wages on social media.

10. Which of the following is an example of a risk associated with technology management within organizations?

   A. Privacy

   B. Data security

   C. Social engineering

   D. All of the above

Appendix A

Answers to the Chapter Review Questions

Chapter 5: Strategic Human Resource Management

1. B. A competitive strategy of differentiation is built on offering high-quality (and often more expensive) elements such as material, service, or functionality, making (B) the correct choice. A cost leadership strategy, (D), is achieved by focusing on a low-cost product. Buyer power, (A), refers to a business being so large that they can leverage the cost of raw materials. Competitive advantage, (C), is what is said to exist when an organization dominates a market due to their ability to produce goods or services more effectively than their competition.

2. D. According to Senge, mental modeling is a form of information processing that is built on a team member's beliefs or attitudes about an organization, making (D) the correct answer. Personal mastery, (A), is focused on achieving an individual vision, whereas systems thinking, (B), is taking a whole view as opposed to an individual view. Team learning, (C), exists when each team member is actively involved in problem-solving, not just leadership.

3. A. The correct answer is (A). A corporate mission statement is one that defines the reason for a company's existence, the purpose of their efforts. (B), values, is a statement of the non-negotiable behaviors that guide a company's decision-making. Corporate governance, (C), is a regulatory effort, and (D) is an effort by individuals to ensure economic, political, and social rights for all.

4. D. The correct answer is (D). When setting a SMARTER goal, it is important to define the desired outcome, (A), ensure that the goal is achievable, (B), that it has an established project timeline, (C), and that key milestones are identified in order to evaluate success, (D).

5. B. The correct answer is (B). Goal setting is part of the strategy implementation phase of the strategic planning process, (A), as is strategy alignment, (C). Strategy evaluation, (D), occurs after an initiative has been implemented.

6. A. The correct answer is (A). In scenario planning, an issue is identified and then leaders come together to make key assumptions, consider systems impact, conduct a risk assessment, study the people impact, and summarize the findings. This data is used to create a response plan(s) should the issue actually arise. A SWOT audit, (B), is a scanning tool used to assess internal strengths and weaknesses and external opportunities and threats. The growth-share matrix, (C), helps organizations prioritize strategies, and setting SMARTER goals is the action planning step of the strategic planning process.

7. C. The correct answer is (C), external. A SWOT audit is an environmental scanning tool designed to identify internal strengths and weaknesses and external threats and opportunities.

8. D. The correct answer is (D), all of the above. Agile is characterized as project planning that is completed in micro phases, seeking feedback from the client and making adjustments as the process evolves until a final, creative product is developed.

9. A. The correct answer is (A). Political forces exist when the politics or governing practices of a country influence how businesses may compete. Economic forces, (B), are factors such

as interest rates or the rate of inflation that drive business strategy. Social forces, (C), are demographic or cultural trends impacting competitiveness, and (D), environmental forces, are factors such as the climate or water availability.

10. C. The correct answer is (C), the Input-Process-Output (IPO) model. The IPO model includes reviewing a company's processes to identify needs. A SWOT audit (A) scans the internal environment for strengths and weaknesses and the external environment for opportunities and threats. (B), PESTLE, examines the political, economic, social, technological, legal, and environmental forces that shape strategic decision-making. The growth-share matrix, (D), is a tool designed to help prioritize strategy.

Chapter 6: Talent Acquisition

1. B. A talent acquisition plan (B) takes into account business strategies related to growth or decline to create a plan of alignment for maximum effect. A succession plan (A) identifies in-house replacements, and a talent needs assessment (C) identifies current and future needs, so both may be necessary components of a talent acquisition plan. A recruitment plan (D) is an HR operational tool used to identify sourcing strategies and may also be included as a component of a larger talent acquisition strategy.

2. C. A programmatic strategy where companies have a systematic method for acquiring target companies has been shown to provide the most valuable results over time, making (C) the correct answer. Larger purchases (B) are not as successful as a systematic approach, and a divestiture (A) would be a strategy from a target company, not an acquiring company. Cultural similarity (D) is important and can be part of an evolving process over time.

3. D. The best answer is (D). A joint venture occurs when two or more companies join together to accomplish a shared purpose over time. A merger and acquisition would most likely result in a transfer of ownership, making (A) and (B) incorrect. A strategic alliance (C) is unlikely to create a new corporation.

4. D. The correct answer is (D), technological forces. Technology has changed the way the world works and thus the skills needed by HR team members. Although a talent acquisition strategy is often focused externally, a robust plan will include reskilling and upskilling of the internal workforce as part of their strategic efforts.

5. C. The correct answer is (C). Cost per hire is calculated by dividing the total number of hires for a given period by the total sum of internal and external recruiting costs. In this case it would be ($20,000 + $15,000) / 26.

6. D. The correct answer is (D). It can be easy to identify a position in negotiation because they often include words such as "won't," "refuse," "never," or "always." The goal in a negotiation is to understand interests as opposed to positions and come to an agreement from there.

7. C. The correct answer is (C). Attrition measures separations that are primarily of the employee's choice, whereas turnover measures all separations, regardless of the impetus. Both turnover and attrition are objective measures that are expressed as percentages, so (A) and (B) are incorrect.

8.   C. The correct answer is (C). The candidate experience has proven to be an important component of the success or failure of a recruiting effort. It is closely tied to other positive outcomes, such as the employer brand and the likelihood of remaining a consumer even if an offer of employment is not made.

9.   B. The correct answer is (B). Demographic factors such as age, race, and gender serve to inform workforce analytics that may then be used to make strategic decisions about the diversity and other needs of the workforce.

10.   B. The correct answer is (B). Assessment centers is a process by which employees are evaluated for readiness to take on a new role. A talent directory (A) is similar to a skills inventory (C), which are methods to track the knowledge, skills, abilities, and other development efforts of a team member. In terms of (D), the question does not give you enough information to determine whether or not the process is legally compliant.

Chapter 7: Employee Engagement and Retention

1.   D. Increased levels of engagement are correlated to many positive outcomes, including safety, positive work behaviors, and increased productivity, meaning a stronger competitive advantage, making (D) the correct choice.

2.   A. Organizational behavior is the multidisciplinary study that pulls from social psychology, applied psychology, human relations, and others. It includes research on how humans are motivated and what drives behavior. Organizational leadership (B) is the study of the impact of leadership behaviors on organizational outcomes, and human resources (C) is the study of the functional areas of HR, such as Total Rewards and Learning and Development. Business management (D) is designed to drive organizational outcomes through strategic planning, finance, and global demands.

3.   B. Job satisfaction is defined as how happy an employee is at work, and it is highly driven across cultures by a sense of achievement, making (B) the best answer. This question is tricky because it includes examples of all of the job attitudes. Loyalty is represented in that Margaret has been with the company for 20 years; however, factors of organizational commitment (A) are less about achievement and more about the organizational culture and leadership. Work engagement (C) is represented in the question with Margaret's near perfect attendance record, yet the question does not talk about the work tasks themselves, making that answer incorrect. A positive attitude (D) is not one of the job attitudes related to employee engagement.

4.   C. The correct answer is (C). Skill variety is the degree to which an employee is able to use multiple skills on the job. A task identity (A) is about how well an employee is able to understand how their efforts affect the whole task, as opposed to only a piece of the work. Task significance (B) is related to how impactful their contribution is, and autonomy (D) is how much independent control the team member has over their role.

5. C. The correct answer is (C), paid volunteer time. Although all of the options have the potential to be correct, paid volunteer time speaks to the need for purpose at work. (A) could potentially be correct, but the question did not give enough information. (B) is more attractive to a mid-mature workforce, and (D) may or may not increase retention depending on how the individual is motivated.

6. B. The correct answer is (B). Both job enlargement and job enrichment are techniques used to develop employees while on their career path. Job enlargement broadens the scope of a job by adding tasks, whereas job enrichment focuses on increasing a job's depth through added responsibilities.

7. C. The correct answer is (C). Although all the options can increase engagement, achievement is the best answer because it has been shown to be more positively correlated with increased engagement across cultures.

8. A. The correct answer is (A). The acquisition stage of the employee life cycle involves recruiting and selection activities. This stage is an opportunity for the employer to communicate the tangible and intangible benefits of coming to work for the employer, thus attracting qualified talent. This often happens through social media, so engaging the passive and active job seekers using the brand online is important.

9. D. The correct answer is (D). Organizational justice refers to the degree to which an employee believes that the process and outcomes of compensation practices are fair. The question does not give enough information for (A), unlawful discrimination, to be true. (B) is an answer distractor, and (C) refers to offering equal pay for equal work, again with the question not providing enough information for this choice to be correct.

10. B. The correct answer is (B). HR systems must align people needs with organizational strategies. This requires asking employees what they need in terms of feedback, connection, growth, tools and (C), technological resources. In turn, research about what other companies are doing (A), the technological capabilities of performance management systems (D), and management input may then be aligned with organizational results.

Chapter 8: Learning and Development

1. A. Option A is the correct answer because the SHRM BoCK domain of People addresses the HR activities that drive individual behaviors. This includes L&D activities that support the traditional HR activities such as Total Rewards, Talent Acquisition, and Employee Engagement. The exam domain of Organization informs L&D practices related to how an HR department is structured and how an organization as a whole learns, making option B incorrect. The Workplace domain (option C) is incorrect since this is the exam domain that addresses the climate in which we ask our teams to perform. HR competencies (option D) are the combined knowledge, skills, abilities, and other characteristics an HR professional needs to perform their work.

2. A. Of the two types of knowledge, tacit is the one that is more subjective, making option A, manager preferences, the best answer. Explicit knowledge can be quantified through the use of tools such as reference guides for general ledger codes (option B), or the use of standard operating procedures on how to place an ad online (option C).

3. C. HR leaders are challenged to find ways to solve organizational problems from a systems view. This means looking at the organization as a whole and finding ways to support outcomes that can address multiple needs, making option C the best choice in this scenario. It would be too soon to immediately go above a senior leader's head and doing so would likely make the R&D manager defensive, thus reducing your influence, so option A is incorrect. Option B may be part of a larger strategy, but it does not address the challenge at hand and thus would not be the best use of your time. Option D will be most effective if you are able to present a solution or other alternative when having the conversation.

4. B. All HR systems must be built around aligning HR systems with organizational strategy, making option B the correct answer. Other advantages of a formal career development process include improving the ability for organizations to attract and keep employees (option A), as career development programs build skills (option C), and communicate to the employee that the employer is invested in their success (option D).

5. D. The best answer is option D. Career planning is the HR activity that helps employees develop a plan outlining the educational or experience activities necessary to grow their career. A career map (option A) is a visual representation of the growth opportunity based on their current role within the organization. Career design (option B) is an answer distractor since it is not a term used in the realm of career management. Career trajectory (option C) is a term used to describe the direction and growth in one's career.

6. D. In order to engage in effective problem-solving through L&D interventions, it is important first to encourage the supervisor to help you conduct a gap analysis to identify the true need, making option D the best answer. Option A is certainly meeting the demand of the supervisor, but you don't yet have enough information to determine if the employee was a poor hire, especially as he is so new. Option B would be a useful option if the gap analyses identifies that the new hire needs more training to resolve the performance challenges. Option C will only be effective once you have conducted a gap analysis to identify the ways that the employee needs to improve.

7. A. The Department of Labor's (DOL) O*Net database defines basic skills as the "developed capacities that facilitate learning or the more rapid acquisition of knowledge," making option A the correct answer. Capacities that facilitate performance in their current role or across jobs are cross-functional skills, so options B and D are incorrect. Option C is not part of the DOL's definition of knowledge, skills, or abilities.

8. A. An organizational analysis seeks to gather data related to an organizational or departmental challenge, making option A the correct answer. An individual analysis (option B) focuses on single employee needs, and a task analysis (option C) is a review of the jobs to identify the main activities, duties, and responsibilities. A gap analysis (option D) looks at current and desired performance and identifies the gap between the two in order to develop intervention strategies.

9. C. The correct answer is option C. Synchronous training occurs when the instructor and students are attending the session at the same time, whereas in asynchronous training, the facilitator and participant do not have to be together at the same time.

10. B. The best answer is option B. A dual career ladder solution is useful for teams of highly competent individuals who do not necessarily promote into people management roles. Option A does not address the heart of the issue, which is this employee feeling valued and able to develop in her role. Option C is not effective, since the promoted employee may not have the skill set in the specific area of developmental need. Option D would have been a good choice if the purpose of the coaching was more aligned with an organizational and individual need (such as people management skills) to maximize the investment.

Chapter 9: Total Rewards

1. B. The best answer is option B. A compensation philosophy is a guiding statement that declares the fundamental belief underlying a compensation structure. Option A, a total rewards strategy, represents the multiple facets of a complex HR system that aligns with organizational goals. A competitive advantage for talent (option C) may certainly be gained through an employer's pay practices, but it is not a term directly related to the field of total rewards.

2. D. The correct answer is option D. A pay structure (option A) serves as the framework from which decisions about pay are made. This includes identifying the minimum and maximum for a job title and creating wage bands (option B) using relevant external market research (option C).

3. B. Any area where there is a disconnect between what an employer says they believe and what they practice has the potential to cause employees to stop trusting the employer, making option B the best answer. There are several reasons why employees stay or leave an employer, so option A is not a good answer. Pay practices are not the primary way to attract and keep talent. Several other factors go into these types of decisions, so option C is not the best answer for this scenario. Option D is not a true statement.

4. A. Remuneration surveys are an instrument designed to collect data related to compensation such as base pay, pay ranges, statutory and other cash payments, paid time off (PTO), and variable compensation, making option A the correct answer. None of the examples in the question are a type of mandatory benefits, so option B is incorrect. All examples could be researched as benchmarks or evidence to use in decision-making, but these examples are outcomes, not research instruments, so options C and D are incorrect.

5. C. Comparable worth is the concept that suggests that jobs with different titles, tasks, duties, and responsibilities but that require similar knowledge, skills, and abilities should be paid equally. It is in place to address the historical pay discrimination against women. Option A is a type of pay at separation, where the employee receives payment in lieu of the right to sue an employer for discrimination. Option B speaks to the degree of openness that an employer allows regarding its pay practices. Option D occurs when the spread between an incumbent and new hires' pay rate is small.

6. D. The court case against the tech companies charged them with suppressing the natural market mechanism of supply and demand by "fixing" wages at a set amount. This is in violation of antitrust laws, specifically the Sherman Antitrust Act, and so option D is correct.

7. B. The correct answer is option B. Workers' compensation laws are required by the federal government; however, states are responsible for program administration. Social Security (option A) and Medicare (option C) are both required and administered by the federal government.

8. C. Pay compression occurs when the earnings difference between an incumbent and new hire is small, making option C the correct answer. It may be a condition of pay equity (option A), but pay compression is the more specific answer. There is no indication that the company is discriminating against Sam, so option B is incorrect, and an unfair labor practice occurs when there is a union present, so option D is incorrect as well.

9. B. Golden handshakes, handcuffs, and parachutes are clauses written into an executive employment contract for various purposes, making option B the correct answer. These clauses may undermine organizational results if they cause short-term thinking, so option A is incorrect. Be careful of any option that includes absolutes such as "always" or "never," making option C incorrect, because these clauses can benefit the organization. Option D is not true.

10. A. The compa-ratio for the HR manager is 62 percent. The compa-ratio is identified by taking the employee salary and dividing it by the market midpoint. You first must convert the midpoint to its annual form by multiplying $66.13 times 2,080 working hours in a year ($137,550). Then you divide $85,000/$137,550 and multiply that number by 100 to convert the number to a percentage.

Chapter 10: HR in the Global Context

1. D. The best answer is option D. The rapid rise of globalization is due to many factors; however, it is growing primarily due to the increased interdependence and interconnectedness among countries, people, and cultures. This is reflected by the migration of the workforce (option A), the opening of more and more developed global markets (option B), and the need and ability to remain competitive (option C).

2. C. The correct answer is option C. Social forces are those that reflect the cultural practices and values of a society. These forces appear as trends or changes to attitudes about families, education, and the way work gets done. Government policies and platforms are the political forces (option A) to which employers must respond. Economic forces (option B) are reflected by interest rates, inflation, and other financial factors, and (option D), technological forces are the impact of device and machine innovation and/or automation on business operations.

3. C. Legal forces (option C) that must be accounted for when designing international assignments include immigration laws, such as work visas and compliance with varying tax laws within and outside of the host country. Political forces (option A) of expatriate assignments that must be managed include the stability of a country's government or dealing with ongoing political violence. Social issues (option B) include the impact of work, schools, and housing structures on the expatriate's family. Environmental forces (option D) that a potential expatriate would consider are those such as the availability of clean drinking water and the desirability of the location of the assignment.

4. B. The best answer is option B, a multinational enterprise, which is a company headquartered in one country with operations in other countries. An applicable large employer (option A) would have been a better choice if the question related to compliance with the Affordable Care Act. Option C is incorrect because the term "domestic employer" refers to a company that operates mostly or solely in one country.

5. C. There are many ways that an organization may expand into an international market. A brownfield operation (option C) is one where an existing building is purchased and developed for use. Outsourcing (option A) occurs when an organization contracts all or part of its business operations to another organization or individual. A greenfield operation (option B) is when an organization expands by building a new facility. A turnkey operation (option D) is when a company purchases an existing business and begins operations.

6. D. The correct answer is option D. Due diligence is comprehensive fact-finding behavior designed to uncover potential risks. Risks are inherent in a merger/acquisition, purchase of turnkey operations, and when addressing the varying labor laws of host countries.

7. A. The correct answer is option A. A geocentric staffing strategy is one where a global organization recruits from anywhere in the world, regardless of their nationality. This means that there is a large pool of candidates from which to recruit and hire.

8. B. Qualitative analysis methods are those that exist as a framework or model, making option B the correct answer. Quantitative methods that rely on objective data and a regression (option C) are a type of statistical analysis that manipulates variables. Trend analysis (option D) is used to anticipate changes based on patterns of behavior.

9. D. Staffing with expatriates creates significant issues that must be addressed and managed on behalf of the international assignee and the organization. Career development (option A) and repatriation (option B) are issues related to the expatriate, and cost control of the assignment (option C) is an organizational need.

10. C. Totalization agreements exist between the Internal Revenue Service and many countries. These agreements are designed to eliminate double taxation for Social Security and Medicare.

Chapter 11: Diversity and Inclusion

1. C. Ensuring that a workforce has diverse talents (A) is not enough as these employees must also be able to use their talents and feel welcome, making C the best choice. Options B and D are best practices to ensure that discrimination does not occur in a company's hiring systems.

2. A. Title VII of the Civil Rights Act of 1964 originally defined race, ethnicity, and national origin as protected from employment discrimination. Factors such as age, sex, disability, religion, and military status have all been added through Title VII amendments or separate non-discrimination laws.

3.   A. Option A is the correct answer because organizations do not have direct control over whether employees choose to unionize. Companies can control the systems designed to promote employees into management positions (B, C), and the hiring practices or job design that require educational degrees (D).

4.   B. As with any organizational strategy, a needs assessment must be completed to identify the gaps and barriers between current and desired state. Coordinating a diversity council to identify these needs will allow HR to design initiatives, such as leadership development (A) or offering language classes (C), which achieve results and that align with corporate strategy. Creating a leadership development initiative for minority groups may very well be a council's recommendation. However, the question notes that these employees are hesitant to apply for promotion, suggesting that there are barriers that must be identified and prioritized before a specific plan is developed.

5.   C. Encouraging diversity of thought is necessary for creative and informed problem-solving and decision-making. Often, an inclusive workplace is derailed in the day-to-day functions, such as meeting participation. By bringing the group together to facilitate a discussion about the importance of diversity of thought, you create the opportunity to identify barriers and include team members in solving inclusivity challenges, even outside of the meeting room. Option A is the antithesis of inclusive practices, so it would not be recommended. Option B is divisive as well, and it can be perceived as gossipy or one-sided. Option D is a good idea, but the question does not note whether these ground rules are already in place, and it is not better than option C.

6.   B. The best answer is B, because training for adults in general is most effective when employees can relate it to their organization or job. Mandating management attendance (A) may increase their awareness of the issues, as will having a diverse workforce in attendance (C). Hiring a qualified facilitator will support awareness initiatives but be most beneficial toward changing behaviors if the training is specific.

7.   B. According to the Bureau of Labor Statistics, Asian women represent 8.6 percent of management roles within organizations, compared with 9.7 percent of Black or African American women, 10.4 percent Hispanic women, and 78.7 percent of White women.

8.   D. It a best practice for HR to have separate, written guidelines for the transgendered community since there are specific issues that need to be addressed. These include the use of pronouns, restroom access, and how to report abusive conduct.

9.   D. Educating leaders and managers is an integral part of any company's DEI initiatives, and employees at all levels need to have a safe place to learn and develop new behaviors, so D is the best answer. Option A is not the best answer because the applicant had not yet been rejected based on her religious attire. Option B is incorrect—the question does not tell us what type of company she applied to, and thus we don't know if attire is a bona fide occupational qualification. Option C is unethical, and it does not promote a culture of diversity and inclusion.

10.   C. Fundamental to the advocacy role for HR professionals is designing, implementing, and auditing HR systems to ensure that they support DEI initiatives, making C the best answer. HR may not be the most qualified to lead diversity training, or to represent the company's DEI initiatives, making A and B incorrect. Option D is correct in that HR should be modeling proper behaviors in all ways, but C better represents how HR can support DEI efforts operationally.

Chapter 12: Risk Management

1. B. The correct answer is option B. Although siloed risk management is more targeted at the departmental level, it is not necessarily more effective. In fact, siloed risk management efforts run the risk of being too operational, ignoring the risk management needs that are identified at an enterprise, strategic level.

2. D. The correct answer is option D. The first stage of managing risk begins by identifying where risk exists. This is often done using qualitative and quantitative assessment tools. Once risks have been identified, risk treatment may begin (option C), such as mitigating (option B) or transferring (option A) the risk.

3. C. The best answer is option C. The primary purpose of any risk management effort is to prevent operational, strategic, and financial losses. This may be accomplished by staying compliant with regulations (option A), such as OSHA and GAAP; aligning with organizational strategy (option B); and taking steps to reduce workers' compensation costs (option D) through increased safety efforts.

4. C. The annualized loss expectancy is calculated using the single loss expectancy; thus the correct answer is $1,200.00. This is arrived at by multiplying the single value amount by the expected number of occurrences ($300 × 4). Challenges to the annualized rate are that if the single loss expectancy rate is not properly calculated to include all potential costs, the annualized rate may be larger than expected.

5. D. OSHA is clear that employers have a general duty to protect their workers from harm, even if there is not a specific standard in place that covers the hazard, so option D is correct. Hazard communication standards (option A) require that employers communicate any safety and health hazards to all affected employees. The duty of good faith and fair dealing (option B) is an exception to the concept of employment at-will, where an employee has a reasonable expectation to be treated fairly in employment. Duty of care (option C) is a phrase used to describe the employer's safety obligations, but it does not exist as an OSHA standard.

6. B. Employees share the burden for their personal safety and health, and this is done by following the code of safe practices, making option B correct.

7. D. Death, lost time injuries, and injuries with modified duty are all recordable, and thus must be recorded on the OSHA 300 log. Other recordable criteria are medical treatment beyond first aid, loss of consciousness, and a significant injury or illness diagnosed by a licensed healthcare professional. Note that all must first be work-related in order to be recordable under OSHA's standards.

8. C. The best answer is option C, workplace violence. The Bureau of Labor Statistics notes that personal relationships are the primary cause of violence against women at work. Prohibiting personal visits is one of many steps that employers may take to prevent a case of workplace violence against women.

9. D. A business impact analysis is a form of risk assessment that should be the first step in building response plans, making option D correct. Once the risks are understood, HR can take on other steps such as identifying the plan objectives (option C), identifying internal and external resources (option B), and communicating with team members (option A).

10. C. The correct answer is option C. The first priority in any emergency is to preserve the health and safety of all team members. In this case, a shelter-in-place is the best course of action since going outside and potentially breathing in a toxic chemical could cause harm. Depending on emergency response plan protocols, you may be responsible for notifying authorities (option A), deploying an emergency response team (option B), or safely looking for hazardous signage to communicate to the teams (option D).

Chapter 13: Corporate Social Responsibility

1. B. The correct answer is option B. The more connected an organization is with its stakeholders, the more likely it is they will have an increased degree of interdependent factors that drive mutual survival.

2. A. The correct answer is option A. Successful CSR initiatives require the commitment of organizational resources, which must be approved by organizational leadership. The government (option B) and (option C) communities are not organizational members, so those answers are incorrect. Employee commitment (option D) will absolutely be necessary, but not in terms of committing resources.

3. D. The best answer is option D. One of the challenges in developing CSR strategies is that they are all important in one way or another. There is no question that basic income (option A), violence against women (option B), and poverty (option C) are issues that must be addressed. However, climate change is an issue that is broadly applicable to the needs of people and organizational competitiveness. This question may be interpreted as a statement of opinion, especially as it contains the absolute of "all," so answering it requires the exam taker to think from the perspective of shared value.

4. D. Option D is the best answer. Option A, lack of infrastructure, is a barrier to commerce, and it creates an inability of individuals to access services for their basic needs. Option B, infectious disease, increases medical waste, affects access to education, and can shut down industries such as transportation. Option C, overpopulation, creates a shortage of resources for food, shelter, land, fuel, utilities, education, and water, and addressing these needs can cause environmental damage.

5. A. The best answer is option A. Corporate social responsibility efforts focus on addressing social, economic, and environmental issues. Corporate citizenship is focused on not causing further harm by complying with various laws and ethical codes of conduct.

6. D. The impact of business practices on the people resources of an organization are many. They include health and safety, wage equity, and respect for human rights. These issues may be addressed by communicating hazards (option A), ensuring fair pay (option B), and ensuring that the rights of all workers are respected (option C).

7.   B. The best answer is option B. The alignment of CSR strategies with business strategy ensures that the committed organizational resources will drive profit and shared value. Value may be defined in monetary and nonmonetary terms, such as protecting resources (option A) and addressing systemic inequities through fair business practices (option D). Option C is tricky since it is also true, but option B, driving profit and value for all stakeholders, is how option C will commit.

8.   C. The best answer is option C. Studies show that qualified employees seek socially conscious job opportunities. By enhancing the employee value proposition, employers may attract these individuals to their organizations. Cost reduction (option A) is not likely to take effect immediately, and protecting assets (option B) is an outcome of sustainable risk management efforts but rarely the driver. The restructuring of work (option D) is the means used to enhance the employee value proposition.

9.   A. There are many benefits to committing organizational resources to addressing the social, environmental, and economic issues targeted by CSR efforts. Strategic benefits include increased brand awareness; modeling of ethical behaviors to team members and other leaders; adding to the employee value proposition; and increased consumer trust.

10. D. The correct answer is option D. Designing and organizing workplace volunteer programs comes with many HR responsibilities. These include recruiting and organizing team members onto projects, taking on a leadership role in opportunities in the community, communicating the benefits of these efforts to the employees, and crafting workplace policies that encourage volunteer activities.

Chapter 14: U.S. Employment Laws and Regulations

1.   B. Under the ADA, an individual may qualify for protection under the act in three ways. This includes if they suffer discrimination based on being perceived as having a disability. An individual may also be protected under the ADA if they have a record of such impairment, such as having recovered from cancer (C), or have an actual impairment, such as asthma (D).

2.   D. Piece-rate systems are allowed under the Fair Labor Standards Act; however, it does not absolve an employer of their minimum wage and overtime obligations. In a charge against Galaxy Home Solutions of Florida, the Wage and Hour Division of the Department of Labor found that the employer failed to accurately keep track of how many hours over 40 in a week their electricians were working.

3.   D. The Federal Employees' Compensation Act is a comprehensive and exclusive program that offers benefits to federal workers who are injured on the job.

4. **A.** In this case, a labor union filed a charge against the administrations charged with protecting their members, not the employer itself for violations related to infectious disease (B), confined spaces (C), or the general duty of employers to provide a safe and healthful workplace (D).

5. **C.** The Consolidated Omnibus Budget Reconciliation Act (COBRA) was passed as an amendment to the Employee Retirement Income Security Act (ERISA) to assure that covered employees maintain the right to purchase health insurance after a qualifying event. (A), the Portal-to-Portal Act, was an amendment to the FLSA. (B), the Equal Pay Act, was an amendment to the FLSA. The Age Discrimination in Employment Act (D) amended the Civil Rights Act of 1964.

6. **D.** The Immigration and Nationality Act, along with its subsequent amendment, the Immigration Reform & Control Act, requires that employers obtain a completed Form I-9 within three days of an employee's first day of work for wages.

7. **A.** The H2A Temporary Agricultural Workers visa program was passed to address shortages of domestic workers by allowing nonimmigrant foreign workers to perform agricultural labor.

8. **B.** The correct answer is (B). In order for behavior to meet the standard of unlawful harassment, the conduct must first be unwelcome. Harassment does not have to be violent (A), nor does it have to result in a tangible employment action (C), such as demotion or termination, to be considered unlawful.

9. **A.** The Uniform Guidelines on Employee Selection Procedures note that all selection tests for hire, promotion training, or other employment-related decisions must meet the standard of validity—that is, they accurately predict what the test was designed to predict.

10. **B.** OSHA 300 logs, the annual summary, and the OSHA incident reports must be retained for five years.

Chapter 15: Structure of the HR Function

1. **C.** The best answer is option C. When a strategic plan targets a large-scale, companywide initiative such as this, it is likely that HR will need to expand their bandwidth using a subject-matter expert. An intern (option A) will not be able to provide the necessary amount of support to achieve these initiatives. Addressing research project diversity (option B) and designing training (option D) may eventually become project priorities once a leader of the initiative is established.

2. **B.** The correct answer is option B. An HR-to-FTE ratio is calculated by dividing the number of HR personnel by the total number of FTEs and then multiplying the result by 100 to convert the number to a percentage. The university has 500 FTEs and 5 HR personnel: 5/500 × 100 = 1 HR team member for every 100 employees.

3. **A.** HR's ability to be effective is driven by the need to be true business partners, making option A the best answer. This may include knowing how to analyze data (option C).

Recruiting (option B) is not the primary job duty of an HRBP as it would be for a recruiter role. Although important, individuals with a positive attitude (option D) are not automatically qualified to work as an HRBP.

4. D. HR professionals in all roles and at all stages of their careers are responsible for their efforts in achieving business goals.

5. B. HR is responsible for adapting their work styles to the needs of other stakeholders, so option B is the best answer. Outsourcing is not a form of integration, so option A is incorrect. Being a point of contact to coordinate IT services does not call upon HR skills, so option C is not a good choice. And option D is an internal function of many HR departments, so processing payroll is not the best example of integration.

6. C. HR staffed in one, centralized location allows for the team to deliver consistent service to the company stakeholders, so option C is correct.

7. B. The best choice is option B. HR practices support many different types of organizational core competencies. A performance-based system that is designed to pay for results can help improve quality outcomes. HR as a core competency refers to using all HR practices to achieve organizational success, so option A is not correct. Option C, a knowledge strategy, would be better supported through selection and training efforts. And option D, supply chain, is unrelated to a performance-based pay system.

8. D. Revenue per FTE is designed to measure organizational efficiencies, so option D is correct. HR expense to revenue, (option A) is useful if you need to forecast costs to complete a department budget. The balanced scorecard (option B) considers multiple factors to determine organizational or the HR department's progress toward goals. Option C, HR expense–to–operating expense, is used to understand how much investment an organization is making into its HR functions.

9. C. Networking is the act of building professional resources from within and outside of the organization, so option C is correct. Listening (option A) focuses on understanding information provided by others. Option B, the exchange of organizational information, is the ability to translate and communicate HR-related information effectively to HR and non-HR individuals, and delivering messages (option D) is the ability to present information in a clear and concise way to a variety of audiences.

10. A. Listening is the skill that involves the message being communicated, the sender of that message, and the receiver, making option A the correct answer.

Chapter 16: Organizational Effectiveness and Development

1. D. The primary purpose of OED efforts is to help measure organizational effectiveness and then develop people (option A), process (option B), or structural interventions (option C) using change management, team, and conflict management skills.

2. C. Organizational development is the degree to which an organization is successful at achieving goals, generating results, and overcoming barriers to performance. Organizational development is a planned effort to overcome barriers by developing solutions and consciously disrupting patterns of individual, team, or organizational behavior through interventions.

3. B. Barriers to organizational effectiveness are often found in the HR systems. This is because HR is responsible to develop systems that support the people practice of the organization. By first looking within the department to find where the practices are falling short, HR can intervene at the root cause and/or cast a wider net if the barriers are not internal. In this case, it is too early to determine why there is such lag time between finding a qualified candidate and making the offer, so analyses need to come before the solutions offered in options C and D. The candidates were not returning calls in the first place, so option A would not be the most effective place to begin.

4. C. The primary purpose of industrial-organizational psychology (option C) is to study how psychological principles affect the workplace, including the impact of individual attitudes and beliefs. Personality assessments (option A) may be used to identify individual characteristics and is one part of the study of I-O, as are many other employment tests. Sociology (option B) is the branch of science that studies human social interactions in all areas of life. Neuroscience is the scientific study of the nervous system, including the brain (option D).

5. A. The Myers–Briggs Type Indicator (MBTI) is not designed to predict behaviors, and thus it should not be used for selection activities. The MBTI is a tool designed to increase self-awareness and is useful for performance coaching and career pathing.

6. C. A team is most clearly defined when a group of people have a shared purpose, making option C the best answer. Note that option A is also a good choice, but because option C is more specific, it is the better answer.

7. D. A job posting is the process of recruiting internal candidates for an open position within the organization, making option D the correct answer. A job description (option A) and roles and responsibilities documents (option B) describe the tasks, duties, responsibilities, and knowledge, skills, and abilities necessary for performance. Job interest cards (option C) are used for employees to express interest in jobs within the organization should they become available.

8. D. A geographic structure is one that is independently managed at a local or regional level, making option D the correct choice. If this organization was centered on customer service delivery, option A would have been correct. If the business was described as having centralized support such as HR, finance, IT, and so forth, option B would have been the better choice. If the situation noted the use of cross-functional teams, then option C would have been the correct answer.

9. C. Change management is the system or process for managing a change initiative, which is the objective of any technological, cultural, or behavioral intervention effort.

10. A. The most innovative and engaged teams are those that have a healthy dose of constructive conflict. The lack of creative problem-solving combined with engagement results suggests that this team is entrenched in artificial harmony, avoiding conflict altogether.

Chapter 17: Workforce Management

1. C. Workforce management is the practice of aligning organizational needs with staffing levels, a major function of Talent Planning and Acquisition (option C). In some cases, employees will need to be developed from within through a company's learning and development activities (option A). In other cases, total rewards systems are used to attract talent (option B), and employees are retained through employee engagement activities (option D). These last three options are only part of a workforce plan, and they serve in a supportive role of talent management in this functional area.

2. D. Once a supply-and-demand analysis has been completed, HR begins the process of developing strategies to address gaps in talent needs. Note that each of the options did not involve implementing any activities. The purpose of workplace plans is to brainstorm and address root causes and then research options to make recommendations to management. The options also addressed internal and external sources for talent through people and structural strategies.

3. B. An iterative (option B) process is cyclical; it begins by defining the boundaries of the content area and then updating the system as new knowledge becomes available.

4. A. Knowledge management programs' primary focus is to retain and allow for efficient transfer of knowledge. Considerations when doing so include compliance issues, such as securing access (option B) and finding ways to use technology to streamline knowledge management systems (option D).

5. D. A rule-of-thumb forecast relies on the general judgment of an experienced subject matter expert, such as a manager, making (option D) the best answer. Option B is a viable option, since a rule of thumb does use forecasted demand, but option D is more specific and therefore a better choice. Option A, situational, is a distractor; it is a theory of leadership, not a type of forecast. Statistical forecasts rely on more objective and measurable criteria, making option C incorrect.

6. D. Building a leadership pipeline is imperative for continued success, and yet there continue to be many barriers to success. Barriers include a lack of qualified talent across all levels (option C), lack of time to design the programs and for leaders to participate (option B), and company budgets being spent on other priorities (option A).

7. A. The path-goal theory has several elements that include leadership behaviors, follower characteristics, and the nature of the task itself, making option A the correct answer. Option B, situational leadership theories, places the most emphasis on the circumstances under which an individual must lead. Option C, transformational leadership theories, focuses on leadership behaviors, and option D, leader-member exchange theory, emphasizes the dynamics of the relationship between the leader and the follower.

8. C. Succession plans have a planning horizon of more than 12 months to allow for adequate development of the candidate. Replacement plans have a planning window of less than 12 months, making option C the best answer. Options A and B determine the learning curve of a candidate, and that is not the primary difference. Option D, urgency of the need, may require that HR seek to buy the talent as opposed to building it from within as part of a succession or replacement plan.

9. B. Navigating the organization is a competency that requires a form of political agility. This is because HR must be able to access and influence the formal and informal hierarchies and systems that exist within any organization and work them to positive effect. Option A is false, since this competency does require interpersonal skills. Option C is untrue because navigating the organization requires both transactional and relational skill sets.

10. A. The company vision is part of an organization's governing beliefs. As an HR sub-competency, it involves defining and supporting a coherent view of the long-term goals of the organization, implying that it must align with the broader, grounded strategic beliefs such as the mission and values.

Chapter 18: Employee and Labor Relations

1. A. Managers and supervisors are the frontline defense for preventing retaliation from occurring—from themselves and from employees. Not only does training managers and supervisors teach them about retaliation, but it also is one way for the employer to establish an affirmative defense against a charge of retaliation should it occur. Option B, promoting a culture of dignity and respect, targets employee morale and harassing behaviors, and it may help to minimize retaliatory behaviors, as would disciplining employees who do retaliate (C). All that said, option A is the best choice.

2. D. The correct answer is option D. The employer of record (option A), a staffing agency that may be the employer of record of the temporary employees (option B), and a union that represents members (option C) are all obligated to protect the rights of the workers, including safety, health, and wages.

3. C. In 2020, the Department of Labor (DOL) identified four factors that indicate whether joint employment exists and factors that do not necessarily assume that joint employment exists. A franchise agreement does not automatically assume joint employment.

4. A. The collective bargaining process includes making decisions about union member wages, hours, benefits, and other terms and conditions of employment (option A). Option B, bargaining units, is the way that represented groups are formed, often by job type. Option C, concerted protected activity, is the right of employees to collectively discuss issues such as wages, hours, and health benefits (the subjects) without interference from their employer. Vocational guidance (option D) consists of standards developed by the International Labour Organization (ILO).

5. C. The International Labour Organization is a tripartite body that sets standards for employment rights and responsibilities. Members are represented by governments, employers, and employees, making option C the correct answer.

6. D. The use of arbitration is an alternative dispute resolution resource that reduces costs and is quicker than litigation for formal employee complaints, disputes, and grievances.

7. C. Alternative dispute resolution encompasses methods that seek to reduce the cost of employment litigation by using third-party decision makers outside of the formal litigation system, making option C the best answer. B is a good option, but employers cannot prohibit an employee from filing a charge with a federal agency, even if it may be one without merit or re-routed due to the presence of an ADR agreement. ADR agreements do not address employee health and safety, so option A is incorrect.

8. B. The ability to enforce noncompete agreements (option B) at a state or a national level can be difficult for employers. This is because employers may not prevent an individual from working. Nondisclosure agreements (option A) are reasonable, since they limit an individual's ability to disclose confidential or trade secrets of the business. Option C, intellectual property rights, are legally binding and thus enforceable. A code of conduct is part of the broader governing employment documents, such as an employee handbook that, when properly written, is enforceable.

9. A. The National Labor Relations Board (NLRB) is responsible for the enforcement of the National Labor Relations Act (NLRA). Section 8 identifies the duty to bargain in good faith during the collective bargaining process, and it defines unfair labor practices when doing so. The Equal Employment Opportunity Commission (option B) investigates unlawful discrimination charges, and the Department of Labor is responsible for standards and enforcement agencies related to most employee rights, including wages, hours, and health and safety. The U.S. Patent and Trademark Office (option D) grants ownership for creative and other inventive works.

10. B. Pluralism is a type of environment where multiple needs, desires, and interests exist within the workplace, and where a participative style is used to negotiate. Option A, a federation, is one or more unions that join together. Option C is a political party that supports large governments, and option D, conservative environment, are those that apply principles of small governments.

Chapter 19: Technology Management

1. A. An HRIS's ability to integrate with other enterprise management systems is critical to offsetting redundancies and inefficiencies. The cost of implementation (option B) and program capabilities (option C) are factors, but the return on investment will be diminished if the program cannot integrate, thus requiring workarounds or creating redundancies. An HRIS's ability to deliver through the cloud is not always desired or necessary, making (option D) incorrect.

2. D. Early iterations of HRI systems were found to be lacking in several ways. Because of their lack of integration with other systems, there were redundant practices (option A) that decreased efficiencies and created disparate systems that lacked coherency (option B). With lack of coherency, any reporting that was available was incomplete, making (option C) among the challenges as well.

3. B. When it comes to handling high-volume exchanges of data, bandwidth (capacity) and latency (speed) are most important. Both of these will help with a platform's ability to store data, such as documentation (option A), streamline employee self-service options, and system integration with other enterprise management software (option C). A platform with the proper speed and capacity will also help improve the user (employee) experience and thus make room to increase the capacity of the HR team (option D).

4. D. For a smaller business, the expense of hiring a full-time team member either in HR (option A) or in IT (option B) may not result in enough of a return-on-investment. The tasks of the IT role do not warrant the scale of an offshoring response, so option C is not the best answer either. Third-party vendors may be selected that are local and responsive and who may build a contract for only the specific needs of the organization with an ad hoc response when necessary.

5. B. When a decision has been made to use a third-party vendor, a request for proposal (RFP) or request for quote (RFQ) is a document that outlines the details of the need. It includes a description of the business, the purpose of the request, and any pertinent details such as budget and timelines. A scope of work may be included in an RFP, but it would not necessarily include enough detail to make a decision, so option A is incorrect. A decision about the resource should not be made before the data is collected, so option C is incorrect. Scanning social media is not going to glean enough information to make a quality decision, so option D is not the best answer.

6. A. A mobile device management policy should clearly outline where smartphone and other device cameras may be used. Option B is unrealistic for most organizations, and option C does not have to be communicated in a formal policy.

7. B. Social engineering is the use of psychological manipulation that targets human fallibility with technology, so option B is the correct answer. Psychological manipulation may include the use of phishing (option A) and other types of unlawful access to information (option C), but these are simply examples of the best answer.

8. C. EIM, or employee Internet management software, is designed with blocking features to prevent access to prohibited websites. Mobile device management (option A) is a policy that outlines the use of personal and company-owned mobile devices. ESS (option B) stands for employee self-service, and EMS (option D) is an enterprise management system, which helps to run operations.

9. B. Employers do not need to have written authorization from an employee to monitor their activities while on company time and on company owned devices, so (B) is the correct answer.

10. D. The use of technology brings with it risks to the employee, the customer, and to the organization as a whole. These risks include exposing confidential information, securing sensitive data, and attempts by hackers through social engineering to gain access to passwords and company servers, making option D the correct answer.

Appendix

B

Summary of Form I-9 Changes

Exam Notables

Form I-9 is required to be completed by employers within 72 hours of a new employee starting work. Though only two pages long, the form can be complicated, and mistakes are costly. Fines for using an expired Form I-9, incorrect completion, or failing to retain the document range from $110 to $20,130 per violation. For example, one business with fewer than 50 employees was fined $40,000 because they could not produce their employees' I-9 forms even though it was later found that they all were authorized to work in the United States. The higher single violation amounts apply to employers who repeatedly and knowingly hire individuals who are not authorized to work in the United States. The purpose of Form I-9 is to verify a new hire's identity and eligibility to work in the United States, so having a compliant process is a critical risk management activity.

The U.S. Citizenship and Immigration Services (USCIS) publishes a guide to help employers comply with their requirements. The Handbook for Employers M-274 was last updated in April 2020, and a summary of those changes is included here. To view or download the document in its entirety, head over to:

www.uscis.gov/i-9-central/form-i-9-resources/
handbook-for-employers-m-274/handbook-for-employers-m-274

Summary of Changes

The purpose of this document is to outline significant changes made to the M-274, Handbook for Employers: Guidance for Completing Form I-9.

Updates Based on Form I-9 Revision

Section 2.0: Clarified who can serve as an authorized representative to correspond with revisions in the Form I-9 Instructions.

Section 12.0: Clarified that the second List B document in the List of Acceptable Documents does not include the driver's license or ID card issued by a state or outlying possession of the United States to correspond with revisions in the Form I-9 Instructions.

Section 12.0: Clarified that the employment authorization document issued by the Department of Homeland Security in List C of the List of Acceptable Documents does not include Form I-766, Employment Authorization Document, from List A to correspond with revisions in the Form I-9 Instructions.

Major Guidance Changes

Sections 4.4 and 6.4.2: Revised guidance to clarify that employers should enter expiration date changes based on automatic extensions of documents in the Additional Information field in Section 2 and have eliminated instructions to have the employee cross out and initial information in the "Alien authorized to work until" expiration date field in Section 1. This ensures greater legibility during Form I-9 inspections.

Section 6.4.2: Revised cap-gap extension document requirements to better align with regulations. Employers will enter the receipt number from Form I-797C, Notice of Action, as the employee's Document Number in Section 2. Form I-20, Certificate of Eligibility for Nonimmigrant Student Status, is no longer required.

New Content

Section 4.4: How to complete Form I-9 with complete Form I-9 with Employment Authorization Documents (EADs) automatically extended by Federal Register notices.

Section 6.2: Guidance on verifying employment authorization for Native American employees born in Canada.

Section 7.1: Guidance for state employment agencies that choose to complete Form I-9 for individuals they refer and for employers of individuals referred by a state employment agency.

Major Clarifications

Section 3.0: The purpose of the Preparer/Translator Supplement.

Section 6.4.1: Determining the document expiration date that F-1 and J-1 nonimmigrant employees should enter in the Section 1 "Alien authorized to work until" expiration date field.

Section 9.0-9.2: How to calculate Form I-9 retention, retention guidelines, and electronic Form I-9 requirements.

Section 10: A review of prohibited Form I-9 practices and penalties and the agencies responsible for enforcement.

Plain Language Updates

Removed duplicate content.

Merged certain sections for better logic flow.

Sections 5 and 6 merged in Section 5; subsequent chapters renumbered.

Section 13.0: Incorporated questions and answers into the body of the handbook whenever practicable to comply with new USCIS style requirements.

Index

D

I

M

N

O

P

T

U

Online Test Bank

Register to gain one year of FREE access after activation to the online interactive test bank to help you study for your SHRM-CP and SHRM-SCP certification exams—included with your purchase of this book! All of the chapter review questions and the practice tests in this book are included in the online test bank so you can practice in a timed and graded setting.

Register and Access the Online Test Bank

To register your book and get access to the online test bank, follow these steps:

1. Go to www.wiley.com/go/sybextestprep.
2. Select your book from the list.
3. Complete the required registration information, including answering the security verification to prove book ownership. You will be emailed a pin code.
4. Follow the directions in the email or go to www.wiley.com/go/sybextestprep.
5. Find your book on that page and click the "Register or Login" link with it. Then enter the pin code you received and click the "Activate PIN" button.
6. On the Create an Account or Login page, enter your username and password, and click Login or, if you don't have an account already, create a new account.
7. At this point, you should be in the test bank site with your new test bank listed at the top of the page. If you do not see it there, please refresh the page or log out and log back in.